COACH K

COACH K

The Rise and Reign of Mike Krzyzewski

Ian O'Connor

MARINER BOOKS
Boston   New York

marinerbooks.com

Designed by Emily Snyder

Library of Congress Cataloging-in-Publication Data has been applied for.
ISBN 978-0-358-34540-4

Printed in the United States of America
1   2022
4500846102

To my world-class big brother Dan, who left us far too soon
Thanks for always having my back
Until I see you again

To the great Mrs. O
Thanks for being a mom to us all

CONTENTS

COACH K

INTRODUCTION

HOSPICE WAS ALREADY IN, and Joe McGuinness needed to tell Mike Krzyzewski something important before he died.

I did not quit.

In his final week, as nasopharyngeal cancer was killing him, the fifty-five-year-old McGuinness repeatedly told his older brother Ed that he badly wanted Coach K to hear those words. Joe had been a small but rugged point guard on Krzyzewski's last West Point team. Coach K would often say that he should have taken McGuinness with him to Duke University, that Joe's defensive tenacity would have made life in Durham, North Carolina, a little easier in the early 1980s.

Their relationship started in 1977 inside the McGuinness home in Nanuet, New York, where Krzyzewski arrived for a recruiting visit like few before it. "We were the traditional Irish family," said Joe's brother Ed. "We always had a million people over."

Joe's grandmother Anne was among those who sat in on the visit—across the table from Krzyzewski—and she was overwhelmed by the fact that the head coach at West Point wanted her grandson. Anne had two boys who served in the South Pacific during World War II, including Joe's father Jack, who spent two years on a PT boat and fought the Japanese in the decisive Battle of Leyte Gulf.

Joe, the middle of his three boys, earned Division I offers from Wagner College and the United States Military Academy while starring at Clarkstown South High School. During Krzyzewski's visit to Nanuet, Joe interrupted the dinnertime conversation by digging a couple of fingers into the cream cake his mother Florence had baked and scooping a divot into his mouth.

Joe was Florence's personal golden boy, so she would have likely let this misdemeanor go. But Coach K? "You're not going to be doing that at West Point," he assured his recruit.

The family's German Shepherd, Luke, nearly knocked a full drink all over the visiting coach. The McGuinnesses had a silly post-dinner tradition of trying to scorch each other with the spoons used to stir their hot tea, and in Krzyzewski's presence Joe playfully burned his grandmother. "Coach K was like, 'These people are crazy,'" recalled Ed McGuinness.

But when Krzyzewski walked out the door that night, there was no doubt Joe was going to play for him. All the McGuinnesses from Grandma Anne on down fell hard for the Army coach, and the Army coach fell hard for them. Grandma Anne would bake and send cookies to Coach K at West Point, and again in his early years at Duke, and when she called his office once to congratulate him on a big victory, Krzyzewski dropped everything to take the call. When he made a recruiting visit to New York City in an attempt to sign Brooklyn high school sensation Chris Mullin for the Blue Devils, Krzyzewski asked Jack McGuinness to join their dinner so he could explain to Mullin's parents what it was like to have a son play for Coach K.

Truth was, Joe McGuinness had been something of a hellion at West Point. He failed a couple of courses as a plebe and struggled to accept the sanctioned hazing from upperclassmen, who screamed in his face when he did not properly square off a corner while walking to class. "They mess with your mind," Joe had said. Asked by his local paper how much he liked military life, Joe responded, "I like to play basketball."

But as a college ballplayer, Joe was exactly what Coach K had envisioned he would be — a pass-first point guard who played the game the way Krzyzewski played it at Army. Reddish and pale, the map of Ireland all over his face, McGuinness was a relentless disruptor when guarding the opponent's most skilled backcourt scorer. In one game against tenth-ranked and unbeaten LSU at Madison Square Garden, "little Joe McGuinness," as the *Daily News* described him, made his mark off the bench. He threw some pretty passes, shut down the Tigers' high-scoring guard from the Bronx, Al Green, and helped Army rally from a huge deficit to lose by only six.

McGuinness made a less favorable impression in a lower-profile matchup with Manhattan. Joe was enjoying a good game when Jim Ward, a guard for the Jaspers, decided to start using his elbows to rattle his opponent. It didn't take much to get Joe's Irish up, and sure enough, McGuinness wheeled on Ward and punched him, earning an ejection. Joe was shampooing his hair in the shower after the game when he suddenly turned to find an enraged Coach K two inches from his face, his jacket and tie taking on water while he started ripping into his point guard.

"You motherfucker," Krzyzewski screamed. "Don't you ever fuckin' put yourself ahead of my team again."

Joe was crushed when Duke hired away Coach K after his sophomore season; he finished his college career at Manhattan, of all places, as a buddy of Jim Ward's, of all people. He played and coached professionally in Ireland and became a college and high school coach back in the States. He won sectional state titles for the varsity boys' and girls' basketball teams at a high school ten minutes from his boyhood home in Nanuet, Albertus Magnus, where he was also the athletic director. Joe never stopped talking about Coach K, never stopped acting like him on the sidelines. Joe's sons Patrick and Conor would watch Duke games and notice disapproving looks on Krzyzewski's face that mirrored expressions on their father's.

"Joe was probably a little crazier on the sideline," said his younger brother, Jack Jr., who would also play for Army. "It takes Coach K a little while to get crazy, but Joe was out of his mind the whole game, pulling his hair out."

Just as Coach K heavily involved his wife Mickie and three daughters in his basketball program, Joe made sure his wife Cynthia and daughter Megan were a constant part of the conversation about his teams. McGuinness learned from Coach K to value end-of-bench reserves and team managers, and he encouraged earnest students who struggled with their studies. "My father brought that to each and every team and class he taught," Megan said.

So it was a devastating blow to the Rockland athletics community when McGuinness received his diagnosis. Krzyzewski was immediately on the phone with a contact he had at Memorial Sloan Kettering in the city — they came to know Joe in the hospital as Coach K's guy — and he put Joe's wife in touch with an oncologist at Duke. Krzyzewski got involved in ensuring that McGuinness had access to the latest trial treatments. He regularly called and texted his former player with words of support, telling him, "You can beat this. Go after it. Never give it an inch."

One day Joe's sister Kate was in the car with him, stuck in Manhattan traffic after treatment, when Coach K called to ask if he could do more to help. The calls and texts helped sustain Joe as his condition deteriorated.

Joe's son Patrick would hand his father his phone with long text messages from Krzyzewski expressing his love for his old point guard. "You could see that after he received a text from Coach K his energy level went up and he was able to get through the day a little better," Megan said.

Krzyzewski was the last man on earth McGuinness wanted to disappoint, so Joe was concerned that he was letting him down when the end-game became clear. Joe fought the cancer so relentlessly that, years later, his siblings would say that they wished he had let go earlier. The chemo wasn't working, and the radiation left Joe unable to speak clearly, or to swallow, or to rest comfortably. "His last few months were absolute torture," Jack Jr. said.

Joe spent his final days inside his home in New City, New York, where he once ran his three kids through basketball drills on the court outside his door. Patrick and Conor grew into accomplished high school and college players and followed their old man into coaching, just as Joe had followed Coach K.

When Krzyzewski's last call came in, Patrick was holding his father's hand. Joe could barely speak. Krzyzewski reminded him how much he loved him, how much he respected him. The coach could not make out a lot of what Joe was trying to tell him, and Joe figured as much. He communicated to his older brother what he needed to share with Krzyzewski.

Ed took the phone and told Coach K that his brother wanted to make sure he knew that he did not give up. "I never doubted that," Krzyzewski responded.

Shortly after that conversation, McGuinness gathered his brother, wife, and children in his living room. Joe was out of his hospital bed and in his recliner when he had his family members huddle like a basketball team would around its coach. They locked their eyes on Joe's and leaned in close to make out what he was trying to say. This would be his final pep talk.

"He still had that Coach K phone call in his head," Megan said. "The principles and values of hard work and of being a good teammate that Coach K instilled in him is the way my father lived. He told us in that last huddle, 'This is what matters most in life. This is our team. We need to always look out for each other.'"

Joe McGuinness died on February 12, 2016, two weeks after Krzyzewski wrote a letter nominating him for induction into the Rockland County Sports Hall of Fame. Coach K cited Joe's on-court leadership and called Joe as good a defensive guard as he had in his five seasons at Army.

When Duke beat Virginia by one point the day after McGuinness died, Krzyzewski dedicated the victory to him, talked to his team about Joe, and had his players sign a game ball that carried the words "In Honor of Joe McGuinness. Duke 63 Virginia 62." Coach K signed the ball and wrote, "For my point guard," and sent it along with boxes of Duke gear to Joe's wife.

More than 5,000 mourners attended Joe's wake and funeral services, including many of his former high school and college players, some of whom served as pallbearers. Just like their father, Joe's two sons would work as counselors at Krzyzewski's summer camp. Coach K met with Patrick and Conor and recounted that last conversation he had with Joe, admitting to the boys that he could not understand much of what their father was saying on the phone. "But I still knew exactly what he was saying," Coach K assured them as he pounded his chest.

Three years later, Krzyzewski was vouching for Conor as he became Army's director of basketball operations. The following year he was calling Joe McGuinness's son the day before Conor was scheduled to undergo surgery for testicular cancer, just to let him know he was praying for him. After the successful surgery, Coach K reached out again to offer encouragement as Conor started two rounds of chemotherapy.

"I'm just the son of a player he coached a long time ago," Conor said. "The fact that he's still keeping tabs on me is just remarkable."

Krzyzewski had spent more than four decades connecting with four generations of McGuinnesses, starting with Grandma Anne, exchanging personal, handwritten letters with various family members, endorsing some for jobs, even sending Joe some old suits of his so he would have clothes to wear as an assistant college coach. Coach K recommended Joe's younger brother Jack Jr. to the West Point coaches in the early 1980s after watching him compete at his Duke camp.

The McGuinnesses all became passionate Blue Devils fans who tracked Krzyzewski's top recruits in high school and didn't miss a game on TV. As a young boy, Joe's son Patrick would slap the floor during basketball camp because he wanted to become the next great guard at Duke. Joe's sister Kate wrote Krzyzewski a letter in 2019 to update him on the family and inform him that her daughter Elizabeth had enrolled in Duke's physician assistant program in pursuit of a master's degree. Coach K said he would help Elizabeth with anything she needed, and he invited the family to a game at Cameron Indoor Stadium, where they sat six rows behind the home team's bench.

To a man and a woman, the McGuinnesses were in awe of Krzyzewski's grace. They couldn't understand how he did it, how he found the time and patience to remain invested in every friend he'd made.

Those close to the living legend with five national titles, nearly 1,200 Division I victories, and three Olympic gold-medal finishes as the leader of Team USA often instruct inquiring minds to look past the talent he has successfully recruited and developed, and the Xs and Os he has drawn on the board. They advise others to focus on Krzyzewski's ability to connect with people from all walks of life, his ability to motivate people to achieve things they did not believe they were capable of achieving, and, above all else, his ability to build lasting bonds with his players, assistants, team managers, childhood friends, and former teammates and coaches.

The secret to Coach K's greatness, his friends say, is found in his relationships. Thousands of them.

Including those with an Irish Catholic family that produced a low-scoring rotation player who spent only two seasons with Krzyzewski, during which Army went a combined 23-28. Coach K told Joe McGuinness's wife that he keeps Joe's prayer card on his desk, and he told Joe's son Patrick that he also keeps a card in his briefcase so that it remains with him everywhere he goes.

As much as nearly anyone else Krzyzewski has met in his seventy-five years on the planet, the McGuinnesses have felt the power of his impact in a most personal way. They saw what he meant to their cancer-stricken loved one. They know that in his final days, Joe effectively sought Coach K's permission to die.

Why has Michael William Krzyzewski been able to move people so profoundly? How did a low-income street kid, the son of a cleaning lady and an elevator operator who got by without high school educations, become quite possibly the greatest college basketball coach of all time?

Before he announced that he would end his forty-seven-year college career after the 2021–2022 season, those were the questions I set out to answer. To understand where Krzyzewski's journey ended, you have to understand where it began. You have to understand his Polish neighborhood in Chicago, and how it fueled the raging fire within.

1

COLUMBO

MICKEY, AS MIKE was often called by the neighborhood kids, was always out there in the schoolyard, all alone with the ball and his thoughts. Friends saw him in the rain, sometimes even in the snow after he was done shoveling the court. He dribbled in solitude and worked on his moves against an imaginary defender while pretending a championship was on the line with a few seconds to go.

Mickey was going places. He figured out early that the game was the vehicle to get him there.

In Chicago, a kid had to learn how to handle a cold, wet basketball, and learn young Mickey did. A local girl, Vivian Przybylo, would be walking to her grandmother's place, or to the neighborhood grocer or butcher, and see the same boy doing the same things on the same Christopher Columbus School court no matter what season it was, or what time it was in the morning, afternoon, or night.

"I don't think I ever passed that schoolyard without seeing him playing basketball, often by himself," Przybylo recalled. "He's the most determined person I ever knew."

Determination was a necessary character trait passed down to the boys and girls who always gathered off Leavitt and Augusta Boulevard at the Columbus elementary school and who would call themselves "Columbos" for life. They were the grandchildren of Polish immigrants who firmly believed in an honest day's work and in the all-American dream that suggested they could someday have lives like those of the wealthy people they labored for.

Krzyzewski's paternal grandparents, John and Sophie Krzyzewski (their surname was printed as "Krzyzowski" in a number of documents), had emigrated from Poland to the United States before the turn of the twentieth century; his maternal grandparents, Josef and Magdalena Pituch, had emigrated from Wola Radziszowska in Lesser Poland Voivodeship after the turn of the century; in some documents they listed their home country as Austria. (Their region was under Austrian control.)

Josef's story was a common one in his Polish neighborhood on the North Side of Chicago in an area that would come to be known as Ukrainian Village. Pituch traveled on the SS *Zeeland* from Antwerp, Belgium, and landed in New York, at Ellis Island, on March 21, 1906. He married Magdalena Daniel in Fayette County, Pennsylvania, three years later. A rugged-looking five-foot-eight, 175 pounds, with brown hair and brown eyes, Josef found work as a coke drawer and as a rigger in a coal mine.

Josef and Magdalena would move from Keisterville, Pennsylvania, to Chicago, where the janitor and homemaker (who went by the Americanized names Joseph and Maggie) lived with their six children at 2039 West Cortez Street. One of their five girls, Emily, married one of the Krzyzewskis' seven children, William, on June 18, 1935. According to the 1940 federal census, the last one taken before their sons were born, Emily made $446 over thirty-nine weeks in 1939 as a machine operator in a cosmetics company (stuffing cotton inside of powder-puff applicators), while William earned $1,560 over fifty-two weeks as an elevator operator in a private building. Emily hadn't attended school beyond eighth grade; William had completed only two years of high school. They wanted something better for their kids.

Their first son, Bill, was more than four years older than Mike, who was born on February 13, 1947. They were raised in the family's brick two-flat on Cortez, starting on the upstairs level and then moving downstairs to the first level when their aunt, Emily's sister Mary, moved out. Big Bill towered over the more athletic Mike. They both received their Catholic elementary school education at St. Helen, a short walk from their well-appointed, if sparsely furnished, home. William and Emily did not want their sons to take the Polish language classes available to them because they knew that a Polish accent, or any discernible connection to the homeland, could put future educational and employment opportunities in jeopardy.

William had changed the family name to Kross to escape the discrimination that confronted Eastern European immigrants in postwar America, and to ensure that he wasn't mistaken for a refugee known as a "displaced person" (DP) from World War II. He was identified as "William Joseph Kross" on his draft registration card, which identified his wife as "Emilia Marie Kross." (William became a private in the Army and received an honorable discharge on January 16, 1946.) Under the section asking the registrar to confirm the truthfulness of William's answers, this notation was made: "Votes under Krzyzewski in 6 precinct 26 ward."

His employer was listed as the Willoughby Tower Building Corporation on Michigan Avenue downtown, where Kross ferried the city's power brokers thirty-eight floors up and thirty-eight floors down, all day, every day, for nearly a quarter-century. Meanwhile, after her husband returned home, Emily caught a bus to the Chicago Athletic Club to scrub floors for its well-heeled members. "My job in the world is to chase dirt," she told her boys. "I do a good job of it. You'll never see dirt anywhere in my house, because I'll chase the heck out of it, and I'm going to beat it."

Back then the Polish kids attended St. Helen, the Slovaks attended Sacred Heart, and discipline was the order of the day in both places. The boys at Sacred Heart often wore corduroy pants to absorb the sting of the nuns' yardsticks. The students in all the city's Catholic schools understood that the educators were always right, and that their parents sided with the nuns and priests in disputes and punished their children — sometimes through physical force — accordingly. But the nuns loved Mike, because he always did exactly what they asked. Decades later, Przybylo was still calling him "the biggest brown nose." Though Vivian beat Mike in a girls-versus-boys mathematics competition in third grade, she recalled him being a whiz in multiplication tables.

Mike was better with numbers than he was with words, and years later he would observe that he might have been diagnosed with attention deficit disorder had he been tested. "I had ants in my pants all the time," Mike would say. And yet he remained a strong student and a committed lieutenant of St. Helen's patrol boys, the seventh- and eighth-graders who helped younger children cross the street. Classmates recalled him getting into trouble only here and there. Mike once earned a dash in conduct on his report card, instead of a letter grade, as did Przybylo, for the felony of talking too much in class. "The dash meant you didn't deserve an F," Vivian said, "but that your parents had to call the nun to get it changed . . . or you would graduate with an incomplete report card."

A year before Krzyzewski graduated, he approached the school principal about assembling a basketball team to compete against CYO (Catholic Youth Organization) opponents. Mike preferred football and baseball at the time, but thought it would be easier to organize a five-man basketball team. Problem was, St. Helen had no gymnasium, no coach, no team, and no interest in fielding one. So Mike effectively started his own league, challenging other neighborhood teams to play his in local parks. Krzyzewski was his team's coach and best player, and along with his friends he took on all comers throughout the city. They walked a mile and a half to some games, rode the bus to others. "No parents involved," Mike said. They rarely lost. He built his first winning program at age twelve.

The Columbos also played baseball, loading their gear into wagons and carrying their bats and bases as they walked into different neighborhoods in pursuit of a game. The Polish kids played the Puerto Rican kids who lived a few blocks away. The Columbos started calling their own team the Warriors, and they wore numbered shirts and black caps distinguished by a white *W.* (Some players wore blank caps because they couldn't afford the extra 10 cents for the white letter.) Mike was a line-drive hitter. He spent a lot of time playing third base, yet he was a fan of the Cincinnati Reds' All-Star Vada Pinson and fancied himself a Pinson-like center fielder.

He played one-on-one stickball too, using a 10-cent rubber ball and a broomstick, with a strike zone outlined in chalk against the schoolyard wall. "Mike made a league out of it," a friend from the neighborhood, Frank Kasprzak, said. About eight individual players represented eight teams—sometimes four players competed simultaneously, using two different strike zones—and Krzyzewski kept track of who won and lost these duels and crowned a champion at season's end. It was sports every day, all day, in the summer, interrupted only by the Krzyzewski family trips to Emily's hometown, Keisterville, Pennsylvania, a 515-mile drive from Chicago. "That was a big thing," Mike said of the trips.

Columbo camaraderie remained a Krzyzewski priority after Mike enrolled at Archbishop Weber, the all-boys high school attended by his brother Bill. They had their rituals. After attending Mass on Sunday mornings at St. Helen, Krzyzewski and Leonard Bryla would head over to Dennis "Moe" Mlynski's house, sit on his wrought-iron fence, and read the *Tribune*'s coverage of the local pro teams. "Mike would bitch and moan that the *Tribune* writers were too critical of the Bears and the Cubs," Bryla recalled. "He thought their coverage was unfair, and he'd be ranting and raving about it."

The nuns told the Catholic school boys that they shouldn't hang out with the public school kids, but the boys never listened. The Catholic and non-Catholic Columbos met on summertime mornings at the Columbus schoolyard, played sports for three hours, stopped in at the neighborhood social center, and then returned home for lunch and maybe a quick viewing of *Bozo's Circus* on WGN. They would head back out for more sports, go home for dinner, and leave again to play more self-organized, self-umpired games into the night.

The games varied, but the group's organizer never did. The Columbos waited at the school in the morning, talking about what they should do that day. "And then normally Mickey would come along," Larry "Mondo Twams" Kusch said, "and say, 'What's going on? Let's get started. Let's do this and that.' He would start things and then sometimes disappear. I don't know if he had chores or what, but he was an instigator. He always got things started, and then he'd come back." (Many Columbos had long, involved stories behind their nicknames; others not so much.)

The youngest of the group, Kusch thought of Mickey "as a dese, dem, and dose guy," like everyone else in the neighborhood. But there was a difference in Krzyzewski's appearance, and in the way he interacted with his Columbo teammates. "He always looked good," Kusch said. "His hair always looked right." Kusch could have sworn that Emily Krzyzewski was ironing Mike's T-shirts, because they always looked better than his. "And if he was quarterbacking and we were playing touch football in the schoolyard," Kusch said, "his plays were always the most meticulous. 'Okay, you go down 10 yards and cut 90 degrees. You go five yards and go 45 degrees this way.'"

The boys worked on their basketball skills, creating shots off the dribble, and sometimes Krzyzewski dragged his foot for an advantage on his defender. "But he got away with it," Kusch said, "because he was so precise in his moves." They used to go to the local gymnasium on Saturday mornings, when there was never any doubting the identity of the game's leading player. "You scored as much as Mike wanted you to score," Kusch said. "He was good at dropping the ball off early and giving us shots, but when push came to shove, Mike would take over."

The Columbos wanted to be on Mickey's team whenever sides were being picked; his presence gave them confidence. As a boy, Krzyzewski had what he called "a very volatile" and "real quick-tempered" disposition on the court and on the ballfield because he so badly wanted to win. "And I wanted to make sure that all the guys on my team felt the same way," he said.

Mickey made the Weber varsity basketball team as a sophomore despite showing up for the first practice with a cast on a wrist that he broke playing touch football. He was a fairly good bowler who threw an effective backup ball—a left-to-right fade for a right-hander—in neighborhood games at Stack and Ryan, where the hourly rate was 25 cents a lane and a strike with the red head pin earned a bowler a free game. When his friends were busy mimicking their favorite pro wrestlers, Mickey assumed the role of Edouard Carpentier, "The Flying Frenchman" who was known for using turnbuckles and ropes to perform his acrobatic moves in midair.

The Columbos were a gang in name only. "Real gangs would drive by and look at us," Kusch said, "and they'd say, 'Leave the Columbos alone. They're harmless.'"

The Polish kids all knew each other's siblings and parents. Everyone was welcome at everyone else's homes, and mothers were free to reprimand other people's kids if their parents weren't around. Emily Krzyzewski, a dark-haired woman with a kind face, would feed a friend of Mike's and bandage him up after a rough day of play, just as the friend's mother would do for Mike. An especially lucky boy would be treated to the chocolate chip cookies Emily loved to bake in her white oven; she pressed exactly three chips into each cookie. When putting together meals and desserts, Emily closely followed directions written on notes stuck to her kitchen cabinets. "As orderly as you could write a game plan," her younger son explained many years later.

The Krzyzewskis didn't have much, but like the rest of their community, they took immense pride in what they did have. The residents all made sure the streets and sidewalks were clean, the flowers were watered, and the small lawns were cut. "It was a very magical neighborhood," Przybylo said. "We were clinging to each other. It was like a security blanket."

Vivian and Mickey were dear friends who could finish each other's sentences, and they dated on and off in their teenage years. Her friends would look Mickey up and down, survey his conspicuous nose and ears, his angular Eastern European features and unspectacular physique, and inform Vivian that he wasn't much to look at. Vivian was never attracted to the cutest guys. She was searching for character and kindness, and for someone who locked his eyes on yours when he spoke. She was searching for someone who didn't look up to people, or down on them.

Vivian was also searching for someone who had a certain aura. And she found it when she sat inside a packed Archbishop Weber High School gymnasium and watched Mickey Krzyzewski take off down the floor.

"People would feed Mickey the ball," she said, "and he could shoot from long distance, off balance, and make the shot . . . He had a magnetism about the way he played. The crowd definitely felt Mike's charisma. When he was going downcourt, the crowd would all stand up because they knew he was going to fly through the air and make the basket."

THE FRONT PAGE of the *Weber News* included a photo of four young men in a library, all dressed in shirts and ties beneath pullover sweaters with large *W*s stitched to the front. Mike Krzyzewski, his black hair in a squared-off buzz cut, was smiling in that picture. He was posing with his fellow se-

nior class officers, including Chico Kurzawski, the class president and heralded football star headed for Northwestern.

Krzyzewski, a member of the National Honor Society, had been elected
Kurzawski's vice president by the senior homeroom officers. He pledged to
do everything he could to help the president "make this a truly great year
at Weber."

But there was really only one way for Krzyzewski to make 1964–1965 a
truly great year — winning Weber's first varsity city championship in basketball.

Krzyzewski had tried out for the football team as a freshman, but on
the second day of practice he watched as new equipment was handed out
to more than two dozen kids who had the CYO connections that weren't
available to him at St. Helen. "And I knew I was better than a bunch of the
kids," Krzyzewski said, "but they were recruited." Mike's temper got the best
of him, and he told himself, "I'm not gonna take that." He quit on the spot
and never returned. The captain of the Columbos would make his mark at
Weber on the court.

Weber was not the easiest place for its 1,200 boys to make the transition to young adulthood. The Resurrectionist priests might give you a quick
whack to the head if you looked sideways at someone or if you didn't walk
down the right side of the hall. At a school assembly, the Resurrection-
ists had their own methods for quieting the unruly: "If you're an enforcer
priest," said Paul Kolpak, a basketball teammate of Krzyzewski's, "you grab
the biggest guy and you make a physical demonstration of him, and the rest
of us got the message."

Krzyzewski's best friend, Moe Mlynski, saw the Resurrectionist priests
and brothers fiercely paddle an entire class at his school, Gordon Tech, if
even one student broke one of their many rules. At Weber, where students
were required to wear a collared shirt, tie, and slacks, one priest carried
around a small Louisville Slugger in his vestment. If he found a boy walking with his hands in his pockets, he would hit the boy on the shoulder with
his bat and ask, "What are you doing, taking inventory? You've only got two
down there. Get your hands out of your pockets."

Another priest, an ex-wrestler, once grabbed two students who were
horsing around in the back of his Latin class, picked them up one in each
hand, and hung them on hooks at the top of the blackboard, leaving them
to dangle and gasp for air for a while before he let them down. Weber, said
Mike Siemplenski, a basketball team manager, "was a no-bullshit place."
Coaches once instructed Siemplenski and another student he didn't get

along with to put on boxing gloves, lace them tight, and beat the shit out of each other until their conflict was settled. Neither boy could knock the other out before reaching the point of exhaustion, and they both retreated to the locker room and lay on wooden benches, missing their next class but having learned a valuable lesson.

Weber was all about self-discipline, even when it came to teaching a boy the proper way to feed himself soup — with the spoon moving away from his mouth, not toward it, to prevent a spill on his white shirt. This was a perfect fit for young Mike Krzyzewski, product of a strict Catholic family and already a believer in structure and organization. He felt at home at Weber, which had a student body that was about 60 percent Polish, 30 percent Italian, and 10 percent Irish and other. The boys were identified by their parishes. Many of the Italian kids were survivors of a 1958 fire at Our Lady of the Angels that killed ninety-two elementary school students and three nuns, including some survivors who were recruited to Weber by the head football coach, Joe Sassano. That powerhouse football team, led by Kurzawski, went undefeated in Krzyzewski's senior year, winning another city championship. That increased the expectation that Krzyzewski — "the Chico of the cagers," the *Weber News* called him — would bring home the school's first title on the court.

In the late fall of '64, when the football team practiced indoors to escape the weather, Kurzawski would watch his friend work on his game on a basket against the back wall of the gym. Krzyzewski would shoot the ball, retrieve it, shoot it, retrieve it, shoot it, retrieve it. Mike had led the Catholic League in scoring as a junior, averaging 18.8 points per game, and here he was as a senior working harder than anyone, getting up shots long after the basketball team's practice had ended.

Krzyzewski was a captain of the varsity heavyweights — the school teams were divided by player size into the heavies, lightweights, bantamweights, and flyweights. He was six foot one, 175 pounds, and wore number 44. In a team yearbook photo, Krzyzewski stood alone in front, ball in hands, while teammates, coaches, and priests stood in rows behind him. The Red Horde was Mick's team.

Al Ostrowski, the head coach, was a young, in-your-face leader who appreciated his point guard's intensity on both sides of the ball. One photo in a Weber yearbook showed a high-jumping Krzyzewski, then a sophomore, knocking his head into the bottom of a gymnasium's wraparound deck. "Mike Krzyzewski hits the ceiling at St. Philip's," read the caption. "Fortunately, it didn't crumble."

In Ostrowski's mind, Mike had a flaw as an underclassman that needed to be fixed: "His only weakness was his lack of confidence in himself and his abilities on the court," the coach said. The way Mike would put it years later, Ostrowski "believed in me more than I believed in me." Coach O was the first man to ever tell him, "You're so damned good." After Krzyzewski had a few poor shooting performances as a junior, Ostrowski sensed that Mike was passing up opportunities he needed to seize. "When you get the ball, *shoot!*" the coach barked at him. Ostrowski threatened to make his point guard run laps if he didn't start firing away. He wanted to bring out all of Mike's talent and leadership ability, and Mike responded, his confidence increasing with each game.

Krzyzewski was described by teammates, managers, and classmates as silky smooth, fundamentally sound, and eager to get out on the fast break. He was a relentless perimeter defender, the kind you did not want guarding you. He was a quick, but not overly fast playmaker, with tremendous vision and a vertical leap that helped him get off a jump shot ripped from the pages of a manual — his body perfectly straight in midair, his elbow tucked, his right arm cocked at a 90-degree angle, his left hand guiding the ball.

After Ostrowski had worked on him, Krzyzewski was the one who made his team believe that it was never out of a game, no matter the score. "A National Honor Society member who ranks twentieth in his class," reported his school paper, "Mike is a cool player who always keeps his head." Teammate Tom Kleinschmidt recalled coming out of the locker room in a big road game, a tense game, after Krzyzewski had made like a coach, relaxing all his fellow Weber players by reminding them that they had succeeded in front of plenty of hostile crowds before.

Mike was quite a sight as he knifed through defenses to score or to hit an open teammate. Even the Columbos who attended Gordon Tech and Lane Tech would spend their Friday or Saturday nights in Weber's gym watching their friend prove himself to be one of Chicago's very best players. After the game, Moe would drive Mick home and tell him how much he enjoyed watching him play. "I can't recall him ever being obnoxious because he'd gotten so good," Mlynski said.

Krzyzewski was dating Larry Kusch's next-door neighbor, Betty Smietana. Mick never lacked for female attention, much to the dismay of his father William, who didn't want his boy distracted. "I don't want my son dating any girls," he told friends. Mick impressed the girls anyway with his athleticism and an appealing sense of humor that he inherited from his mother, the family's answer to Lucille Ball. "Every Columbo girl in my group had a crush on him at some point," said Linda Wolczyz, who did not date Krzyzewski. "He just knew what to say and how to say it."

Mike was a class officer for three years, a member of the National Honor Society and French Club for two, and the Sock Hop Committee for one. If something troubled Krzyzewski in his personal life, he would turn to his geometry teacher, Father Francis Rog. They would talk in the cafeteria about life and about faith. "He explained things in a way which made me feel less guilty about just being human," Krzyzewski explained. He later told Moe that during his time at Weber he thought of becoming a priest. "Father Rog and he would talk about that," Mlynski said. "Mick always wanted to be a teacher, and to help people, and he thought maybe that was a way."

Krzyzewski knew he wanted to impact others the way Father Rog and Coach O had impacted him. While he tried to figure out his precise calling, Krzyzewski tore up the Catholic League, to the delight of packed and chaotic Weber crowds of about 1,500, sometimes up to 2,000, in the same gym that held Friday assemblies and Mass and sock hops. The Red Horde was always one of the best-conditioned teams around. More disciplinarian and motivator than master strategist, Ostrowski made Krzyzewski and his teammates run laps around the court, upstairs to the second level, across the bleachers, and back down again when they didn't listen to his instructions, which wasn't often.

Krzyzewski, Kleinschmidt, and Len Koplitz led the Red Horde to a 13-2 record in its nonleague ("exhibition") season before rolling through the North Section of the Catholic League, a rough-and-tumble league shaped by Big Ten physicality and an unwritten code that called for hard fouls on ball handlers who ventured into the paint. Krzyzewski routinely delivered more than 20 points per night as he chased a second consecutive Catholic League scoring title. He scored 27 in a convincing victory over St. Philip, avenging Weber's only league defeat, and was chiefly responsible for the eight-game winning streak Weber carried into its second game with Loyola.

On that Friday night, February 26, 1965, Krzyzewski put on a show at the best possible time in front of a crowd at Loyola that, the *Weber News* reported, included more Red Horde fans than Ramblers fans. Loyola was up 12 in the third quarter before Weber cut it to 5 for the start of the fourth. As was his habit in these situations, Krzyzewski took control of the game, scoring 18 of his 33 points in the final quarter to give Weber a 69–58 victory and, of greater consequence, the North Section championship.

"This may be the last time Mike Krzyzewski will play against us," Loyola coach Gene Sullivan said afterward, "but from what I've seen tonight, I've seen enough of him to last me the rest of my life."

Krzyzewski had worked so long and so hard for this moment. Sometimes when practicing by himself, Mike bounced the ball against the Weber gym wall to simulate a teammate throwing him a pass, and then counted down the seconds in his head before taking and making a shot to win the North Section title. He now owned that title. He now had scored more than 1,000 points in his varsity career. The school paper described him as "poetry in motion," and "the best basketball player in the history of Weber High School." Coach O praised his point guard's leadership and wondered if people understood "the excellence of Mike as a person." He said that Krzyzewski had a chance someday to play pro ball.

The Catholic League playoffs called for the top seeds from the North and South Sections to cross over and play the second-place teams from the opposite section, meaning Weber would be paired against Mount Carmel, an opponent it had already beaten twice in the exhibition season. The Weber boys felt good about their prospects as they entered DePaul University's Alumni Hall on Saturday, March 13, excited to compete in a big-time college environment. But on this night Krzyzewski would learn for the first time the unforgiving reality of sudden-death March basketball.

Mount Carmel's Tom Kilmartin, a six-foot-three senior, scored his team's first three baskets and out of nowhere had the game of his young life, sinking shot after shot from the corner as Weber struggled to recover. The Red Horde trailed virtually the entire night, stunning many in the crowd of 4,100, including Moe Mlynski, who watched Mount Carmel's defenders successfully double-team Krzyzewski. "They just changed their whole defense to stop him," Moe said. "Weber wasn't able to adjust."

As soon as Mike helped cut the deficit to 51–45, Kilmartin, who would finish with 27 points, responded with a few more baskets to build an insurmountable lead. It was a big upset, by a large margin. The 73–56 victory sent Mount Carmel to a Catholic League final it would ultimately win.

"Weber's Mike Krzyzewski, who paced the Catholic League in scoring, had another good night, with 22 points," read one newspaper account. "But he didn't get enough help from his teammates."

Ostrowski and his players were gutted by the shocking end to their season. Krzyzewski had tears in his eyes when he walked out of the arena with Mlynski, who had never seen his friend more upset over a loss. "He was so distraught," Moe said. It was a tough way for a decorated player to go out.

Krzyzewski still hoped to find a major college interested in an average-size point guard with a jump shot, a willingness to play defense, and an ability to work around his lack of superior foot speed. At the same time, a twenty-four-year-old rookie head coach at Army needed to find athletes willing to be pushed beyond their physical and emotional limits while forming a team that could beat far more talented opponents.

Robert Montgomery Knight was talking to the Loyola coach, Sullivan, who identified the Weber star as the Catholic League's finest player, and Knight made an appointment to meet with Krzyzewski in Weber's cafeteria. When the sit-down happened, Mike's teammates couldn't help but stare.

At six five, Knight had been a large presence as a bit player on Ohio State's 1960 national championship team. Now the second-youngest major college coach in America, he was only six years older than Krzyzewski, who was already certain of three things in life: (1) He wanted to become a high school coach; (2) he wanted to become a high school teacher; and (3) he wanted absolutely no part of serving in the Army. Mike had no knowledge or understanding of the military academy and preferred to keep it that way.

But Knight was already a developing force of nature, and when he met with William and Emily Krzyzewski as well as Mike that night, he made a compelling case for West Point. Emily and William had labored for so long for the kind of distinguished families that sent their sons to West Point, and now here was the military academy's representative sitting before them and recruiting one of their own.

Emily and William were very different personalities and played very different roles in Mike's life. Emily was the one who sat him down before he attended Weber and told him, "I want to make sure you get on the right bus." Mike assured his mother that he knew the route, including Division to Grand. "Michael," Emily responded, "that's not what I'm talking about." She always called him Michael when she had something profound to say. "Tomorrow you're going to meet new people," Emily continued. "You're going to get on a different journey. The bus that you drive, make sure that it's the right one. Make sure that you only let good people on it. And if you get on someone else's bus, make sure it's with someone who's good." It was the best advice young Krzyzewski ever received.

With a smile, Emily would ask her son, "What are you going to do when you grow up and stop playing basketball?" Emily was always there for Mike; she attended his games (sometimes without telling him) and lavished him with praise when he returned home. Her husband was just as proud of Mike, though he was too busy working to go to the games or to spend any quality time with him. "He talked about me a lot," Mike would say, "but hardly ever to me. I knew my dad loved me. He just let me have my freedom."

When William was done as an elevator operator, he would open a small restaurant in Chicago's factory district to serve the city's laborers, and then a tavern on the South Side; neither venture did much to elevate his family's financial standing. William worked, and worked, and worked some more, then came home and smoked cigarettes before falling asleep in his favorite chair. He would rise early to start another workday, usually with a very strong cup of coffee. Mike's teammates and closest Columbos didn't know anything about his father for a good reason — Mike didn't know much about him either.

William did teach Mike a valuable lesson when he was a young boy, after Mike sneaked into his parents' bedroom and pulled some coins out of the pants his dad always draped over the back of a chair. When William asked Mike if he had lifted the money, Mike denied it, but later confessed. William told his son that he had taken and spent a coin that carried sentimental value for him, and that he was very disappointed in him for stealing and lying. Mike long remembered how his father's disapproval made him feel: "It set me on a path where I knew I never wanted to feel that way again."

More than anything, William and Emily shared the same fierce devotion to their sons and spent whatever extra money they could save on their Catholic educations. Emily owned only two dresses, and she didn't see the need to spend money on a third. Those dresses were always spotless and perfectly ironed — West Point style — as they hung in her closet.

As they were finishing up their chat with Knight, William Krzyzewski, who hadn't said much that night, turned to his son and announced, "Well, Mike, I think West Point is where you ought to go to school." This was a dream come true for Mike's parents: William had changed his name to mask his family's identity and background, and he simply could not believe that the military academy, a symbol of American might, wanted a Krzyzewski.

He also could not believe his son's response to the offer of a free education at such an elite institution. "I don't want to be a soldier," Mike told his parents. He didn't want to carry a rifle, and he didn't think Army was the right place to make the transition into a career in teaching and coaching. Mike said no to Coach Knight, hoping to land a scholarship at one of a handful of Division I schools that had shown interest, including Wisconsin of the Big Ten and Creighton, a Jesuit university in Nebraska.

Emily and William were not giving up that easily. "I can't believe he's not taking this opportunity," they repeatedly said to each other. They spent two weeks ripping into their younger son in kitchen-table conversations they conducted in Polish, loud enough for Mike to hear in the living room. Occasionally, just so their boy got the point, they would blurt out in English, "Stupid Mike!"

Stupid Mike leaned on Coach O for guidance. "Mike and his mother came to our home, sat at the kitchen table, uncertain where Mike should go," Ostrowski said. "And as his coach, I knew Army was the best choice. He reluctantly took my advice."

It was a turbulent time in the country, a year and a half after President John F. Kennedy had been assassinated in Dallas. Congress had just passed the Voting Rights Act, designed to end discrimination against African Americans in the voting process. The nation's involvement in Vietnam was growing; President Lyndon Johnson was about to call for another 50,000 ground troops to be sent there, and he would soon double the number of men to be drafted, up to 35,000 per month.

Some of the Columbos were more concerned than Mick was about the war and his postgrad military commitment. American Marines were only weeks away from engaging in the first major ground battle of the war, Operation Starlite, on the Van Tuong Peninsula, where U.S. forces would win a fierce firefight lasting days. And yet Emily and William were equal parts exhilarated and relieved when their son changed his mind and committed to the military academy. (Coach Knight liked to spin the five-year commitment to active duty as a guarantee of employment after graduation.)

When Mike went to inform his best friend of his choice, the two sat on Moe's fence near the schoolyard, the same fence where Columbos often hung out late on Friday nights.

Moe had no idea where West Point was located. "Isn't that where all the presidents go to school?" he'd asked Mike earlier, after Knight first showed interest. When Mike told him that he would be a cadet after all, Moe was taken aback, but excited for his friend. "He was coming out of the neighborhood," Mlynski said, "and doing something big."

Whatever Mick ended up doing, he would do it as a Krzyzewski, not a Kross. Some of his cousins had changed their name, just as his father had done. (The English translation of "Krzyz" is "Cross.") But when he was a kid visiting his Uncle Joe, a Chicago cop, at Christmastime, Joe would greet him at the door and ask, "What's your name?" Mike would always answer, "Krzyzewski," and his uncle would respond, "Don't you forget it. I want you to be proud of who you are, your heritage . . . Don't change your name."

All the old-timers in the community were proud of Mick, proud that he didn't give an inch to a society that often mocked the Polish and their descendants. They were proud that Mick would represent them at a world-class academy, among the very best young men America had to offer.

Meanwhile, Vivian Przybylo felt badly for Mick's girlfriend Betty. Krzyzewski was sitting outside Betty's apartment with her neighbor, Larry Kusch, whose mother had just signed a contract to sell their home. The Kusches were moving to a place 10 miles from their cherished neighborhood, and as the three of them sat there talking, Larry felt the weight of the moment.

"We all had our own angst about it," he said. The neighborhood was changing, the world was changing, and Krzyzewski was leaving Betty and the Columbos and the rest of his friends to go to a place that seemed a million miles away.

"On that day Mick told us he was going to West Point," Kusch said, "I thought, 'This is going to be the end of us.'"

The end of innocence on the North Side of Chicago. And for Mike Krzyzewski, the beginning of a long-term partnership with a volatile genius.

2

COACH KNIGHT

On JULY 1, 1965, Mike Krzyzewski marched straight into the living hell known as Beast Barracks. This is what they call cadet basic training at West Point, and for the 1,200 entering freshmen, or "plebes," at the all-male United States Military Academy, the exercise was best described as the opposite of what their high school classmates were doing all summer — chasing girls, playing ball, and drinking cold beer on the nearest beach or bay.

Beast Barracks, or Beast, was designed to turn a boy into a man by breaking him down physically, psychologically, and emotionally, and then building him back up into an officer and warrior who could someday manage any life-or-death crisis he might face in some faraway land. For the better part of two months, the plebes were deprogrammed and forced to embrace a new normal that their bodies and minds begged them to reject. From sunup to sundown, from Reveille at 6 a.m. until Taps at 10 p.m., they were verbally humiliated by superiors and limited to only three acceptable responses: (1) "Yes sir," (2) "No sir," and (3) "No excuse, sir." The plebes were told that one out of every three of them would not make it to graduation day. The freshmen who thought that West Point would be, in the words of one recruit, "an advanced Boy Scout camp" never stood a chance.

As an incoming cadet most interested in playing basketball, Krzyzewski knew right away that he'd had it much better with the punitive priests back at Weber High. Their heads shaved, their uniforms perfectly pressed, the new cadets were required to walk briskly — with erect posture and eyes trained straight ahead — as they robotically squared off every hallway and stairwell they encountered on post. They were also required to have full command of what was called plebe knowledge. The plebes had to memorize a mind-numbing series of trivial facts — the items on a daily menu, the number of gallons in Lusk Reservoir (92.2 million), the number of lights in Cullum Hall (340), the number of days until Army beat the hell out of Navy in football, you name it — and recite those facts to upperclassmen without advance warning.

Rising above the west bank of the Hudson River in all its gray Gothic glory, West Point inspired fear in all plebes. Older cadets were forever shouting spittle directly into the faces of new cadets, barely an inch away from nose-to-nose contact, while correcting the most benign and incidental errors. Plebes were berated if their brass belt buckles weren't fully polished, or if they had failed to spit-shine their boots and shoes. (The toes and heels received particular scrutiny from the upperclassmen.) The plebes had to practice bracing, or pulling back their chins until they disappeared under their wrinkled gullets, to enhance their posture. They even had to practice bracing while eating, which one cadet described as a fate worse than death.

The plebes were required to collect the older cadets' laundry and mail, among other things, while enduring day after day of marching, weapon training, tactical drills, and calisthenics. Misconduct could lead to room confinement, or to a one-hour punishment tour spent walking back and forth across the Central Area. Violations of the Honor Code ("A cadet will not lie, cheat, steal, or tolerate those who do") could result in immediate expulsion. Plebes were not permitted to quit the academy on their own until three weeks had passed, though Krzyzewski, like many of his classmates, thought of quitting as much as he thought about anything.

Hazing at West Point wasn't what it was in the draconian days that preceded the 1900 death of a plebe named Oscar Booz, who died of tubercular laryngitis allegedly because cadets had repeatedly poured Tabasco sauce down his throat. A congressional committee had been assembled to investigate, and a cadet named Douglas MacArthur, who had been forced to do deep knee bends over broken glass until he passed out, was among those who testified about hazing. The committee found evidence of severe misconduct at West Point — some plebes were forced to sit on bayonets — and Congress moved to outlaw acts it found "of a harassing, tyrannical, abusive, shameful, insulting or humiliating nature." MacArthur tried to effectively eradicate hazing from the academy after he was named superintendent in 1919, but much of what was known as the fourth-class system remained in place by the time Krzyzewski arrived forty-six years later.

One day Krzyzewski was stopped on post by two upperclassmen, who demanded to know his surname. "Krzyzewski, sir," he said. "What kind of name is that?" one responded. "Well, Mr. Alphabet, or whoever the hell you are, your shoes are cruddy. You're a crudball." Krzyzewski's roommate had earlier splashed mud on his shoes while stepping in a puddle. "No excuse, sir," the plebe told the upperclassmen. Krzyzewski later screamed at his roommate for earning him demerits, though on further review he realized he needed to accept responsibility for the mistake. The man in his mirror was ultimately to blame for neglecting to change his own shoes.

Another day a fellow plebe and basketball teammate named Gary Eiber was talking about academy life with Krzyzewski, enjoying a rare break as they waited on line to get back into the barracks. "And then suddenly Mike's eyes got as big as saucers; he looked scared," Eiber said. "There was an upperclassman I hadn't seen, and we were supposed to be at attention. I got chewed out royally, but Mike didn't, because I was doing all the talking ... There's probably not an eighteen-year-old kid who goes in there, even if you're a tough guy, who doesn't have tears in his eyes before he's done."

The plebes lived three to a room, and all they had was each other. The Corps of Cadets was divided into four regiments with companies identified by letters of the alphabet. Krzyzewski was assigned to E-3, part of the Third Regiment. "The motto of the company was 'not excessively eager,'" said one member, Bob Baldwin. "It wasn't a bunch of super-strivers." It was a randomly selected group of twenty-five men from around the country who represented, according to another E-3 member, Cary Gaylord, "the biggest bunch of cutups you could possibly imagine."

For example, E-3 plebes tore up pieces of bread and put one piece on each shoulder of an unsuspecting classmate, promoting him to "bread colonel" as he unknowingly walked about the mess hall with bread on his shoulders. By all accounts, Krzyzewski rarely engaged in the silliness. "He was too busy for it," Gaylord said. "And because of how hard he was working, everybody loved him."

Baldwin cited a very specific reason Krzyzewski stayed clear of the horseplay. "We had some guys in E-3 who were way out there, and they were good friends with Mike," Baldwin said. "But Mike didn't run with them ... In those days, if you had a cadet disciplinary thing against you, you were off corps squad."

Corps squad meant intercollegiate athletics. And for the two-time leading scorer in Chicago's Catholic League, intercollegiate athletics meant basketball.

He started building his relationship with Bob Knight early in his plebe year, when the Army coach converted his hilltop home on post into a sanctuary for his beleaguered recruits. Eiber, who had played on Knight's junior varsity team at Cuyahoga Falls High School in Ohio, recalled that during the weekend hours when plebes were allowed to walk about, Knight and his wife Nancy, also from Orrville, opened their house and put mattresses on the floors and offered the boys ice cream and cake. "Mike and I and other plebes would go up there and watch TV and sleep and pig out and chill out," Eiber said.

But if the first-year cadets thought that Knight would be anything but the most demanding and verbally degrading authority figure they would meet at West Point, they were in for a surprise. As much as they needed a break from the hazing and bracing while scrambling into formation before dawn and marching to Washington Hall for meals and to Thayer Hall for classes, Knight was not about to provide one in basketball practice.

Knight had been a star high school athlete, but at Ohio State he was a limited offensive player and a lead-footed defender on some outstanding Buckeye teams that were coached by Fred Taylor and featured future Hall of Famers John Havlicek and Jerry Lucas. (An Army media guide a few years later would claim that Knight had "an outstanding basketball career at Ohio State University.") He was a reserve who averaged 3.7 points per game on the school's 1960 national championship team. He did score the basket against Cincinnati that sent the 1961 NCAA finals into overtime, a game Ohio State would lose. But as a senior, Knight wasn't one of the eight Buckeyes who played in the 1962 finals rematch with Cincinnati, also won by the Bearcats. He left Columbus bitter over his playing time, or lack thereof. "The brat from Orrville," Taylor had called him. A forgettable player, Knight wanted to make up for it as a coach.

Eiber had felt Knight's wrath while playing for his Cuyahoga Falls High School junior varsity team. Knight pulled him aside in one practice, after Eiber had dropped a few balls, and repeatedly fired underhanded passes at him from close range — the fireball drill, they called it. "It was like dodge-ball," Eiber said, "but you don't have a choice to dodge it."

Knight rolled balls onto the court in practices and ordered opposing players to dive for them and fight for possession. He broke a clipboard in his first game coaching tenth-graders. He conducted a six-hour practice after his Cuyahoga Falls team lost its opener in the final seconds, to Kent Roosevelt, which prevailed on an absurd shot from behind the backboard that deflected off the glass and dropped in. The Cuyahoga JV finished with a 13-3 record, but more than half a century later Knight could still provide vivid details of the shot that dealt him his first defeat as a basketball coach.

Taylor, of all people, persuaded a friend of his, Army coach George Hunter, to give an assistant's job to Knight, who had to enlist to work at West Point. Knight was sent to Fort Leonard Wood in the Missouri Ozarks for his basic training. After Hunter got fired, his replacement, Taylor "Tates"

Locke, kept Hunter's commitment and assigned his young assistant to run the plebe team.

Locke was nearly as volcanic as Knight. He once ended up with more than two dozen stitches in his hand after responding to an intramural basketball loss by punching out a window, and he reportedly traded blows with Knight — himself an intramurals madman — during a heated pickup game. But they made for a formidable partnership. Locke went 40-15 in two seasons with the varsity and made two trips to the National Invitation Tournament semifinals before he shocked the academy by leaving for Miami of Ohio in May 1965. Twenty-four-year-old Knight, private first-class in the U.S. Army, was named his successor a couple of weeks later, after he interviewed for an assistant's opening at Duke University. He was making $99 a month at the time.

Knight was in the Krzyzewski home shortly thereafter, talking about how his team would compete with, and defeat, bigger, stronger, and faster opponents. Now Mike was living the Knight system as an ineligible player — freshmen were not permitted by the National Collegiate Athletic Association (NCAA) to compete in varsity sports. The program started in the fall, when Army players put on combat boots and jogged up the hill to the home of West Point's storied football program, Michie Stadium, where they ran the stairs and worked on their vertical leaps. Coaches weren't allowed to oversee or attend workouts until the official start of practice on October 15, but a defiant Knight sat in the highest and darkest corner of the gym and watched as his Cadets played in pickup games. (The Army team was called the Cadets before its nickname was officially changed to the Black Knights years later.)

Army's home arena was a dusty, drafty, cavernous red-brick field house down on the river; one veteran referee called it "the coldest place in the world." A biting wind came off the Hudson and cut through incoming spectators on game nights and through outgoing cadets on practice nights while they were racing from their quick showers to get to the mess hall before dinner shut down. Knight had to fight for his space in the field house, as it was used by a number of the academy's varsity teams, including mighty football late in its season. He ordered tarps to be hung around the court for privacy while the track team ran on the perimeter oval; Knight, of course, could get easily annoyed by all the hustle and bustle. Once, while some nuns were being given a tour of the gym, the coach had to be asked to curb his profane language until the nuns were ushered out the door.

Krzyzewski was the point guard on Army's plebe team, and after Knight temporarily lost some upperclassmen to academic troubles, the plebes practiced with the varsity while running the upcoming opponent's offense. On most days, the starters and reserves actually viewed Knight as their primary opponent. One of his Cadets said that a number of players vomited during or after their first practice — or at least suffered the indignity of dry-heaving if they had no food in their bellies to expel — and that it only got tougher from there.

Knight wanted his practice to be the most exacting two hours his athletes endured every day, which was saying a mouthful at the academy. No student in America confronted a daily schedule like that of a student at West Point. The cadets were up and in formation outside their barracks at a time when most college students were rolling over in their beds, preparing to sleep another four hours and blow off yet another morning class. They marched to a 6:30 breakfast inside Washington Hall, where more than 3,000 plebes, yearlings (sophomores), cows (juniors), and firsties (seniors) ate three meals together, ten to a table. Cadets attended classes over six days, including Saturday mornings, followed by Saturday parades on The Plain, the green 40-acre field about 150 feet above the river where the Corps of Cadets marched to patriotic band music in their gray wool coats, black tar bucket hats, and white pants and gloves, with rifles tucked against their shoulders.

Besieged by advanced math courses and the math textbook known as "the Green Death," they were graded every day, in every class, on the endless road to a bachelor of science degree. Like all plebes, Krzyzewski needed to take a physical education course that included boxing, swimming, wrestling, and gymnastics. Mike boxed a few rounds with Baldwin and held his own. Yet, as a consequence of growing up in a big city, Krzyzewski had no idea how to swim. He was a member of the "rock squad" — the group that needed to be taught the fundamentals that would save them from drowning. During class, one of Krzyzewski's basketball teammates, Dick Simmons, noticed that Mike's big toe and neighboring two toes seemed to be fused together. "Almost like he had a fin," Simmons said. "So he got a lot of shit from us about that."

As part of the rock squad, Krzyzewski said, he had to team up with "a number of other guys in fatigues and boots and learn how to swim in survival swimming." Part of his training called for him to travel the length of the pool while carrying a brick in each hand, a task he never completed. Again, it was Chicago's fault. "The closest we ever came to water was an open fire hydrant on hot days in the summer," Mike joked.

Krzyzewski was no expert in gymnastics either. One of his instructors, Richard Cardillo, who was also the assistant officer's representative for men's basketball, made Krzyzewski climb ropes and jump over various hurdles in exercises the plebe found to be a waste of time, even if they helped prepare him for the infamous beat-the-clock, indoor obstacle course test that plebes had to pass. If a drill wasn't developing him as a point guard, Mike wasn't terribly interested. "I had him run and jump off a springboard and do a vault," Cardillo said. "He'd run into the vaulting horse once in a while instead of going over it."

Mike wasn't used to losing, or to making a fool of himself, so only the potential humiliation of his parents kept him from walking out of the academy, flying home, and seeing if the coaches at Creighton or Wisconsin would take him in on the rebound. It wasn't just swimming and gymnastics; Krzyzewski didn't know how to put up a tent either. He nearly flunked electrical engineering and French, even though he'd been a member of Weber's French Club. Mike was just trying to survive each day so he could advance to the next one. It's the West Point way.

Two Columbos, Moe Mlynski and Ed Stanislawski, flew out to New York to visit/comfort their friend. They slept overnight in the Port Authority Terminal in Manhattan, caught an early morning bus to West Point, and found Krzyzewski waiting for them at the academy gates. He was so happy to see someone from home, he had tears in his eyes.

If Krzyzewski had any break at all, it came inside Washington Hall, where, under the stained-glass windows and state flags and the massive mural depicting history's greatest military battles, varsity athletes sat together at corps squad tables, with no bracing required during meals. The recruited athletes were not generally a privileged set within their companies, but the relaxation of rules at the dining table was a cherished exception. Dinner ended at seven, giving the plebes three hours to study before it was lights out. Their course load was so intense that freshmen sometimes studied after hours, under their bed covers, with the aid of flashlights.

At Central Gym and in the field house, Knight thought he needed his own brand of hazing to mold Army into a team that could compete. With the academy's height limit set at six foot six (an occasional waiver allowed for players a bit taller), he had no choice but to emphasize defense, discipline, and conditioning. That was the reason why Joe Lapchick, the St. John's coach, had likened a game against Army to a trip inside a "human meat grinder."

The one NBA-level player on Knight's first team, six-foot-six Mike Silliman out of Louisville, Kentucky, could have played for just about any major college in the nation, and he would captain the 1968 U.S. Olympic team that won gold in Mexico City. Had Silliman not wrecked his left knee in a January 1966 game against Rutgers, Knight might have accomplished what his predecessor, Locke, did not — win the then-prestigious National Invitation Tournament in Madison Square Garden.

Army beat Manhattan and upset San Francisco in the first two rounds of the fourteen-team NIT, and the Cadets had top-seeded Brigham Young in deep trouble in the semifinals before the officials made what Knight described as an "atrocious" and "gutless" blocking call on Army star Bill Helkie that fouled him out. "I thought Knight was going to lose what little religion he had that night," said one of his players, Bob Seigle. The Cougars won by six, and afterward Knight told reporters that his kids had "sweated blood" all year in practice. "And then he walked outside into the hallway and he went after [referee] Lou Eisenstein again," Seigle said. "If he got his hands on him, there's no telling what would have happened."

This was the varsity program that Krzyzewski entered as a sophomore in the fall of '66, after spending his freshman year, in Seigle's words, "as a starry-eyed cadet who didn't care anything about the military stuff." That characterization was disputed (somewhat) by Krzyzewski's company mates. Gaylord conceded that Mike was never interested in trying to persuade people he was a model cadet, but insisted that "he was good at what he did." Said Baldwin: "He was not an indifferent cadet. He was not a slacker. He was not a guy who people thought was just here to play basketball."

Krzyzewski averaged 11.3 points per game for a winning plebe team and compensated for his moderate foot speed with a mental agility and court awareness that kept him a step or two ahead of the play. Knight noticed, and he made plans for Krzyzewski to play significant minutes as a yearling doing what he did best — taking charges on defense and deliberately running Knight's reverse action offense, which required players to reverse the ball from one side of the court to the other while setting screens. This was the system run by one of Knight's mentors, Pete Newell, who had won NCAA and NIT championships and an Olympic gold medal. (Knight had a West Coast wise man in Newell, a heartland wise man in Hank Iba, and an East Coast wise man in Clair Bee.)

Meanwhile, the Army coach continued to punish his Cadets in practice so that the games would come easier to them and West Point would remain the best defensive team in America. His players wore white Converse high-tops, khaki-colored gym shorts, and gray T-shirts that carried the AAA (Army Athletics Association) logo. Knight had every minute of every drill planned out, and a horn would blow when it was time for his players to move to the next station. The players' practice uniforms were completely soaked through when the final horn was blown.

The Cadets were forever running the zigzag drill, a quadriceps-burning exercise for defenders forced to slide their feet, stop on a dime, and reverse field on a 45-degree angle as an offensive player tried to advance his dribble. In another drill, Knight had defensive players scramble into position to take charges from offensive players going full speed to the basket. The Army coach also summoned his Cuyahoga Falls days by positioning two lines of Cadets opposite each other, rolling out a ball, and ordering the two players at the front of the lines to dive for it. The loser of that battle had to stop the winner from scoring — at all costs. If you didn't dive for any loose ball in the vicinity, you needed to find a new sport. Hitting the floor was everything at Knight's West Point.

"The loose ball drill would not be over," said six-foot-six forward Mike Noonan, "until there was blood on the floor."

One day Eiber, a six-foot-six, 200-pound forward, looked across the court to find the six-foot, 180-pound Krzyzewski (he had been listed as six foot one at Weber) as his opponent in the loose ball drill. Eiber shrugged at Mike. "He was all business," the forward said. "I dove for the ball, knocked him out of the way, and got the ball. And when I went down to make the layup, Mike jumped on my back to stop me from scoring."

Knight surely approved. Tall and fit and wearing a crewcut, Knight looked young enough to join his players in drills, to be *one of the boys*. He never let them feel that way. "The only thing I had to do was duck the folding metal chairs; Knight threw those like frisbees in practice," said Wade Urban, a reserve guard. "Those things would sail into the stands . . . He was a wild man. He only knew one style, and that was to break you down." After he once made a mistake while playing defense, Urban recalled, Knight stood five feet behind him and fired a ball right into the back of his head, knocking him out. "They hauled me off the floor until I came to," Urban said. "That was my first combat experience, with Bob Knight."

Urban was hardly the coach's only target. Simmons, a six-foot-six sophomore, had played for an easygoing high school coach in Chico, California, who went by his first name. The day Knight picked up Simmons, then an incoming freshman, at LaGuardia Airport was the day Dick realized he would never be calling his coach "Bobby."

A high-leaping shooter who didn't play physically enough for Knight's liking and who struggled to dribble the ball, Simmons was on the receiving end of many eruptions. When he'd awkwardly try to back his way into the basket to protect the ball from a smaller defender, Knight would scream at him, "Come here, Mary Alice, you big pussy!" Knight would storm down the court with his index finger pointing at Simmons, and then he'd repeatedly pound his knuckle into the player's chest while screaming profanities in his face. Years later, after seeing action in the war, Simmons told people that being a company commander in Vietnam was easier than participating in Knight's basketball practice.

"We hated him," Simmons said.

The players constantly griped about Knight's tyranny, with one exception. "Mike Krzyzewski would never say anything," said one member of the basketball program. "He was on the quiet side, more stoic than anything. He never joined in the complaining about Coach."

Not that Knight spared him any abuse. The coach who called his sophomore point guard "Kre-shef-ski" instead of the proper "Sha-shef-ski" struggled with his given name too. During Krzyzewski's first two seasons, Knight later joked, he thought his point guard's name was "GoddamnitMike." Mike once called his mother to inform her that his coach kept calling him all these nasty things. "At least he's talking to you," Emily Krzyzewski told her younger son. "If he stops talking to you, then you're in trouble."

Knight had a talent for ripping his players during shooting drills — *You're shooting it on the way down; shoot at the top of your jump and then come down!* — and he never believed in Krzyzewski's aim, despite his high school scoring titles. As forcefully as Al Ostrowski told Mike to shoot, Knight was telling Mike not to shoot. The coach made it clear to Mike that his job at the point was to protect the ball, distribute it to the frontcourt players inside, and play defense.

The 1966–1967 Cadets lost their first three games, including the home opener against Princeton, the only visiting team to win at West Point in two years. Krzyzewski, who wore number 12 in his home whites and number 13 in his dark road jersey, scored only four points in his first varsity game, and one of the New York papers spelled his name "Kruyzenski" in the box score. After being held scoreless in his second game, a blowout loss at Syracuse, Army's point guard could find his name in the next day's box score as "Krsy'ski" in the *Syracuse Post-Standard*. The following morning, after a seven-point defeat at Cornell, the *Rochester Democrat and Chronicle* got closer in documenting Krzyzewski's 3-for-12 shooting, 8-point performance by spelling his name "Kryzewski," before the *Ithaca Journal* finally got it right but celebrated by accidentally publishing Krzyzewski's line twice in the box score. Mike was probably not as upset about the printed errors as his coach was about the fact that he took a dozen shots.

The Cadets gathered themselves and easily defeated Lehigh and Holy Cross at home before taking a pre-Christmas road trip into Big Ten country. Down 14 to Purdue with two minutes to play, the brilliance of Army's six-foot-six Steve Hunt — who would finish with 27 points and 12 rebounds — and some missed Boilermaker free throws helped cut the deficit to four in the final seconds. John Mikula made two foul shots with one second left to make it a two-point game, and then a Purdue player committed an inexplicable mistake on the inbounds pass: he threw the ball down the other end of the court and watched it go untouched out of bounds, giving Army the ball under its own basket.

Ed Jordan, a six-foot-three guard, then caught the inbounds pass to the right of the foul line and immediately launched a jumper before the buzzer sounded; it went in to send the game into overtime. Purdue somehow recovered, controlling the extra five minutes to win by 10 — after Hunt became the fifth Army player to foul out — but the Cadets' startling comeback gave Knight a renewed feeling of confidence as he prepared for an emotional return to Ohio State.

The Army coach wanted this one, badly. His Ohio State teams had never lost inside their home St. John Arena during Knight's three varsity seasons, and the former Buckeye reserve intended to keep his personal undefeated record intact.

The Cadets had the game in their hands too, unnerving Ohio State with their man-to-man defense and taking a 45–36 lead in the second half. They were trying to hang on at the end, holding a one-point lead with a little more than a minute to go, when Ohio State's Steve Howell scored off an offensive rebound to make it 60–59. Howell stole the ball from Army on the next possession, and when the final score of 61–59 was in the books, Knight had finally lost a game at St. John Arena. The *Dayton Daily News* described him as "a sick young man."

"He was really broken down," confirmed Army's senior captain, Dan Schrage.

The Cadets spent the days between Christmas and New Year's in North Carolina for the Charlotte Invitational, where they blew out Fordham (Krzyzewski cracked double figures with 10 points on 5-of-7 shooting) before missing another opportunity against an opponent from a heavyweight conference when they lost to Maryland in the final, 57–54. According to an eyewitness, after tournament organizers wheeled the runner-up trophy into the Army locker room, "Knight turned around and spit on it."

His team then ripped off six consecutive victories, four of them before a home crowd inside the arena that Knight wanted to have the feel of a giant pit. "It's a big coliseum with a court surrounded by dirt," Urban said. "When you play in our field house, it's like going into the sixth level of hell."

Near the end of the season, Krzyzewski had a breakout offensive performance against Rutgers, playing more like he'd played in high school by scoring 17 points — or five more than were scored by his counterpart at point guard, a Rutgers senior named Jim Valvano — in a 77–59 victory. The Cadets beat New York University, and then met Navy in a regular-season finale that meant everything. Army-Navy in basketball was not Army-Navy in football, but it was close enough. The Cadets hadn't lost to the Midshipmen since George Hunter was coaching at West Point in 1963, and Knight knew that a defeat would cost his team any chance of reaching the NIT for a fourth consecutive year.

A capacity crowd of 4,500 assembled inside Navy's field house on the annual weekend when the two military academies competed in eight sports. The Midshipmen had the better of it early on, but a Krzyzewski basket late in the first half gave the Cadets a lead, at 28–26, that they never surrendered. Krzyzewski made a long jump shot early in the second half and then a banker to help Army secure control of what would be a 64–54 victory that featured four Cadets in double figures, including Krzyzewski with 13. Knight actually did let his point guard shoot once in a while, though some indignities lived on. The Associated Press dispatch from Annapolis misspelled Mike's name as "Kryzewski" and "Kryyzewski."

The Cadets had won three in a row and ten of their last twelve to finish 13-8, and as a local and Madison Square Garden favorite, they were confident the NIT would reward them with a bid. "But the year before we got there Knight got a technical and they didn't invite us back," Schrage said. Knight's tirades during and after the BYU defeat had likely cost his team. Some New York sportswriters were in the habit of calling him "Bobby T," as in "Technical."

It was a disappointing end to a first varsity season for Krzyzewski, who averaged a respectable 5.3 points. He wrote letters during the season to his old neighborhood friend Vivian Przybylo, who was away at college. Vivian and the Columbos caught a game here and there, and they cringed when Knight screamed at Mickey from the bench. Al Ostrowski was a hard-ass at Weber, but Knight was an entirely different animal. Still, Krzyzewski seemed to weather his storms without much problem.

"Every letter I got from him, it was two lines of, 'Hi Viv, how are you?'" Przybylo said. "And then it would be a huge story of the last game he played with the score in big letters. Basketball was everything to Mick."

From the letters Przybylo could tell that Mick was very lonely at West Point. Between his sophomore and junior years, they got together with the rest of the Columbos and relived their glory days on Augusta Boulevard. The world was exploding around them in the long, hot summer of 1967.

Antiwar advocates and civil rights leaders were condemning the conflict in Vietnam. More than 150 riots would break out in American cities like Newark, Minneapolis, Milwaukee, Detroit, and Washington, DC. Chicago was largely spared until the following spring, when rioting followed the assassination of Dr. Martin Luther King Jr., and the following summer, when police clashed with protesters at the Democratic National Convention.

Mick was trying to savor life away from the academy and back on Cortez, eating his mother's home-cooked dinners and three-chip chocolate chip cookies, when he met a dark-haired United Airlines flight attendant named Carol Marsh at a small gathering of friends. She was, in the parlance of the day, a knockout. Krzyzewski liked her legs, and truth be told, she liked his too. One skeptical Columbo, Larry Kusch, took one head-to-toe survey of Marsh and said, "No way. Mick's got no chance. He is dating out of his league."

Marsh grew up a Washington Redskins and New York Yankees fan who adored Mickey Mantle and went by the nickname "Mickey." Her brother was a college baseball player; she could talk sports with the best of them. Marsh did not have much else in common with Krzyzewski. "I'm a WASP and a Baptist who grew up in Alexandria, Virginia," she would say. "I like country music. Mike likes Motown."

Mike loved Motown, though he was hopelessly lost as a dancer. He asked Marsh to join him for a Martha Reeves and the Vandellas concert at the 250-seat Whisky A Go Go on the corner of Rush and Chestnut, where admission was $3.50, plus a two-drink minimum at $1.50 a pop — a good deal to hear the group sing its 1967 hit "Jimmy Mack." Krzyzewski and Marsh had enough fun for Mike to later write her from West Point to ask if she would go to a Bears game with him, though he confessed to her, for some ungodly reason, that she was his third choice for the date. Marsh got over her anger, attended the game, and ultimately changed her nickname from "Mickey" to "Mickie," to avoid sharing the same name as her new boyfriend.

Knight didn't want his players to have serious girlfriends — he saw them as distractions — but his point guard didn't really care. Soon after Krzyzewski met Marsh, he walked into the room of his E-3 company mates Robert Hoffman and Bob Baldwin. "Mike was real quiet about it," Baldwin recalled. "He didn't say, 'I met the girl I'm going to marry.' But Mike was definitely smitten."

Krzyzewski told everyone in his company that he was serious about his relationship with Marsh. "Mike zoned in on Mickie very early and never wavered from it," Cary Gaylord said. So it surprised nobody when Marsh showed up at Army's 1967–1968 season opener at Princeton, the eighth-ranked team in the nation, and a perennially strong Ivy League program that had won twenty-five games and reached the NCAA Tournament the year before.

Marsh had put in for a transfer from Chicago to New York before she met Krzyzewski, and she was now living in the city with three roommates. They would take weekend drives up the Palisades Parkway to West Point to meet up with Mike and his roommates — when they had time off — and sometimes Mike and his roommates would make the 50-mile southbound drive to meet up with them. The cadets thought the long-haired kids in the city smoking pot were from a different planet, and those long-haired kids thought the same of the cadets. And yet Krzyzewski and his friends were not as clean-living as their appearance suggested. "I made mistakes as a college student," he would say years later. "I did some crazy things on weekends in New York. You drink. You dance. You stay out all night. You do all the things that kids do."

Krzyzewski and Marsh were enjoying each other's company and growing closer. She would tease him that she preferred the playing style of Louisiana State's phenom Pete Maravich, who averaged 44 points per game during his college career, to the deliberate approach Knight forced on his point guard. "And that would just drive Mike insane," Mickie said.

When Marsh realized she was not scheduled to work any flights on December 1, she decided to grab a roommate and drive her red Volkswagen Beetle to Princeton for the big opening game, without telling Mike. Marsh drove right into a heavy snowstorm, and when she pulled off the highway in search of refuge, she unwittingly found and checked into the motel that was housing the Army team.

The Cadets would lead Princeton for most of the game before a packed house in Dillon Gym, yet the Tigers recovered late to give their rookie coach, Pete Carril, his first victory at the Ivy League school. Krzyzewski fouled out after scoring four points.

The following morning Knight had an argument with a team manager, who would quit the program. The Army coach then walked into the hotel restaurant to find his players eating breakfast together, while Krzyzewski and Marsh were eating at a separate table. Knight turned to face them; Marsh later told people that she had never seen a stare quite like it. "And then Knight went crazy," recalled Mike's teammate, Dick Simmons. He was raging over the fact that Mike wasn't sitting with his fellow players, and over his erroneous assumption that his point guard had spent the night with his girlfriend. Knight told his point guard that he was in danger of being removed from the team.

"That was my introduction to him as a basketball player," Marsh would say of her boyfriend. "I kind of learned that if I was going to go to games, I should keep a low profile." Krzyzewski was angry when he later met with Knight to explain that he hadn't stayed with Mickie and that he'd earned the benefit of the coach's doubt. Knight relented. As the prototypical coach on the floor, Krzyzewski was the only player who could have persuaded him to stand down.

Sophomore guard Jim Oxley spoke for many Cadets when he said, "We all tried to protect ourselves from [Knight's] wrath." Bill Schutsky, the outstanding player and captain of the 1967–1968 team, often thought of quitting because of Knight, who was particularly rough on his leading scorer. In the locker room, Knight once "fired" Schutsky as captain, then asked his players to vote for a new one; when they unanimously voted to restore Schutsky, Knight told them, "Okay, that's the answer I wanted." Schutsky made a habit of running down the side of the court opposite the coach, leaving his fellow forward, Mike Noonan, to catch an earful near the Army bench. Noonan would later go to Airborne Ranger School, where he lost 30 pounds over nine weeks of food and sleep deprivation. "And there's nothing in Ranger School," he said, "compared to preseason practice with Coach Knight."

The players looked for comic relief wherever they could find it. One day in the mess hall, where plebes were required to cut equal pieces of dessert for everyone at the table, Noonan decided he wanted the entire black forest cake for himself. He tried to steal the piece reserved for Jim Oxley, and a food fight ensued. Krzyzewski responded by grabbing a healthy portion of the cake and smashing it into Noonan's shocked face. "Not because he favored me over Noonan," Oxley said, "because we were all friends. But he thought Noonan was getting the better of me, and Mike didn't like that."

In Knight's practices, the Cadets did find a temporary sanctuary in the company of assistant coach Al LoBalbo, a defensive specialist from the Bronx. LoBalbo was a prince of a man who took the big men to one end of the floor and talked to them, gently, while Knight was tearing into the guards downcourt.

Colonel Tom Rogers, an officer representative and Knight aide, was another voice of reason to whom the beleaguered players could turn; Krzyzewski was particularly close to the colonel. Rogers and his fellow rep Major Richard Cardillo, the gymnastics instructor, would host the players' girlfriends at their houses while the players were restricted to the barracks. Cardillo's wife Inez had the plebes over for a Thanksgiving dinner that Krzyzewski still counted among his West Point highlights decades later.

Inez had ordered her young son Robert, a ball boy, to never repeat any of the curse words he heard from Coach Knight during the games. Robert's father was charged by his superiors to keep a close eye on Knight, to ensure he adhered to the academy's rules and values. He saw himself as more of a father figure to Knight than as an assistant and tried to tell the coach that his anger was getting in the way of his talent.

And yet there was one thing Cardillo emphasized with the West Point administrators and civilians who asked about Knight's considerable warts: he knew how to win and what it took to win, and the young men on his team who were being prepared for combat needed to learn how to win. That was something nobody could take away from Knight.

Knight could blow his whistle at any moment in any practice and identify what every player had done right and wrong on the previous sequence. He became the first Army coach to win twenty regular-season games when he presided over a twelve-game winning streak in 1967–1968 that started with a late Krzyzewski free throw that helped beat Yale by a point and included a dramatic 55–54 comeback victory at St. John's, which had held a 12-point halftime lead. After Schutsky fouled out late, Krzyzewski and his new backcourt partner and road roommate, Oxley, made big back-to-back baskets to give the Cadets the cushion they needed. Oxley's extended family was seated behind the Army bench, including six of his aunts. Afterward they circled Oxley and staged what he called an intervention. "That guy [Knight] is absolutely crazy," they told him. "You cannot stay here." The Cadets were so giddy over the result that they threw Knight in the shower. "That's the first time we had a public display of affection with him," Noonan said.

Army was being patient with the ball on offense, thanks to Krzyzewski, a critical development for an undersized and underskilled team in a college basketball era without a shot clock or a three-point line. The Cadets also led the nation in defense, surrendering only 57.9 points per game. So they had a chance to compete in the NCAA Tournament, which had surpassed the NIT in prestige and now crowned the school recognized as the sport's national champ.

Knight had a team that Simmons called "a bunch of slow white guys," and though he still didn't have a single African American player on his varsity, Knight saw where the major college game was heading — or better yet, where it had already arrived. With an all-Black starting five, Texas Western had beaten all-white Kentucky two years earlier for the national title. West Point had not opened its doors to many Black cadets; the academy graduated fewer than ten per year into the early 1970s. Its lack of diversity did nothing to attract the great African American athlete.

Those athletes were playing for civilian schools in the NCAA Tournament. Knight explained to his team that with Lew Alcindor in the middle of John Wooden's UCLA dynasty and Elvin Hayes averaging 37 points per game at Houston, Army had no shot to beat either school in the twenty-three-team NCAAs, but he thought the Cadets had a reasonable shot to win the sixteen-team NIT. He asked them to decide what they preferred to do.

The Cadets voted unanimously to bus down to the big city and take their chances in the Garden. In the first round, they were paired against Notre Dame — on St. Patrick's Day weekend. The Army–Notre Dame rivalry that played out in Yankee Stadium in the 1940s was everything to college football; Army–Notre Dame in the Garden in the 1960s was significant enough to college basketball to draw a national TV audience.

Schutsky was unstoppable in the first half, scoring 22 points to give Army a one-point lead at the break. "And then it felt like to us that the refs came out in green outfits," Schutsky said.

The Irish blitzed Army early in the second half, scoring 12 of the first 14 points to seize control of the game. The Cadets rallied, but their frontcourt players were plagued by foul trouble and their starting backcourt of Krzyzewski and Oxley combined for just 10 points, making Schutsky's final performance in an Army uniform (31 points) nothing more than an interesting footnote to Notre Dame's 62–58 victory. The defeat was especially painful for Knight, who punched the side of the bus on the way home to West Point. But there was one Cadet who was taking it harder than anyone, the same junior whose picture ran in newspapers across America the following day, courtesy of an Associated Press photographer who captured the outstretched point guard trying and failing to stop Notre Dame's Mike O'Connell from scoring near the baseline.

Mike Krzyzewski was crying in the locker room. "A good Catholic kid like him, he did not want to lose to Notre Dame," Noonan said. "He was crestfallen. It was televised back to Chicago, and he'd just lost to the big Catholic school. I said to him, 'Mike, you're going to be okay. You've got next year.'"

BOB KNIGHT TRULY believed he was turning boys into men and officers. A number of his West Point players told people decades after leaving the academy that they would still run through a brick wall for him. Why? Wade Urban, senior guard, said that Knight taught him how to react in a split second, under pressure, in a crisis, and that his coaching helped him survive two ambushes in Vietnam. David Kremenak, senior forward, said that Knight was one of two people outside of his family to visit him in Walter

Reed Army Medical Center after he suffered brain damage from being run over by a jeep.

But his style of coaching put his athletes under so much stress that it occasionally broke them, temporarily or permanently. Simmons, a senior starter and son of an Army National Guard member, quit the team before the 1968–1969 season. He was the rare athlete who wanted to be in the Army and wanted to serve in Vietnam more than he wanted to focus on sports; he was also tired of Knight calling him "Mary Alice" or "Alice" or just plain "pussy."

Simmons reconsidered, however, and rejoined the team shortly thereafter. And then there was his fellow senior, Steve Hunt, one of the most talented big men to ever play at the academy, the country's second-best shooter as a junior with a field-goal percentage of .621. Hunt, said Urban, "hated Knight with a passion." The coach got on his center about his weight, and Hunt wore a sauna suit to try to improve his fitness. He had injured his back in preseason, exacerbating the situation; still, Knight's verbal attacks on Hunt picked up in intensity. Hunt played below his standards in the first three games of the 1968–1969 season, including a two-point effort against the Temple Owls; he'd scored 26 against them the previous season. The center decided after that game that he would never again play for Knight.

Simmons said that the coach had gone ballistic on Hunt during one halftime rant, calling him "a son of a bitch" before benching him. "The next day I saw Steve Hunt," Simmons recalled, "and he said, 'I'm not putting up with that shit.'" Another player said that Knight had grabbed Hunt in the locker room, and that the player knocked the coach's hand away and told him not to touch him again. Major Richard Cardillo recalled a post-practice scene of the coaches and players walking up the metal stairs in the field house before an irate Knight "got hold of Steve Hunt and hauled him into a locker."

Simmons also recalled walking through the field house when one of Army's veteran track coaches stopped him and said, "Mr. Simmons, all the coaches know what's going on at practice. And we want you to know that we're with you guys. The only piece of advice I'd give you is, 'Don't hit him.'"

Krzyzewski, the only logical choice, was voted captain before his senior season. Beyond his play, Mike was a valuable asset to the coaches when they brought high school prospects on post. "He could never get enough of what we were doing in recruiting," said one of Knight's assistants, Don DeVoe. "He never let us down in that regard. The Vietnam War was really starting to pick up . . . and we felt it was really critical that kids understood what they were about to do if they went to West Point."

Krzyzewski was also Knight's much-better half on the court, a disciplined leader who was calm and reassuring when his teammates needed support. "I got into some trouble with Coach Knight, like all of us did, and I remember Mike having my back, patting me on the butt, telling me it would be all right," said the graduated Schutsky. Mike Gyovai, a six-foot-five center Knight called the toughest player he ever had, once broke teammate Alan Fenty's jaw with an elbow while they tangled under the boards in practice. Gyovai went to Krzyzewski, not Knight, to say he thought it would be best for the team if he quit; the point guard talked him out of it.

Doug Clevenger, a talented sophomore forward, once had a heated confrontation with Knight during a scrimmage that escalated when the coach called him, by one teammate's account, an "insolent bastard," or a "lowlife sonofabitch," by another's. Clevenger shouted back at Knight and started walking off the floor before Krzyzewski intercepted him. "Mike went over to bring him back in line," Gyovai said, "and was like, 'Where the hell are you going?'"

Krzyzewski had earned so much respect from players and coaches over his first three years in the program, said classmate Simmons, that Knight asked him to run practice in his place if he had to slip out of the gym for a quick meeting. Urban said that if the coach had a question about somebody on or around the team, "he wouldn't go to that individual, he'd go to Mike and ask about him." Cardillo recalled that after one of Knight's halftime tirades, which included objects being thrown around the locker room, Krzyzewski calmed everyone down once the coach stormed out of the room. "Mike was a healer," Cardillo said. "He tried to fix things."

Krzyzewski won his first six games as captain, starting with an actual double-figure scoring performance against Lehigh (14 points, including 12 foul shots in 15 attempts) and concluding with two decisive free throws against Bradley in the Kentucky Invitational. In that game Krzyzewski suffered a bloody eye injury that was caused, according to Knight assistant Dave Bliss, by a Bradley player who gouged Krzyzewski. "Mike was one of the toughest players I've ever seen," Bliss would say.

That toughness was tested after Army lost to host Kentucky and its star center Dan Issel in the tournament final, reportedly inspiring Knight to spit on a runner-up trophy for the second time. The Cadets dropped their next four games, and Knight had his players write him a letter on why they thought they weren't winning. In his note, Dick Simmons told him, "This whole program is against you, the coach." As captain, Krzyzewski felt entirely responsible for the losing; he just couldn't understand why it was happening. "It was the toughest period of my life as a player," he would say.

The schedule eased up enough for Army to win four consecutive games before traveling to the Bronx to play the Fordham Rams, whose senior captain, Frank McLaughlin, was tired of watching his teams get physically manhandled by the Cadets. "We're not going to let them beat the shit out of us this time," McLaughlin told his teammates in a meeting. So Fordham fought fire with fire, winning by a 52–42 count, and when it was over Knight got into it with Fordham coach Ed Conlin, a former Rams star and first-round NBA draft pick.

McLaughlin was on the narrow stairway that both teams used to exit the court. "And the next thing you know Knight and Conlin are yelling and screaming at each other," McLaughlin said. "I just remember overhearing Knight later saying, 'I wasn't able to hit him, but I was close enough to spit on him.'"

Ten days later, with Rutgers up two in the final seconds of a contentious game, Knight was actually one of the few members of Army's traveling delegation who *didn't* completely lose his cool. Clevenger put a hard foul on the home team's Doug Brittelle, and the two started swinging at each other, with Clevenger landing a clean punch. Gyovai ran from the other end — with Krzyzewski trailing him — and did what he called "a gorilla stomp" on a fan, one of several who had run out of the boisterous crowd of 2,800 and onto the court. "The cops had to come out on the floor, and I ended up in the seventh row of bleachers, with fists flying," Gyovai said.

The Scarlet Knights finally beat an Army team that had long dominated them in their annual series. The two schools were jockeying for an NIT bid, and with Vietnam becoming an increasingly unpopular war, Army was something of an unwelcome guest at liberal Northeast schools. It was getting tougher and tougher to persuade prospects to commit to the academy, according to DeVoe; Wade Urban said that he had heard opposing fans in different gyms call the Cadets "baby killers." So it wasn't a terrible surprise that, as Army headed for the locker room following a player-fan melee, a spectator reached over the railing and tried to hit the oblivious Knight in the back of the head.

The man missed, but the Knight colleague walking behind him, Bill Parcells, did not. Parcells was an Army football assistant, and a good friend of Knight's. He watched NFL games (including the New York Jets' shocking upset of the mighty Baltimore Colts in Super Bowl III) in the basketball coach's basement and played pickup basketball games with Knight and other prominent figures stationed at West Point, such as Norman Schwarzkopf and tennis champion Arthur Ashe. Parcells also scouted opponents for Knight and sometimes sat with him during games.

Seeing what the spectator attempted to do, Parcells nailed him with a hard punch to the head, leaving the man slumped over the railing and apparently unconscious. In the locker room Parcells informed Knight of what had happened, and of his concern that he might get arrested. The Army basketball coach told Parcells to put on a cadet's long gray coat and black hat and then told his players to surround the football assistant and act as his protective cocoon on their walk to the bus. They escaped New Jersey without further incident.

Army led the nation in defense, again, which proved to be too much for Pittsburgh, Iona, and NYU in consecutive victories at West Point's field house. The Cadets then traveled to Annapolis to face Navy on March 1; the Midshipmen had never beaten Knight as an assistant or head coach. Sitting in the sellout crowd of 4,595 was U.S. Army Chief of Staff General William Westmoreland, who nine months earlier had been replaced as commander of American forces in Vietnam following the Tet Offensive.

The Cadets dominated the Middies, both under the boards and all over the court, building a big lead and forcing Navy to foul and send them to the line. Krzyzewski took the most free throws, nine, and made seven of them in what would be a 51–35 triumph, improving Army's record to 14-8 and keeping alive its NIT hopes. Knight knew that beating Navy meant as much to Krzyzewski as it did to him. He awarded his senior captain the game ball.

But the moment was stolen from Krzyzewski in the immediate wake of the game. A call had come in with terrible news from Chicago. Krzyzewski's father, William, had been ill, and the family hadn't wanted to concern Mike while he was studying and playing at West Point. Mike's best friend on the team, Oxley, remembered Knight summoning Mike for a talk on the team bus. When the point guard returned to his seat next to his backcourt partner, Oxley asked, "Is everything okay?"

"No," Mike said. "My father just died. We're going out to Chicago tomorrow."

William Krzyzewski was fifty-eight when he died of a cerebral hemorrhage on Sunday, March 2, 1969. Oxley said that Mike spoke about his mother all the time at the academy, but seldom about his father, other than to say that he was an elevator operator who had changed his name to Kross on some paperwork. (The *Chicago Tribune* obituary was printed under the boldface name "Kross" and identified Mike's father as "William Kross [Krzyzewski].") Inez Cardillo, the officer representative's wife, recalled seeing William Krzyzewski at one Army game — a rarity, since the people in Mike's life barely remembered seeing his father anywhere. "He was just so very proud that Mike was able to go to West Point," Inez said.

Knight drove his point guard to the airport early in the morning, in dangerous wintry conditions, and gave him some pocket cash in case he needed it, NCAA rules be damned. There were two games to go, but the coach told Krzyzewski to take care of his mom, to take as much time away as he needed. Knight told him he would meet him in Chicago.

Sure enough, Knight left his team and was back in the Krzyzewski home that night for the first time since his 1965 recruiting visit. "He came in and loosened his tie," Mike would recall. "He sat around the kitchen table—Polish people sit around the kitchen table and eat all the time. My mom had some Polish food on the table, and Coach would just grab it with his fingers. It was very relaxed—just the sort of thing my mom needed."

Knight was showing his human side again, at the most critical time. "It was as if nothing else mattered to him right then other than helping my mom and me," Krzyzewski would say. The Cadets were 14-8 and needed to beat Colgate and Rochester to qualify for the NIT, and yet their coach was willing to miss multiple practices to be there for his captain. Knight stayed through the Wednesday morning funeral at St. Helen before traveling back to New York. Mike's father was buried at Saint Adalbert Catholic Cemetery; the tombstone was paid for by the government because of William's military service and carried the name "Kross," which William had used in the Army. Mike said goodbye to his mother, relatives, and friends, and though Knight had excused him from the trip, he made it back to West Point in time to catch the Thursday bus to Colgate.

Krzyzewski scored 13 points in a 73–49 rout and held the Red Raiders' star, Rick Caputo, to 1 basket and 5 points, 15 below his average. Krzyzewski always covered the other team's highest-scoring guard, spending more time and energy on limiting the opponent's stat line than on inflating his own. Mike grinded every day without airing any complaints or making any excuses.

Just like his old man.

ON TUESDAY NIGHT, March 18, 1969, Mike Krzyzewski was a college student with a plan. He was scheduled to graduate from the academy in June and then to marry the love of his life, Carol "Mickie" Marsh, hours later. But on that March night in Madison Square Garden, Krzyzewski cared only about the NIT game he had to play.

Army had beaten Wyoming in the first round, holding the Cowboys to 34 points below their scoring average, to advance to their second-round meeting with South Carolina and its legendary coach, Frank McGuire. The son of a New York City cop, McGuire had unleashed a fellow New Yorker named John Roche, a sophomore guard who averaged 24 points per game and was named Atlantic Coast Conference Player of the Year. Roche was everything Krzyzewski was not at Army.

"You're not allowed to shoot," Knight told Krzyzewski before the South Carolina game, as if that were some kind of new development. "You take a shot and I will break your arm."

Krzyzewski's chief assignment was to contain Roche — and contain him he did. Roche took 20 shots, and missed 16, while Krzyzewski tracked him baseline to baseline before a crowd of more than 12,000. Army controlled the entire game, taking an eight-point halftime lead before beating the taller, favored Gamecocks, 59–45. Oxley, Simmons, and Clevenger scored in double figures for Army, but it was Krzyzewski who defined what would be his last victory as a college player. He even deferred on a wide-open jumper near the foul line, if only to avoid seeing if Knight was serious about his threat. "As I cocked my shooting arm," Krzyzewski would recall, "my whole life passed before me. I passed off. We won. So it worked."

Krzyzewski made seven of his nine foul shots to finish with nine points. Afterward, Knight praised his defense, playmaking, and selflessness. Army would lose to Boston College in the semis, and then to Tennessee in the consolation game, but in the end these Cadets would be remembered for the adversity they overcame and for the captain who steered them through the turbulence they encountered — on game nights as well as in practice.

MIKE KRZYZEWSKI DID NOT graduate near the top of his West Point class of 800 cadets who survived the rigors of the academy, but he was not among the 400 fellow plebes who did not make it to the finish line. "We were in the lower half," said classmate John Legere. "The smart guys wore gold stars on their collar. I don't think Mike and I were offered those."

Krzyzewski's teammate Wade Urban placed Mike's class ranking at 563 out of the 800, right behind Urban's 562. "The only time I was ever ahead of Mike," he said. On his way out the door, Krzyzewski absorbed one last round of hazing in his class yearbook, which explained that his name was pronounced "Kriz-il-lon-ski or some other variation" and mocked the size of his nose by stating that his "success in the future will rank with such notables as Durante, DeBergerac [sic], and Pinocchio."

All 800 graduates threw their caps into the sunny sky at the June 4 ceremony inside Michie Stadium, four days before President Richard Nixon met with the president of South Vietnam, Nguyen Van Thieu, to inform him that he would be reducing the more than half a million U.S. troops in Vietnam, and six weeks before Neil Armstrong set foot on the moon.

In his half-hour speech during the ceremony, General Westmoreland challenged the cadets to stand strong against those who were protesting the war and the system that developed men to fight it. Krzyzewski was not scheduled to go to Vietnam, at least not yet. He was scheduled to marry Marsh at the Catholic chapel on post four hours after he graduated.

Emily was there when her younger son wore a bow tie as part of his uniform on his wedding day; Mickie's long dark hair looked striking against her white dress and veil. Mike's brother Bill was his best man. The union of Krzyzewski and Marsh was one of fifty-nine West Point weddings that week, all handled by the cadet hostess, Dorothy Schandler. The academy weddings that got the most press coverage were those of a retired army colonel's twin daughters, who both married West Pointers, and of the cadet who married a descendant of Benedict Arnold.

But on that glorious bluff above the Hudson on June 4, 1969, two people came together to form a most unlikely power couple. Mickey and Mickie were not going to change America, but they were going to change the landscape of American sports.

3

HOOSIERS

As MIKE KRZYZEWSKI and his friends on the All-Army basketball team headed to practice, they saw the injured men who had returned from the jungle. The team worked out on a court below the Letterman Army Medical Center at the Presidio of San Francisco, where they shared the gym with amputees in rehab sessions and young soldiers with prosthetic legs walking about or shooting baskets from wheelchairs.

The players were moved by the sight of the wounded warriors, who were the same age they were. "You would think of the many kids you went to high school with who went to Vietnam," said one of Krzyzewski's teammates, Brad Luchini, a former player at Marquette. "You felt very fortunate, and in some respects you almost felt guilty that you were not over there."

Krzyzewski and his West Point backcourt partner, Jim Oxley, knew some cadets from their classes who had been killed in Vietnam. The bloodshed was on their minds every hour of every day. They were very cognizant of the fact that they were getting to play basketball, as part of their postgraduate military commitment, while many Army grads were off fighting a war that was opposed by the majority of Americans and had inspired the protests of hundreds of thousands of demonstrators marching through major cities.

After graduation, Krzyzewski had spent six months training to be a field artillery officer at Fort Sill in Oklahoma. His next stop was Fort Carson outside of Colorado Springs, where he was stationed for eighteen months. Krzyzewski was assigned to an artillery unit as its executive officer and put in charge of six self-propelled Howitzers. "If five were pointing one way and the sixth was going in a different direction," he said, "I knew enough to turn the sixth one around."

Once a week Krzyzewski played basketball with the Fort Carson soldiers he was charged to lead. Carson's commanding officer, Bernard Rogers, had been West Point's commandant of the Corps of Cadets, and he wanted the former Army point guard on the fort's team. He didn't care that Krzyzewski's supervising colonel preferred that his officers avoid fraternizing with the enlisted men.

The *Fort Carson Mountaineer* newspaper welcomed the basketball team's new recruit with this lead paragraph: "K-R-Z-Y-Z-E-W-S-K-I. Crish-ev-ski — or something like that. Sounds like something you might read on a pickle jar, doesn't it?" Krzyzewski became the star player and head coach, and in February 1970 he beat Fort Riley for the Fifth Army championship. It was clear early on that Mike would give Mike far more freedom than Bob Knight ever did. "Mike Krzyzewski was the big gun for Carson Thursday," reported the *Colorado Springs Gazette-Telegraph*. "He poured in 28 points." Krzyzewski won the Fifth Army title again the following year, making 11 consecutive free throws and scoring 23 in the Mountaineers' comeback victory over Fort Leonard Wood. All that success at Carson, Krzyzewski said, "was more for my playing than my coaching."

He did a lot of winning for another coach, Hal Fischer, a civilian employee at the Presidio base who held a status that was the equivalent of a colonel's. Fischer was a card-carrying hard-ass whom Bill Walton, a teenage member of his 1970 World Championship tournament team, would decades later call "the scariest, meanest person I ever met." Fischer often told his teams, "If you don't play hard, you're going straight to Vietnam." It never seemed like he was kidding.

Fischer invited West Point officers Krzyzewski and Oxley, a fifth round draft pick of the New York Knicks, to try out for his All-Army team, which included the six-foot-nine Darnell Hillman, a high-rising forward from San Jose State; Don Crenshaw from USC; Art Wilmore from San Francisco; and Fran Dunphy from LaSalle. Oxley had a house on post at the Presidio, the scenic waterfront base near the Golden Gate Bridge, and over time he invited Krzyzewski and Mickie and their infant daughter Debbie to live with him. Krzyzewski and Oxley and their All-Army teammates traveled up and down California to face club teams of former college players who were not in the kind of wartime shape that the Army players were in. Fischer used a run-and-gun style on offense and a pressing approach on defense — to wear out his opponents — and he built a winning streak that exceeded 100 games.

"Teams stayed with us the first five minutes of the game," Oxley said, "and then their tongues would start hanging out and we would just destroy them." All-Army was the Harlem Globetrotters and everyone else was the Washington Generals. Many times Fischer even brought along his own refs to officiate the games. He had complete command of his program, at all times. During team practices, if a stray general happened to wander into his gym, Fischer wasn't afraid to toss him out.

Some of his players thought he had a kind heart beneath the gruff exterior. Luchini described Fischer as a marshmallow held too close to the fire — crusty on the outside, soft on the inside. "He was a character," Oxley said. "And he felt like he never got the credit he deserved. He was always telling us essentially how good he was."

Fischer took All-Army on the road to win the armed services tournament against Navy, Air Force, and the Marines at North Carolina's Camp Lejeune (a tournament he won nearly every year), and then he led an All–Armed Forces all-star team to London, Kentucky, for the national AAU (Amateur Athletic Union) championship, which it won. Fischer took his title teams around the globe on goodwill tours to compete in places such as Lebanon, Greece, Italy, Germany, Syria, and Iran. On pregame layup lines, while Hillman and others put on a dunking show for the international crowds, Krzyzewski, Oxley, and Dunphy stayed in the rebounding line because they couldn't get over the rim.

On a trip to Tehran for the world military championship tournament, which Fischer's all-stars would win, some players felt an anti-American sentiment in the air, others did not. They were all struck by the perpetual presence of armed security forces in the streets and around the team. Krzyzewski and Oxley roomed together in Iran, and they heard dogs barking all night long, at least until rounds of gunfire suddenly silenced them. "The next day they would serve us some kind of stew, and we would not eat it," Oxley said. "We thought for sure there was dog in that stew." They met with the shah of Iran's brother, and they ate at the same U.S. embassy where the hostage crisis would unfold in 1979–1981.

Just like at West Point, Krzyzewski was known more for his toughness than for his talent. Luchini recalled the point guard catching an elbow to the face in practice. "I don't know if Mike's nose was broken, but there was some blood," he said. "And he never stopped." But Fischer, a scout for the Knicks, saw Krzyzewski as more of an assistant coach than a player. "Hal relied on Mike to do the scouting of other teams, to really run practices," Oxley said. "Mike really embraced that role."

His teammates understood that Krzyzewski made up for his physical limitations by seeing things on the floor that even Fischer didn't see. Also noteworthy was the way Krzyzewski, an officer, treated the enlisted players. "Some of the officers on the base would be sure to let you know there was always a distinction," Luchini said. "With Mike, there was never anything like that. His actions just left you feeling comfortable being around him."

Krzyzewski loved his experience with Fischer, his first and last coach after Knight, and credited him for being open-minded when his de facto assistant had a strategic suggestion to make. "He gave me an opportunity to express my ideas," Krzyzewski said. "He wanted to hear what I had to say."

More than anything, Fischer gave Krzyzewski and the other players an escape from the everyday horrors that tens of thousands of young American men were facing in Southeast Asia, including some of Mike's teammates at West Point. Basketball kept Krzyzewski out of the line of fire, even after he was sent overseas for a required thirteen-month unaccompanied tour. Mike was on a list for a potential deployment to Vietnam, but in part because of the gradual pullout of U.S. forces, he was sent instead to South Korea, where he was stationed at Camp Pelham, eight miles from the Demilitarized Zone (DMZ) separating the Republic from North Korea.

Krzyzewski was an artillery liaison officer in the Second Infantry Division and commander of the recreational compound. He played fast-pitch softball, among other activities, and was "very, very competitive in it," said Oxley, whose unaccompanied tour in South Korea, at Camp Casey, overlapped some with his teammate's.

As a coach-player of the team representing the Eighth Army, the forces protecting South Korea, Krzyzewski won the United States Army Pacific Command Championship. His MVP award in that tournament earned him another few months on the All-Army and All–Armed Forces teams, playing for Fischer.

Like all West Point graduates — and all Bob Knight players — Krzyzewski had been trained to embrace the necessity of winning. It bothered him that the American game plan in Vietnam did not appear to make winning the top priority. Krzyzewski said that his friends and classmates who fought in the war "had a regulator put on them. I never wanted to be part of something like that." He would have gone to Vietnam if ordered — he lived by duty, honor, and country after all. But while in South Korea, Krzyzewski was not about to volunteer to make the trip. "There's five minutes to go in the game and you're not gonna win," he said. "We're getting the hell out of there. I didn't want to go in the game."

Krzyzewski was lonely in South Korea, desperately missing his wife and nineteen-month-old daughter Debbie, who were living with his in-laws in Virginia. His unaccompanied tour meant just that — he was to be unaccompanied by any family members for its duration. In an era without cell phones and email, FaceTime and Zoom calls, it was awfully difficult to be a world away from your loved ones.

"I felt cut off from everything I cared about," Krzyzewski would say. "You had nothing going for you, *nothing.*"

So with not much time left in her husband's stay in South Korea, Mickie decided to make a little unauthorized trip, with Debbie in tow. Krzyzewski's wife and daughter were not permitted to stay on the base, so they secretly lived in a supply room for three full months. Yes, a supply room. Oxley thought his friends were crazy for trying to pull this off without getting caught, but pull it off they did.

Mickie slept on a cot, cooked with a hot plate, and used the women's room inside a base movie theater to take a shower every night while her husband stood guard outside. One night Mickie was reminded of how perilously close they were to a war zone — or at least to potentially hostile North Korean forces on the other side of the DMZ — when gunfire rang out near their supply room/apartment, leaving her terrified. Mike assured Mickie that it was only a drill. She asked him how he might respond if they were ever confronted by real-world enemy units.

"I'd get all my men together, and we'd throw basketballs and popcorn at them," Krzyzewski joked.

Meanwhile, back in the States, Bob Knight had left West Point for Indiana University and big-time Big Ten basketball and the academy had hired Villanova assistant Dan Dougherty to replace him. Dougherty had an opening for a head basketball coach at the academy's prep school at Fort Belvoir in Virginia, 20 miles south of Washington, DC, and Knight talked up Krzyzewski when he worked with Dougherty at the summer camp run by Villanova coach Jack Kraft.

Dougherty called Krzyzewski and asked if he would be interested in coaching at Fort Belvoir. "I didn't tell him, 'You're going to make $100,000 if you take the job,'" Dougherty recalled.

Even if he had offered only a plane ticket, gas money, and $25 a week for expenses, Krzyzewski would have agreed to spend the final two years of his five-year military commitment doing what he first talked about doing in high school — coaching his own team. At the time, Dougherty had no idea that he had just placed his own successor in the Army coaching pipeline.

IN THE FALL OF 1973, Krzyzewski started working with the player who would change his life. His name was Gary Winton, and he was a six-foot-five bull of a young man out of Brewer High School in Somerville, Alabama. He was the son of a World War II veteran, the grandson of a World War I vet, and a member of his school's junior ROTC program. When he got the offer from the United States Military Academy, via a one-year stay at its prep school at Fort Belvoir, Winton did not need much time to deliberate.

"We were sharecroppers, just a regular everyday family," said Winton's sister Lou Ellen.

Krzyzewski needed Winton badly; he had lost nearly every game in his first year coaching the prep school. "Horrible" was the way a friend and former West Point roommate, Mike McGovern, described that season. "I think we won two games, three tops, though we did beat Navy Prep." McGovern, Mike, and Mickie commiserated in the local Hot Shoppes and, out of desperation, scribbled on napkins the potential lineup changes that could stop all the losing.

Mike had gone 24-5 in one year coaching at Fort Carson, and 15-1 another year in Korea. As a player, he had known nothing but relative success at Weber and Army and then complete domination as part of Fischer's service teams. He was not going to relive year one in year two at Fort Belvoir, where he served as a training officer. That year Krzyzewski's team would play the typical Army Prep opponents — a hodgepodge that included military academies and freshmen and junior varsity clubs from local Division I schools — and win at a staggering rate despite minimal resources.

"We played in a Quonset hut gym," recalled Vance Herrell, starting point guard, "and we'd go to games with a box lunch of a ham sandwich and an orange and boiled egg. The bus was OD green, Army green. We were playing at Virginia Tech or Virginia or George Mason, where the facilities were outstanding, and here we were, lowly little Army Prep. We took our frustrations out on the teams we played. Coach instilled in us greatness and molded that into a team."

Herrell was one of Krzyzewski's first recruits. The Army Prep coach had called him to ask him to send tapes of his play. "He said his name, and he told me his Polish history," Herrell recalled. "The only thing I knew that was Polish was dill pickles and sausage. I asked him to spell his name, and when he did I said, 'Oh my goodness.'"

Some of the players called Krzyzewski "Coach K," to make things easier when talking among themselves. Almost all of the boys at the Fort Belvoir school were there to try to improve their grades and earn entry into West Point. Playing basketball would help. Playing winning basketball would help even more.

Krzyzewski installed a man-to-man defense and a motion offense, similar to what Knight started running at Indiana. Sometimes the coach got on the floor and showed his players what he needed from them; he was still in fighting shape, and he was only eight years older than the kids he was teaching. "He still had his ball-handling ability, and he could score against us when he wanted to," Herrell said. Krzyzewski stressed ball movement, screening, spacing, and finding the open man. "Coach taught us to be more selfless," Herrell said. "And when things broke down, we got the ball to Gary."

Winton was unlike anyone the Army Prep starters and reserves had played with in high school. He was a country-strong, fat-free forward who ran the floor and didn't need to lift weights to become an immovable force under the basket. "Just an unbelievable player," said his six-foot-three teammate Rick Johnson. Winton averaged 24 points and nearly 20 rebounds a game for Krzyzewski, whose stature as a young coach was starting to grow along with his military rank — he was now a captain in the U.S. Army. But it was clear early that Krzyzewski would not run a team exactly the way Knight had run his at West Point.

"He wasn't a screamer, he was a technician," said Johnson. "I don't remember Coach ever getting upset with us."

Army Prep played twenty games and won eighteen, though the boys of Fort Belvoir did not have a postseason to qualify for. "Our playoffs were Navy Prep and the Navy plebes," Johnson said. "And those were the two games we lost." Krzyzewski's players beat every college team they faced, yet lost to the opponents that forever define a season within the Army program. Decades later they were still complaining about some of the fouls called against them in those Navy games. Of greater significance, they were still talking about the bond they shared with their coach.

"He instilled in us a love for each other," Herrell said. "He had the ability to bring out the best in us, things we didn't know we had inside."

MICKIE KRZYZEWSKI WAS NOT sold on the basketball life when Bob Knight invited her husband to join his staff, as a graduate assistant, in Hoosierland.

"Going to Indiana was totally against my wishes," she said.

Mickie was no fan of Knight's, dating back to how he had treated her boyfriend after that Princeton game Mickie attended in 1967. She had made it clear to people that she had no desire to ever again spend any time around that man. But her concerns about the Indiana move were bigger than that. Mike was a U.S. Army captain with a steady income, the war was effectively over, and Mickie thought they could raise a family in prosperity with her husband as a career officer. She pressed her case in vain; Krzyzewski resigned his commission and accepted Knight's offer. His dream was to coach, and he couldn't turn down even an unpaid position in the Big Ten. Mike, Mickie, and Debbie were heading to Bloomington, where Knight was already building a juggernaut.

Right around the time Richard Nixon resigned the presidency in the wake of the Watergate scandal, Krzyzewski enrolled in Indiana's business school, thinking he could pursue an MBA while learning how to run the equivalent of a Fortune 500 company in his industry — a Division 1 basketball program. Yet his main education would take place in Knight's classroom, the gym, where the Hoosiers had long listened as their head coach told stories of how tough his former Army players were, stories Knight never shared with the Army players themselves. Krzyzewski showing up for fall practice, in the flesh, was a big deal to the Hoosiers.

"It was nice to finally meet somebody who lived through Coach Knight for four years at Army," said Steve Green, a senior forward who would be the leading scorer on the 1974–1975 team. "We figured they'd all have to be dead."

Green recalled the twenty-seven-year-old Krzyzewski giving the Hoosiers peace of mind by talking to them about Knight, explaining him and his ways. "It was all positive," Green said. Krzyzewski helped run some drills, but he wasn't quick to jump on anyone's ass; he knew Knight did enough of that for everyone involved. As they stood under a basket during one practice, Krzyzewski leaned over to Green and said, "Geez, he never worked us this hard at Army." The player shot the grad assistant an incredulous look. "That's all we've been doing these years, trying to outwork you guys," Green told Krzyzewski. The Indiana senior wore that concession like a badge of honor as he approached his teammates and said, "You can't believe what I just heard from Mike Krzyzewski."

Knight and Krzyzewski and the rest of the Hoosiers put on a clinic in the selfless virtues of team basketball. They steamrolled through the Big Ten, crushing Ohio State by 31, Michigan State by 52, Michigan by 14, Iowa by 53, Minnesota by 20, Northwestern by 26, Wisconsin by 20, Purdue by 33, and on and on. Knight's brilliance was no longer tempered by the physical limitations of his players at Army. Indiana had high-profile recruits and All-American players, and yet they shared the ball as if they were unaware of their prominence in the game. No single player averaged 17 or more points per game on this team; four averaged between 11.8 and 16.6 points.

Krzyzewski soaked it all in while he took his business classes and cleaned up on his intramural basketball team. It was easy to get caught up in all the winning as Indiana ran its record to 10-0, 15-0, 20-0, and perhaps Knight sensed that when he challenged his former Army point guard one day in practice. Krzyzewski was a helpful, if quiet, presence in the gym, often working with the Hoosiers' guards. "We just knew him as Mike, who thinks he wants to be a coach," recalled John Laskowski, Indiana's sixth man. The players liked Krzyzewski, though many couldn't correctly pronounce his name, advancing a postgraduate trend that started at Fort Sill, where a frustrated host at the officers' club once announced, "Lieutenant Alphabet, your table is ready."

Knight decided for this one particular scrimmage that Coach Alphabet would assume a bigger role than he was accustomed to. Knight split up the first unit and the second unit and suddenly asked Krzyzewski to coach the starters. The stunned grad assistant tentatively approached the first unit's huddle.

"This is the first time Mike is put in this situation," said Laskowski. "We're the number-one team in the country, Mike has sixty seconds to talk to us, and Knight is watching."

Krzyzewski stood before Scott May, Quinn Buckner, the six-foot-eleven Kent Benson, Green, Bobby Wilkerson, and Laskowski — all future NBA players — and completely froze. "Mike does not say a word. *Not a word*," Laskowski recalled. "He doesn't know what to do."

Knight stared at the silent Krzyzewski, the anger rising from his toes. The head coach headed straight toward his assistant and started profanely tearing into him. In conclusion, Knight shouted, "Now get in there and start coaching this fuckin' team." Krzyzewski spit out a few clichés and sent the first unit out onto the court. "It was a learning lesson Knight set up for him," Laskowski said.

Krzyzewski learned so much from his old Army coach that year about the daily price that needed to be paid in pursuit of perfection. At the same time, he was warned by a couple of Knight mentors, Pete Newell and Hank Iba, to be himself if and when he became a head coach and to take only pieces of Knight with him.

There would be no national title for the 1974–1975 Hoosiers, who were 31-0 entering the NCAA Tournament's Mideast Regional final in Dayton, Ohio, where they met Kentucky. Near the end of Indiana's regular-season blowout of the Wildcats, Knight argued with his counterpart, Joe B. Hall, near midcourt and slapped the back of Hall's head hard enough to knock him forward, enraging the Kentucky side. So for Knight, this rematch was a Shakespearean tragedy waiting to happen. Hall had told people that he would never forget the way Knight humiliated him in Assembly Hall, and on March 22, 1975, it was payback time.

May, the Indiana star, was making his first start since breaking his arm a month earlier, and instead of the 25 points he scored against Kentucky in December, he managed only two in the rematch. Hall switched from a zone defense to man-to-man and ordered his players to plow through Indiana players who were setting (often illegal) screens; he completely outcoached his former friend, who without question had superior talent on the floor. Knight's celebrated defense surrendered 92 points in the two-point loss, wasting Benson's 33-point, 23-rebound performance and leaving the coach's young son Timmy in tears on the bench as he was comforted by Green, the senior who would not be returning for what would be the following season's championship run.

"It was going to be UCLA and Indiana in John Wooden's last game," Green said of the NCAA final that never happened, "and I guarantee you, we were going to win that game for our coach against UCLA. That was going to happen." A stickler for NCAA rules, especially those forbidding extra benefits for student-athletes, Knight told associates that he did not respect Wooden because he believed cheating was part of UCLA's pyramid of success.

Krzyzewski watched as Knight built and navigated a perfect winning machine, then saw how quickly it all unraveled in the sudden-death madness of March — before anyone was calling the NCAA Tournament "March Madness." Krzyzewski learned from the genius of Knight, and also from the hubris of Knight. Several Indiana players felt that their coach's head slap of Joe B. Hall gave Kentucky an emotional edge in a rematch that was never going to be easy for the nation's top-ranked team to win while playing with a diminished Scott May.

The following year, the Hoosiers went 32-0 in becoming what remains the sport's most recent unbeaten champ, and still players who competed on both teams felt that the 1974–1975 edition was superior. "It's not even a debate," Quinn Buckner said.

Bob Knight never coached a stronger team, and Krzyzewski had a front-row seat for it all. This advanced education in Bloomington proved invaluable when news broke that the United States Military Academy had fired Knight's successor, Dan Dougherty, and was in the market for a new head coach.

MIKE KRZYZEWSKI HAD never even been a full-time college assistant when he stood among the small handful of finalists vying for the open Army job. Bob Seigle, a West Point faculty member who was a senior basketball player during Krzyzewski's plebe year, was a member of the athletic board charged with finding the right candidate. So was Colonel Tom Rogers, Knight's old officer rep who had grown particularly close to Krzyzewski after Mike's father died in 1969.

Dougherty had finished his fourth season with a 3-22 record and with a 31-66 record overall. Seigle said it was tough to watch that last Dougherty team because it played hard and then "found more ways to lose games in the last ninety seconds than I've ever seen in my life."

West Point needed a closer, and the board had more than 120 applicants to choose from. Two candidates separated themselves from the pile: Princeton assistant Gary Walters—who played with Bill Bradley on the Tigers' 1965 Final Four team and had college head coaching experience at Middlebury and Union—and the twenty-eight-year-old Krzyzewski.

Seigle, Rogers, and former Army guard Dick Chilcoat were all pushing hard for Krzyzewski, whom some on the committee referred to as "Kruzew-ski." The older colonels involved in the search couldn't understand why Seigle, Rogers, and Chilcoat were so high on the young, relatively inexperienced candidate.

But they didn't eliminate him. Knight called the West Point athletic director, Jack Schuder, and told him, "If you're serious about getting a good coach, Mike Krzyzewski is the only guy I'd recommend." On his job interview at West Point, Krzyzewski ran into a surprised Winton, his former player, and told him he was in the running. "I sure hope you get it," Winton responded. Krzyzewski aced his interview. He brought with him a printed plan for how he would restore the dormant Army program to its standing under Knight.

"We said, 'This guy has talent, and we want young and hungry,'" Seigle recalled. "But they outvoted us and offered the job to Walters." Colonel Gilbert Kirby, head of the Department of Earth, Space, and Graphic Sciences, offered the Princeton man a modest salary and a house on post—a bid that Walters just used to get a better deal at Dartmouth. Crestfallen and a bit peeved, Kirby turned his attention to the runner-up in the derby. "I suggest we offer the job to this 'Kruzewski' kid," he said. The pro-Krzyzewski committee members looked at each other and laughed. "And we all said, 'Okay, let's do it. When we come out of here, we're in total agreement. It's a unanimous decision that we ask this kid Mike to coach.'"

Funny how things work out. At one point during their deliberations, Brigadier General Fred Smith, dean of the academic board and head of the search committee, turned to Seigle and said, "You know, this guy 'Kruzewski' didn't do much in the Army." And the colonels involved in the selection process weren't thrilled that Krzyzewski had resigned his commission.

Seigle dropped his pen and looked straight into the dean's eyes. "I said,

'Dean, we got more Army officers here than are concentrated anywhere in the world. We're not looking for another Army officer. We're looking for a basketball coach.'"

"You know, you're right," the dean responded.

Krzyzewski was named head basketball coach of his alma mater on April 15, 1975. Mike's wife Mickie made him swear that he wouldn't shut her out of anything in the male-dominated world at West Point, which was still a year away from admitting its first female cadets. Krzyzewski assured Mickie that she would always be a full member of his team, with full privileges, and that they would rise or fall with Army basketball together.

Starting with the old field house near the river, home to so many memories, Mike and Mickie took one look around and realized that the rebuilding had to begin right there. "Mike decided we had to fix the locker room," Seigle said. "We got in there on our own and repainted the place, stripped down the lockers. We were all painting the bleachers. Mike, Mickie, the assistant coaches, everyone."

Krzyzewski did this after being told by athletic department officials that they didn't have the money to hire professionals to do the job. The new coach made a deal with them for the wooden bleachers: *You buy the paint, we'll do the painting.*

Painting, stripping, scrubbing — that's how a Polish kid from Chicago got things done. Mike was willing to work from his hands and knees, just as his parents did, because he was raised to believe that nothing worthwhile is ever attained without hard work — and because he desperately wanted to make Army basketball his ticket to the big time.

4
COACH K

THEY WERE JOKING around on the other bench, laughing at Mike Krzyzewski's team. Army was scrimmaging with Penn State behind closed doors; after the first ten minutes, the top seven members from each side sat down and allowed players number eight through fifteen to compete against each other for the next ten minutes. During that session, Penn State's starters and top reserves were having a little too much fun at the expense of Army's nonrotation players.

Krzyzewski was doing a slow burn on the sideline. Like any good West Point man, he wasn't about to let an opponent from a civilian school — or any school — mock an earnest circle of West Point cadets. Krzyzewski knew he was entering his first season as a college head coach with a short supply of talent on the first unit, never mind the second and third units.

He accepted the fact that there would be long and painful days and nights while trying to rebuild Army basketball. That didn't mean he would ever subject his players to unnecessary indignities. So before his best players returned to the court for the final ten-minute session of this preseason scrimmage, against Penn State's top seven, Krzyzewski told them, "I do not want them to score a point for the first six minutes. Not one foul shot or one basket, nothing. I want them to know and feel what Army defense is like. I want to let them know that we don't like what just happened."

The Cadets looked at each other as they tried to process their rookie coach's mandate. *How are we going to keep them scoreless for six minutes?* the senior captain, Tom Valerio, asked himself. Some players thought that Krzyzewski was merely trying to set an impossible standard so he could feign outrage over their failure and order up a punishment practice after the Nittany Lions had left on their bus. Either way, Army's players could feel

Krzyzewski's intensity as he glared at them and demanded that they make their opponents pay for their disrespect.

And so, on their coach's orders, the Cadets hit Penn State with a fury that had probably never been seen before in a meaningless college scrimmage. They got up in the Nittany Lions' faces on defense, guarding them nose to nose for the length of the court. They started diving for loose balls, taking charges, and contesting every pass and shot. "We were playing like it was the NCAA finals," Valerio said. After more than three scoreless minutes, the Nittany Lions cried uncle and called a time-out. Nobody on their bench was laughing.

Continuing the assault when play resumed, Army cleared the six-minute mark without surrendering a point. Penn State looked equal parts rattled and dismayed. "I think they probably were saying, 'These cadets are mad men. What the heck are they feeding these guys?'" Valerio said.

Only this wasn't about what Penn State's players were feeling. It was about what Krzyzewski's players were feeling. The veterans on his roster had grown accustomed to losing, and losing big, and their coach was showing them a potential path to victory. The Cadets were almost never going to outscore anybody; they would have to win on effort and execution, with effort being the more important of the two. In that scrimmage, Valerio said, "Coach was building our confidence up about being a great defensive team. And you get a little swagger in that. You felt that when you walked onto the court in a game . . . you were going to make the other team really have to work for every basket and every inch of the floor. It was a special moment."

A moment that was fleeting for the senior captain as the season opener against Lehigh approached. Valerio said to himself, *Wow, this is great. But I can't believe that I'm only going to get to play for him for one year.*

At age twenty-eight, with virtually no college basketball coaching experience, Krzyzewski knew that his alma mater was the only Division I school in America that would have even interviewed him for a head job. The brick field house on the river was even busier and noisier than during Krzyzewski's playing days: the track, lacrosse, and baseball teams sometimes practiced in there, along with the equestrian team. "You had horses in there, all kinds of stuff going on," said one of Krzyzewski's assistants, Bob Hutchings. The staff would drop curtains around the court for some semblance of privacy, but they didn't much help when a starting pistol would go off at the track to start a sprint.

As Krzyzewski had done when he was a Cadet, his players practiced drawing offensive fouls on teammates going full speed to the basket. They would work on closing out hard on shooters, all but submarining them.

(Sometimes the shooter would come down with both elbows to retaliate against a submarining defender.) They would dive on the floor in practice and all but maim each other for control of loose balls.

Tempers would naturally flare in a competitive environment where stressed-out students, awake since the predawn hours and already worn out by the marching, classwork, and hazing from upperclassman, were ordered to challenge one another physically and mentally. Krzyzewski's gym, said Vance Herrell, the Army guard who had also played for Mike at Fort Belvoir, "was not a sanctuary. It was about business. There were fistfights during practice, but once that was over we went into the locker room and it was a team." (One player said the fistfights were an everyday occurrence.) Like Knight, when Krzyzewski wanted to blow off some steam of his own, he would join other coaches and staffers in playing pickup games that were treated with NCAA Tournament urgency. "When he fouled me," said team manager Bill Wechsler, "I would end up in row 3 of the stands."

Players received sheets of paper outlining Army's offensive and defensive principles. Krzyzewski spent far more time drilling his players in how to shut down opponents than in how to beat them off the dribble. "I want you to pick them up when they come out of the locker room," he told his players, "and follow them to the bench." When he wanted to turn to the hated drill that required defenders to move their feet and maintain a proper stance while shadowing crossover-dribbling ball handlers the length of the court, he would shout, "Ball and a partner, zigzag." One player said, "Your heart would flutter when you heard that." Army constantly worked on box-outs under the boards and on halfcourt offense and defense; the Cadets rarely went full-court early in the preseason. Over the first three weeks of practice, said freshman guard Pat Harris, "I thought we were in soccer camp. We did so many defensive drills, I don't know if we ever touched a basketball. He was developing our culture."

Krzyzewski's plebe class included prospects, such as Harris, Scott Easton, and Matt Brown, who had been recruited by Dan Dougherty before he was fired. Brown, a six-foot-five guard from York, Pennsylvania, the most talented member of the class, was impressed that Krzyzewski was a West Point graduate. Easton, a six-foot-seven shooter from Grove City, Pennsylvania, recalled Krzyzewski making him his first recruiting visit after he was hired; Easton's brother Tim, a team manager at Army, had played for Mike at Fort Belvoir and spoke highly of him. Harris, an Irish-Catholic point guard and construction worker's son from the Bronx, recalled his high school coach at Mount Saint Michael telling him that Dougherty was being replaced by "a young whippersnapper from the academy, and I can't pronounce his name."

Krzyzewski arrived at Harris's apartment to secure his commitment and quickly won over the recruit's parents, the way Knight had won over his in Chicago. "His sincerity was just flowing out in that meeting," Harris recalled. "My father said, 'That's the kind of man you want to play for.'"

Krzyzewski pushed his players hard on the new equipment that Arthur Jones, inventor of the Nautilus, had brought to West Point for the academy's athletes to sample. Brown said that the weight work prepared him for the rigors of Division I basketball. A classmate, Tom Spellissy, was so exhausted by his first two experiences on the Nautilus machines that he walked out of the gym and vomited on the sidewalk.

The first-year coach was introducing his players to a level of mental toughness — a Bob Knight level — that they had never before seen. Krzyzewski "loved Coach Knight," Spellissy said. "He always talked about Coach Knight." Now Mike Krzyzewski *was* Coach Knight at Army, and he saw himself, Knight's point guard, in his own players. Krzyzewski mirrored his mentor's approach to practice — minus the physical contact with the Cadets — by making them run, run, and run some more. When he was through with his Cadets in wintertime workouts, Krzyzewski sent them out of the field house, with wet hair, into the chilled, dark night and an unforgiving wind known as the Hawk that came off the frozen river as they headed up the hill, racing against the clock to make it to the mess hall for dinner. Sometimes West Point basketball players made that walk through six to eight inches of snow.

Over time, Easton would say, "that walk becomes a part of your soul. You play a game in that atmosphere, that field house becomes your battlefield, your domain, your enclave, your cave. You're going to have a warrior mentality. You feel that you're not going to let anybody come in there and win. And that's how we felt as a group."

The Cadets felt that way as they approached the season opener. They spent a rainy, foggy Thanksgiving Day on a largely empty campus with Krzyzewski, his wife Mickie, and their daughter Debbie; they all ate in the mess hall before gathering at the coach's hilltop house on post for more team bonding into the night. The following evening, Friday, November 28, 1975, was Krzyzewski's grand debut against a Lehigh team that was also coming off a disastrous season (1-23) and was also being led by a twenty-eight-year-old rookie head coach, Brian Hill.

Krzyzewski said of Army's prior season, "I have completely dismissed the thought of last year's record from my mind, and I believe those players who were a part of it have done the same." He junked Dougherty's fast-break offense and zone defense in favor of a motion offense and a man-to-man defense with a ball-you-man approach — a stance requiring a defender to use his peripheral vision to eye the ball handler and his assigned offensive opponent at all times.

Wearing their gold tops over their white uniforms with black and gold trim, Army warmed up in front of a boisterous crowd of 4,000 that included cadets who were gearing up for the next day's trip to the annual football game against Navy in Philadelphia. The football program had crumbled in recent years and entered this final game with a 2-8 record and a 5-26 record over the last three seasons. West Point was ready to win again at something, anything, and basketball was a pretty good place to start.

"I want to see you looking at me," Krzyzewski barked at his players, "not staring at the ground or the wall." On his chalkboard he had written next to the names of his starters the numbers of the Lehigh starters. And then he unleashed his players on the visiting Engineers, who had no idea what they had signed up for. Lehigh scored the first two points of the night, then got completely shut down by the Army defense. The Cadets scored 17 consecutive points as their packed house roared its approval. "Lehigh was like a deer in the headlights," said Harris, the reserve guard. "I don't think they ever saw defense played that well."

Army surrendered only 10 points in the first half — ten — and took a 19-point lead into intermission. The Cadets were all over the floor, crash-landing out of bounds in pursuit of loose balls. Krzyzewski had been up off the bench, nervously working the sideline and the refs and profanely imploring his team to never let up.

Outside of the head coach's one grad assistant season at Indiana, none of the Army assistants — Pete Gaudet, Bobby Dwyer, Hutchings, and former Krzyzewski teammate Bill Schutsky — had any college coaching experience at all. "We were all scared shitless about whether we could turn this around and be competitive," said Gaudet. "There was an unknown, with all the freshmen who came in and the other guys who had just lost and lost and lost. But we absolutely did not let [Lehigh] play. I didn't know if anyone was able to prepare a team mentally to play that hard and kick another team's ass."

The Cadets scored 56, and didn't even let their opponents get to 30. The senior team managers, Bill Wechsler and Jim Moerkerke, who had lived through a lot of losing in the Dougherty years, saw the field house come alive like it hadn't since the Knight years. "From the fans it was like, 'God, what happened to the Army team?'" Moerkerke said.

Valerio and Gary Winton each finished with 15 points (Winton also grabbed 13 rebounds) while Lehigh was busy missing 35 of its 44 field-goal attempts. "I got what I wanted," Krzyzewski said afterward. "Full effort."

He was 1-0 as a college head coach. In the following day's *Newburgh Evening News,* Bo Gill wrote of Krzyzewski's Cadets: "They ran with gusto, they swarmed over the enemy offense like hornets, they drove for the loose basketballs and did just about everything that could be expected of a first-game team Friday."

The winning Army players took an early Saturday morning bus to Philly to watch Navy nearly shut out West Point for a third consecutive year. Krzyzewski didn't make the trip; he was too busy preparing for the next opponent, Upsala College, and for a season that would reestablish Army as a regional presence and a team absolutely nobody would cherish facing.

The Cadets won their first three games. They were losing to Pitt-Johnstown in the final minute, which was something of a surprise, when Krzyzewski called time-out, looked his players dead in the eye, and barked, "We're going to win this game." It was the first time Krzyzewski had ever entered a huddle and said those words to a college team that was confronting an endgame deficit, but it would not be the last. On command, West Point forced a couple of turnovers and won the game.

Though Krzyzewski had a program centerpiece in Winton, the most talented player in Army history, and a gifted freshman in Matt Brown (the NCAA started allowing freshmen to play varsity basketball in 1972), his team could not compete with eleventh-ranked Tennessee and its high-powered pairing of Bernard King and Ernie Grunfeld; King scored 39, and Grunfeld 20, in a 99–69 victory in December's Volunteer Basketball Classic. And yet, six weeks later, Army displayed enough skill and heart to carry a seven-point lead over fourteenth-ranked St. John's into the final minutes of regulation before losing in overtime.

"A basketball game with Army can no longer be considered a small skirmish," said St. John's coach Lou Carnesecca.

The Cadets won their final two games to finish with a respectable 11-14 record, punctuating the season with a 16-point victory over Navy before 4,600 fans in the field house. Winton scored 31—his fifth game of more than 30 points in a little more than a month. The sophomore was thrilled to be reunited with his coach from his prep school days. On a regional level, Winton could be the type of player who carried a Division I program to unexpected heights. The type of player who propelled his coach from the field house to the penthouse.

· · ·

THE FOLLOWING SEASON, after winning its first seven games, Army missed some free throws and blew a seven-point second-half lead in a loss to South Alabama in the final of the Birmingham Classic. If Mike Krzyzewski was in a foul mood, a Christmastime trip to his hometown of Chicago for a game against DePaul would surely cheer him up.

Krzyzewski took his team to the White Eagle banquet hall, the neighborhood place run by Vivian Przybylo's father, Ted. The players met a number of their coach's old friends and couldn't get enough of the endless supply of Polish dishes that came their way. "Oh my God," said Vance Herrell, "it was so good, we ate until we were sick."

The game was played in DePaul's Alumni Hall, where Krzyzewski had lost his final high school game in a stunning playoff upset. He was back home in front of his fellow Columbos and, of course, his mother Emily, who was still just as committed as ever to an honest day's work.

DePaul had a future NBA first-round draft choice in Dave Corzine, a six-foot-eleven center who towered over the quicker, more athletic Winton. Determined to play his taller opponent aggressively, Winton was called for three fouls in the first eight minutes. Corzine ultimately grabbed 18 rebounds and outscored the Army star 22–17, and the Blue Demons won by a 77–66 count, sending Krzyzewski into a short Christmas break with seven victories and two defeats.

The Cadets were fully expected to extend their losing streak to three when they were matched against Florida State in the first round of the Vermont Classic. Like most early-season, holiday-time tournaments, the Vermont Classic was set up for the host school to face the marquee invitee in the final. Vermont was supposed to beat Yale on one side of the draw, and Florida State was supposed to beat Army on the other — but on a brutally cold night in Burlington, Winton was hell-bent on making up for his performance against DePaul and his teammates were hell-bent on letting him, showing patience on offense against the Seminoles and constantly working the ball inside. Winton scored 34 points, and with their smart help defense, the Cadets honored their coach with a hustle play that converted potential defeat into victory.

Army was up one in the closing seconds when a Florida State player headed toward the basket and a trailing Cadet, Scott Easton, recalled a drill out of the Krzyzewski/Knight playbook — a drill requiring a scrambling defender to beat a full-speed-ahead offensive player to a spot and draw a charge at the expense of his physical well-being. Easton executed it perfectly, cutting off the Florida State driver, planting his feet, and sacrificing his body. "And we were fortunate enough to get the charge," Easton recalled. "I made both free throws to win the game."

Krzyzewski called the 72–71 upset "a great win for us and it's our biggest win in our two years at Army." One of his reserves, Herrell, credited the coach for instilling a strong sense of belief in his team. "He made us feel like we belonged," Herrell said. "That it was not an upset if we just play and do the things we were supposed to do."

The following night, West Point struggled at the foul line, missing 12 of 22 attempts, but still held a 50–49 lead over Yale with five seconds to go. On the final possession, Yale's Dick Shea took the inbounds pass and drove the ball left into two defenders, Matt Brown and Pat Harris, who kept him from releasing his jump shot before the buzzer.

The defensive stop gave Krzyzewski something that Bob Knight and Tates Locke and every West Point basketball coach before them had never managed: a tournament title. Yet a reporter on-site noted that the Cadets weren't particularly demonstrative in celebrating their victory or the naming of Winton as the tourney's MVP.

"Our basic philosophy is to always play up to our potential," Krzyzewski said. "Winning is simply a by-product of hard work, a fleeting thing. Only hard work remains. Our kids realize that, and that's why they were a little glum after the game. I was very proud of the way they felt because it means they understand what we are trying to get across in this program."

Army was now 9-2, and Krzyzewski was the toast of the post at West Point, where he sometimes wore a pinstripe suit on game nights and other times colorful sweater vests and plaid pants with his jackets and ties. His buzz cut was long gone, replaced by near-Beatles-length hair that flowed over his ears. He was some sideline sight as he demanded that his players get their hands into the opponent's passing lanes and reminded them that every single loose ball had to belong to Army. "An easy man to get along with off the court, he is all business when it comes to the game of basketball," read his bio in the team's media guide.

Krzyzewski's nasal voice could carry across a gym or an arena; it was the kind of command voice they teach and expect out of leaders at West Point. He wasn't afraid to use profanity in that command voice, whether it was directed at the officials or his own team. When his cheeks were red, his lips were pursed, and his black eyebrows were rising into his head, Krzyzewski was an intimidating, in-your-face presence. There was a reason, after all, that the players "called him Coach K and some other names as well," Pat Harris said through a laugh.

As for his assistants, Krzyzewski sometimes kept them at his house until 4 a.m., watching films and reviewing scouting reports, but he always gave them room to make a meaningful impact on the team. "For every game we played he always asked for the coaches' input at halftime," Hutchings said. "He gave us something specific to look at in the first half, and before he'd talk to the team at halftime he'd say, 'What do you see? What do you think?'"

The Cadets were 16-6 when they hosted the Iona Gaels, who were coached by the former Rutgers guard whom Krzyzewski had competed against, Jim Valvano. The thirty-year-old son of a Long Island high school coach, Valvano was funny enough to be a stand-up comic and charismatic enough to seduce the kind of recruits Iona had no right landing. He was a fast-break talker, an English major and voracious reader who loved poetry and quoted Shakespeare, and a man who lived from whim to whim.

He had almost nothing in common with the Army coach, other than an ethnic Catholic background and an outsize nose. Krzyzewski had very little use for Valvano, who had beaten him the year before in their first meeting as head coaches. The Gaels arrived at West Point with a modest 13-9 record, but they were closing hard on a six-foot-eleven center from Long Island named Jeff Ruland, arguably America's number-one high school player, who would reject Indiana and Kentucky in favor of a smaller school close to home. This was the time for Krzyzewski to beat Valvano, and beat him he did.

Suddenly, with Valvano behind him, Krzyzewski had a shot at a twenty-win season — just two years after Army's twenty-two-loss season — and the school's first appearance in the NCAA Tournament. In Annapolis, the Cadets survived a late Navy rally that Krzyzewski called "a real fistfight out there," before adding, "I guess that's the way Army-Navy games should be." Both head coaches were assessed technical fouls in front of a Halsey Field House crowd of 5,200.

West Point played Seton Hall next in the four-team Eastern College Athletic Conference playoffs. Two more victories, and Army would claim the conference's automatic bid; one victory and the Cadets could possibly earn an invitation to the NIT. Krzyzewski had already beaten Seton Hall and its silver-tongued coach, Bill Raftery, at home, and now he needed a victory on a neutral-site court (St. Peter's in Jersey City) to get one more crack at the likely winner in the other semi, St. John's.

But Raftery had a tough little Jersey guard, Nick Galis, who accepted the challenge of containing the six-foot-five Brown. Winton pounded away against the Seton Hall frontcourt, collecting 29 points and 12 boards, but Galis held Brown to 13 points while scoring 18 himself and dishing for 11 assists. Seton Hall went on a 14–2 run in the second half and won, 77–71, to crush Army's NCAA hopes.

The Cadets beat Manhattan in the consolation game in Madison Square Garden to make it a twenty-win season, no insignificant achievement given the state of the program Krzyzewski inherited. "I'm hoping to hear from the NIT pretty soon," he said after the Manhattan victory. The *Sunday Daily News* published a photo of a young girl holding a basketball with both hands and wearing a dress that was graced by an *A,* for Army. "This doll is Debbie Krzyzewski, 6, Army coach's daughter," the caption read. One player recalled Krzyzewski summoning his daughter to the practice court and saying, "Hey, Debbie, stance," and watching her drop down into a perfectly balanced defensive stance — with palms up, of course.

Krzyzewski never heard from the NIT selection committee; Seton Hall and Rutgers were the only New York area schools chosen for the sixteen-team field. A couple of weeks later, the Metropolitan Basketball Writers Association named Krzyzewski its Coach of the Year, an honor he also earned for District II from the National Association of Basketball Coaches (NABC). But Mike was 0-for-2 in his attempt to reach a national postseason tournament, after Knight took Army to the NIT four times in six years.

No athletics official or academy administrator at West Point was demanding more of its head coach. Krzyzewski was the only one demanding more of Krzyzewski.

IN THE WINTER OF 1977, the academy no longer looked like the one Krzyzewski entered in the summer of '65. The first class of women, 119 strong, had joined the Corps of Cadets in 1976, and the all-white basketball teams Krzyzewski had played on and captained were now integrated with African American athletes such as Winton and Clennie Brundidge. One bench player, Vincent Brooks, who would become the academy's first African American First Captain of the Corps of Cadets, said he was surprised by the amount of racism and hate mail he had to endure at West Point — generated not by his role on the basketball team, but by his role as the highest-ranking member of the cadet chain of command. "You could feel very alone," said Brooks, who years later became the commanding general of the U.S. Army Pacific.

Division I college sports were increasingly shaped and dominated by African American athletes, and Winton embodied that new reality. Described by the *New York Times* as an "antipersonnel tank with sneakers," Winton would obliterate the school career scoring and rebounding records with 2,296 points and 1,168 boards, proving that a great Black athlete could thrive at West Point. One who hoped to follow was Gilbert Shepherd of El Paso, Texas, a lightning-quick, five-foot-eleven guard from Eastwood High who patterned his game after NBA All-Star Nate "Tiny" Archibald. Though he was the son of a lieutenant colonel and Vietnam vet, Shepherd had barely heard of West Point; he thought it might be in Indiana.

On arrival at Army, Shepherd was thrown into a workout that included some head-to-head scrimmaging against the head coach. "Coach K was a cheater," Shepherd recalled. "Man, he was tough. He would hit me in the stomach, grab my jersey, and push me around. I hung with him, but man, I said, 'This guy is a son of a bitch.'" The staff saw Shepherd's obvious athletic talent in practice as a plebe — the whole team saw it — but he was hanging on by a thread academically.

"The math kills everybody at West Point, the athletes," Shepherd said, citing calculus, physics, and chemistry.

Shepherd struggled some in practices but maintained that he was a game-day player, and he couldn't understand why Krzyzewski didn't give him more playing time to add foot speed to the backcourt. He was much quicker than the starting point guard, Pat Harris, and a better defender and driver to the basket. If Krzyzewski had a not-so-subtle affinity for gritty, white, and physically limited Catholic school kids, it made sense: he was one of them, "and I was not in that mold," Shepherd said. (At the same time, he said Krzyzewski's treatment of him, which included throwing a blackboard eraser at him in one locker-room session, "definitely wasn't racial." Shepherd added that when the coach got mad, "it was scary.")

Jon Hyman, a white freshman guard out of San Antonio, recalled Shepherd consistently blowing past him and everyone else in defensive drills. Hyman thought his fellow Texan could have gone down as one of the best players in West Point history.

"For some reason Mike didn't like him," Hyman said. "I don't know what it was . . . Mike started Pat Harris over him, but Gilbert was a far better athlete."

When Krzyzewski recruited him, Shepherd said, he told him that Army would play in the Sun Bowl tournament in El Paso, Gilbert's hometown. And Krzyzewski kept that promise in Shepherd's second year, when the Cadets upset nineteenth-ranked Kansas State and nearly beat Memphis State in overtime in the final.

But the coach didn't play him for even one minute in either game, humiliating Shepherd in front of family and friends. Shepherd hung around for a small handful of games before finally breaking the news to his coach that he was done.

Shepherd eventually faced potential expulsion from the academy over his failings in the classroom, but when he went before the academic board, a surprise guest appeared to speak on his behalf — Mike Krzyzewski. Shepherd recalled his former coach telling the board that he was responsible for bringing the athlete to West Point, and that he knew when he was recruiting Shepherd that the prospect would struggle with the academic demands. Krzyzewski asked the board to consider his former player's strong work ethic and to give him another chance. "For him to come to the board meeting and speak up for me," Shepherd said, "it said a lot about his character."

The board granted him a reprieve, and Shepherd graduated with an engineering degree. Even with the cadets he "missed on," Krzyzewski made a difference. But he didn't miss on many.

Despite Shepherd's experience, Krzyzewski's ability to connect with his athletes, to inspire them, was his most obvious strength. He built bonds with his players during extremely physical off-season pickup games on post. "We would run him off picks and obliterate him," Hyman said. "The guys would say amongst ourselves, 'Did you get a chance to hurt Coach?' . . . Mike played like he was a cadet, and we brutalized him. It was our fun to be able to do that with him, and Mike never complained about it."

Krzyzewski told his team that football was a collision sport and basketball was a contact sport, and that preparing for contact was a must. He ordered his players to set hard picks on him during demonstrations in practice, just as they would in pickup games, and they eagerly obliged. If the Army coach didn't like the way his Cadets were taking charges, he'd plant himself in the paint, order a player to bowl him over, and scream as he fell backward to the floor.

Krzyzewski earned their respect by never showing any fear. In one heated practice, Winton, who maxed out on every Nautilus station, was ready to engage the barrel-chested Brundidge, an All-American tight end. Just as they were going chest-to-chest, recalled team manager Jeff Anderson, "here's Mike Krzyzewski walking into 500 pounds of flaming meat fighting each other. He took charge. It was, 'This is my team and we're not doing this,' and they backed down."

The Army coach could motivate with words too. Krzyzewski once pulled aside his point guard, Harris, and told him he needed him to shoot more, not only because he had a good touch, but also because he would hurt the team if he allowed defenses to lay off him on the perimeter — something Krzyzewski would have loved to hear from Knight. "I never played a game where I looked over my shoulder and thought, *Oh, did I do the right thing?*" Harris said.

Krzyzewski empowered his chief decision-maker on the floor, telling him to attack a vulnerable defense in tense endgame situations rather than first looking to call time-out. Harris applied the message at the end of the Kansas State upset, when he gained possession of the ball in the final seconds of a tied game and fired a pass into the corner to Brown, who sank the winning jumper.

Over the years at Army there would be multiple stories of an enraged Krzyzewski pulling a Knight — for example, returning from a lost road game in the middle of the night and ordering his team to immediately change into practice gear for a two-hour workout. "His eyes could burn a hole right through you," Scott Easton said.

But the softer, human side was there, shaped in part by his wife Mickie, the more endearing side of the partnership. They were living in a modest Merritt Road home on the hill — in a parklike setting near one of the chapels — with daughters Debbie and Melinda, or Lindy, who was born in April 1977. Mike had kept his promise to Mickie that he would not hide her away in the male-dominated domain that was West Point; she was a visible and significant figure around the team and the program, much to the players' delight.

"She was like our mom there," said Spellissy. On weekend gatherings for the plebes at the coach's house, Easton said, "Mickie would answer the door and give you a hug. She really helped him. It was critically important at Army that you felt you were a part of a family, that you weren't stuck in this stark, gray stone military fortress overlooking the Hudson River. You had Mickie Krzyzewski hugging you and giving you ice cream."

The Krzyzewskis' nurturing was there for everyone. "They treated the managers just as good as he treated Gary Winton," Anderson said. "Mickie and Mike opened their house, and their daughters were little toddlers in cheerleader uniforms. They were all in."

Though some players considered Mickie the program's matriarch, others saw her more as a caring big sister. "She would talk to us as young men on how we should treat ladies, as cadets," one player said. "She told us to always be gentlemen. She would say, 'I know you guys are horny.'"

Her husband was pretty good at keeping them focused. Krzyzewski won ten consecutive games to close the season, including another victory over Valvano's Iona and Jeff Ruland, who scored 17 but made only 5 of 12 field-goal attempts and 7 of 15 foul shots. After Army's 63–61 victory, an Iona player told the Cadets' Harris, "God, you knew a lot about us," a concession that amounted to another Krzyzewski triumph over Valvano.

West Point beat Seton Hall for a second time in the 1977–1978 season, this time overcoming a Winton injury near the end of the first half. Winton pulled his left calf muscle and appeared questionable at best for the second half, as he was reportedly in agony on the training table.

Borrowing from New York Knicks captain Willis Reed, who famously hobbled out of the Madison Square Garden tunnel with a badly injured leg before Game 7 of the NBA Finals and helped beat the Los Angeles Lakers and Wilt Chamberlain, Winton limped through the Nassau Coliseum tunnel and joined the Army bench five and a half minutes into the second half. He took the floor four minutes later, with the game tied, and eventually scored the first six points of overtime for West Point's eleventh straight victory. "It was a very emotional experience for me," Winton would explain.

And for his head coach too. It would be Army versus St. John's in the final, and Krzyzewski was 0-3 against Lou Carnesecca. Now he had another shot at the St. John's coach with so much on the line. A victory might not just send the Cadets to the NCAAs for the first time but could also help elevate Krzyzewski to a job in an elite Division I conference, to essentially allow him to follow the path that Knight took from Army to Indiana only in half the time.

But St. John's was the one opponent in the region that wouldn't give in to Army's tenacity and technique. The Cadets' slow-paced motion offense, designed to cover their relative lack of athleticism, asked players to put stress on defenders by passing, cutting, and screening for teammates. "We don't have the talent to make up for lapses on the court," Krzyzewski said. St. John's did have that kind of talent, along with the toughness and size to neutralize West Point's approach. It would take a Herculean performance from Winton to prevail, and the senior was playing on one leg.

Winton answered the challenge, scoring 25 points, just as Carnesecca figured he would. "Like Willis Reed, the Trojan horse," said the St. John's coach, "and out of him come 9,000 guys." Problem was, with 1:28 to go and Army trailing by four, Winton was called for a foul by one official — his fifth, disqualifying him from the balance of the game — and for a technical by another official for hanging on the rim (after he was pump-faked into the air) in an attempt to avoid fouling St. John's Gordon Thomas and to avoid further injuring his leg. Thomas sank both ends of a one-and-one and then made a technical foul shot while Krzyzewski shouted in protest that he wasn't given ample time to replace Winton. Official Ed Batogowski suddenly whistled the Army coach for yet another technical, this one of the two-shot variety.

"It's really tough to lose it like that," Krzyzewski said.

Though the NCAA dream was dead, and though Krzyzewski had hurt his team at the worst possible time, the 19-8 Cadets still made their first postseason appearance of the post-Knight era when the NIT selected them for its sixteen-team field. "I think we proved we belong in the NIT and I think we have the best player in the East in Gary Winton," Krzyzewski said. "But we don't beg." The NIT selection committee gave Army a road game against 21-6 Rutgers on March 9. Krzyzewski's last impactful trip to Rutgers, as a player, had unfolded nine years earlier, when a late brawl inspired Knight's buddy Bill Parcells to punch out a fan.

There would be no punch-out this time, just a knockout. "We brought the entire Corps of Cadets to Rutgers," said Matt Brown. "But they had James Bailey, a first-round pick in the NBA." Rutgers still had a number of players from its 1976 team, which had carried a 31-0 record into the Final Four. Winton was still limited, and the six-foot-nine Bailey proved to be the kind of explosive frontcourt force that Army was not accustomed to seeing.

Army's season ended at 19-9. "I can't be upset after a competitive game like this," Krzyzewski said.

He was upset, though, that he would never again get to coach Winton, who had made him a winner at Fort Belvoir and again at West Point. Krzyzewski revealed after the season-ending loss that Winton didn't just have a calf injury; he was playing through a stress fracture in his left foot. "I just wished I had him back for four more years," Krzyzewski sad.

In the weeks ahead, Krzyzewski did not get the big job offer that would have moved him into the upper echelon of Division 1 college basketball. He would need to put in more time at the military academy, without his star player, to prove himself worthy of a major conference job. And that promotion, like every promotion at West Point, would not come easily.

ON SATURDAY AFTERNOON, February 9, 1980, Mike Krzyzewski was being harassed by a chicken. He was coaching against Jim Valvano in Iona's Mulcahy Center, and Valvano, ever the showman, had decided to hire the San Diego Chicken, for two reasons: (1) To entertain the 3,209 fans in the building and the regional TV audience; and (2) to annoy the shit out of the West Point man on the other sideline.

Valvano was successful on both fronts. Krzyzewski was already annoyed before the opening tip, when he saw the Iona coach embracing one of Army's players, John Vislosky, who had grown close to Valvano at a summer basketball camp in the Poconos. "I happened to look over and I could feel his eyes burning into the back of my head: it's Coach K on the sideline watching this greeting of old friends at midcourt," Vislosky said.

"In the middle of Valvano hugging me, the San Diego Chicken is behind

Krzyzewski humping his leg . . . I did not get off that bench the entire night. He didn't look at me or talk to me . . . The San Diego Chicken bothered Coach K the whole game."

During one Army huddle, Krzyzewski was drawing up instructions on his board when Ted Giannoulas, in costume, approached him from behind and started making silly gestures behind his head. "I've got to figure Valvano told the Chicken, 'This is your target,'" Vislosky said. "And Coach K turned around, and I thought he was going to coldcock the Chicken. An assistant pulled him back, but man, his face got beet red."

Iona won easily, 67–54, late in a magical 29-5 season for Valvano that included a Garden beatdown of a Louisville team that would win the national title. The day after his loss to the Gaels — his second straight loss to Valvano, whom he now despised — Krzyzewski blistered Vislosky over every move he made in practice. "I couldn't do anything right," Vislosky said. "I never told Valvano how much he screwed me over."

Army was in tenth place in the eleven-team ECAC Metro Conference, with a record of 7-15. Mike Krzyzewski was not used to being 7-15, and he wanted nothing to do with anyone who might be comfortable being 7-15. Especially with Valvano at 18-4.

It had been a turbulent two seasons for Krzyzewski. In December 1978, team manager Tim Easton was killed in a car accident in West Germany, and his brother Scott was beyond devastated. Tim had been his role model. "I would not have even considered attending West Point had he not been there," Scott said. Though a couple of serious knee surgeries had cost him a chance to play, Tim was beloved by the athletes he had helped. His death, said one player, "sucked the whole wind out of our team." At Tim's funeral, Krzyzewski walked beside Scott Easton behind the hearse carrying his brother from the chapel to the West Point cemetery.

Army finished the 1978–1979 season at 14-11, punctuated by Krzyzewski's first loss to Navy as a coach or player. The significant players who had largely covered for the graduation of Winton — Brown, Brundidge, Harris, and Easton — were now graduating themselves, leaving Krzyzewski with massive holes on his roster. During the off-season he interviewed for the Vanderbilt job but lost out to Virginia assistant Richard Schmidt. He would spend at least another season at his alma mater, hoping against hope for the best outcome.

Meanwhile, Krzyzewski and his assistants, including enlisted man Chuck Swenson, a former graduate assistant and student manager under Knight at Indiana, were still painting the field-house bleachers and sweeping the dirt off the field-house floor — tasks no other Division I staff had to undertake. Swenson drove with Krzyzewski down to the city every week for media luncheons with the other local Division I coaches at Mamma Leone's. Jimmy V of Iona, Looie Carnesecca of St. John's, P. J. Carlesimo of Wagner, Bill Raftery of Seton Hall, and Tom Penders of Columbia and Fordham were all blessed with a gift of gab that more or less eluded Krzyzewski. "He'd get up there and mumble his way through," Swenson said. "He gave our SID report."

That report wasn't terribly hopeful for year five. Krzyzewski didn't want to talk about 1979–1980 as a rebuilding season because he didn't want to give his players an excuse to lose, but facts were facts. Krzyzewski looked at the talent Valvano had landed from Long Island alone — Kevin Hamilton, Glenn Vickers, and especially Ruland — and realized he could never match that haul at a school with a postgrad military commitment. Krzyzewski had done commendable work in rebuilding the program. "But it's still hard to convince someone who's six-nine and good to come to West Point," he said.

Even before dealing with the losing of the 1979–1980 season, Krzyzewski got caught up in an international incident started by — who else? — Robert Montgomery Knight, who had asked him to join his U.S. team staff for the Pan American Games in Puerto Rico in the summer of '79. One morning, while the Americans were practicing in a gym outside of San Juan, Knight got angry that the Brazilian women's team — scheduled to practice next — was making noise while waiting inside the gym. According to a police officer on the scene, Jose Silva, Knight took ugly Americanism to new depths, saying, among other things, "Take those whores out of here." The coach and the cop ended up in a nose-to-nose confrontation, with Krzyzewski standing only a few feet away. Silva said that Knight called him the n-word and "broke my chin" with a punch to the face. Knight denied using the racial slur and said he only knocked away Silva's hand after the officer jabbed a finger in his face and poked him in the eye.

Silva put the U.S. coach in handcuffs and drove him to the police station, where he was briefly detained. The Americans beat Puerto Rico for the gold medal, and Knight was charged with aggravated assault, a misdemeanor, by a district court judge in San Juan. He refused to return to the island to stand trial and was convicted and sentenced to sixty days in prison and fined $500. Krzyzewski insisted that his former West Point coach never punched the cop and never used racist or demeaning language in the incident. "Coach Knight is a tough man but he's honest," Krzyzewski said. "If he were a coach from some other country, this whole thing would've been forgotten. They're just giving him a raw deal."

When it came to boorish behavior, Krzyzewski was never confused with his mentor. But everyone at West Point knew that he had his Knight-like moments. There existed a Jekyll-and-Hyde dimension to Krzyzew-ski, and few people knew that better than John Vislosky, who recalled his mother serving the coach a halupki dish during his recruiting visit to their Philadelphia area home and the coach loving it. The prospect would give Krzyzewski—a dedicated Motown fan—a tape of the fifty greatest Mo-town hits. "You would have thought I gave him the golden chalice," Vis-losky recalled.

Many of the cadets appreciated the family atmosphere that Krzyzewski created around the team. But one day after the holiday break, Vislosky showed up late for practice—his father, a Navy veteran of World War II, had driven him from their home to the academy through a terrible snow-storm. Krzyzewski didn't even acknowledge Vislosky's father on arrival. He just tore into his six-foot-six forward and future Green Beret and even threw a chair in his direction.

"It was not a chair at me, it was a chair instead of me," Vislosky said. "I was late to practice, and on top of that I sucked at the practice. We were on the court when he [threw the chair], and Gaudet grabbed it and went over to Mike to calm him. When that chair flew, everybody froze like in an old Western when the piano stopped playing."

A former high school English teacher, Pete Gaudet often played the good cop to Krzyzewski's bad cop, and the team appreciated his human touch. Gaudet was also a master at putting together scouting reports and teaching big men how to operate in the post. It's just that Army didn't have much size or talent in the post, or on the 1979–1980 roster for that matter. That's why the Cadets were 7-15 after their loss to Valvano and the San Diego Chicken. "We competed literally forty minutes every game, and probably even over-achieved," said Marty Coyne, a junior forward and one of the leading scor-ers on that team. "I know it sounds strange given the record, but we were overmatched every single game, and we were in almost every game. We fought like crazy."

Krzyzewski did have one player, in addition to Coyne, who inspired fear in opposing defenses, one player who would have been a factor on any team in any conference in America. Bob Brown, named to Michigan's all-state high school team alongside Earvin "Magic" Johnson, had decided to play for the Michigan Wolverines before Krzyzewski showed up at his house and started talking. The son of a Marine and Korean War vet, Brown fell in love with West Point on his first visit. He embraced the family atmosphere, Brown said, "even though every plebe told me I'd be crazy to come here, go to Michigan, [Army's] like being in prison."

The Michigan coaches also told Brown he was crazy. The future four-star general and commander of the U.S. Army Pacific scored more than 1,200 points for Army before suffering a knee injury that cost him any shot at the NBA. "I learned more leadership on the basketball court than anywhere else at West Point," he said. "Coach K got everything he could out of a team with very little talent . . . He's the greatest I've ever seen leadership-wise in getting the most out of people."

One night in the Bronx, after Brown finished off a spirited comeback with an 18-foot baseline jumper to beat Fordham, 71–70, Krzyzewski exercised that leadership with his best player. "He came up and said, 'Hey, now play some defense.'" Brown recalled. "He could have at least said, 'Nice shot,' first."

Krzyzewski once kicked Brown out of practice for throwing an elbow and knocking out a teammate during the ol' loose-ball, anything-goes, two-man drill. The next day a frustrated Brown went to see Krzyzewski. "And I came away ready to go through a brick wall for him," Brown said. Krzyzewski was never afraid to send his best players and leaders to the showers. One part-time Army assistant, Denny Carroll, said that Krzyzewski preplanned practice ejections to send various messages to his team. "It was, 'I'm going to throw so-and-so out of practice today just to see how he reacts,'" Carroll recalled.

Krzyzewski tried everything he could with the 1979–1980 team; Brown said he even played the theme song to *Rocky* before one game. His fellow junior, Coyne, said that Krzyzewski had never coached better than he did that season, when he kept reminding his players of how hard they were competing. "You looked at him during the losing," Coyne said, "and there was no wavering, no pouting . . . So we never gave up on him."

The Cadets entered their final game of the year with an 8-17 record. They faced Navy in the field house, and the Midshipmen never stood much of a chance in front of the typically animated cadet-and-civilian crowd. They scored a grand total of 12 first-half points against a smothering Army defense; the Cadets' slowdown offense was good enough for a 9-point halftime lead. In the second half, after Krzyzewski implored them to never let up, to finish the season with a fury, Army made 11 of its first 14 shots and built a 20-point lead with eight and a half minutes to play. Brown and Coyne combined for 32 points. The final score, 53–48, was the closest Navy got over the last thirty minutes.

Krzyzewski was glowing in the immediate wake of this necessary triumph. "I may be disappointed with our final record, 9-17," he said, but not with "our effort or progress," adding, "We've come a long way."

In the end, when measured against the bottom-line standard of wins and losses, Krzyzewski had to be honest with himself: his program was going in a dangerous direction. He did not want to coach teams that fought hard while losing seventeen of twenty-six games. He did not want to recruit at a school that afforded him no chance to sign the best available prospects.

When he left his tiny locker room and office inside the cavernous field house on February 23, 1980, Krzyzewski was hoping he had represented Army basketball for the final time. He just needed one school, one athletic director, to believe he was meant to coach much better players on a much bigger stage.

THE ATLANTIC COAST CONFERENCE Tournament was unfolding in Greensboro, North Carolina, and Tom Butters, athletic director at Duke University, was sitting next to a former Duke basketball star, Steve Vacendak, a dozen rows up from the court. Butters had offered Vacendak the position of associate athletic director, and the former NBA draft choice and ABA player had accepted and was scheduled to start on the payroll in a few months.

Butters didn't have months to wait. He turned to his new hire and said, "Steve, your first responsibility is to find us a basketball coach." Vacendak did a double take. "I was stunned," he said. "I had no idea." Vacendak had been busy running his own team at Division III Greensboro College and had not been following published reports that Duke was about to be in the market for a new coach. In his mind, the school already had a basketball coach, and a very good one, in Bill Foster, who was currently going up and down the Blue Devils' sideline.

"It's not official yet, but Bill has resigned and is going to be the head coach at South Carolina," Butters told him. "You have an unlimited budget. Go out and develop a pool of individuals you think would be successful at Duke."

It was a hell of a first assignment. Just two seasons earlier, Foster had led the Blue Devils to the national championship game in St. Louis, where they lost to Kentucky. Right now the popular coach was in the process of winning the ACC Tournament for the second time in three years. *And he was leaving? For South Carolina?*

People in the know realized that Foster was obsessed with North Carolina coach Dean Smith and with the Tar Heels' exalted standing locally, regionally, and nationally. They saw that Foster had a strained relationship with Butters, that Foster felt underappreciated, and that, among other things, he was angry over the fact that the coaches' parking lot at Cameron Indoor Stadium devolved into a mess when it rained. "They battled a lot," Duke star Gene Banks said of his coach and Butters. Or as Banks's teammate Kenny Dennard put it, Foster "had a serious relationship problem with Tom Butters."

Amid the chaos, Duke beat Maryland in the ACC final on a Mike Gminski tap-in. The following day, with his team starting preparations for the NCAA Tournament, Foster made his resignation official, effective the end of the Duke season, though he did not yet confirm the obvious — that he was heading to South Carolina.

Vacendak was already putting together his list of candidates for Butters. He was a smart choice to run the search for Foster's successor: a former ACC Player of the Year who had helped Duke reach the 1966 Final Four, he had played with Connie Hawkins on the ABA champion Pittsburgh Pipers. His list would include his good friend, Old Dominion coach Paul Webb, and Boston College's Tom Davis, Kansas State's Jack Hartman, Duke assistant Bob Wenzel, and Mississippi's Bob Weltlich, a former Knight assistant at Indiana and West Point.

Butters was familiar with all of these candidates, of course, but he wasn't familiar with the only other name on the list. "You like defense, Tom," Vacendak told the AD. "You should look at Mike Krzyzewski at Army."

While working for Converse and living in Annapolis, Maryland, a few years earlier, Vacendak had taken a call from his former high school coach at Scranton Prep in Scranton, Pennsylvania, Jack Gallagher, who was a close friend of Knight's. Gallagher advised him to attend an Army-Navy game and check out the Cadets' promising young coach. Krzyzewski invited Vacendak, who attended nearly every Navy home game, to sit in on his staff's pregame meeting at the Holiday Inn. The Cadets beat the Midshipmen, 54–53, "and I thought Mike did a masterful job of nailing that Navy team," Vacendak recalled. "I thought it was very concise. He just had a real penetrating way of putting together the game plan."

Gallagher called Vacendak again three years later, after Foster's resignation, to ask if he would be interested in Krzyzewski, and Vacendak assured him that the Army coach was already on his list. He told Gallagher to make sure Krzyzewski applied for the position; the Duke official thought it important that candidates formally apply to show their interest in the program. At the time, on Knight's recommendation, Krzyzewski was already in talks with Iowa State about its opening; Army assistant Bobby Dwyer told his boss that they could establish a recruiting pipeline from Chicago, Krzyzewski's hometown, to Ames, Iowa.

Butters called Knight and, just to make sure, asked if he would be interested in coaching Duke: Knight playfully dismissed his friend's offer and pushed hard for Weltlich, who had grown up in Knight's hometown, Orrville, Ohio, and been taught by Knight's mother in second grade. The Indiana coach also mentioned former assistants Dave Bliss and Don DeVoe as being worthy of consideration. When the Duke AD asked him about Krzyzewski, Knight told him that the Army coach was a man of high character, a leader who possessed "all of my good qualities and none of my bad ones."

Butters asked Krzyzewski to meet him in Lafayette, Indiana, where Duke was set to play the University of Pennsylvania in the NCAAs. Krzyzewski won his three-hour meeting with Butters before Foster won his game with Penn, and so everyone agreed to meet again days later in Lexington, Kentucky, where the Blue Devils would face Kentucky in the Sweet 16.

Iowa State had offered the Army coach its job, and though Knight thought his Midwestern protégé would find a better fit (and less pressure) with the Cyclones, Krzyzewski preferred to take the huge gamble of waiting on the Duke job. He had no guarantees in Durham. If he lost out on Duke after rejecting Iowa State, Krzyzewski would almost certainly end up back at Army, where another losing season could take him off the high-major radar and leave him to fight for his mid-major life over the next few years.

Krzyzewski left more than a dozen inches of snow behind in West Point and made the trip to Lexington, where he met with Butters, Vacendak, and Duke chancellor Ken Pye. Staying near the designated meeting spot, the three school officials walked down the side of an interstate highway that was under construction to get to the hotel, Pye was chugging along, struggling to keep up with the former professional athletes. They met for nearly four hours, and all came away believing they might have found Foster's replacement. Only Butters was not sure that he could follow his heart and instinct on this one.

"Let me see if I got this right," Butters said to Vacendak. "You want me to hire a coach with a losing record at Army whose name I can't spell or pronounce?"

"That's right," said Vacendak, who challenged his boss to have "the nuts" to hire Krzyzewski.

Signed by Branch Rickey, Butters had pitched in forty-three major league games for the Pittsburgh Pirates in the early to mid-1960s before suffering a severe whiplash injury in a car accident that ended his career. He became a fundraiser and head baseball coach at Duke and, in 1977, an athletic director who was known for being direct, fearless, principled, and perceptive when it came to reading people.

He saw Krzyzewski as a sincere and dedicated thirty-three-year-old man, and as someone who understood the value of defense better than any other candidate. Some Duke staffers wanted to stay in house with Wenzel, who was actually younger than Krzyzewski and had no head coaching experience. The two top officials in the school's sports information office, Tom Mickle and Johnny Moore, preferred Wenzel because of his institutional knowledge and his success in recruiting; he'd helped sign the centerpieces of Foster's '78 Final Four team, including Jim Spanarkel, Mike Gminski, and Banks, a Philly high school sensation and Duke's first McDonald's All-American. Yet Wenzel never gained any real footing in the race.

"I think Tom Butters was greatly influenced by Bob Knight," Wenzel said. "At that time Knight was the king of basketball."

Knight's first choice, Weltlich, didn't think he had a good interview with Butters. Though he also interviewed at Iowa State, Weltlich wasn't desperate for a new job; he thought he had a solid team returning at Ole Miss. Butters remained intrigued by Vacendak's good friend, Old Dominion's Webb, who had been a college head coach for more than twenty years and was coming off a 25-5 season and a trip to the NCAA Tournament. Years later, when he took his wife and a couple of friends on a summertime visit to Duke, Webb ran into Butters, who told him he had truly wanted to hire Webb for the job. "But I couldn't get Mike Krzyzewski out of my mind," the AD said.

The Blue Devils' loss to Purdue in the regional final in Lexington sent Foster on a private plane to South Carolina. Butters started to close in on a Foster replacement. The contenders Weltlich, Webb, Wenzel, and Davis were known to those who were covering and following the search — but one additional contender was not. Duke's sports information office was asked to do whatever it could to keep that name a secret. "Butters continued to tell Mickle and me, 'Don't let the media know about Krzyzewski,'" Moore said.

Though it would be widely reported that Butters invited Krzyzewski to bring his wife to campus, the AD's wife, Lynn, recalled that the Army coach had called the house and, with Butters not home, asked Lynn if he should bring Mickie to Durham. "I answered for Tom at that point," Lynn said. "I thought that would be a good idea . . . I remember Mike was hoarse. He had a different voice when I picked him up at the airport."

Lynn drove Mike and Mickie to their home on St. Marks Road, where the finalists met with the Butters family, including teenagers Jill and Bret. Lynn recalled that during Krzyzewski's visit she thought he was kind, organized, and good with her children. The family tried to remain neutral as the candidates came in one by one; they liked all the coaches, especially the one they already had a relationship with, Wenzel. But there was something about Krzyzewski.

"We all loved him," recalled Jill, who at the time was preparing to attend Duke. "He was the most like my dad. My dad was a man of very few words, and when he spoke you just listened. And Coach K was the exact same way. There was no air about him, no ego about him. I could tell from the second I met him that he was a very principled, direct, honest man full of integrity."

Jill's brother Bret recalled looking Krzyzewski in the eye and feeling that "he was completely sincere in what he was telling you." When the family meetings were over, Butters asked his wife and children to write down the name of the candidate each would pick to be the next Duke basketball coach. "The question Dad had was, 'Who would you like to play for?'" Bret recalled. Butters also told his family members, with a wink, "I will not hire him unless you can spell his name."

Lynn, Jill, and Bret grabbed pens and scrap paper, sat at the kitchen table, and made their choices.

They all spelled the name correctly — K-R-Z-Y-Z-E-W-S-K-I.

On their walk across campus, Mickie surveyed the Gothic buildings and the overall beauty of the place and told Mike, "Don't screw this up." He needed to survive another round of interviews: the finalists would appear before Duke's Athletic Council at the home of Chuck Huestis, the school's vice president for business and finance. Butters had Krzyzewski go last before a panel that included Duke chancellor Ken Pye. After interviewing the five candidates, the council informed Butters that he was free to pick any of them.

He still did not offer the job to Krzyzewski, who was starting to regret his rejection of Iowa State. Vacendak drove Krzyzewski and his wife to the airport; Mickie took a plane to Washington, DC, to pick up their daughters at her parents' home in Virginia. Mike was about to board his plane to New York when Vacendak got paged just as he was leaving the airport. It was Butters.

"Where are you?" Butters asked.

"I'm walking out of the airport," Vacendak responded.

"Where is he?"

"I left Mike at the gate. He's getting ready to get on the plane."

"Go back and get him. Don't let him get on the plane."

"What's this all about? You can't do this, Tom. Are you going to interview him *again?*"

"No, I'm going to offer him the job. But don't tell him."

Krzyzewski heard his name paged before seeing Vacendak hustling back to the gate to tell him he needed to stick around. The Army coach was hardly thrilled. "What's going on?" he asked in an annoyed tone. "Well, Tom wants me to take you to dinner," Vacendak responded sheepishly. Krzyzewski shook his head in disgust. What was wrong with these people? What possible questions were left for Butters to ask? What did Krzyzewski have to do to finally get the offer?

Vacendak took him to a steak dinner at the Angus Barn and never told him that the offer was coming. Butters had asked Vacendak to keep Krzyzewski occupied for about an hour and a half so he could get everything organized, so for an hour and a half Vacendak talked to the candidate about the weather, their families, their playing careers, everything but the only thing on their minds. "It was an awfully long dinner when you have the information that I had," Vacendak said. Finally, he told Krzyzewski that Butters was ready to see him one last time. Vacendak drove him back to Huestis's home in Durham, where Butters asked him, simply, "Will you take the job?"

Butters did not have to ask twice. Mike Krzyzewski became the nineteenth head coach of Duke University's men's basketball team.

The AD and the coach talked and talked about their new alliance, and Mike didn't get to call Mickie until midnight. She had grown concerned, practically terrified: she couldn't reach him at their West Point home, and when she called the airline she was told that his flight had landed on schedule.

"Where have you been?" she asked in a frantic tone.

"They called me back," he responded.

"*They called you back?* They can't make up their minds."

Mike explained that Butters had summoned him from the airport back to Durham to ask him one last question. Mickie was beyond angry, at least until her husband revealed that the question was whether or not he wanted to coach the Blue Devils. She immediately wanted to know one thing. "How much are we making?" Mickie asked.

"I don't know," he said. "I never asked. Tom will be fair."

Fair, the way Butters defined it, amounted to a $40,000 wage for five years. Around 6:30 the following morning, Krzyzewski called Dwyer in his apartment in Highland Falls, New York, and said, "I need you down here in Durham tonight." Dwyer's jaw almost hit the floor. "Mike!" he said. "You got the job?" Once Krzyzewski confirmed that he was indeed the new head coach at Duke, Dwyer booked a flight and stuffed some clothes into his suitcase.

Swenson was also stunned that his boss had landed the Duke job.

Krzyzewski asked the assistant to join him in Durham too, though Swenson was more than a bit afraid of the prospect of recruiting against Dean Smith. Now Butters and Krzyzewski, hired under the veil of secrecy, had to go explain the whole thing in a press conference that night, Tuesday, March 18, after the *Durham Morning Herald* had surveyed the Weltlichs, Webbs, and Wenzels and printed across the top of its sports section the headline, "Duke's New Coach? He Begins with 'W.'" Had Krzyzewski rejected Butters, the AD was prepared to offer the job to one of the *W*s, Webb. But that was never happening. Duke's man came with a surname that began with a *K*.

"Most of the players just call me 'Coach K,'" Krzyzewski said.

Butters stood before a small, jam-packed conference room on the first floor of the school's public affairs building, and addressed the same reporters who had never mentioned Krzyzewski as a candidate during their coverage. The AD was as blunt as ever. "For the sake of accuracy, if indeed accuracy means anything," he said, "the job was not offered to anyone else. He *is* my first choice, and he will *remain* my first choice. Coach Mike Kre-shev-sky."

One reporter in attendance admitted that the group was "almost blind-sided" by this announcement. Butters had just taken a leap of faith that stunned athletic administrators across the country. Krzyzewski walked to the podium and turned to his left to acknowledge the one person in the room who clapped: "Thanks a lot for all the support," he said with a smile. Wearing a tan sports coat, white shirt, and a dark blue tie with a knot slightly askew, his straight, jet-black hair parted to the side and still covering most of his ears, Krzyzewski faced three rows of reporters in folding chairs, a photographer kneeling in front of him, and some TV cameras on tripods, another on a man's shoulder. He looked young up there, but you could see the Army in his bearing. Krzyzewski stared straight into the bright lights as he spoke into an unwieldy tangle of microphones.

"It's K-r-z-y-z-e-w-s-k-i," he said. "And if you think that's bad, it was a lot worse before I changed it." He said he was fine with being called Coach K, but added that his players needed to know how to spell and pronounce his surname before they graduated.

Krzyzewski said he was not shocked that he had beaten out more experienced candidates. "I felt this was a position right for me," he said. As for whether or not he would coach and carry himself like his mentor, the overlord of the Hoosiers, Krzyzewski said, "I benefited greatly from working with him. I also learned things from Dave Bliss and Don DeVoe. But I'm a different person than [Knight] is. I think the principles he teaches are excellent. But I think you make a mistake trying to be somebody else."

Butters was beaming, though the tone of the following day's newspapers didn't quite reflect that mood. "Duke selects Army's loser!" read a headline in the *Dayton (Ohio) Daily News.* The headline in the weekly magazine edition of Duke's student paper, *The Chronicle,* was: "Krzyzewski: This Is Not a Typo." The name game was played in dispatches around the country, with many publications going with "Kre-Shef-Ski" as the correct pronunciation, and others going with "Kre-Ches-Skee."

Of course, Krzyzewski would return to West Point to say goodbye to the young men who had given him everything they had. The players gathered in the field-house bleachers. They described the vibe of the meeting as somber. They recalled that Krzyzewski was emotional when he thanked them, but that he didn't speak for long. He gave them all firm handshakes and wished them good luck.

Back in Durham, about three months after Butters hired Krzyzewski, Vacendak walked down to the construction site where towering light stanchions were being installed at Duke's Wallace Wade Stadium. He asked the foreman if he could spare two giant lug nuts that were bigger than his fist. Vacendak took them to a sporting goods store, had them mounted on a plaque, and gave the plaque to Butters with this brass-plate inscription:

"It took a pair this big to hire the right man."

5

LOSER

ONE SECOND REMAINED on the clock, and North Carolina led Duke by two. Mike Krzyzewski was drawing up a play on his clipboard, and the Duke Blue Devils were not listening to him. Actually, they were listening to him. They just had no intention of doing what he was asking them to do.

This wasn't West Point, after all. This was Bill Foster's Duke team; Bill Foster's two senior forwards, Gene Banks and Kenny Dennard; and Bill Foster's home crowd inside Cameron Indoor Stadium for the final game of the 1980–1981 regular season. The players and the fans did not want their old coach to leave for South Carolina, but leave he did, giving Krzyzewski his big break. And now, with his 14-11 team about to inbound the ball against its Tobacco Road rivals, the North Carolina Tar Heels, in an attempt to send the game into overtime, Krzyzewski was busy wasting his time instructing his players to set up the tying jumper for a sophomore sharpshooter named Chip Engelland.

Dressed in jacket and tie, Coach K was sitting inside a circle of Blue Devils with a pen in his right hand and the board in his left. Banks was on one side of the huddle, and Dennard, with a towel over his left shoulder, was on the other. "We looked at each other when he drew up the play," Banks said. They had been teammates and friends and fellow campus hellions for four seasons. Nothing needed to be said.

The whole season had been a fight for Krzyzewski — a fight for acceptance at Duke, a fight for respect in Dean Smith's neighborhood, and a fight for control of a team dominated by two senior party boys who had no use for some Bobby Knight knockoff who, they thought, wanted to turn the basketball season into a joyless military drill.

It was the team captains, Banks and Dennard, against the coach some at

Duke called "Captain" as a nod to his rank in the Army. When Krzyzew-ski held his first team meeting after his hiring, Banks and Dennard were off taking their own personal spring breaks from campus. Banks had gone home to Philadelphia, and Dennard had headed down to Key West and the bar at the Pier House Resort & Spa on Duval Street. There, while drinking his third or fourth tequila, Dennard was watching TV when the local sports anchor announced that Duke had hired a new basketball coach. "Uh oh," the Duke forward said to himself. "I'm not there."

Banks learned the news of Krzyzewski's hire on TV too, while sitting in his mother's kitchen. He had never heard of Coach K before that day. Dennard had heard all about him after attending Howard Garfinkel's Five-Star Basketball Camp in Honesdale, Pennsylvania, in 1976. A small-town country boy raised outside of Winston-Salem, Dennard put himself on the major-college map at the camp, not by scoring, but by drawing charges and diving for loose balls without any regard for his bloodied elbows. "I looked like I fell off a Harley," he said.

Krzyzewski sent him handwritten letters about the West Point program and dispatched his assistant, Bobby Dwyer, to visit his home. For some rea-son, Dwyer wore red bell-bottom pants and a white silk shirt on the trip. "He looked like he'd come out of a '70s pimp movie," Dennard said. "My mom looked at him and she goes, 'This is how they dress at Army?'"

Dennard picked Duke, and one local reporter bet another that the kid wouldn't score 100 points in his college career, in part because he was in the same recruiting class with West Philadelphia High School's Banks, who, be-sides being Duke's first McDonald's All-American, was arguably the nation's top high school player from a group that included Michigan's Magic John-son and New York's Albert King.

Paired with established stars Mike Gminski and Jim Spanarkel, the two freshmen helped Duke reach the national championship game in 1978. The following year, Foster caused a stir by giving the starting point guard job to a white transfer from Indiana, Bob Bender, instead of the Black incumbent who grew up in Durham, John Harrell, who had been a solid first-string quarterback for the NCAA runner-up after transferring in from North Car-olina Central. "That divided the team," said Banks, who thought that Fos-ter had "alliances" with Duke's top white players and who saw a wide gulf between the overwhelmingly white school and the African American com-munity in Durham.

"The racial part, that bothered me," Banks said. "When we lost games, I got blamed. When we won games, the credit went to Gminski and Spanarkel. My junior year I let my Afro grow out. That was my rebellion. I had blinders on in some ways. I was still getting the popularity and attention, so I had the freedom to speak and to do things . . . But a lot of Black Durham thinks Duke is a white institution. The only Black people at Duke were the workers."

Site of the historic Royal Ice Cream sit-in in 1957, when African American protesters were arrested for trespassing while sitting in the whites-only section of the ice cream shop, Durham had finally desegregated its restaurants, schools, hotels, and movie theaters in the 1960s; Duke desegregated its undergraduate schools in 1963, but the university still had no Black faculty, administrators, or trustees.

Like every old Confederate city, Durham struggled to come to terms with its racial past. The lingering tension did not prevent the gregarious Banks, nicknamed "Tinker Bell," and the reckless six-foot-eight Dennard, known in some circles as "Crash," from forming a fun and fierce partnership in Foster's final years. Banks called Dennard "the craziest white man I've ever met." They established a tradition of hugging and screaming during pregame introductions, to the delight of the Cameron crowd, and their athletic, high-flying exploits on the fast break — along with their relentless commitment to having a good time away from the gym — made them campus legends. The city kid and the country boy showed the university and the community something they didn't often see. "We helped break down some of the racial barriers," Dennard said.

By the time Krzyzewski walked into their anything-goes world, the seniors were most definitely set in their ways. At West Point, the players said, "Yes, sir. No, sir." At Duke, Banks and Dennard said, "I do my own thing, sir." They rarely had to pay for meals in local restaurants, and the school community treated them like NBA stars.

When Banks and Dennard returned to Durham from their vacations, they met with Coach K for the first time. Krzyzewski gave Dennard a look that said, *Where have you been?* though he didn't say it out loud. "He did say, 'Listen, I'm not Bobby Knight,'" Banks recalled. "That was the first thing he said to us." Krzyzewski talked to them about their responsibilities as seniors and showed them a fresh design for Duke's uniforms.

And then Coach K's Blue Devils played the season that was to be expected from a circle of accomplished veteran players and a new coach who wanted to change everything about Foster's team, especially the way it played defense. Krzyzewski had once told an Army assistant that he would never coach in the South, not after his West Point team got a bum whistle at Virginia Tech ("They cheat down there," he said). Yet now his Southern career started, fittingly enough, with a November 18, 1980, exhibition victory over the touring Polish national team in Cameron. The Blue Devils then gave Krzyzewski his first regular-season victory, over Stetson, in the home opener, and his second over South Florida in a game in Tampa attended by New York Yankees owner George Steinbrenner.

But the third game was the first real test: the first meeting between Krzyzewski and Dean Smith. The forty-nine-year-old Smith was in his twentieth season as North Carolina's head coach. He had led the Tar Heels to five Final Four appearances and had done everything at Carolina except win the national championship. He was the son of prairieland teachers and churchgoing Baptists in Kansas; his father Alfred, also a coach, ignored the racist locals and school board members and placed a Black student on his 1934 Emporia High School basketball team, which won a state title. Dean was a member of the 1952 Kansas Jayhawks team that won the national title, but the five-foot-ten guard did a lot more sitting and listening to his coach, Phog Allen, than actual playing on the court.

Later, as a North Carolina assistant, Smith defied segregation by sitting with a Black pastor and theology student in a Chapel Hill restaurant frequented by the team. (The restaurant's manager knew Smith to be a member of Frank McGuire's staff and allowed a waitress to serve them.) In the mid-1960s, Smith helped a Black graduate student buy a home in an all-white Chapel Hill neighborhood and signed Charlie Scott as the university's first Black scholarship athlete. He had become an imposing force in the community and in the gym.

It was an interesting journey on the way there. Smith got the job after McGuire was forced out in 1961 in the wake of NCAA sanctions and point-shaving allegations involving players. The university chancellor, William Aycock, gave Smith a simple charge: don't embarrass the university. The school actually deemphasized basketball, forcing Smith to try to work around the travel and recruiting restrictions put on his program. By January 1965, tired of the post-McGuire mediocrity and angered by a four-game losing streak, Carolina fans were hanging the coach in effigy. His players ripped down the dummy and took out their frustrations on Duke a few nights later. Two years after that, Smith made his first trip to the Final Four.

He became the revered head coach of the basketball team nearly every North Carolina schoolboy dreamed of playing for. The Tar Heels enjoyed a statewide popularity that eluded fellow Atlantic Coast Conference members North Carolina State, Wake Forest, and certainly Duke, a private university with no shortage of wealthy prep school kids from the Northeast. Smith used that popularity to the hilt in recruiting, landing many of the best in-state prospects and expanding the program's long-established reach into New York, McGuire's backyard. His winning percentage in recruiting as well as on the court wasn't hurt by the fact that he always got the benefit of the doubt from game-night officiating crews — at least that's the way his fellow ACC coaches saw it.

Working at a campus nine miles from Chapel Hill, Krzyzewski knew that Smith was the man to beat if he wanted to lead Duke to the ACC mountaintop. They had next to nothing in common. Smith was from the heartland; Krzyzewski was from the Second City. Smith was a Democrat; Krzyzewski was a Republican. Smith opposed the Vietnam War; Krzyzewski had prepared to fight in the Vietnam War. Smith was a Baptist who never used profanity; Krzyzewski was a Catholic who cursed like a drunken sailor. Smith was a chain smoker; Krzyzewski saw smoking as a sign of weakness. Smith liked to play golf; Krzyzewski liked to play tennis.

Unsurprisingly, there were sparks between them at the end of their first encounter, on December 5, 1980, in a tournament known as the Big Four that included the four ACC schools in North Carolina. Duke and Carolina played before a lively Greensboro Coliseum crowd of 15,000 that left the players saying the game had an NCAA Tournament vibe. With Duke down one in the final seconds, Dennard was around the rim in pursuit of Vince Taylor's missed 15-footer when he was called for offensive goaltending. The Blue Devils then intentionally fouled Carolina's Jim Braddock, and as time expired Smith walked toward Krzyzewski with his hand extended. Coach K kept his hands at his side.

"The damn game isn't over yet, Dean," he barked at Smith. Only after Braddock took his free throws to officially end the game would Krzyzewski shake the winning coach's hand. From 10 feet away, Carolina assistant Roy Williams watched the two men scowl at each other before going their separate ways. Williams's first thought about the defiant Krzyzewski was, "My gosh, come on, big fella. You don't have to be like that." But then Williams was struck by a second thought: "This is a competitive guy. He has the right to his own standards. And he was right: the game wasn't over."

One of Duke's assistants, Rick Johnson, who had played for Krzyzewski at Fort Belvoir, recalled that when the Duke coach returned to the Coliseum floor to watch Wake Forest hammer North Carolina State, a section of Blue Devils fans gave him a standing ovation. "I thought, *Wow, this is good,*" Johnson said.

The feeling didn't last. The following night Duke was beaten easily by North Carolina State and its own first-year coach, Krzyzewski's old nemesis from Iona, Jimmy Valvano, who had landed the job in Raleigh nine days after Krzyzewski was hired in Durham.

"We were terrible," Krzyzewski said of the loss to State. "We weren't ready to play." The Blue Devils recovered to win some nonconference games, but they then lost another five straight against ACC opponents, including a rematch with North Carolina in Chapel Hill that turned into a seemingly routine 15-point victory for the home team. "This wasn't the kind of UNC-Duke game that everyone had told me about," said Sam Perkins, a Carolina freshman. "After we got ahead, they had nothing. They weren't intense."

Those words were daggers to Krzyzewski, who demanded intensity above all else. His motion offense and man-to-man defense were not working to anyone's satisfaction, and he did not have a reliable center to replace the graduated Gminski.

But the Blue Devils' biggest problem was the relationship, or lack thereof, between the head coach and his starting senior forwards. One prominent Duke player said that Banks and Dennard felt like they were running the school, and that when Krzyzewski took the job by the throat they thought, *Who the fuck is this guy?* One of Duke's bench players in the 1980–1981 season, Gordon Whitted, thought of everything Foster had built and decided, "You can't really call it Coach K's team. It was Gene Banks's and Kenny Dennard's team."

Banks and Dennard were still pining for Foster. "Bill really took care of us," Banks said. "Nothing illegal, but he really spoiled us a lot." He could make them laugh too: Foster kept a spray can with the words BULLSHIT REPELLENT printed on it, and he'd pull it out and spray it whenever a player went off on a tangent.

Krzyzewski had no time or patience for such nonsense. Emerging from his closet-sized Cameron office, wearing a T-shirt, tight coach's shorts down to his midthigh, tube socks, and white Adidas sneakers, Krzyzewski would show up to his choreographed practice with a script that accounted for every minute, including when, exactly, water breaks would start and finish. Banks and Dennard had little use for this West Point structure.

"Coach K struggled with Gene and Kenny," said student manager Nick Gravante, "and they struggled with him . . . They never really acted up in terms of being disrespectful to him, but you could tell the way they rolled their eyes that it was a real adjustment for them."

Krzyzewski would roll his eyes too, in his own way. Speaking of Banks and Dennard, he would tell people, "I have to make it through one year with them. Just one year." And yet he had no problem with how his seniors competed on game night, as both ran the floor with abandon and could jump, score, and handle the ball.

"But off the court," recalled junior guard Vince Taylor, "good luck . . .

Kenny was going to do whatever the hell he felt like doing. Foster let them be who they were."

Coach K, on the other hand, installed a curfew to keep his seniors in check. As much as Banks and Dennard missed Foster's freedom, they also missed his philosophy on defense, which revolved around zone principles. Foster used the zone to protect Gminski from foul trouble and to hide whatever physical deficiencies might show up against a more high-powered opponent. A number of Foster's holdovers, including six-foot-eight Mike Tissaw, worried that Krzyzewski's man defense wouldn't work against more talented ACC teams. Banks and Dennard asked Krzyzewski to consider switching to zone at times to better suit the players Foster had recruited, and Krzyzewski declined.

"He was 100 percent Bobby Knight as far as his offense and defense," Dennard said. "I used to giggle that with the motion offense and man-to-man defense, you don't need coaching. I don't think we ever called a play. We just had this motion thing."

Krzyzewski did alter his offense in the middle of the season when, according to Dennard, he told his players that he wanted to see at least five passes per possession before a shot was attempted, and that he wanted the ball in Banks's hands for most of those shots. This would be Duke's "Pentagon" offense, which called for the Blue Devils to spread the floor and patiently wait for opportunities for Banks to go to work against his defender. Krzyzewski's slowdown summoned his West Point days and was met with skepticism from some of his veteran players.

It worked on the road against Valvano's Wolfpack in Coach K's first victory over a conference opponent. Krzyzewski also surprised Banks, who scored 23, by playing some zone on the other end of the floor. "He did earn my respect because he wasn't so headstrong," Banks said. Whitted observed that a number of Blue Devils looked at Krzyzewski differently after he made that temporary concession on defense. "I think that really helped the team in its relationship with Coach K," he said.

Outside of his clashes with Banks and Dennard, Krzyzewski had healthy relationships with the majority of his players. He invited them all to his small house for Thanksgiving dinner; the place was so cramped that the dinner table had to be extended through a door and into a hallway. Jim Suddath, a senior bench player, became one of Krzyzewski's most passionate supporters after the coach inherited him and a persistently troublesome knee that required multiple surgeries; the coach allowed him to rehab his way back into the rotation. Suddath was moved by how Krzyzewski provided an example to his young athletes in the way he treated his wife and two daughters, involving them in the program as much as possible. He was also moved by Coach K's unbending honesty with the team. "He never once lied to us for the whole year I was under him," Suddath said.

Another senior reserve, Larry Linney, a defensive specialist and one of only four Black members on the team, had a more complicated relationship with the coach. One teammate called Linney, a philosophy major, "the smartest person in the room." Banks recalled that Linney would sometimes leave Krzyzewski "flustered" when pressing him on social and racial issues and asking questions Coach K didn't have answers for. In a video interview with Krzyzewski's wife Mickie, who did a series of them on players as students, Linney described Duke as "a racist institution." Linney later wrote a letter to the daily student newspaper, *The Chronicle,* chastising the Duke students who held up the image of a white woman in a swimsuit whenever a Black Alabama player took a free throw and disclosing that he had heard racial slurs from the crowd during the season.

Though he didn't believe Krzyzewski was particularly sensitive to his concerns, Linney gained respect for his coach after showing up late for a game against North Carolina State. Linney told Coach K that he was late because he was the point person for an event that his historically African American fraternity, Omega Psi Phi, had been hosting with a U.S. congressman he admired, and that he thought this part of his Duke experience was more important than a basketball game. Krzyzewski responded that night by giving Linney more playing time than usual.

The following week, with eleventh-ranked North Carolina in for the final game of the regular season, Linney, Suddath, Banks, and Dennard were honored at Cameron as departing seniors. Krzyzewski gave Linney the start. Banks was introduced last, of course; he'd just become the third player in Duke history to score at least 2,000 career points, joining Gminski and Spanarkel.

The Cameron crowd of 8,564 roared when a pregame spotlight followed Banks as he walked into the darkened arena with a bouquet of flowers, hugged Dennard, and lifted the flowers toward the roof. Soon enough, Banks was circling the court and throwing yellow and red roses into the stands, one at a time. Unlike Foster, who had decided to retire Gminski's number 43 the year before, Krzyzewski had decided not to retire Banks's jersey, number 20, but Banks was still going out with a ceremony that outdid them all.

The finish on this day would be as thrilling as any in a rivalry that spanned more than sixty years. With two seconds to play, the Tar Heels holding a two-point lead and Duke holding just one time-out, the Blue Devils were about to inbound the ball 94 feet from the basket when Smith — celebrating his fiftieth birthday — handed a gift to Krzyzewski by calling his own time-out to set up his defense. This allowed Coach K to instruct Dennard to fire a pass to the other side of midcourt, where Chip Engelland would receive it and immediately signal for time with one second left, giving Duke a chance to inbound closer to the basket.

In that first huddle, Whitted turned to Suddath and said, "That's not going to work. That's stupid." Yet it did work. So the Blue Devils formed that second huddle, and Krzyzewski drew up the play on his board for the six-foot-two Engelland, using one of the best players in school history, Banks, as a decoy. Dennard, the wild child from the South, locked eyes with Banks, his kindred spirit from Philly. "That ain't happening," was Dennard's interpretation of Banks's look. They'd been speaking with their eyes like this since they were freshmen playing pickup games in the intramural gym in August 1977.

"We all knew Kenny would throw it to Gene," Whitted said. "Everyone in the gym knew it. Probably Coach K knew it too."

Dennard walked toward the official standing on the North Carolina side of halfcourt and planted himself out of bounds. With the entire sellout crowd on its feet, he took the ball and watched as Taylor whiffed on his attempted screen for Engelland, who cut from around the midcourt line toward the near hash mark. Dennard faked a two-handed pass to Engelland and fired it instead to his intended target all along. Banks caught the ball above the foul line and quickly turned to find the taller Perkins, with his seven-foot-six wingspan, closing hard on him.

Banks had no choice but to release the shot right away, a millisecond before the buzzer sounded, and to launch it as high as possible. Decades later, he still had no idea how he got the ball over Perkins's outstretched left arm. The shot took forever to come down, and when it splashed through the net the building exploded, Dennard threw his arms in the air, and his teammates mobbed Banks. Krzyzewski was swinging his fist on the sideline and jubilantly waving his players back to the bench.

Duke was not about to lose in overtime. With nineteen seconds to go, Banks gathered a loose offensive rebound and scored his 24th and 25th points on a layup to give the Blue Devils a 66–65 lead. The Tar Heels' Mike Pepper missed an open jumper with three seconds left, and suddenly Mike Krzyzewski had the biggest victory of his coaching life — his first victory over Dean Smith. The fans stormed the court and lifted Banks in the air, and then Dennard, who had cleared the 1,000-point career mark during the game. The Duke veterans had beaten their hated rivals to finish the regular season with a respectable 15-11 overall record, 6-8 in the league.

The Blue Devils lost to Maryland in the first round of the ACC Tournament, then won two games in the NIT before falling to Purdue without the injured Banks. But Coach K's first year at Duke had already climaxed when he skipped off the Cameron court, clapping his hands and pumping his fists after the victory over Carolina. "This game definitely belonged to our seniors," Krzyzewski said.

Coach K was smart enough to never say a word to Banks and Dennard about that final play, that final audible. "He never once said, 'You son of a bitch, you broke that play,'" Banks would say decades later.

That night, while Dennard and some teammates attended a Bruce Springsteen concert in Greensboro, their coach celebrated by spending a quiet night with Mickie; their third daughter, Jamie, was born nine months later. "My shot created Jamie," Banks would say through a laugh. "I was very proud of my coach. He made me realize he's a man and not some machine."

ON DECEMBER 12, 1981, Kate McGuinness traveled to Princeton to see the man who had coached her brother Joe at West Point. Duke had just lost to the Ivy Leaguers, 72–55, to start the season with its fourth loss in five games, when McGuinness met Krzyzewski outside the losers' locker room to say hello and ask about his family. Coach K talked excitedly about his newborn baby, Jamie, his third daughter, but looked a bit distraught when the conversation turned to his team.

"I think they're going to give me another year to turn this around," he said.

"I hope so," McGuinness responded.

Krzyzewski had coached only thirty-five games at Duke, and already he was worried that he might be losing his grip on a dream job. In fact, he was so concerned that, after talking to Kate, he temporarily left his team in the Princeton locker room to go somewhere to be alone with his thoughts. Dwyer went looking for him; walking down a long, empty hallway, opening this door and that door, he finally opened one with Krzyzewski behind it.

He was sitting by himself, crying. Dwyer sat down next to him.

"What can I do?" the assistant asked.

"Nothing," the head coach responded. "Just give me a few minutes."

Krzyzewski never wanted to show any weakness, especially in front of a family, the McGuinnesses, that knew him as one of the toughest men around. The previous summer, Kate's brothers Joe and Jack attended

Coach K's summer basketball camp at Duke and played in lunchtime counselor games with Krzyzewski, who took no shit from anyone.

"He would knock you on your ass and he didn't care," said Jack, then a high school underclassman. "I had a friend who came with me, and he fouled [Krzyzewski] hard. The kid was fourteen years old, and Coach K got right in his face."

Duke had been playing basketball since 1906, when the school was known as Trinity College, and none of the eighteen men's coaches before Krzyzewski had ever opened a season at 1-4. Coach K roasted his team after the Princeton loss and told reporters he had never felt so gutted after a defeat in his seven seasons as a college head coach. Foster's Duke team had beaten Princeton by 36 points two years earlier.

"We were disgraced tonight," Krzyzewski said. "It was a total collapse. Everything we did was wrong, and everything they did was right. We're going to have to back up and see what the hell we're doing wrong. I really don't know what to say. Nobody was more embarrassed than I was."

The seeds for this collapse had been planted during recruiting season, when Krzyzewski put a full-court press on some of the top high school prospects in the country and failed to sign any of them. This wasn't a shock to one widely respected scout who knew him, Tom Konchalski, a New Yorker who told it straight to big-time and small-time coaches alike. Konchalski was skeptical when Krzyzewski brought West Point assistants Dwyer and Chuck Swenson with him to Duke. Though Dwyer saw himself more as a recruiter than an Xs and Os guy, Konchalski said, "I just didn't think it was going to work. They're going into a conference, the ACC, with barracudas and sharks. I thought there was no way they were going to be able to recruit against those schools."

Krzyzewski was among the finalists for two New York high school stars, Chris Mullin and Bill Wennington, and for West Virginia's Jim Miller, Florida's Rodney Williams, New Jersey's Tim Mullen, California big man Mark Acres, and Indiana big man Uwe Blab, who grew up in Germany. Krzyzewski had traveled to Florida to wrap up Williams's supposed commitment to Duke at his high school postseason banquet, only to be told on arrival by the prospect's coach that Williams had suddenly decided to attend the University of Florida. (Coach K still honored his pledge to speak at the banquet, even though his lost recruit was not in attendance.)

The one near-miss that hurt him the most was Mullin, a sweet-shooting swingman from Brooklyn. Dennard, of all people, had helped Krzyzewski chase Mullin by writing letters to him. "When he came on campus," Dennard said, "I may have given him his first beer." Gminski took some time

away from the NBA's Nets to take Mullin and Wennington out to a restaurant near Duke. The assignment of Nick Gravante, the manager, was
to escort his fellow Brooklynite Mullin to frat parties around campus.
Like Gminski, Gravante didn't see Mullin choosing the Blue Devils over
the hometown favorite, St. John's. "He didn't show any fire in the belly for
Duke," the manager said.

Krzyzewski did show considerable fire in the belly for Mullin. He fell in
love with him at Five-Star camp, and grew close to Mullin's mother Eileen.
He had Swenson practically live in Brooklyn for a while, where the Duke
assistant made regular trips to the deli that Mullin frequented, just to bump
into him. Krzyzewski returned to New York right after the six-foot-six lefty
led his Xaverian High team to the state championship, but on arrival, he
discovered that Mullin had just signed with Lou Carnesecca and St. John's.
Krzyzewski was as dejected as his assistants had ever seen him. He told one,
Swenson, that he didn't think the St. John's coaches knew how good of a
player they were getting. "Mike was crestfallen," said Konchalski, who sat
with him that night. "It was like he'd been punched in the stomach, and the
wind had gone out of him."

The Mullin miss inspired Coach K to listen to tapes made by the motivational speaker Denis Waitley on the psychology of winning; he ordered
his assistants to listen to them too. In the end, because he finished second
on six of his prime targets, Krzyzewski was left with one gifted Foster-era
senior in Taylor, a pair of reliable junior shooters in Engelland and Tom
Emma, and almost nothing else. After landing only Doug McNeely in his
first class, Krzyzewski settled for a four-man class that included just one
future starter, six-foot-seven Danny Meagher. Dean Smith, meanwhile,
improved a loaded North Carolina team that had lost the national title
game to Indiana by signing two McDonald's All-Americans from in state
—Buzz Peterson and a six-foot-five swingman from Wilmington named
Mike Jordan.

The Blue Devils had no center, no size, and no chance to compete with
the heavyweights atop the ACC. The most fight they showed all year came,
predictably enough, from their head coach. Krzyzewski watched as Wake
Forest coach Carl Tacy—angry over an official's call—accidentally bumped
into Engelland on the Cameron sideline during Wake's 15-point victory on
Coach K's thirty-fifth birthday in February. The home coach responded,
according to the *Charlotte Observer,* "like he had spotted a live grenade."
Krzyzewski got in Tacy's face and later asked, "What was expected of me
when I saw my player bumped? Just sit there?"

Duke had opened the season in Cameron with a double overtime loss to

Vanderbilt and its five-foot-eleven guard, Phil Cox, who scored 30 points. When the six-foot-five Taylor complained about having to cover a much smaller, quicker opponent, Krzyzewski screamed at him, "I don't give a fuck. You're good enough to do it. Now you go out and fuckin' do it."

Taylor did lead the ACC in scoring, and he rang up 35 points in a dramatic triple-overtime victory over Clemson in his final game at Cameron, Krzyzewski's 100th career win against 87 defeats. Coach K did finally relent and sometimes deploy a two-three zone, a weapon that was particularly effective in victories over Auburn (and freshman Charles Barkley) and Rutgers. But the Blue Devils lost at home to Appalachian State and to Davidson (in its own Iron Duke Classic), and on the road to Stetson. They lost by 38 to Louisville, and they lost a 40–36 game to a stalling Maryland team that kept Duke's entire front line from scoring a single point. The Blue Devils lost seven of their last nine games after Krzyzewski guaranteed in the preseason that his team would be playing its best basketball at the end of the year.

Duke finished 4-10 in the ACC and 10-17 overall after getting hammered by Tacy and Wake, 88–53, in the first round of the ACC Tournament. No Duke coach had ever lost seventeen games in a single season. To make matters worse, Coach K's buddy, Valvano, finished 22-10 with an NCAA Tournament appearance in his second season at North Carolina State. To make matters much worse, Dean Smith finished 32-2, seized the regular-season and postseason conference crowns, and finally won the national title as freshman sensation Mike Jordan turned into Michael Jordan with a jumper to beat Georgetown. At the New Orleans site of Smith's breakthrough, Krzyzewski busied himself campaigning with other ACC coaches for the approval of a shot clock to eliminate delay tactics and increase scoring.

But to improve Duke's uninspiring offense — and prevent North Carolina from dominating the league — Krzyzewski simply needed to sign better players. Against the odds, he had landed a class of recruits who had gotten everyone's attention, including Smith's. The singular question that defined these prospects was clear:

Would they develop in time to prevent Mike Krzyzewski from getting fired three years into his five-year deal?

THE NIGHT OF JANUARY 5, 1983, was supposed to be a time for Coach K to finally flex his high-major muscle. His Duke Blue Devils were hosting a team from the bowels of Division I, Wagner College of Staten Island, the kind of opponent Krzyzewski might struggle with at Army but certainly shouldn't here in the ACC.

Duke had started relatively slowly at 5-4, but that was to be expected with a lineup now dominated by freshmen. These weren't your average freshmen, however, even by ACC standards. These newcomers represented the best recruiting class in America, even better than a Dean Smith class that added the two most heralded prospects in North Carolina, Curtis Hunter and Brad Daugherty.

Desperate to make up for his recruiting failures the previous year, Krzyzewski altered his approach: instead of chasing more than two dozen high school stars, Coach K decided to focus all his efforts on a handful of players he felt the Blue Devils had a good chance of signing. Duke printed up 5,000 brochures about Krzyzewski and his program to mail to recruits around the country who might not have even heard of the coach, and Krzyzewski sent Dwyer and the twenty-eight-year-old Swenson to find him high-end ACC talent. During one midseason stretch, Swenson spent thirty-four of forty-eight days on the road recruiting.

He made numerous four-and-a-half-hour drives on barren I-76 from Denver to the southwestern Nebraska town of Grant, population 1,300, just to close the deal on six-foot-eight Bill Jackman, who had received a lesson over the phone from another Duke assistant, Dwyer, on how to pronounce Krzyzewski's name. When Coach K visited the Jackman home, he told the family he erred in recruiting twenty-five players the previous year, and was going after only seven this time around.

Krzyzewski later scored decisive points with the family on two ethical fronts: When informed by Jackman that a famous NBA player representing his former school had given the family brand-new sneakers, Krzyzewski told him that he didn't want to know the name of the school and that he should send the sneakers back. And when Jackman said that he would likely take a recruiting visit to Hawaii as something of a vacation, Krzyzewski told him it wasn't fair to the Hawaii coaches to waste their time unless he was serious about joining their program.

When Jackman broke his home state's heart by picking the Blue Devils over the Cornhuskers, some 14,000 Nebraskans, including the governor, signed a petition imploring him to stay, but his mind was made up. Eleven days later, with Swenson doing the grunt work, Krzyzewski used his hometown connections to land six-foot-six Weldon Williams of Chicago, who had been recruited by Indiana coach Bobby Knight.

Swenson was again the point man on six-foot-eight Jay Bilas of Rolling Hills Estates, California. Coach K flew out from Durham for one-night stops just to watch Bilas play, practice, or even compete in a pickup game. He followed up almost every conversation with Bilas by sending a personal letter, usually handwritten, with impressive cursive penmanship.

Swenson applied a lot of pressure on the big man to commit, and one night Bilas grew so frustrated over the assistant's persistence that he slammed his mounted rotary phone against the wall next to his family's washing machine, only to have the phone fall into the machine. Bilas's mother Margery was angrier at her son than she was at Swenson; Krzyzewski called to apologize and smooth everything over.

One competing college coach used Duke's failures early in the 1981–1982 season against Krzyzewski in a phone call to Margery Bilas that went like this:

COACH: Have you ever heard of Appalachian State University?
MRS. BILAS: No.
COACH: Well, they just beat Duke last night. If your son is thinking of going there, you might want to think about it.

Jay Bilas assured his mother that Duke wouldn't lose again to Appalachian State if he played for the Blue Devils, but she told Coach K about the phone call and told him she was concerned about his program. "So am I," Krzyzewski responded. "That's why I'm recruiting your son."

Unlike other recruits, Jay wasn't worried that Krzyzewski's coaching style might be as tempestuous as Knight's, but he did ask Coach K if he was a yeller and screamer. "If you screw up, I'm going to let you know about it," Krzyzewski told him. "I'm not going to tap you on the shoulder and say, 'Come on, you can do better.'" That was a good enough answer for Jay.

Bilas went to lunch with Krzyzewski at a local Mexican joint, the Original Red Onion. Jay's bill came out to $7 or $8, and Coach K made him pay for his own meal. Every other coach who had taken Jay to lunch picked up the tab, in violation of NCAA rules. Impressed by Krzyzewski's integrity, and hoping to establish the kind of bond with his college coach that he never felt with his high school coach, Bilas picked Duke over Iowa, Syracuse, and Kansas in January 1982. Three down, three to go for Krzyzewski, who was about to land the player he needed above all others.

Johnny Dawkins, a six-foot-two guard from Washington, DC, was built like a one-iron and could slice through defenses like only one or two other high school guards in America. Dwyer was the lead assistant on this one, and it was never going to be easy, not with Georgetown's John Thompson, Notre Dame's Digger Phelps, and Maryland's Lefty Driesell — himself a Duke grad — pushing hard for the point guard. The Blue Devils had started tracking Dawkins in the tenth grade, and Krzyzewski watched him in the summer in DC's Jelleff League. On flights to DC during periods when coaches weren't allowed to talk to high school prospects, Dwyer wrote Johnny long letters that he handed off to the kid's coach.

Dawkins said he read every one of those letters. But enough people told him he would be crazy to pick a struggling program with a struggling young coach that he told his father, a former Green Beret, that maybe Duke would never win under Krzyzewski.

Johnny Sr. stared at his son. "Are you good? Are you good?" he asked.

"Yeah, I'm good, Dad," Johnny Jr. responded.

"Then don't worry about it," Johnny Sr. said with a shrug. "They'll be good also."

Taylor hosted Dawkins on his campus visit; Krzyzewski told him this was the one recruit Duke absolutely had to get. Taylor showed the kid his nice third-floor apartment, a single, on campus, and Dawkins figured, incorrectly, that he would be assigned the same kind of living quarters. Krzyzewski announced on March 13 that Dawkins had committed to Duke, a stunning development.

Coach K then moved to close on Mark Alarie, a six-foot-eight forward from Phoenix who had been leaning heavily toward Stanford, at least until its head coach, Dick DiBiaso, was forced out.

Swenson had been working Bilas and Alarie hard, sometimes commuting between Los Angeles and Phoenix to watch them play and leaving laundry in both places to be picked up on his next trip. He first saw Alarie at a tournament in Sacramento; he needed to sit through only the first half to make his evaluation. Swenson ran to a pay phone, dialed up Krzyzewski, and said, "I found somebody better than Bilas." Of course, Coach K was needed to secure the signature. As a recruiter, the Duke head coach was always prepared. He carried his own spoon in his shaving kit on the road so he could use it for his nightly serving of ice cream before going to bed.

Alarie called Krzyzewski "clearly the most energetic and passionate" coach who visited with him; the recruit noticed that the Duke coach had goose bumps on his arms when delivering his pitch. "It's hard to fake goose bumps," Alarie said. Four days after the Dawkins announcement, Alarie declared that he too would attend Duke.

David Henderson, a six-foot-five forward, was the final member of the class to commit, and the only one from North Carolina. He was a small-town kid who grew up a North Carolina State and David Thompson fan, and he was planning to play for the Wolfpack until he saw Krzyzewski charge Carl Tacy in protecting his player in that Duke-Wake game. *I can play for that guy,* Henderson told himself.

Krzyzewski had also been a regular attendee at Curtis Hunter's South Durham High games, but Hunter picked the Tar Heels three days after they defeated Georgetown for the national title, leaving Henderson as a much-valued consolation prize and giving the Blue Devils four prospects — Dawkins, Alarie, Bilas, and Henderson — placed by the Gannett national newspaper chain in the nation's top fifty.

It was a staggering haul for a coach who was in the middle of a 10-17 season at Duke, two years after a 9-17 season at Army. Krzyzewski was thrilled that he would finally have depth and competition on the roster in year three. "But I've told the people coming in that if they think everything is going to be great, it's not," he said. "Any time you have so many new people coming into a group of fifteen, you have potential problems."

The first problem was matching up with the Tar Heels. North Carolina and Duke players often competed against each other in the summer, sometimes in Chapel Hill and sometimes at Cameron Indoor Stadium or at Duke's auxiliary facility, Card Gym. During their first week in Durham, the Duke freshmen headed to the Carolina campus to play in pickup games at the school's old Woollen Gymnasium. They were wearing Blue Devils gear, which attracted a lot of attention, especially from Jordan, who wanted to teach America's number-one recruiting class a harsh lesson in Tobacco Road diplomacy. "Jordan's only thought was, 'Come on, let me show you how futile it's going to be for you when you play us in the regular season,'" Alarie said.

They were sitting under the basket, waiting their turn, when Jordan hit his head on the backboard while dunking the ball. Amazed, Alarie looked at Bilas and thought to himself, *What have we gotten ourselves into?*

The same could be said of the Duke intrasquad games between the hotshot freshmen and the upperclassmen, who had no interest in surrendering their principal roles on the team. "The seniors said, 'Okay, motherfuckers, you think you're good? Let's see,'" Jackman said. Jackman recalled the freshmen beating their elders in their first encounter, a brutally physical game that included fisticuffs. Word got back to the coaches that the kids had prevailed, Jackman said, setting a tone for the season.

Mike Tissaw, one of the seniors, said that before the coaches were allowed in the gym under NCAA rules, the Blue Devils heard that Krzyzewski wanted the freshmen to be on one team. As official practices got under way, Tissaw noticed that the hyped-up freshmen were allowed to hack away at the less talented seniors without getting fouls called on them. Tissaw grew so upset with Krzyzewski over this double standard that he nearly took it out on Alarie's handsome face after the freshman got away with a couple of particularly hard fouls. Alarie was terrified that the rugged senior was about to punch him out.

"I knew that I was getting away with what I wanted to get away with; the players figured that out very quickly," Alarie conceded. "And I knew it was unfair [to the seniors], but I still wanted to win and you've got to take advantage of what they were calling."

As the early regular-season games unfolded it was clear that Alarie and Dawkins were the team's most talented freshmen, with Bilas and Henderson not far behind, and that Tom Emma and Chip Engelland, who was not a strong defender, were the seniors who would continue playing meaningful roles. Tissaw had been reduced to a nonpresence. Duke opened with a tight victory over East Carolina and, as Bilas had predicted, beat Appalachian State in the second game to avoid a second embarrassing loss to the Mountaineers. Then the Blue Devils lost four straight, including a 104–91 defeat at the hands of top-ranked Virginia and seven-foot-four center Ralph Sampson, who had 36 points and 14 rebounds.

Coach K was on edge. So were the members of his first full recruiting class — Meagher, Jay Bryan, Greg Wendt, and Todd Anderson — and the one recruit from his first year, McNeely, who had been hurdled by the freshmen. Krzyzewski had been using as many as four freshmen in the starting lineup. He had predicted there would be problems with so many newcomers, and sure enough he had problems.

"Small things set people off that year," Bilas recalled. "After a tough practice once . . . a couple of guys hung around and started shooting halfcourt shots for a dollar. We were screwing around before we left the gym an hour after practice was over, and one assistant had walked through and seen us doing that. The next day we got bitched out for screwing around. We weren't in a bar, we were shooting halfcourt shots. It was like, 'Can't we have any fun?'"

The Blue Devils won home games against Davidson, New Hampshire, and George Mason, teams they were expected to handle, before they met Wagner, a team they were expected to destroy. The Seahawks had gone 4-22 the previous season under P. J. Carlesimo, and they had dropped seven of their first nine games under first-year coach Neil Kennett, including a 50-point loss to the University of Nevada–Las Vegas the previous week. They had already played three games in the ECAC Metro Conference and had lost all three to St. Francis (New York), St. Francis (Pennsylvania), and Long Island University by double figures.

Kennett had not acquired any film of Duke until the day of the game.

He watched it quickly at the hotel, diagrammed a few plays, and then conducted a walk-through with his team. The Seahawks showed up at Cameron hungry, literally—they thought they were being served steak and lasagna for their pregame meal and ended up with only salad instead. "So we had a little attitude going into the game," said Bobby Mahala, a fifth-year senior guard.

Wagner caught a major break, as Duke students, notorious for their witty and sometimes offensive behavior toward the opposing team, were out of session. They were not in their usual positions right on top of the court, screaming Staten Island put-downs into the Seahawks' ears. "But it still seemed like when you walked in there, everybody knew everybody," Mahala said. "The refs knew everybody too. It was one big party."

Except that no form of home-cooking from the officials could save the Blue Devils on this night. Wagner showed no stage fright in front of a relatively small crowd of 5,500 and showed no fear of their hosts and their acclaimed freshmen. The Seahawks were smaller but quicker, and Mahala, a future New York City fireman who flourished under Kennett (less so under the far more abrasive Carlesimo), outscored Dawkins 25 to 18 and stripped him on back-to-back possessions. Duke struggled against the zone (Wagner usually played man-to-man) while the Seahawks shot 57.6 percent from the floor against Krzyzewski's man defense, without a single made basket feeling fluky.

Early in the game, after Wagner made a few plays, Mahala surveyed the look of uncertainty in Duke's eyes and told himself, *We've got these guys.* Late in the game, during a time-out, Kennett surveyed the look of belief on his players' faces and told his assistant, Joe Servon, "They believe we will win this game. I guarantee you we will win this game."

Duke's coaches couldn't believe they were losing in their building, to this opponent, and to a scoring guard with thinning hair who they thought looked about thirty-two years old. But lose they did, 84–77, and there would be a reason why Krzyzewski, when he ran into Mahala years later at a basketball clinic in Toronto, told the former Wagner player, "You sonuvabitch, you almost got me fired." As the teams left the court that January 1983 night, they heard fans screaming for Coach K's head. "You could hear them yelling all kinds of nasty stuff," Mahala said. "It was, 'You guys stink. How can you lose to these guys?'"

The Blue Devils heard even worse from their crowd as they passed some adult fans who were hanging over the railing, including members of the program's Iron Dukes booster club who were screaming at Krzyzewski, calling him a loser and a bum. Alarie recalled running off the floor to escape the humiliation of it all. "They were hecklers," the freshman said. "They were saying, 'You're out of here, Krzyzewski. You're an embarrassment, Krzyzewski.'" Alarie recognized some of the longtime boosters who were shouting and didn't forget their faces.

Coach K heard it all, of course; he had no choice but to hear it. Duke fans didn't hang him in effigy the way Carolina fans had with Dean Smith. "But they wanted him out of there," Jay Bryan said of the fans. As unnerved as his players were, and as distraught as he was, Krzyzewski remained gracious in his praise of Wagner and Mahala. "We could have played them another forty minutes," he said, "and we still would have lost. We couldn't handle number 10."

The following morning Krzyzewski's wife Mickie called Duke's assistant sports information director, Johnny Moore, looking for her husband. Moore knew where to look for Coach K. He drove to Cameron, walked into the back area of the locker room, and found his basketball coach rewinding his way through the most disturbing parts of the Wagner loss, over and over and over again.

"You okay?" Moore asked him.

"Nope," Krzyzewski responded while keeping his eyes on the film.

"You need anything?"

"Nope."

Moore called Mickie and assured her Mike was okay.

Some of his players were teased at the mall for losing to Wagner. Around the same time, Jackman and a couple of other freshmen joined Krzyzewski at an Iron Dukes luncheon. The players didn't speak; Coach K did all the talking. And when he was through, the boosters started shouting out questions about why the Blue Devils weren't playing zone defense, and Krzyzewski responded that he believed firmly in man-to-man. "We were looking at each other like, 'This is crazy,'" Jackman said of the players. "Nobody on our team could cover Ralph Sampson or Michael Jordan, but Coach K said, 'I don't play zone.'"

The walls seemed to already be closing in on Krzyzewski, and it was getting hard to see his escape route out. Krzyzewski did learn something in that crushing Wagner defeat that might have provided some long-term benefit. Twenty years later, when he attended the funeral of Carlesimo's father, Krzyzewski saw a vaguely familiar figure approach from the side: it was Wagner coach Neil Kennett.

"Coach, I'm sure you don't remember me," Kennett said.

"Oh, I remember you," Krzyzewski responded. "You're the guy who beat me. And you're the reason why I never took another team lightly the rest of my life."

DUKE LOST ALL FOUR of its 1983 games with Dean Smith's Tar Heels and Jim Valvano's Wolfpack by an average margin of 19 points. This wasn't like losing games to Kentucky or UCLA.

"We couldn't even hide in our own cul-de-sac," Johnny Moore said. "We've got to go to work and to lunch and dinner every day with Carolina and State fans."

And yet the divide between Krzyzewski's talent and his chief rivals' talent was not Duke's biggest problem. That was the divide between Krzyzewski and Bill Foster's last holdovers.

To begin with, Krzyzewski's style of coaching was an acquired taste for all team members. Nobody was fully prepared for his relentless profanity or his ability to make you feel smaller than a referee's whistle. "I'd never been dressed down like that," Jay Bilas said, "and it wasn't just me. Just about everybody else felt that way too. It was really intense and loud and personal. Not demeaning, but crushing." In other words, Bilas said, "there was a Bob Knight air about things with Mike."

Krzyzewski threw team members out of practice if they didn't dive onto the floor with enough purpose for a loose ball. When watching film, he had a rewind button that he would keep pressing to harp on mistakes. The Blue Devils grew to despise that button, as Coach K never hesitated to explode on erring players in front of their peers. Most of the freshmen figured this was just part of the major-college deal, a rite of passage from high school to the upper reaches of Division I. But Foster's guys — Engelland, Emma, and Tissaw — embraced very little about Krzyzewski. "That was not a healthy relationship between him and them," recalled Bilas.

The seniors did not mistreat the freshmen at all, according to Bilas and Alarie, but the lack of trust between Foster's players and Foster's successor shaped the season. Exacerbating the disconnect was the feeling that Krzyzewski's job was in danger. Tissaw said that even the school's professors expected that Coach K would not last much longer at Duke. The Blue Devils' radio voice, Bob Harris, sat with an emotional Krzyzewski in the old coaches' locker room when Coach K, his chin quivering, defended his aversion to playing zone defense, saying, "If they just leave me alone and let me build it the way I know I can, it will work." But would they leave him alone?

"We could sense an enormous amount of pressure," Bilas said. "It was everywhere. There were very few supporters that we knew of. Every time you turned around he was getting criticized . . . We had all kinds of Iron Dukes chirping. Honestly, I didn't care for our older fans back then. They wanted him out."

The Iron Dukes started calling its club the Concerned Iron Dukes. "They were concerned about me being their coach," Krzyzewski acknowledged. Some Duke fans were actually rooting for their team to lose in order to im-prove the odds of a coaching change. One Iron Duke member, the father of Alarie's girlfriend, took the boys to dinner one night and told them that boosters had signed a petition calling for Coach K's ouster. Bilas was angry and surprised. *Why would you tell me that?* he thought to himself. *I don't want to hear that.*

Bilas told Alarie and other teammates that he would immediately trans-fer from Duke if the very reason he chose the school — Krzyzewski — was escorted out the door. Like his classmates, Bilas had plenty of time to pivot to other schools and reshape his college basketball career. The seniors did not have that option. As their roles and minutes diminished over time, a couple of those seniors could be heard barking in the locker room to sig-nify their place in the doghouse, angering Krzyzewski. "I don't have a dog-house," he yelled. "If you're sitting on the bench, it's for a reason."

The Cameron locker room was too small to fit a doghouse anyway. The players were crammed into their rectangular, wire-meshed, side-by-side lockers, and they sat in chairs — planted in front of their stalls — designed for much smaller people. Krzyzewski often addressed his team near a door with the slogan WINNERS NEVER GIVE UP printed above it.

Only some Blue Devils did consider giving up. Tissaw recalled a team meeting in a dorm room that was attended by the majority of Blue Devils, including the freshmen, who were, in the senior's words, "very, very con-cerned about Krzyzewski's approach. People started talking about transfer-ring." Tissaw recalled that one issue raised in the meeting revolved around the way Krzyzewski "was speaking to some players, and treating some players."

One prominent member of the Duke program had met with some of the players and told them, "Get the hell out of here. He's a terrible coach." Jack-man, who had seen his playing time decrease and who had family issues at home, was already thinking of transferring to Nebraska. (He would leave Duke for the Cornhuskers after the season.) As he started losing his sense of belonging in Durham, Jackman chose not to reach out to Krzyzewski, the assistants, or his closest teammates, Bilas and Alarie — a regret he car-ried for decades. He listened to some team elders who thought he needed a new school and a new coach. "I didn't side with them," Jackman said, "but I heard what they said: 'This is a sinking ship. Get out.'" In the final analysis, Jackman said, "We had a lot of dissension on the team."

That was evident after the final regular-season game, another blowout loss to Michael Jordan and the Tar Heels. The ACC had elected to experiment with a three-point goal and a thirty-second shot clock to quicken the pace; Jordan made 5-of-7 threes and scored 32 points to beat the Blue Devils by 24, giving them a record of 11-16 overall, 3-11 in the conference, as they entered the ACC Tournament. Duke ended up as the second-worst team in the ACC five years after Foster's Blue Devils ended up as the second-best team in the country. Engelland scored 30 in his Cameron farewell, but it was a perimeter shot launched by Tissaw — a card-carrying bricklayer who had not scored a point all year — that caught Krzyzewski's attention during film review.

Coach K was watching on the 16-millimeter reel, repeatedly hitting that damn rewind button on Tissaw's shot, before he said, "You know what you're saying to me when you're taking this shot? You're saying, 'Fuck you.'" Tissaw didn't hesitate: "Coach," he said, "if I wanted to say 'Fuck you,' I'm just going to say it to your face. I'm not going to take a jump shot."

The room fell silent. Soon Duke would prepare to get destroyed by Ralph Sampson one last time.

The night before the Blue Devils' opening-round tournament game against Virginia, Krzyzewski visited his players' hotel rooms in Atlanta for individual pep talks. The Cavaliers had beaten Duke by a combined 34 points in their two regular-season meetings, and Krzyzewski knew his team needed to be at its very best to stay in the game. He told Jackman that, as a bench player, if he saw his teammate Alarie struggling with his confidence — especially in response to a dominating Sampson performance — he should go over and reassure him during the game. "I'd never before seen Coach go around to everybody's rooms before bed and tell them their roles like that," Jackman said.

Nobody expected it to work, and it didn't. Though Sampson picked up three early fouls that sent him to the bench, keeping it relatively close in the first half, the Cavaliers completely dominated in the second; their 109–66 victory represented the biggest blowout loss in Duke's seventy-eight-year basketball history. The game marked the third time that season that Virginia had topped 100 points against Krzyzewski's man-to-man. As if that weren't enough, Sampson accused Bilas of playing "dirty basketball" in the paint. The towering Virginia center logged only fourteen minutes (and scored 18 points), though some on the Duke side thought that Sampson had been on the floor too deep into the rout, and that his coach, Terry Holland, had run up the score. After Holland also accused Bilas of playing dirty, an angry Krzyzewski confronted him in the hallway and started a shouting match.

Bilas denied everything except the accusation that he had just gotten his ass handed to him. "They kicked the shit out of us," he said.

Duke fans in attendance were not pleased with the effort. "We got booed coming off the floor," Swenson said, "and people were yelling, 'Dumb Polack,' at Mike." On the way back to her hotel room, Mickie Krzyzewski stopped in Duke's hospitality suite and heard some Iron Dukes scheming to get her husband fired. Johnny Moore passed by the same suite and heard the Iron Dukes — the Concerned Iron Dukes — complaining about Krzyzewski. "You could hear them from the hallway," Moore said.

Mickie ended up crying in her room, fearful that Mike was done at Duke. To escape their grim reality, the Krzyzewskis ventured out into the dark, rainy night and joined Bobby Dwyer, Moore, Duke sports information director Tom Mickle, and a couple of highly respected writers, the *Washington Post*'s John Feinstein and the *Durham Morning Herald*'s Keith Drum, on a search for some comfort food. They pulled up to a Denny's just off the interstate around 2 a.m. and headed to a back corner table.

"The first thing we did was remove the knives," Moore said through a laugh.

The group had yet to order when Moore grabbed his glass of water and raised it toward the ceiling. "Here's to forgetting tonight," he said.

Krzyzewski told Moore to lower his glass, then lifted his glass and proposed his own toast.

"Here's to *never* fucking forgetting tonight," he said.

SAVING COACH K

MIKE KRZYZEWSKI WAS sitting across from his boss, looking worried that he was about to lose his job. His team had just been crushed by Wake Forest the night before, and the man who had hired him, Tom Butters, had asked for Coach K to be sent to the athletic director's office as soon as he arrived at Cameron that morning.

Butters often arranged to meet with his coaches in their offices to give them a sense of home-court advantage. When he was summoned to the AD's office instead, Krzyzewski knew it had to be important. He had been up all night with his assistants watching and rewatching the horror film that was Duke's 31-point loss to Wake Forest — Coach K's eighth straight loss to the Demon Deacons — and he was trying to process the circumstances that led to the meeting before he walked into it.

Duke had started the season with a 14-1 record that was largely assembled against lesser nonconference lights, but it included a 78–72 victory over a Virginia team no longer anchored by Ralph Sampson; the Houston Rockets had made the seven-foot-four center the number-one overall pick in the NBA draft. For the first practice of the 1983–1984 season, Krzyzewski posted the 109–66 score from their ACC Tournament loss to Virginia in lights. Before Duke's victory over the Cavaliers ten months later, Krzyzewski's blackboard — normally littered with Xs and Os and pregame notes — had only one thing on it: "The number 43," recalled Mark Alarie, referring to the margin of defeat. "He doesn't forget slights or disrespectful treatment."

Krzyzewski had told his players after that rout, "I don't want you to ever forget what this feels like." They didn't. And yet even after securing a measure of revenge against the Cavaliers in their ACC opener, the Blue Devils were back in crisis mode, in part because of the way their fans treated Maryland senior Herman Veal in their second ACC game, an 81–75 Terrapins victory on January 14.

Accused by a female student of sexual misconduct, Veal had been placed on disciplinary probation the year before and banned from postseason play after a student judicial board ruled that he had violated the school's code of conduct. When Veal was introduced in the pregame, Duke fans threw women's underwear and condoms in his direction. The sound of the condoms hitting the floor, the Maryland forward would say later, "sounded like rain falling." Though Veal was never charged with any crime, and though the university ultimately cleared his record, he was subjected to a vile chant about rape.

Duke students had earned their reputation for the kind of intelligent mockery of opponents that would soon make "Cameron Crazies" a nationally recognized description of their crowd. Every game night a few thousand surrounded the lower arena, stood almost right on top of the coaches, players, refs, and credentialed press, and shouted and chanted insults at anyone perceived to be an impediment to victory.

For the most part, when Duke students ridiculed a coach's wardrobe or a player's height or haircut, opponents accepted it as a somewhat humorous part of the Cameron experience. But the Veal incident was different. The crowd's behavior was clearly in very poor taste. "Herman was pissed before the game," recalled Maryland coach Lefty Driesell. "I said, 'Let's go out there and win this game for Herman,' and we did." Ken Denlinger of the *Washington Post* rightfully ripped the Duke student body in his column, and he wasn't the only journalist to take issue with Blue Devils fans. As race was forever an issue at Duke, it wasn't lost on many observers that a white college crowd seemed to take particular delight in taunting Black athletes.

On January 17, the same day a white Duke junior wrote an opinion piece in *The Chronicle* explaining that he hung a Confederate flag in his room as "a reminder of the honor and grace of the chivalrous Old South," the student paper ran a story under a front-page headline that read, "Duke Fans Scorned Nationally." The university's vice president for student affairs, William Griffith, decried the student body's attempt to "intimidate and dehumanize the visiting players." In a letter that he sent to all students and signed "Uncle Terry," Duke president Terry Sanford asked them to "think of something clever but clean, devastating but decent, mean but wholesome, witty and forceful but G-rated for television, and try it at the next game." Sanford finished the letter with this dagger: "I hate for us to have the reputation of being stupid."

That night, with his program suddenly feeling under siege, Krzyzewski completed a brutal four-day period with that blowout loss to Wake and with this concession: "We just played horribly. When I say 'we,' I mean the whole group — coaches and players." Back in Durham, he caught a few hours' sleep after his all-night film session with his assistants in the coaches' locker room, and then returned to his small Cameron office, where he was redirected across the building to Butters.

What is this all about? Krzyzewski thought to himself. The losses to nationally ranked Maryland and Wake Forest were dispiriting reminders of the past two seasons, the bad ol' days, and the crowd behavior was no positive reflection on Coach K, who did nothing about it. And of course, the previous spring, Jim Valvano's NC State pulled off an all-time miracle run to the national championship, punctuated by a last-second victory over heavily favored Houston on perhaps the most memorable night in college basketball history. No witness would ever forget the Dereck Whittenburg heave and the Lorenzo Charles catch and buzzer-beating dunk that sent Valvano scrambling onto the Albuquerque court in vain pursuit of someone to hug.

Krzyzewski sure wouldn't forget it. Jimmy V had become a national media darling while a relatively new cable TV phenomenon, the Entertainment and Sports Programming Network, or ESPN, was making its mark in college basketball and promising to turn characters such as Valvano into richer, more marketable men.

At the end of his third year at NC State, a 24-mile drive from the Durham campus, Valvano had won an NCAA title and an ACC Tournament title and compiled a 62-33 overall record. At the end of his third year at Duke, Krzyzewski had won two NIT games and compiled a 38-47 overall record, including a 2-4 record against NC State. The last two national championship coaches, Valvano and Dean Smith, were living next door to Krzyzewski, who was feeling immense pressure to keep up.

But Coach K did land the nation's number-one recruiting class two years earlier, and he had since added an All-American high school point guard in freshman Tommy Amaker, who had already made impactful plays in the victory over Virginia — Krzyzewski's first after seven losses to the Cavaliers. Duke had started building team chemistry on a summer trip to France and a series of games against French clubs. And besides, the Blue Devils were 14-3. A soft 14-3, perhaps, but was it even possible to fire a coach in the middle of a season with that kind of record?

A year earlier, when he followed an 11-17 season with a 10-17 one, Krzyzewski asked for a meeting with Butters because he was worried that his 38-47 record would get him fired. "I knew I would end up with something in basketball," Coach K would tell a few administrators and coaches years later at a University of Rhode Island ethics seminar, "but I was worried about my assistants. When I met with Tom, I told him if he was going to fire me, tell me now and I will work on getting my assistants other jobs."

Back then, Butters didn't say anything in response. He had already stared down a deep-pocketed booster who was in the habit of giving Duke about $100,000 a year, and who made it clear that he didn't want "that dumb Polack to come back." Butters told the man he didn't want his money anymore.

When Krzyzewski said what he said about getting fired and helping his assistants land on their feet, Butters pulled out a folder and asked him to start reading the terms of his employment contract at Duke. "When I got to the part about it being a five-year contract, Tom stopped me," Krzyzewski said. "Tom said, 'Mike, sixty days before that contract ends, you and I will meet here and discuss your future at Duke. And not a day sooner.'"

And yet Krzyzewski was now being called to Butters's office fifteen months before the contract's expiration date. He might have been even more worried had he been aware of a conversation the AD had had with Bob Knight. Tom Miller, the head coach at Cornell and a former Krzyzewski teammate at Army, was sitting in the Indiana basketball office when Knight's longtime secretary, Mary Ann Davis, told him that Butters was on the phone.

"The gist of it was Butters calling and saying, 'Bobby, what do I do? The alumni are on my ass. He's got two years left on his contract, and the alums are all over me,'" Miller recalled. "Coach Knight said, without hesitation, 'The only thing you can do is extend his contract to shut them up.' He said it as fast as you can say something. And then there was dead silence."

Miller couldn't hear precisely what Butters said next. "But I could tell what was going on," Miller said. "There was a pause, no conversation for ten seconds. I'm sure Butters was saying, 'Are you kidding me?' Maybe it was, 'I'm calling Coach Knight and he'll let me off the hook and say he understands you have to do what you have to do.' He was looking for a little validation. Was Butters looking for an out because he wanted to justify what he was doing next to the alumni, or to placate the alumni because they were on his ass? And say, 'Hey, this isn't working out. It's time after the three-year experiment to pull the plug on the Polish kid.'"

Maybe Knight's advice had no impact on Butters, maybe it did. Either way, after a worn-out Krzyzewski took a seat, his expression tight and his small mouth all but disappearing from his face, the AD paced back and forth in front of him. As he later relayed the exchange to his son Bret, Butters told

Krzyzewski, "I want to talk to you about your job." Coach K jumped right in and talked about finishing second in recruiting for the likes of Chris Mullin and Uwe Blab, and then following up those near-misses with the Dawkins, Alarie, Bilas, Henderson class that ranked as America's finest. "Coach was trying to explain to him," Bret Butters said, before his father stopped him and said, "No, I want to talk to you about your job."

Then the imposing AD looked straight at his coach and told him, "We've got a public who doesn't know how good you are. We've got press who are too stupid to tell them how good you are. And the biggest problem right now is I'm not sure you know how good you are."

Butters then pulled a document out of his drawer and slid it across his desk to Krzyzewski. "I'm going to do something about your contract," he told the coach. "I'm going to tear the son of a bitch up."

As Krzyzewski began reviewing the papers in his hand, he realized that Butters had just handed him a new five-year deal to run through the 1988–1989 season. Coach K was stunned; his eyes filled with tears. A year earlier, his contemporary and rival, Valvano, had been given a ten-year extension by NC State. Valvano already had a national championship ring, endorsement deals with Mountain Dew and Hardee's, a book deal, his own signature sportswear line, and the attention of an NBA franchise, the New Jersey Nets, who wanted to airlift him out of Raleigh and fly him back to his New York market roots.

What did Krzyzewski have, other than the new contract in his hands?

"Tom, you don't need to do this," he told the AD. Butters assured him otherwise.

Now everyone needed to decide when it made sense to announce the extension. First, Duke had to get through its next home game with the undefeated and top-ranked North Carolina Tar Heels in three days, its first home game since the Maryland debacle. On January 20, the day before the UNC game, *The Chronicle* published a letter from Krzyzewski to what he called "the Best Fans in College Basketball." Coach K made no reference to his new contract, but he sure sounded like a secure and confident man. "I guess that there has been more written about all of you this week than there has been about the Super Bowl (you know, that's the game played the day after *the game,* Duke-UNC)," he wrote. "You have taken some shots, some fair and some unfair. I know because I have also taken a few this week.

"I want you all (that's about as Southern as a Polish kid from Chicago can get!) to know that the players and coaches consider you as part of the team. You are the best! You give us more support than any student body in the country . . . One of the main reasons we are able to recruit young men from throughout the country is because of the great basketball atmosphere here at Duke. We have even made tapes of you in all of your splendor to show just how wild and crazy Cameron can be. Thanks for being you."

Coach K went on to write that there had been "a couple of times when we have done some things in poor taste. I really do not think we need to curse (I'm attempting to correct that in my own vocabulary) or be abusive. Everyone around the country is doing that and we certainly do not want to be like everyone else . . . Let's get together on Saturday and start doing everything in a class manner."

This was hardly a strong rebuke — barely a rebuke at all, considering that senior Duke administrators had threatened to remove abusive students from the North Carolina game and require them to appear before the school's undergraduate judicial board. Coach K met with students a couple of hours before tipoff to remind them to maintain their enthusiasm while keeping their conduct in check. But as it turned out, the only Blue Devil supporter who would need to apologize for his or her behavior after the Saturday night game was Krzyzewski himself.

The students acted in Cameron almost as if they were attending a church social. They wore makeshift halos made of coat hangers and foil, gave the officials a standing ovation, and hung signs that read, A HEARTY WELCOME TO DEAN SMITH and WELCOME HONORED GUESTS. Rather than rage against the refs with a chant of "Bull-shit" after a call went against Duke, the students chanted, "We beg to differ." Even though North Carolina senior Matt Doherty, from Long Island, had described the Cameron crowd as "just a bunch of rude northerners who study too much and release it on the opposing players," the Duke students were gracious hosts to the Tar Heels. They even shouted, "Hi Dean," when the Tar Heels' coach entered the arena, though Smith (unlike some ACC coaches) never found the Duke students funny, clever, or cute; he was offended by the amount of cursing from the Cameron crowd.

It was a hell of a game too, one Duke appeared about to win before the 13-0 Tar Heels were saved by Michael Jordan and freshman point guard Kenny Smith. Krzyzewski's man defense forced Carolina into 24 turnovers and inspired the Blue Devils to think, with five minutes to play, that they were about to bring down their well-behaved house. "Then Michael took off," said Duke forward Danny Meagher. "Every year we play them he does that."

After Dean Smith praised Duke's effort and performance to reporters and called Krzyzewski's team one of the best he'd faced, a steaming Coach K changed the conversation upon sweeping into the interview room under the Cameron stands. Smith had jumped all over one of the officials near the end of the first half, and with 4:26 left, while trying to get a substitute checked into the game, the frustrated Carolina coach pounded the table while trying to hit the courtside buzzer and accidentally hit the scoreboard button and added 20 points to the Tar Heels' total.

Krzyzewski was furious that Smith wasn't assessed a technical foul, especially since the Duke coach was rightfully hit with one — for berating a ref — in the final seconds of the 78–73 defeat. Tired of the pounding his team's fans had taken, and perhaps fueled by the knowledge that he had a fresh five-year deal in his hip pocket, Krzyzewski chose to fire away at Duke's critics and at the favorable treatment he thought was granted to Smith.

"I want to tell you all something," he started. "When you come in here and start writing about Duke having no class, you better start getting your heads straight because our students had class and our team had class. There was not a person on our bench who was pointing a finger at the officials or banging on the scorer's table or having everybody running around on their bench. So let's get something straight around here and quit the double standard that sometimes exists in this league. All right?"

Coach K specifically defined the double standard as "one for Dean Smith and one for the rest of us." Krzyzewski thought that press coverage in the area was slanted toward Carolina and away from Duke in part because of the state's long-standing obsession with the Tar Heels and in part because Carolina grads held influential jobs with local media outlets. He wasn't afraid to rage against that bias and to accept the beating he took for saying what he said at Smith's expense, knowing that he was now in a better position to weather this storm and those that might follow.

Duke decided to announce the new contract before the Blue Devils' next game, against Valvano's defending national champs, at Cameron. Some university officials thought that would be a mistake, since Krzyzewski had a hard time beating Valvano. Wouldn't it make more sense to publicly disclose the news before a game Duke was more likely to win?

In announcing the news, Butters said of his coach, "We offered the first five years on what we thought he could do. Now, this five is on what I know he can do and what he's in the process of accomplishing . . . He deserved it, he's earned it, and the university is extraordinarily pleased with him as a man and as a coach."

Krzyzewski spoke of how much the commitment would help the Blue Devils in recruiting. "One thing we're striving to do is to develop continuity," he said. "I've always believed I had the support, but only through ways like this will everyone understand."

And then Krzyzewski went out and lost again to Valvano, 79–76, Duke's fourth consecutive ACC defeat. That result, on top of the contract news, did nothing to dissuade the Concerned Iron Dukes and other Blue Devils fans who thought Coach K was overmatched. Krzyzewski's young daughters had been hearing about it in school; the impact of losing on school-aged children in a passionate college sports town is among the steepest prices a beleaguered coach can pay. Butters was facing heavy criticism too, for sticking with a coach many believed he should not have hired in the first place. The Concerned Iron Dukes wanted him out along with Coach K. The letters got angrier and the phone calls grew more alarming. Butters received multiple death threats immediately after the announcement of Krzyzewski's extension.

His wife Lynn fielded a middle-of-the-night call from a man who threatened to kill her husband. When she crawled back into bed, unnerved, Butters asked his wife who was on the phone. "I don't know," she said, "but it was someone saying some awful things about you." Butters responded, "Would you mind starting the car this morning?" They both cracked up laughing.

Bret Butters, then in college, once went to a baseball field and sat in a chair waiting to fight an anonymous caller who had challenged his father; the man never showed up. Bret's sister Jill, then in high school, was there when the calls came in after her father extended Krzyzewski's deal. "It was hard to hear," Jill said. "It was, 'We know where your dad is. He's not coming home tonight' . . . He was in the paper all the time, and people didn't like him, but we did. It was tough, but that's the normal we grew up with."

One prominent member of the Duke basketball program thought Tom Butters had little choice but to double down on Krzyzewski. "If he fired Coach K," the person said, "then Butters was going to get fired next." Regardless, Butters and Krzyzewski were in it together, and if the Blue Devils kept losing games across the balance of the 1983–1984 schedule, the extended partnership was going to end up looking like a really bad idea.

Instead, Duke won its next eight games, including back-to-back road games against Clemson and Georgia Tech; yet another victory over Virginia; and two more over the teams that had sent Krzyzewski spiraling into that meeting with Butters, Maryland and Wake Forest. Duke fans flooded the Cameron court after Alarie's layup in the final seconds of overtime beat the Demon Deacons, who had erased a 20-point deficit in regulation. The victory marked the first time Coach K had defeated Wake and its coach, Carl Tacy, in nine attempts. Krzyzewski closed out the winning streak by beating Valvano at his place, Reynolds Coliseum, also in overtime. Suddenly the Blue Devils were ranked fourteenth in the nation. They had won five of six conference road games and, at 22-5 overall and 7-4 in the ACC, they appeared set to earn Krzyzewski's first NCAA Tournament appearance in nine years as a head coach.

Krzyzewski's breakthrough recruiting class had grown up in its sophomore year, with Alarie a force up front and Dawkins joining Gene Banks and Mike Gminski as the only sophomores in Duke history to crack 1,000 career points. The arrival of Tommy Amaker, a true quarterback, had liberated Dawkins to be his best self on the court. Krzyzewski had been watching Dawkins play summer league ball when he followed through on an AAU coach's suggestion to check out his tiny high school junior, Amaker. Krzyzewski walked up to Amaker's mother after watching his game and said, "Mrs. Amaker, your son is going to look great in Duke blue." Young Tommy would later ask the nice man from Duke who was recruiting him if he acted like Bobby Knight when coaching, and Krzyzewski would assure the point guard that wouldn't be the case.

Krzyzewski's assistant Bobby Dwyer had been the point man on Amaker, out of Falls Church, Virginia, just as he had been on Dawkins. The very first time Krzyzewski saw Amaker play, before his junior year of high school, he told Dwyer, "That's my point guard. I want that kid. We've got to get that kid." Dwyer got him, in part, by traveling to the DC area every Tuesday and Friday after January 1, watching Amaker practice in the afternoon and then Dawkins play at night.

But Dwyer had gotten engaged, and his fiancée wanted to start a family; after the dreadful end to year three, he told his boss he didn't want to spend his life on the road anymore. "Bobby," Krzyzewski said, "you understand you can only leave Duke one time, right?" Dwyer understood. He said he was interested in running the Division III program at the University of the South in Tennessee. Coach K told him he would do everything he could to help him.

To replace Dwyer, Krzyzewski hired Bob Bender, the former Duke player who had become a Duke fundraiser. He also moved Colonel Tom Rogers into the director of basketball operations position and brought in Pete Gaudet, his assistant and successor at Army. Gaudet had been fired after two seasons with an overall record of 12-41. He had spent a year coaching a Kuwaiti club team run by the king's son, who paid the American in cash; Gaudet used it to buy a station wagon colored Carolina blue. He was advised not to park it in the Duke lot.

Krzyzewski's other assistant from West Point, Chuck Swenson, was still on the Duke bench that his buddy Dwyer had just vacated. The two had collected a stunning array of prospects; Swenson didn't even know how good his own recruits could be until he watched them as sophomores take down Vanderbilt in the 1983–1984 season opener. He was so moved by the potential they showed that night that he walked into the bathroom inside the coaches' locker room and started sobbing.

Three and a half months later, in the semifinals of the ACC Tournament in Greensboro, the Blue Devils faced the top-ranked North Carolina Tar Heels, who finished the ACC regular season at 14-0 by outlasting Duke in double overtime in Michael Jordan's last game at UNC's Carmichael Auditorium.

Krzyzewski promised his gutted players that they would finally beat Carolina the next time they met, but few people among the 16,662 who gathered in Greensboro for the rematch believed that Jordan wouldn't prevail again. A day after his team survived yet another overtime game (against Georgia Tech) in their opener, Krzyzewski told the Blue Devils, "We expect to win this game. If we win this game, we are going to walk off the court. We are not going to celebrate. We are going on to our next opponent." In other words, Coach K told them, *Act like you've been here before.* Even if they hadn't.

On this magical postseason day, Krzyzewski's program came together like never before. Dawkins was Dawkins, and Alarie, leaping higher than he did as a freshman, showed all of his athletic grace in scoring 21 points. A muscled-up Jay Bilas, who had pounded the weights in the summer to avenge the ass kickings he took as a freshman, led both sides with 11 rebounds, and David Henderson, an overlooked but valuable tweener, contributed 14 points, 6 assists, and some timely defense on Jordan. A year earlier, on the team bus back to Durham after another loss in Chapel Hill, Henderson had severely reprimanded freshman Bill Jackman for raving about Jordan like some starry-eyed fan.

Now the Blue Devils were leading the Tar Heels by two with three seconds to play when Matt Doherty tried to inbound the ball. The Carolina senior had visited Duke as a high school recruit and didn't see enough talent around Gene Banks and Kenny Dennard to sign on. Doherty saw enough talent out there now, especially in Alarie and Dawkins.

"But they weren't James Worthy and Michael Jordan. They weren't Sam Perkins," Doherty said later. "They were very good players, and Coach K brought the best out of them by creating that culture of togetherness and toughness, and by giving them room to play."

Krzyzewski stood to Doherty's left before the play unfolded, nervously motioning at his defenders and shouting, "No fouls. No fouls." An official waved for Coach K to back up before he handed the ball to Doherty, who was standing right in front of the Duke bench. Twice Doherty faked a two-handed pass toward midcourt before he fired a hard overhead pass down the near sideline toward Jordan, who was streaking into the corner about 65 feet away. The ball was too wide for Jordan and crashed into the Carolina bench. Duke ball. The Coliseum exploded. The Tar Heels would actually get off another shot, after a foul on the Duke inbounds and a Dawkins miss at the line, but Perkins's desperation heave was a prayer unanswered.

Three years earlier, Mike Krzyzewski had beaten Dean Smith with a Bill Foster team. Now he had finally beaten Smith with a Mike Krzyzewski team.

His wife, Mickie, stood and clapped and planted her hands on her face in disbelief. Her husband wandered onto the court, almost in a daze, then walked into the arms of the most important player he ever recruited. Krzyzewski pulled Dawkins in for a tight hug and wouldn't let him go. The coach buried his face in his point guard's right shoulder and closed his eyes. "Coach," Dawkins said, "I thought we were supposed to walk off the court like we expected to win."

"Johnny," Krzyzewski responded, "just be quiet and let's enjoy this."

The Blue Devils jumped into each other's arms. Krzyzewski hugged Henderson too and lowered his head into the forward's chest. His Duke team had just beaten the best of the best, and perhaps that breakthrough inspired an emotional letdown in the Blue Devils' loss to Maryland the following day in the ACC Tournament final, and again in their opening NCAA Tournament game against Washington.

Krzyzewski knew his program and his school had to start expecting success and building on it rather than treating it as a surprise to be celebrated. That's why, after the Duke bookstore made bumper stickers showing the score of the game — Duke 77, North Carolina 75 — Krzyzewski ordered the bookstore to get rid of them. "I don't want our name ever with any other team's name," Coach K announced. He was not going to be happy until the Blue Devils stood alone on top of the sport.

He now knew that was possible. Mike Krzyzewski now knew that he was a good enough coach, with good enough players, to follow Smith and Valvano and win a national championship. It was just a matter of doing it.

THEY WERE SURROUNDED by their parents and their fellow students on the Cameron floor, microphones in hand. It was Sunday, March 2, 1986, and the five seniors who had changed everything at Duke were savoring the most memorable basketball day of their lives.

The Blue Devils, the number-one team in America, had just beaten number-three North Carolina to win the program's first outright regular-season ACC title in twenty years, and the seniors were finishing their Cameron careers going 15-0 at home on the season. Krzyzewski had never won a championship of any kind in his previous nine years as a Division 1 head coach, and at game's end he threw his arms toward the roof in touchdown form and let out a roar from his toes.

But this was also about those kids who believed in him as high school players, back when very few people believed in Duke's head coach. Johnny Dawkins, Mark Alarie, Jay Bilas, David Henderson, and Weldon Williams all stayed four years for this crowning moment.

Their junior season had been something of a disappointment, though Krzyzewski did earn his first NCAA Tournament victory (over Pepperdine) before his team was eliminated by Boston College. Coach K's frustration that year was best captured by his actions after an embarrassing 18-point loss at North Carolina State. Back at Duke late that night, as he stood before his team in the locker room, Krzyzewski held a framed picture of Alarie diving for a loose ball. "Are we ever going to see this again?" he barked at the junior forward before slamming the picture to the floor and sending shards of glass flying everywhere. For good measure, Krzyzewski grabbed Alarie's picture and ripped it up right in front of his player.

Coach K didn't need to draw on his inner rage nearly as much during the 1985–1986 season, not after he had landed two McDonald's All-Americans the previous year, point guard Quin Snyder and six-foot-ten Danny Ferry of Maryland's DeMatha Catholic, son of former NBA player Bob Ferry and a pupil of the legendary high school coach Morgan Wootten. Before practices at Duke, Ferry would sit courtside and study Krzyzewski's detailed schedule of drills for the day. Coach K told his assistants in a meeting that he was tired of his player trying to gain a competitive advantage on his teammates. "The next day Danny looked at the schedule," recalled Pete Gaudet, "and Mike had written, 'Fuck you Ferry.' And Danny never looked at the schedule again."

Duke opened the season 16-0 before meeting 17-0 North Carolina in an epic January encounter in the brand-new Dean E. Smith Student Activities Center, a monument to the coach that was six years in the making. The Tar Heels could not afford to lose that game, so they didn't. Duke recovered from this defeat, and from another at Georgia Tech, to win the final thirteen games on the regular-season schedule, including this farewell-to-Cameron game for the senior class, an 82–74 victory over Carolina.

The Class of '86 scored 80 of Duke's 82 points. During the postgame ceremony, when the seniors were swarmed by classmates who had remained on campus — during spring break — to celebrate them, Henderson called his time at Duke the best four years of his young life. Bilas and Alarie thanked the student body for sticking with them through the struggles of their freshman season. "I don't think anything could be finer than beating Carolina," Alarie said. The Blue Devils spent the next few weeks testing that claim.

They beat Georgia Tech in the ACC Tournament championship game, 68–67, when Amaker gave defensive help to his backcourt partner Dawkins, who was trying to stay in front of his four-year rival, Mark Price. The Tech point guard was forced to pass to the less dangerous Craig Neal, who missed the potential winning jumper, sending a delirious Krzyzewski back into Dawkins's arms. Coach K had matched Valvano's total of ACC Tournament titles. Now he needed to match Valvano's total of national titles too.

Seeded the number-one team in the NCAA Tournament, Duke was paired against number sixty-four, Mississippi Valley State, in the Greensboro Coliseum. It was the Blue Devils against the Delta Devils in the Blue Devils' backyard, and it was supposed to be a nationally televised blowout on ESPN. Instead, it became a harrowing test of Duke's resolve.

Fast and fearless, Mississippi Valley State turned a three-point halftime lead into a seven-point second-half lead that left Krzyzewski and his players pondering the catastrophic consequences of defeat. Dawkins was always ready to be the Blue Devils' savior if they ever needed one. And now they needed one. *We're not losing this game,* he told himself. *We're not ending our careers like this.*

He scored 29 of his 27 points in the second half, 15 in the final 16:56. Dawkins was the difference between an unmitigated disaster and a trip to the second round. He was the one who liberated the Blue Devils to chase the championship with freedom.

They dominated Old Dominion in the second round and then beat DePaul by seven in the Sweet 16 in the New Jersey Meadowlands. In the East Regional final, Mike Krzyzewski, West Point Class of 1969, would have to beat the United States Naval Academy to advance to his first Final Four.

Of course, this was not the Navy team that Krzyzewski routinely defeated as an Army player and coach. This was a Navy team built around a colossus, six-foot-eleven David Robinson, the nation's most feared shot-blocker and rebounder; the most dominant player to ever suit up at a military academy, he'd grown four inches since enrolling as a freshman.

The day before the game, when Navy coach Paul Evans and some of his team members were holding a press conference, Krzyzewski noticed that the players were wearing T-shirts and sweats. "How come you guys aren't in uniforms?" he joked. "When I played at Army, Coach Knight always made us wear our uniforms everywhere. I hope you get demerits for that stuff."

Coach K was determined to keep it light. He said of Robinson, "I have three daughters, and I read them bedtime stories. But I never knew that Cinderella was seven feet tall and blocked two hundred shots in a season." Of Navy's Polish-American point guard, Doug Wojcik, Krzyzewski said, "If you checked his family background, there have probably been six or seven letters knocked off [his name] over the years. Kind of like me."

But in private, Krzyzewski was a complete wreck before this game. He could not bear the thought of Navy costing him a trip to Dallas for the Final Four. He told his players, "I'm a West Point graduate. No matter what, I just can't lose to Navy. I might get drafted if we lose." Coach K actually told his players they would be dead to him if they lost to the Midshipmen. He devoted his usual pregame prayer on the bench, while making the sign of the cross, to the cause of avoiding personal humiliation in the Meadowlands. "Please God," Krzyzewski whispered. "Not Navy."

The Midshipmen never stood a chance. Krzyzewski ordered four men to crash the boards instead of the usual three, holding back only Amaker, and the Blue Devils found enough vacated lanes in the Navy zone to grab 18 offensive boards in the first half alone. They won the rebounding battle on both ends, 34–15, over the first twenty minutes and 49–29 for the game. "I didn't expect them to kill us on the boards like that," said Robinson, who finished with 23 points and 10 rebounds.

Dawkins would deliver the game's signature shot, racing downcourt near the end of the first half and rising up for a reverse dunk as his rump crashed into Wojcik's head. Duke won by 21, and it could have won by 30 or more; Krzyzewski dialed back the attack out of respect for a military academy. Taking it all in from the Meadowlands stands was a New Jersey high school freshman and North Carolina Tar Heel fan named Bobby Hurley, who that day started falling in love with Duke's coach and its style of play.

Lacking a true center, Duke didn't block many shots or throw down many thunderous dunks. Krzyzewski had spent his first college job with the Indiana Hoosiers of the mid-1970s, a team, Coach K said, that scared you in warm-ups. "We have very good players," Krzyzewski said, "but we don't look like a great team when we're warming up or walking through airports."

It was clear now, however, that Duke did have an advantage in coaching in nearly every matchup. "He's a cross between Jim Valvano and Bobby Knight," Alarie said of Krzyzewski. "He's in between. He's a disciplinarian in a loose environment. He coaches in a very friendly atmosphere, but he has the ability to get the most out of his players."

Krzyzewski was known to assail his own very friendly atmosphere with a barrage of profanity, in practices and in games, that would even make his coaching mentor blush. "People think he must be a clone of Bobby Knight, but he's much different," Dawkins said. "One time instead of practicing, we played volleyball. Another time we played softball."

The Blue Devils would have to play hardball in Dallas. Their coach promised a surplus of emotion, and a hell of a celebration, if they won two more sudden-death games.

MIKE KRZYZEWSKI HELD UP his right hand and motioned for his team to slow it down, to work the forty-five-second clock. Duke, in white, was holding only a four-point lead over Louisville, in red, with just under seven minutes to play on Monday night, March 31. Krzyzewski was gambling that methodical execution would give the school its first national championship in any sport.

Louisville had beaten Louisiana State in one Saturday semi, and number-one Duke had beaten number-two Kansas in the other, largely because Alarie held Jayhawks star Danny Manning to four points. Duke entered the championship game with a 37-2 record. No team in the history of the sport had ever won more than thirty-six games.

Would Duke go down as the greatest team of all time with a victory over Louisville and its coach, Denny Crum, a former UCLA player and assistant? Were the 1986 Blue Devils better than all ten champions assembled by Crum's mentor, John Wooden? Better than Knight's 32-0 Indiana Hoosiers team ten years earlier?

Knight had spent the weekend in Dallas in full support of his protégé, wearing a GO DUKE button. A year after Knight achieved a new level of infamy by hurling his chair across the court during a game against Purdue, Krzyzewski asked the two-time national champion and coach of the 1984 Olympic gold-medal winning team to speak to the Blue Devils the day before they played Louisville; Knight told them to remember what carried them to Dallas and to avoid deviating from it. "I love Coach Knight," Krzyzewski said. "He's like a member of my family."

But Coach K didn't act like Knight in the lead-up to the big game. As he did before facing Navy, Krzyzewski remained in a loose and playful mood with reporters. He joked that he would have put Crum's name on his Coach of the Year ballot if they had allowed Polish coaches to vote. He talked about Tom Butters sticking by his side during the tough times and about university administrators who were forever firing coaches. "If you checked their personal backgrounds," Krzyzewski said, "they've probably been married four or five different times." To play along with the relentless media interest in his ties to Knight, Coach K explained that he had learned the basic principles of his motion offense and man defense from the former Army coach. "But I didn't learn the motion offense playing for him because it's an equal opportunity offense," he said, "and he didn't give me an equal opportunity to shoot at West Point."

When Krzyzewski made his big move with a small lead over Louisville, CBS analyst Billy Packer, a former Wake Forest player, said on the broadcast that it was a mistake to play slowdown with seven minutes left. "It's very difficult if the [shot] clock works down with, say, six, eight seconds to go to get off a good shot against a team like Louisville . . . I think it takes away your momentum and it really causes you to have to take some tough shots."

And just like that, the Blue Devils went cold. They did not make a field goal over seven minutes and nine possessions, missing 10 straight shots. (Henderson and Dawkins did make free throws in that stretch.) Meanwhile, six-foot-nine Louisville center "Never Nervous" Pervis Ellison took control inside, using his length to play above the shorter Duke frontcourt. As the momentum shifted to the Cardinals, Krzyzewski chewed anxiously on his gum.

Dawkins had scored 15 in the first half but was smothered in the second. Two plays in the closing five and a half minutes would tell the story of how the winners separated themselves from the losers. On one, Louisville's Milt Wagner scored a basket on a baseline drive while being fouled by Bilas, who was trying to draw a charge, leading to a three-point play. On the second, with Duke down one, Ellison beat Bilas and Alarie to a Jeff Hall airball under the basket and put it in to give the Cardinals a 68–65 lead with forty seconds to go.

No coach, and no program, had practiced drawing charges and blocking out opponents on rebounds more than Krzyzewski and Duke, and yet they went 0-for-2 in those fundamentals with their season on the line.

Another two points from Ellison, on foul shots, pushed the Louisville lead to five with twenty-seven seconds left. He hadn't even turned nineteen years old, and he had collected 25 points and 11 rebounds against the Duke seniors up front. "We knew we had to deal with Milt Wagner and Billy Thompson, but we did not see Pervis Ellison beating us," Henderson said. "We thought we were, along with Kansas, the two best teams, and once we beat them in the semis we absolutely believed we were going to win."

Did they believe too much? Was Duke's confidence replaced by hubris? "We got past who we thought was the team we had to beat to win it, Kansas, and that's not a great psychological position," Alarie said. "You're not supposed to go into games thinking you're supposed to win."

Bilas finally ended the Duke field-goal drought on a follow with eighteen seconds to play. After Krzyzewski was done screaming at an official for a foul call, CBS play-by-play man Brent Musburger teed up Packer about his earlier criticism of the Duke coach for working the clock, saying, "I dare say he may be regretting that move right now." The analyst responded, "It took away a lot of momentum, and it took Johnny Dawkins out of the game."

Ferry scored on a put-back with three seconds left before Wagner, the fifth-year senior, made two free throws to seal it, leaving the Blue Devils staggering toward their bench while the Louisville band played on. The Duke players took their seats, buried their heads in their hands and towels, and watched another team celebrate what they had thought would be theirs. They hadn't lost a game in more than two months. They'd forgotten just how horrible defeat felt.

UNIVERSITY OF LOUISVILLE, NATIONAL CHAMPIONS, read the big Reunion Arena scoreboard. The Cardinals' band started playing Queen's "Another One Bites the Dust." Amaker hugged Dawkins on the bench. Their teammates watched the Louisville players and coaches climb up ladders to cut down the nets.

"They will go down as the greatest non-great team ever," Valvano said of the Blue Devils.

It was a harsh epitaph to accept for Dawkins, who had scored 2,556 points in his career, almost exclusively without a three-point shot, and for Alarie, who scored 2,136, and for all five seniors. They took a lot from Krzyzewski over four years, both before and after the intense pregame speeches he made with goose bumps covering his arms. Bilas was forced to cover taller, superior opponents in the middle after Coach K failed to keep a recruiting promise to move him out of the center position after his freshman year. They were all berated, cursed out, drilled into submission, challenged on the smallest details, forced to run the mile in a certain time. They all responded to Krzyzewski's coaching. They gave him seven consecutive victories over Virginia after that 43-point loss in the '83 conference tournament final. Their leader, Dawkins, gave Coach K 133 consecutive starts and never once cheated him on effort.

But now it was over between Krzyzewski and the class that saved him. In Duke's hushed locker room, Dawkins was overcome by the shock and sadness of it all. He started thinking about everything that had transpired over four years. "It's like when you die," he said, "and your whole life passes in front of you. You never get over those things."

Krzyzewski would not get over this. His team was a tired team in the deciding sequences against Louisville. "It was a shock," said Krzyzewski's assistant Chuck Swenson. "We played with a frustration in that game we didn't normally play with."

Coach K's players partied together through the night in their hotel, and some never went to sleep before the morning trip to the airport. The Blue Devils were welcomed back to Durham the following day by a crowd on the campus quad that showered them with the love and appreciation they had earned, but their head coach knew he hadn't given his team its best chance to win. He knew he had probably cost Duke the national title by trying to manage the clock when he did, retreating from the approach that had earned his team the lead and forcing his players to take tough shots at the worst possible time.

"That's his explanation for why we lost," Alarie said. And that explanation would haunt Coach K for years until he finally did something about it.

7

CAN'T WIN THE BIG ONE

A YEAR AFTER BOBBY KNIGHT cheered for his team at the Final Four, Mike Krzyzewski lost to him in the NCAA Tournament's Sweet 16. Alaa Abdelnaby, a six-foot-ten Duke sophomore, said that Coach K seemed a little tighter in that game than in others. "You could see it on him," Abdelnaby said.

University of Colorado coach Tom Miller, former West Point player, sat in the stands for Indiana's six-point victory that night and concluded that his former teammate had deferred to his former coach. "I felt like Mike really didn't go after him," Miller said.

As it turned out, the chemistry between mentor and protégé worked in the Hoosiers' favor. "They're extremely well coached; they should be," Knight had said of the Blue Devils. "I taught the son of a bitch how to coach." On the bench that night, and in practices before the game, Duke walk-on Jon Goodman could see what he called "just a different Mike Krzyzewski . . . You could always see him up for the challenge against Dean Smith or Jim Valvano, and he very much felt equal to everyone else. I didn't sense he felt equal to Bobby Knight. He was so respectful and deferential to him . . . This one was almost a do-your-best kind of thing."

Duke's best wasn't good enough, and nobody seemed terribly upset about that. After eliminating the Blue Devils, Knight said, "Mike is as close to me as any player I've ever had. I didn't particularly enjoy coaching against him." Asked about Knight, Krzyzewski promised, "I'll be rooting for him the rest of the way."

The Hoosiers won the national championship, Knight's third. The three most significant coaches in Krzyzewski's life — Knight, Smith, and Valvano — now had a combined five.

Duke won another ACC Tournament title in March 1988, and then another NCAA Tournament regional final in the New Jersey Meadowlands, where senior stopper Billy King helped shut down the top-ranked Temple Owls and their freshman sensation, Mark Macon. In between, Duke played the first two rounds of the NCAAs in the Dean Smith Center, of all places, where the sights and sounds of Blue Devils fans chanting "Go to hell, Carolina, go to hell," angered the UNC reps in the building and convinced them that inviting the tournament to Chapel Hill probably wasn't a great idea.

But Duke was outclassed in the national semifinals by Danny Manning and a Cinderella Kansas team. Krzyzewski's weekend got worse when he learned that a thief had broken into his Durham home by kicking in a back door, stole the coach's 1987 Chevrolet Celebrity, and used it in a break-in at another home. Krzyzewski asked his former Army player and current Duke volunteer assistant Scott Easton, a future FBI anti-terrorism agent, to stay with his family, including his mother, the next time he left town.

Easton had also been called on to sit with the players at dinner during the season to check the pulse of the team, to survey the chemistry between certain Blue Devils, and to find out if anyone was dealing with a family problem at home, or with a girlfriend issue on campus.

Relentless attention to detail, coupled with Coach K's raging quest for perfection, created a West Point–like standard of precision and accountability that occasionally led to an extra 5 a.m. practice. After Duke beat Stetson the year before at Cameron — but only by three points — Krzyzewski shattered his clipboard by firing it above his players' heads and into a locker room wall. "We thought he would tear his shirt off like the Incredible Hulk," said one player. "He went nuts. You have to play Duke basketball to his level of expectation." Another time, after North Carolina State's Rodney Monroe picked apart the Blue Devils' defense, Krzyzewski stormed onto a quiet bus and shouted, "Why couldn't we guard Rodney fuckin' Monroe?" before he started calling out individual players.

Krzyzewski demanded excellence from the end of his bench too. Sometimes during film review he'd hit pause and air out the walk-ons for being bad teammates, for not giving the rotation players any discernible energy or support. That's why the Blue Devils were the Blue Devils, and why they won twenty-eight games during 1987–1988. And yet, in retrospect, their biggest victory that season unfolded on November 11, more than two weeks before the opener, when a six-foot-eleven high school senior from outside of Buffalo, New York, Christian Laettner, announced that he had picked Duke over North Carolina and Virginia. Krzyzewski had beaten Smith on Laettner just as he had beaten him on Danny Ferry.

Raised in the small, rural village of Angola near Lake Erie, the son of Bonnie, a third-grade teacher, and George, a printer at the *Buffalo News,* Laettner was named by Bonnie after her favorite Marlon Brando characters — in *Mutiny on the Bounty* (Fletcher Christian, lead mutineer) and *The Young Lions* (Christian Diestl, conflicted German soldier). Christian was a tough kid toughened up by his brother Christopher, who was older by four years. Their wrestling matches sometimes ended with one in the hospital getting stitches to close a cut on the back of the head. They used to play baseball in the backyard with a tennis ball so that they didn't break any windows, and when they ran out of tennis balls, they would use the caps from milk bottles and see who had the hand-eye coordination to hit those. They played dodgeball in the pool and pegged each other in the face. And in pickup basketball games, Christopher, a rugged six foot two, never missed an opportunity to bloody Christian's lip or dig an elbow into his ribs. "When I kicked his ass," Christopher said, "he never stopped. He always came back, where most kids four years younger would have given up and walked away."

One day when Christian was fourteen years old and about six foot seven, he'd had enough. For the first time he got the better of his older brother in a fight that turned heated in the bedroom they shared. "I never got an ass kicking like that in my life," Christopher said. The boys never battled again.

The Laettners never had any extra money, yet somehow raised their four children (Leanne was between Christopher and Christian, and Katie was the youngest) and paid the mortgage on their Church Road home. The kids walked about 150 yards up the street in the summertime to pick tomatoes and green beans, hoping to sell their pickings for $3 so they could head to the ice cream store. "I don't know how my parents put food on the table," Christopher said, "but we were never hungry. We had a roof over our head. To us we were living in paradise."

The four kids were talented athletes, but Christian was different. He could walk on his hands at age six, and despite the fact that he had high arches and crab toes — "The ugliest feet you ever saw," George said — Christian was nimble for his size. To improve his footwork and athleticism, George had him work with a local boxing trainer once a week. Christian would jump rope, work the speed bag, and occasionally even spar with the seventy-something trainer.

Bonnie wanted her son to spend his high school years at Nichols, northern Buffalo's answer to Exeter and Andover, an exclusive coats-and-ties prep school with a tree-lined campus and a stately nineteenth-century feel. But middling exam scores, an August birth date, and some questions about

Christian's maturity compelled the Laettners to have their boy repeat the eighth grade, at Nichols, before he moved up.

The Laettners couldn't afford the Nichols tuition without their son's help. Christian had to wash windows, paint walls, rip up old rugs, and strip and varnish the gym floor to help cover the cost of his private education. He was serving as a maintenance man for his classmates, the sons and daughters of people with a lot more money than the Laettners. "Everyone there knew he was poor," his brother said.

Everyone also knew that Christian was a hell of a basketball player. He scored more than 2,000 points and won two state titles at Nichols, and Krzyzewski was among the many major-college coaches who badly wanted him. Bonnie was an early proponent of Notre Dame, and Christian and Christopher were on the South Bend, Indiana, campus when Digger Phelps and the Fighting Irish upset number-one North Carolina. They were treated like royalty, and Christopher told his brother, "You've got to go to Notre Dame." But Christian wanted to play in the storied ACC, the conference that best fit his finesse game.

His final two were Duke and North Carolina. The Tar Heels had already won a national title, and Laettner was intrigued by the idea that he could be the one to make history in Durham. He started following Duke during their '86 run, and he liked what he saw and heard from the Blue Devils in their press conferences before the title game against Louisville. "All the kids were really open, really funny, seemed really nice," Laettner said. "They were having a good time. I like that. From then on I said, 'I've got to check out Duke and see how it is.'" On November 11, ten days after he finished visiting the Duke campus, Laettner announced he was committing to the Blue Devils, a bulletin that, strangely enough, compelled his mother to start crying. When Christian asked her what was wrong, Bonnie said, "I just love, love Dean Smith."

Recruiting expert Bob Gibbons listed Laettner as the sixteenth best prospect in America, fifteen spots behind Georgetown-bound Alonzo Mourning. Crawford Palmer, a big man from Arlington, Virginia, who had also committed to Duke, was ranked sixty-second on Gibbons's list. And yet, during a sluggish summer performance in an overseas series of games against European national teams, Coach K warned his big men that Palmer was preparing to come in and take their playing time. "He didn't even mention Laettner," said Mike Brey, the twenty-nine-year-old assistant who replaced Chuck Swenson in 1987.

Duke's staff did not know exactly what it had in Christian — and neither did the senior star, Danny Ferry, when he elbowed the freshman in the mouth on a drive to the basket in their first one-on-one, simply to test his resolve and introduce him to Duke physicality. Laettner was never going to back down from a challenge; his brother Christopher had made certain of that.

In a scrimmage held before about 700 high school coaches, Laettner was dominating Ferry and everyone else, while Brey, who had helped the legendary Morgan Wootten coach Ferry at DeMatha Catholic, was staring at Duke's graduate assistant, Tommy Amaker. "Tommy and I are looking at each other from the baseline to halfcourt," Brey recalled, "and we're going, 'Are you shitting me?' The clinic ends and there must've been fifteen coaches who came up and asked, 'Coach Brey, did you know Laettner was this good?' We're like, 'Oh yeah, we'd evaluated him.' Come on, if anyone tells you they knew Laettner was that good, they're lying."

Laettner averaged only 8.9 points and 4.7 rebounds as a freshman and started fewer than half the games. But he sounded content when he called home and talked about the way Krzyzewski was coaching him. "There are no rules," Christian told his brother. "What do you mean, no rules?" his brother responded. Christian explained that Coach K believed in case-by-case flexibility, that he had seen too many military men boxed in by too many rules at West Point. Christian relayed Krzyzewski's philosophy to his brother this way: "You've got to look at an eighteen-year-old as a flower growing in a vase. That flower is going to grow as much as the vase allows. If you have too many rules, that flower is not going to grow. If you open up the vase, you allow the flowers to blossom."

Laettner found a kindred spirit and now best friend in classmate Brian Davis, an overlooked recruit from Maryland, and showed just how comfortable he was in his Blue Devil skin late in the season, starting with the ACC Tournament championship matchup with North Carolina at the Omni in Atlanta.

Dean Smith had earlier created a bit of a firestorm by wondering why J.R. Reid, his six-foot-nine junior, was being asked about the possibility of turning pro after Ferry wasn't asked the same questions the year before, and by stating his displeasure with crowd signs that read J.R. CAN'T REID. The North Carolina coach compared the treatment of two of his Black players, Reid and Scott Williams, to how two of Krzyzewski's white players were treated. "Danny Ferry and Laettner didn't do as well on their total college board scores as Reid and Williams," Smith said. "It's kind of a racist remark, and it really bugs me."

Furious that any coach had named his players in that context, Krzyzewski was ready for full-contact engagement with Smith when Duke attempted to win its second consecutive conference tournament title and its third in four years. The Blue Devils had beaten the Tar Heels three times in the 1987–1988 season — *three times* — and Smith was concerned that Krzyzewski had already built a program superior to his. The Tar Heels hadn't won the conference tournament or reached the Final Four since 1982, and here were the Blue Devils now doing both on an almost annual basis. The year before, Dean Smith had finally quit what once was a three-pack-a-day cigarette habit. It was one less thing for Krzyzewski to needle him about.

The game mirrored a Green Bay Packers–Chicago Bears game from the '60s, all blocking and tackling, blood and guts. Courtside witnesses called it the most intense and violent Duke–North Carolina game they ever saw. Krzyzewski shouted at Williams for knocking Laettner to the floor, and Smith shouted at the Duke coach to stop talking to the Tar Heel players. "Fuck you, Dean," Coach K responded.

When it was all over, Laettner had scored more points than any Tar Heel (15) on only six field-goal attempts and led Duke in rebounding (7) in only twenty-six minutes. Meanwhile, Ferry had a nasty boxer's cut under his left eye, Reid had a boxer's mouse under his eye, and Williams said he had a dislocated shoulder and "a concussed head." The Tar Heels, 77–74 victors, celebrated in their locker room by spraying cans of Sprite on one another. The celebration didn't last for long: that evening the NCAA Tournament selection committee sent one second seed, Duke, to nearby Greensboro, while sending another second seed, North Carolina, back to Atlanta. Smith was angry that the losers in the Omni ended up with a more favorable first-round site and with an easier draw in the East Regional than the Tar Heels got in the Southeast Regional, where they would lose to Michigan in the Sweet 16.

The Blue Devils defeated South Carolina State and West Virginia in Greensboro and ended up back in their home away from home, the Brendan Byrne Arena in the New Jersey Meadowlands, where they had qualified for the Final Four in '86 and '88. After delivering a double-double (10 points, 11 rebounds) in a regional semifinal victory over Minnesota, Laettner introduced himself to the country as a superstar in the making in Duke's Elite Eight matchup with Georgetown and the number-one player in Christian's recruiting class, six-foot-ten Alonzo Mourning.

It was no contest. Mourning admitted that he spent the afternoon "moving in slow motion" while the Blue Devils attacked the basket and the moment with ferocity. Though Duke's six-foot-four Phil Henderson authored the signature moment in the form of a monstrous dunk over Mourning, it was Laettner who made the biggest impression. He scored a game-high 24 points by making nine of ten shots, shaking off a Mourning rejection of his first attempt — ninety-one seconds into the game — with a quick follow-up basket. "A big play for our confidence," Krzyzewski said.

Laettner added nine rebounds, four assists, one rejection of a Mourning shot, and one rejection of the notion that he might have been haunted by his failure in this very building four weeks earlier. With one second left against Arizona and Duke trailing by a point, Laettner had missed the front end of a one-and-one to give the Wildcats the victory. His coach had hustled out to comfort him. "Christian, you didn't lose this game for us," Krzyzewski told him. "If you'd made the free throws, you would have saved us."

Laettner never needed consoling; he proved that before 19,514 Meadowlands fans who watched Duke beat Georgetown, 85–78. Mourning scored only 11. "In the second half," Laettner said, "he wasn't talking as much as he was in the first half." Said Mourning: "I played against Laettner before in high school all-star games. I knew he was a good player. He didn't surprise me."

The same could not be said of Krzyzewski. "There's no way I thought Christian could do that," he said. Of course, Coach K had talked up a different incoming big man over the summer; Crawford Palmer did not get off the bench against Georgetown. He'd been averaging only five minutes a game.

On the way to the Final Four, again, Krzyzewski was asked the inevitable questions about the pressure to finally win it all. "That's not the one thing I want more than anything else," he said. "I'd have to have my head examined to think that's the one thing I want more than anything else, a national championship . . . I'll compete out there. But I'm not going to let it possess me."

Duke lost again in the national semis, this time to a Seton Hall team coached by Krzyzewski's friend P. J. Carlesimo and resilient enough to turn an 18-point first-half deficit into a 17-point victory in the Seattle Kingdome. The Blue Devils unraveled, in part, because of an injury suffered by starting forward Robert Brickey, and in part because Laettner fouled out with 9:26 still to play. This was the final college game for Ferry, who scored 34 points, and for Quin Snyder, who was raised nearby.

"We started out playing like men," Henderson said, "and finished up playing like little boys."

Krzyzewski cried when he addressed his departing seniors. "Blame me," he said. "I'm the constant around here. I've been around when we couldn't win the big one." Duke had been to seven Final Fours, more than any school that had yet to win it all.

Back in his hotel suite, watching tape of the game around midnight, Krzyzewski heard a knock on his door. Laettner. "Coach, are you all right?" he asked. "Are you okay, coach?"

Sleepless in Seattle, Krzyzewski was a million miles from okay. He clearly had his franchise player for the next three years in Laettner, but now he needed to surround him with more talent. Starting with a quarterback.

AS A LITTLE KID in Jersey City, New Jersey, Bobby Hurley wanted to play for the Tar Heels. He attended North Carolina's camp and dreamed of someday running Dean Smith's offense from the point. But like Laettner, Hurley fell hard for the '86 Duke team. He still loved Carolina blue, and as the all-everything quarterback of national powerhouse St. Anthony — coached by his legendary father, Bob Hurley Sr. — he felt honored when Smith showed up to watch him play. But Smith was also recruiting another McDonald's All-American point guard, New York's Kenny Anderson, the national player of the year who would sign with Georgia Tech. "We'd like to have Bobby and Kenny," Smith explained. "I just didn't think that would work," Hurley said.

For a while Bobby assumed that he would end up in the Big East, probably at Seton Hall, maybe at Villanova. For the gritty son of a gritty coach (and probation officer) from a gritty city playing in a gritty league, that made all kinds of sense. "Bobby wasn't going to Duke," his father said. "Duke was a very preppy school. This kid growing up in Jersey City, he's going to Seton Hall if he stays home, or to Carolina or Villanova or Syracuse or Georgia Tech, which is less preppy than Duke. He's not going to Duke. It was too much of a rich-kid school from where we were from."

But then the Hurleys met Mike Krzyzewski. Bob Sr. recalled playing against him when he was a freshman at St. Peter's College and Krzyzewski was a plebe at West Point. Bob Sr. said he scored 20 points in the second half of that freshman game, an Army victory, then ate dinner with the Cadets in the mess hall. The Irish-Catholic coach from Jersey City and the Polish-Catholic coach from Chicago had a lot in common. "It was ethnic, it was Catholic, it was city, it was family," Bob Sr. said. "This is my oldest child. I needed to know we were a lot alike, and we were."

Bobby loved his visit to Durham, where he felt that the passion for basketball was just as intense as it was back home. He loved the barbecue at Coach K's house, where the entire team mingled with Krzyzewski's family and watched college football. Hurley felt comfortable, felt at home, partly because he already had a long-standing relationship with another Jersey guy, Alaa Abdelnaby. "It also didn't hurt that the national Player of the Year is taking you around campus and hanging out with you," said Hurley, referring to Danny Ferry. Krzyzewski joined his recruit on the flight back to New Jersey and pushed him for a commitment, as Duke had another high school point guard, Chris Reynolds, as a potential backup plan.

"He was going on and on about the program," Hurley said. "I was just wiped out."

Bobby headed to the cramped Jersey City bingo hall, White Eagle, where the St. Anthony team often practiced. He went downstairs to work out in the weight room, and his father joined him. "I want to go to Duke," he told his old man. "What?" Bob Sr. said. "We just started the process."

Bobby was sure. Krzyzewski reminded him of his father, a coach who was relentless in driving his players to be better, but who was fair. Bobby liked the fact that Coach K played his position, and that he shared his urban, blue-collar roots.

Coach K arrived later that day for his scheduled home visit at the Hurleys' red-brick row house on Ferncliff Road in a melting-pot Jersey City neighborhood known as Greenville. "It wasn't a recruiting pitch," recalled Bobby's brother Danny. "I felt like I was meeting Bob's coach. A partnership was already formed." Bob Sr. recalled that his wife, Chris, made a great chicken parm for Krzyzewski and his assistants. At one point, Bobby called his parents into the kitchen and confirmed to them that he had found his new home. "It feels right to me," he told them.

And then Krzyzewski did something he never did with his point guards, or with anyone else. At the start of preseason practice for the 1989–1990 season, Coach K handed Hurley the ball, literally, and told him the Blue Devils were his team. Krzyzewski had prided himself on never promising starting roles or playing time to anyone, for any reason, before those roles and time were earned. Year after year, some of the nation's top high school prospects swore that Krzyzewski was the only recruiter who did not promise them a starting spot, not to mention pricey side benefits outlawed by the NCAA. But now Coach K was putting a freshman in control of his offense before he had made a single good decision in a single official practice. He thought Hurley was that special.

On cue, Laettner was more outraged by this move than any other member of the team. He called his brother at home. "Christian was so pissed," Christopher said. "He didn't feel Bobby earned it." According to Hurley's father, Laettner took his concerns straight to Krzyzewski, who told the six-foot-eleven sophomore, "Do you see what our choices are at point guard now? Why do you think Bobby came here, Christian? He watched us practice last year."

Krzyzewski kept a close eye on the Laettner-Hurley dynamic all season. Bobby competed like mad defensively, pressuring opposing ball handlers the length of the floor, and he set an NCAA record for freshmen with 288 assists. Yet he would make only 35 percent of his shots and average nearly 4.5 turnovers a game, giving Christian the openings to rebuke him. That Hurley started all thirty-eight games pissed off Laettner too. "Bobby would say, 'I'm going out in the parking lot and fight him after practice,'" Bob Sr. said. "Mike would calm him down and say, 'It's just what Christian sees in you.' It was Christian being Christian, constantly trying to get a rise out of people."

Laettner lived to torment others; his favorite author was Stephen King for a reason. Hurley didn't think he deserved the verbal abuse, and he once asked Krzyzewski to order Laettner to stop. "Tell him yourself," Coach K responded. Hurley did just that, and Laettner backed off — temporarily, anyway. Soon enough, there came a day when Hurley finally boiled over and decided he'd had enough of Laettner's bullshit. His method of conflict resolution during a pickup game was to drive into the lane, spot his much bigger tormentor rotating toward him, and then, from point-blank range, intentionally fire the ball right into his face. "He went down for a second, dazed," Hurley recalled. "He got up and chased me around the gym."

Eleven inches taller and about 100 pounds heavier than Hurley, Laettner wasn't about to track down the point guard. But no matter how maddeningly arrogant Duke's center could be, nobody could deny his talent, or his fearlessness, or his hunger to be great. As a basketball player, Christian Laettner seemed to have a magical quality. Now the coach had to put him in position to use it.

MIKE KRZYZEWSKI WAS screaming right in a Duke student's face, nose to nose, and that student was not a basketball player. He was a terrified 140-pound reporter for the school newspaper, *The Chronicle,* who had a hidden tape recorder running in his book bag that would change the way America looked at the beloved Coach K.

Andy Layton had received permission from *Chronicle* editor Craig Whitlock to, in his words, "wire myself" in case this meeting turned as ugly as it had indeed turned in this moment. It was Monday night, January 15, 1990, and the coach who had led the Blue Devils to three Final Fours in the last four years had invited the newspaper's sports staff to a sit-down inside the Duke locker room. Layton figured it might be bad. He had no idea how bad.

Three days earlier, the student reporter had printed his prediction of a

Maryland victory over the Blue Devils, inspiring the Cameron crowd to boo him on his way to his courtside seat. After Duke's 91–80 victory on Saturday the 13th, a school official advised Layton that Krzyzewski was furious with him, and that it might not be the best idea to enter the locker room. Trying to avoid a scene, Layton decided to cover the Maryland locker room and to send a *Chronicle* colleague in to cover Duke.

On Monday, Krzyzewski's secretary, Donna Keane, called *The Chronicle* to set up the appointment with her boss after the reporter Brent Belvin wrote a piece grading the Blue Devils on their performance through fourteen games; he had given the team an overall B+ and did not give any rotation player a grade lower than C+. Keane described the meeting's purpose as a chance for the student journalists to get to know more about the coaches and players they were writing about. "Look," Layton told Whitlock, "in the event something goes wrong here, it's going to be my word against his word . . . and I'm not going to be credible." After checking the legality of taping Krzyzewski without his knowledge, the editor gave his man the green light.

When the ten *Chronicle* staff members were escorted into the locker room, they found ten empty chairs in a semicircle. They were asked to take their seats and to wait until practice ended. Soon enough, team managers, trainers, players, and assistant coaches filed in, surrounded the reporters, and then waited in silence. Finally, Krzyzewski came barreling into the room.

"He comes in like an absolute house afire," Layton recalled. "I saw on his face sheer anger. Everybody knew he was an intense guy. Everybody knew he could get really angry. We'd heard stories about a road trip back from Virginia when he was screaming the whole way back, and about him shattering pictures that were taken off the wall. At that time, he ran hot. He came into the room . . . and it was intimidating."

Krzyzewski went on a profane eight-minute rant. He was angry at Belvin, the fact that he felt the need to grade his classmates, and the fact that — in Coach K's opinion — his assigned grades weren't high enough. He was angry at Layton. He was angry at everyone.

"I just wonder where your mindset is that you don't appreciate the kids in this locker room," he barked at the reporters. "I'm not looking for puff pieces or anything like that, but you're whacked out and you don't appreciate what the fuck is going on and it pisses me off . . . and I'm suggesting that if you want to appreciate what's going on, get your head out of your asses and start looking out for what's actually happening."

Coach K told Belvin his article "was full of shit" and "an insult to me" and added that his team deserved an A+, not the B+ assigned by the student reporter. Krzyzewski said he was also upset that Layton had written a profile on Maryland's Walt Williams rather than on his own player, Greg Koubek, and that *The Chronicle* had picked Duke to lose against Maryland and Georgia Tech.

"He got up in my grill," Layton said. "It was R. Lee Ermey in *Full Metal Jacket* with Matthew Modine. It was straight out of Paris Island. Coach K was literally screaming in my face while close enough to kiss me. He was leaning over me, yelling in my face at the top of his lungs . . . It's scary when you're five foot eleven, 140 pounds, and you're surrounded by big people. I've never had anyone get up in my face ever . . . My heart was racing. I was scared for my own well-being."

Layton said he was legitimately concerned that Krzyzewski might slap him in the face. When Coach K was done shouting, he abruptly walked out and the reporters were escorted out of the room. Rodney Peele, the paper's sports editor and one of the journalists present, called the experience "humiliating" and said that Krzyzewski acted "as if we worked for him."

Out in the parking lot, Layton pulled his recorder out of his black book bag to show his shell-shocked colleagues, and their eyes nearly popped out of their heads. They all made their way back to *The Chronicle* offices on the third floor of the Flowers Building on the school's West Campus and informed Whitlock of what had gone down. The initial newsroom debate revolved around the question of whether Krzyzewski's tirade was off the record. Everyone who had witnessed it (and the tape recorder) confirmed that Coach K had never requested that the meeting be off the record.

Layton typed up a transcript, and Krzyzewski and athletic director Tom Butters were contacted for comment. Coach K declined to offer anything for the story other than, "It was a personal thing, and I wanted to let them know how I felt." Butters sounded a little more forceful than that. "If *The Chronicle* chooses to make an issue of it," he warned, "then I'm gonna look at it very, very closely and somebody's gonna come out the loser."

Krzyzewski's planned ambush, right in front of his team in his team's domain, might have been a ploy to show his players just how much he supported them. Coach K never would have tried this with professional beat reporters from the *Raleigh News and Observer,* the *Charlotte Observer,* and the *Durham Morning Herald,* which published an account of Krzyzewski's verbal onslaught off the tape provided by *The Chronicle.* Coach K had always erroneously viewed the student newspaper as an extension of the school's sports information office, said the former *Chronicle* writer and editor-in-chief who covered Krzyzewski's first Blue Devils team, Jon Scher.

Under the headline "Men's Basketball Coach Blasts Chronicle Writers" — on the same day Duke was set to play at North Carolina — the newspaper turned what Coach K thought would be a private smackdown into a public display of his temper, paranoia, and naïveté when it came to student journalism.

"We might have been a convenient target to go after to make a point to his team; I don't know the answer to that," Whitlock would say. "The stuff we wrote was so vanilla, so mild, it's hard to imagine if he got that worked up over it. Or if he's got some temper issues. We pulled back the curtain a little bit on him . . . I think it was shocking to the rest of the country."

The story was picked up everywhere in the coming days. National TV networks called for copies of the Krzyzewski audiotape; one offered money for it. (*The Chronicle* turned them down.) "Coach K. Gives Stately Duke an Undignified Jolt," read one headline on the front page of the *New York Times* sports section. The day after the *Chronicle* story hit, North Carolina's student paper, the *Daily Tar Heel,* ran a story, headlined "Krzyzewski: From Classy to Classless," that opened this way:

"Professionalism. Class. Intelligence. Maturity. Personality. These are the things people like about Duke coach Mike Krzyzewski — and these are the things Krzyzewski threw out the window . . ."

The *Daily Tar Heel* story said that the paper's reporters had "never received a response even close to Krzyzewski's from any coach." One of its own sportswriters said that Dean Smith had never confronted him on anything he had written, and that the Tar Heel coach "has too much class to do that."

Krzyzewski knew he needed to fix what he had broken. This was a big deal to Duke administrators, especially to the university president, Keith Brodie, who had succeeded Terry Sanford in 1985. On the one hand, school elders did not want to criticize the figure (Krzyzewski) and the program (men's basketball) that had represented what Whitlock called "the golden goose for the university." On the other hand, they did not want to criticize their own students, journalists in training who did not deserve to be berated by an employee and who had done so much good, meaningful work at an institution that, unlike North Carolina, did not have a journalism school.

"The university was paralyzed," Whitlock said. "They didn't know what to do. They didn't say anything."

Krzyzewski finally did. He asked for a meeting with Whitlock and the ten reporters he'd blasted (nine would be in attendance). They gathered, not in the locker room, but in Cameron's Hall of Fame room, with no Duke players or staffers invited to be present. Coach K said that he regretted using profanity in the Monday night meeting, and regretted holding it in the locker room, but that he "wouldn't change the substance of the meeting." Krzyzewski actually claimed with a straight face that he was not trying to intimidate the student journalists. He said that *The Chronicle*'s access to the team would not be cut, but he offered no apology for his conduct. On the claim that his secretary shouldn't have advertised the sit-down/ambush as a get-to-know-you-better session, Krzyzewski said that the reporters should have known better and that "if you expected brownies and milk or whatever, I think that would be naive on your part."

When Coach K was making the few concessions he made over the course of the hour, Layton said, "it felt like somebody had a gun to his head. He was saying it through his teeth." When the meeting ended, all parties were eager to move on.

Krzyzewski had established a bond with the student body, his cherished "sixth man," and that bond was never more obvious than it was at the biggest games, especially the North Carolina games on campus, where students would spend days and weeks sleeping in tents erected outside of Cameron to be in place for admission. That was the demand for Duke basketball, for Mike Krzyzewski basketball. Students took turns manning the tents while their fellow residents attended classes. Coach K sometimes sent pizzas to the tent village. He sometimes invited the diehards into Cameron for a pep talk or to share a scouting report or game tape.

The village even had a name—Krzyzewskiville. Man, he'd come a long way from spelling and pronouncing his name at his opening press conference in 1980.

He still had no national championships after those three Final Four trips. When Mike Krzyzewski assailed *The Chronicle* for giving him only a B+, he forgot that an A+ in college basketball isn't earned in a screaming match. It's only earned on the last Monday night of the season.

"*RUN SPECIAL.*"

His team down by a point, Mike Krzyzewski barked that command at Christian Laettner with 2.6 seconds left in overtime of Duke's East Regional final against Connecticut at — where else? — the New Jersey Meadowlands. UConn's Tate George, who had made a remarkable catch of a full-court pass and subsequent shot with one second left to beat Clemson in the Sweet 16, had just nearly intercepted a Hurley pass that bounced off him and out of bounds to give Duke a chance. Krzyzewski had drawn up a play in the huddle for one of his three senior starters, Phil Henderson, to take the shot.

But then Krzyzewski saw something in the Huskies' defense: they weren't covering Laettner, the inbound passer, so Krzyzewski told him to scrap the play and run "special." The Duke center mouthed the instruction to his roommate, Brian Davis, who was positioned near the three-point line. The other three Blue Devils on the floor were oblivious to the audible. When Laettner was handed the ball, Davis took a jab step toward the basket, then cut hard back toward his best friend, who passed him the ball. Davis caught it and immediately passed it back to the streaking Laettner, who took one left-handed dribble, left his feet near the foul line extended, double-pumped under a lunging UConn defender, and sank the floater for a 79–78 victory.

Krzyzewski threw up his arms and screamed as he hopped onto the court, before quickly throwing his arms down to his side and walking over to hug Connecticut coach Jim Calhoun. Out of the manic pile of Duke bodies spilled two players wrapped in a hug, holding onto each other for dear life: Hurley and Laettner, number 11 and number 32, exchanging profanities and expressions of love. Down in Dunedin, Florida, where Laettner's brother had just finished umpiring a Phillies–Blue Jays game and calling every close pitch a strike to speed things up so he could catch the end of Duke-UConn, Christopher was high-fiving Blue Jays players over Christian's remarkable shot.

Duke was making its third straight trip to the Final Four, and its fourth in five years. North Carolina? The Tar Heels hadn't been to the national semis since they won it all in '82. North Carolina State? The Wolfpack hadn't been to the national semis since they won it all in '83, and now Jim Valvano, who once had Krzyzewski's number, was suddenly in far greater danger of losing his job than Coach K was in his early years at Duke.

Valvano had been under intense fire since the release of a book, *Personal Fouls,* that alleged academic corruption and racism at NC State; in response, the NCAA put his program on two years' probation for rules violations involving the improper sales of sneakers and complimentary tickets. People close to Valvano, who had already lost his athletic director's post amid the controversy, swore that North Carolina grads in the media were not interested in doing Jimmy V any favors in their coverage and pointed out that the coach was not directly implicated in any violations. But the controversy, combined with revelations of his team's dreadful overall academic performance, left Valvano vulnerable despite the '83 title.

The Blue Devils blitzed Arkansas in the national semis in Denver, winning by 14 and surviving the mile-high altitude, the Razorbacks' "Forty Minutes of Hell" pressure defense, and the intestinal flu and diarrhea that besieged Hurley, who was seen scrambling off the court to get to a bathroom. Even before Duke advanced to play Jerry Tarkanian's Runnin' Rebels of the University of Nevada–Las Vegas in the final, Krzyzewski was asked about his growing collection of near-misses. "I think our approach to the tournament has been a good one," he maintained. "I know I haven't won a national championship, but we think we're doing things the right way."

His opponent, Tarkanian, was also without a ring. An owlish man with dark, hooded eyes who spent his game nights nervously chomping on a folded towel, "Tark the Shark" was college basketball's ultimate renegade, forever fighting with the governing body he called the N-C-2-A, which seemed to delight in tracking his every rule-breaking or -bending move. The UNLV program stood in direct contrast to the Duke program. Tarkanian believed in giving second, third, and fourth chances to players, most of them African American, who might have fallen short of the academic or disciplinary standards of detached administrators who had no understanding of what those players had to overcome in their communities. Krzyzewski, on the other hand, was picking almost exclusively from the sons of stable, two-parent households and never from the junior-college circuit that Tarkanian frequented.

"Battle of Good vs. Evil?" was one predictable major newspaper headline among many, given the matchup of a largely Black team from a public research school and a team with a history of white stars representing a private school often grouped with Stanford and the Ivy League. Krzyzewski did what he could to quash that angle, declaring his respect for UNLV and maintaining that the Blue Devils were hardly the choir boys the media made them out to be.

When Duke was last matched in the final against another largely Black team, Louisville, the media had seemed smitten with the Blue Devils' storytelling charms. "When we played in '86," Krzyzewski said, "people tried to do the same thing, portray us as Snow White." One of his players in '86, Jay Bilas, now Coach K's graduate assistant, recoiled at the media portrayals of Duke and Vegas and reminded everybody that UNLV's starting point guard, Greg Anthony, was vice chairman of the Nevada Young Republicans. "He would've been Entrepreneur of the Year at Duke," Bilas said. "How do you think Laettner and Hurley would've been viewed in Vegas uniforms? It's ridiculous."

If nothing else, opposites attract and make for good TV. Duke-Vegas figured to be a hell of a show, and CBS unwittingly added to its appeal. On the eve of the game, the network shockingly fired its signature play-by-play voice Brent Musburger and announced that the NCAA final would be his farewell call. Given that the news broke on April 1, many assumed that the firing was an April Fool's joke. It most certainly was not.

Krzyzewski knew that Vegas presented a most formidable challenge. Though the Rebels did not play the kind of competition that Duke faced in the ACC, they were a juggernaut defined by fiercely determined players in the likes of Larry Johnson, Stacey Augmon, Greg Anthony, and Anderson Hunt. UNLV was an opponent that would demand the very best of the Blue Devils. And Krzyzewski knew Sunday that his team would surely not be able to give its best. The day after Hurley played through illness against Arkansas, after Abdelnaby described his ghostly pale skin as translucent, the point guard was ordered to stay in bed. Hurley was visited by his Duke classmate, Debbie Krzyzewski, who described his coloring as green and his eyes as sunken and dark. "It was so sad to look at him," the coach's daughter said. Bobby needed IV fluids and a lot of chicken soup. Duke staffers put a humidifier in his room and hoped for the best.

They got the worst instead, as a weakened Hurley was no match for the swarming Rebels he encountered. The freshman had the same amount of combined points and assists (five) as he did turnovers against UNLV, who ran the Blue Devils off the floor and out of the building. Duke's defenders had been dropping low in their stances and slapping the court with their palms over the past couple of years when in dire need of a stop, but there was no reason to bother on this night. Over the course of the game, one columnist wrote, the Rebels were "blowing by Hurley as if he were some child who had wandered out of the stands and onto their floor." Krzyzewski left his point guard in the game until the bitter end.

"I think he knew it destroyed me to be out there and to feel that humiliation and pain with 10 million people watching," Hurley said. Krzyzewski wanted his point guard to be embarrassed and angry that he had responded to the biggest moment with his worst performance, just to make sure he never let it happen again. When it was mercifully over, Hurley was too emotionally spent to cry. He was empty, broken, just like the rest of his team.

The final score, 103–73, represented the biggest margin of victory in NCAA championship game history. During Duke's second-half time-outs, Laettner said, "none of the players had a clue what to do. We all looked to Coach to pull out a miracle."

"I think that's the best a team has ever played against me," Krzyzewski said. "I'm in awe of what they did to us tonight."

Coach K went out of his way to praise the UNLV players as "class kids" who were "so gracious after they won." But in the locker room, while making sure to thank his seniors for everything they gave him, Coach K lit into his team for its indifferent effort with so much on the line. He simply could not tolerate a defeat that came with no dignity attached to it.

"This is never going to happen again to this program," Krzyzewski raged. "I'm never coming back to another locker room like this one." Over his four-year career at Duke, Hurley never saw his coach angrier after a game.

Krzyzewski was angry at himself too, for not inspiring enough competitive fight from the bench. Back at the team hotel, the same Iron Dukes boosters who had wanted him out in the early years were busy in their postgame reception complaining that Coach K still couldn't win the big one. Hurley's parents, Bob Sr. and Chris, could barely process what they were hearing as they made their way around the room.

The Hurleys told the boosters that no other coach could have led these Blue Devils to the national title game, and that Coach K's best was yet to come.

Meanwhile, Krzyzewski was in his suite with his family and his staff, trying to recover from the devastation of it all. His mother Emily, brother Bill, and sister-in-law Pat were in the room. At one point, piercing the funereal mood of the occasion, Emily shouted to get her son's attention.

"Mike," she said, "don't worry. You'll do better next year."

8

CONQUEST

THE DUKE COACHES were talking on the bus, out of earshot of their players. They did not have to sell a false sense of confidence if their student-athletes couldn't hear them. This was when they could be human. This was when they could express doubts.

"Goddamn," one of them said, "we've got to deal with Vegas again."

Mike Krzyzewski had just beaten Lou Carnesecca's St. John's team to become the first coach to advance to four consecutive Final Fours since John Wooden made it to nine in a row at UCLA. "Wow," Carnesecca said after losing the Midwest Regional final in the Pontiac Silverdome. "It's not by accident that they got to five Final Fours in six years. That's not by chance. It's skill. It's hard work and it's excellent leadership."

Krzyzewski had supplied that leadership again during the 1990–1991 season, and yet when the Blue Devils were on the bus after beating St. John's by 17 points, his assistants were worried. Their next opponent, in Indianapolis, would be UNLV. The Runnin' Rebels had clinched their own return to the Final Four the day before when they defeated Seton Hall for their forty-fifth consecutive victory, a streak over two seasons that included their historic 30-point takedown of Duke in the final.

Krzyzewski usually sat in the second row of the bus (often watching game tape), right behind longtime trainer Max Crowder, with the assistants right behind Coach K. Mike Brey and Tommy Amaker, who had been promoted to full-time assistant to replace Bob Bender — now the coach at Illinois State — were busy sharing their concerns about facing the team that had destroyed them the previous year.

"Tommy and I were like, 'Oh shit. How do we stop their fast break? Nobody can guard Larry Johnson,'" Brey said.

And then they heard that unmistakable voice. "Hey, man," Krzyzewski said, "we've got a date with destiny."

A date with destiny? Or a date with a dynasty?

"Mike was so freakin' serious about it," Brey said. "Only he could say that after what happened to us."

Krzyzewski told his players on that bus, "We are going to win." In fact, he was speaking confidently about his Final Four matchup even before Duke beat St. John's in the Elite Eight. He sat with his best boyhood friend and fellow Columbo, Dennis "Moe" Mlynski, in their hotel hours before the St. John's game and told him, "If we're fortunate enough to win today, I know how we can beat UNLV next week." The details would come later.

KRZYZEWSKI HAD ALMOST passed up this opportunity the previous spring. The pressure to finally win it all — along with the lingering wounds from *The Chronicle* incident — were wearing on Coach K enough for him to consider a unique remedy: leaving. His friend Dave Gavitt, former Big East commissioner, had been named the new boss of the Celtics, and Krzyzewski conceded in late May that if he were contacted about their coaching vacancy, "I would look into it. The Celtics are one of the marquee franchises in America."

Gavitt knew Krzyzewski from their shared association with USA Basketball: Gavitt was president and Krzyzewski would be head coach of the upcoming Goodwill Games and FIBA World Championship teams. Gavitt met with Krzyzewski for several hours in Durham to try to persuade him to move to Boston, and Coach K began pondering the opportunity while playing racquetball later in the day. Celtics legend Red Auerbach, franchise overlord, met Krzyzewski and Gavitt for a two hour–plus lunch in Washington, DC. Auerbach reportedly needed convincing that a college man like Coach K was the right fit for the Celtics.

As the story unfolded, Hurley was among the Blue Devils concerned that they were about to lose their coach. The point guard called Krzyzewski and reminded him that he had promised during the recruiting process that he would stay at Duke for the long term.

Coach K fired right back at Hurley, saying, "Well, you said you were going to be a heck of a player here too." Krzyzewski was on offense now. He was the one being recruited this time, and it felt pretty damn good.

"I would be a fool not to listen," Krzyzewski said, "especially with Dave running it. Whether I'd do it is another thing."

The previous June, while participating in an International Institute for Sport ethics summit at the University of Rhode Island, Krzyzewski had breakfast with a few fellow attendees, including longtime college adminis-trator Dick Quinn, who asked him if he would ever leave Duke for the NBA. Krzyzewski told him the story about the good faith Butters had shown him in his office after year three in Durham. "Why would I ever leave a job at Duke," Coach K told Quinn, "when they were willing to give me every chance to succeed, and go to the NBA where a coaching tenure of five years is considered long?"

Krzyzewski would pull his name from Celtics consideration, explaining to reporters, "It wasn't anything to do with money or anything like that. It came down to what I liked doing and what I think I'm well suited for, and that's working with college athletes. I love the kids on my team. I think you have to find your place . . . Sometimes after ten years, you lose track of some of the little things. The things that make this something special."

TEN MONTHS LATER, Coach K believed that his team was now special enough to beat UNLV. He knew that he had a week to prepare for UNLV this time around, not a day and a half. He knew that Christian Laettner and especially Bobby Hurley were better players than they were the year be-fore. More than anything, he knew that he was suiting up a freshman who brought a talent, grace, and athleticism never before seen in a Duke basket-ball player.

Grant Henry Hill was the six-foot-eight son of Calvin Hill, a Yale gradu-ate and four-time Pro Bowl running back for the Dallas Cowboys, and Ja-net Hill, a Wellesley classmate of Hillary Rodham Clinton's and a promi-nent teacher, scientist, corporate consultant, and former special assistant to the secretary of the Army. Krzyzewski knew that he needed Hill, out of Reston, Virginia, to take the final step of winning a national title, as much as he once needed another DC-area prospect, Johnny Dawkins, to launch his program.

But Calvin Hill, who also played for the Washington Redskins, was a huge Dean Smith fan, and when he woke up in Chapel Hill after spending a day with Smith, he suggested to his son that they cancel their appointment at Duke. "We've been to the Promised Land," Calvin said. "Let's go home." Grant reminded his father that it would be rude to bail on Krzyzewski, so they made the short drive to Durham.

Hill was impressed by Coach K's obvious hunger, his apparent bond with his team, and his honesty in the largely dishonest business of recruiting. "You can be special," Krzyzewski told the prospect, "but it's going to depend on you." As always, Coach K promised nothing but an opportunity.

Krzyzewski visited the Hills at their home, followed by Smith, and then the Hills were scheduled to take a weekend trip to the University of Michigan, where the Wolverines' second-ranked football team was hosting top-ranked Notre Dame. Michigan AD Bo Schembechler, the titanic football coach, offered the Hills sideline passes for the game, and Calvin wanted to attend. Problem was, Grant had already decided he was going to spend his four college years in the state of North Carolina. Though he was the one who thought the Hills shouldn't cancel on Duke, Grant was now advocating that they cancel on Michigan.

"Well, we'd be going to go see the game," Calvin said.

"Well, it would be disingenuous to be there knowing that I'm not going to go there," Grant responded.

Calvin initially thought it wouldn't be a mortal sin to be disingenuous for a few more days, then realized his son was right. All the schools that recruited Grant showed integrity, and Grant and his parents needed to respond in kind. "Usually a father teaches his son," Calvin said, "and in this case it was a son teaching his father."

At decision time, something Krzyzewski said during his visit resonated with the Hills. Coach K noticed that Grant was planning on visiting the University of Hawaii, an odd school to include among the basketball heavyweights on his list, and wanted to know why. When Grant told him that the family liked living there when his father played for the Hawaiians of the World Football League, Krzyzewski turned the tables on the recruit.

"You need to understand that when people set up these visits, there's an outlay for the expense," Coach K told Grant, "but they also think there's a chance they'll get you. I'll never be disingenuous to you. I'll always be honest. And I just think your visit, especially for a program like that, might take an opportunity from someone who would've gone there and might not now get to visit."

Krzyzewski had given the same speech to a recruit from the early '80s, Bill Jackman. Just as Grant was serving as his father's moral compass during the process, Coach K was now serving as Grant's. The pride of South Lakes High School called Smith and the other coaches with the unfortunate news. On September 20, 1989, Grant Hill made his commitment to Duke official. "I just felt comfortable with Coach K and his program and felt that I could fit in there," he said.

Hill was still seventeen years old when he arrived at Duke, and his addition changed everything. He was the kind of high-powered frontcourt athlete not found on Duke teams of the past, the kind who could be the difference between finishing second and finishing first.

In his opening team meeting in the fall, with every player's eyes locked on his, Krzyzewski was confident enough in his roster to announce, "We're going to win the national championship." It was a bold thing to say given the loss of three senior starters and three of his top four scorers in Alaa Abdelnaby, Phil Henderson, and Robert Brickey, and given the return of nearly all of UNLV's firepower. Krzyzewski said it because he needed to say it. His team, his program, his everything had been humiliated by the Rebels. He needed his young athletes to hear it, and to feel his unbending belief in them. "It was a forceful, impassioned message," said team manager Mark Williams, who was in the room. "He said it with conviction."

And for the most part the Blue Devils played the season as if they believed in what their coach had told them. Of course, there would be adversity to overcome on the long and perilous road back to the NCAA final. Duke got blown out in its first ACC game, at Virginia, and on the three-and-a-half-hour bus ride back from Charlottesville, while the upperclassmen were smart enough to converse in a whisper, a German-born and -raised freshman named Christian Ast made the mistake of laughing out loud at something, drawing Krzyzewski's ire.

Coach K was already so furious over his team's performance that his rage had earned him a technical foul during the 81–64 defeat. Hurley missed seven of his eight shots and committed eight turnovers. His backcourt partner and fellow sophomore, Thomas Hill, missed four of his five shots, and the entire team went 21 for 56 from the floor. Christian Laettner's 27 points and 10 rebounds were all that kept this conference opener from being a complete embarrassment. So when the Blue Devils returned to Durham late that night, Krzyzewski ordered up an immediate practice, during which a stray elbow from freshman Antonio Lang broke Grant Hill's nose.

With Hill out, Duke responded to the punishment practice by thrashing Georgia Tech in its ACC home opener, 98–57. On the same night Dean Smith secured his 700th career victory at Maryland's expense, Coach K gave his friend Bobby Cremins his worst defeat in ten years at Georgia Tech. Billy McCaffrey, Duke's sophomore shooting guard, showed no signs of an earlier ankle injury in scoring 29 points, and Hurley recovered from the Virginia game to deliver 13 points, 9 assists, and some tough defense on the Yellow Jackets' Kenny Anderson, who needed 25 shots to score his 25 points. Of the 41-point margin of victory, Krzyzewski said, "I was amazed by it, because I came into the game wondering if we can beat them."

These were strange times in the ACC because of the sudden absence of its biggest personality, Jim Valvano, who had been fired by North Carolina State in the wake of the investigations into his program. He became a broadcaster for ABC and ESPN, and nobody doubted that he would grow into a formidable TV star. Valvano had known for a while that he wouldn't survive the scandal at State. In a December 1989 home game against East Tennessee State, he told the visitors' coach, Les Robinson, a North Carolina State grad, "Les, this might be a damn good place for you to coach. My ass is out of here at the end of the year." A stunned Robinson did indeed replace Valvano at his alma mater.

The change in Raleigh broke up the trio of ambitious coaches in their early thirties who had arrived in the ACC around the same time. "They used to call Mike, Jimmy, and myself 'the young guns,'" said Cremins, who played on the South Carolina team that lost to Krzyzewski's Army team in the 1969 NIT. "We all knew Dean Smith was at the top of the mountain."

During one league meeting, tired of Smith's habit of always making certain he was the last man to arrive, Valvano grabbed Krzyzewski and Cremins and headed out into the lobby, where Jimmy V handed a doorman $20 to alert them when Smith showed up. Sure enough, after the three coaches spent twenty minutes hiding in the men's room, the doorman entered to tell them that the legend was in the house. Valvano then led Krzyzewski and Cremins back into the meeting, walked right up to Smith, and said, "Hey, Dean, how are you doing? Great to see you. Sorry we're late." Everyone, including Smith, got a good laugh over that.

But Krzyzewski had supplanted Smith as the ACC's man to beat after Duke's Final Four runs became as much of an annual March event as New York's St. Patrick's Day Parade, and after Coach K outrecruited Smith for the likes of Danny Ferry, Christian Laettner, and Grant Hill. "Mike was very underrated as a recruiter," Cremins said. "I think in recruiting his true personality came out. He's very quiet and very unassuming, and I think as time went on he got rid of that MO. When Mike went into [a player's] home, he was not unassuming or quiet."

Krzyzewski won his second outright ACC regular-season title with an 83–77 victory over North Carolina in what had become widely known as the Dean Dome, completing a season sweep of Smith. The moment represented a significant breakthrough for Hurley, who had been ineffective in three previous matchups with King Rice, including an 0-for-7 performance in Duke's victory in January, when the opposing point guards got into a scrap. Rice had consistently gotten in Hurley's face and under his skin with trash talk that made the sophomore from Jersey City appear to be the fragile player he most certainly was not.

Hurley decided in this game to say nothing to his nemesis, to ignore his antagonistic methods. He scored eighteen points, made four of six three-pointers, and dished out six assists while holding Rice to seven points and five assists. "Today I wasn't flustered at any time," Hurley said. "Even against their pressure, I felt good, confident. I wanted to win this one so badly . . . and not just because of King."

This was what Krzyzewski had always seen in Hurley, and he had come up with an inspired way to help Bobby honor that vision. Coach K asked assistant Pete Gaudet to piece together video clips of Hurley at his whining, pouting, wailing, and blaming worst, so he could sit down with his quarter-back and show him the impact of his dreadful body language.

"Bobby talks with his face," Coach K said. "I tried to tell him: 'Do you re-alize the power you have?' He didn't. I also told him: 'You have to hate see-ing yourself that way in order to break that habit.'"

They sat alone in the dark and watched this horror film together. Taken aback by the images, Hurley vowed to make changes. "If I make a bad pass, if I take a bad shot," he said, "I can't let that affect the next series of plays." Hurley realized it wasn't enough to show a maniacal daily work ethic, espe-cially on the defensive end, to ride the bike or do the StairMaster for up to forty-five minutes after games and practices. Hurley now understood that he had to lead in other ways too. He also understood that he needed to re-pay Krzyzewski for letting him play through mistakes, and play freely, de-spite some freshman-year calls for his benching.

"Playing for my dad in high school," he said, "I internalized every mis-take and every loss, and it would just eat me alive if I was doing things that weren't successful. I found myself again in that spot as I navigated deeper waters at Duke, as I was figuring out my identity at that level. Coach K showed me my negative emotion and lashing out at teammates and officials, and he made that the primary thing I had to get better at. And I became way more consistent. The fire I had, I started to control it better. And I give credit for that to Coach K."

The Tar Heels were not going to let Duke beat them three times in one season as they had three years earlier; they won their ACC Tournament fi-nal matchup by 22 points, and Krzyzewski did not overreact. He surveyed his 26-7 team, a team that had gone 16-0 at Cameron and was now head-ing into the NCAA Tournament as a number-two seed in the Midwest Re-gional, and wrote "0-0" on the Duke board. "Everybody's that way right now," he said. "I look at the whole season as a journey. Wins and losses are all part of that."

On the bus, Krzyzewski sensed that his team deserved the benefit of the doubt, that it was a lot to ask the Blue Devils to beat an excellent North Car-olina team again. He also sensed that his players needed another dose of the confidence he'd given them in that first team meeting. So, on March 10, four days before the Blue Devils played their opening NCAA Tournament game, Krzyzewski told them exactly what he had told them five months earlier:

"We're going to win the national championship."

WHEN THE BLUE DEVILS returned from Pontiac, Michigan, winners of a fourth consecutive regional final, they had precious little time to catch their breath. They had defeated their four NCAA Tournament opponents — Northeast Louisiana, Iowa, Connecticut, and St. John's — by an average of nearly 19 points, but there were tense moments along the way: Duke was leading Northeast Louisiana by only six at halftime in the Minneapolis Metrodome when Krzyzewski decided it was time to smash up a chalkboard. It worked. Duke won by 29.

But now Krzyzewski was focused on the night Duke lost by 30. He had a coaches' meeting that included Jay Bilas, the center on his '86 team and now a grad assistant and Duke Law School student. The topic: Should Krzyzewski show his players the tape of their emasculating loss to UNLV to prepare them for the rematch?

"Do we really want to show that?" said Bilas, who wanted to keep the film sealed. "Mike was adamant. 'Oh no, we're going to show them every mistake we made.' His message to the team basically was, 'If we clean up this and clean up that, our mistakes led to that margin. If we clean that up, it's going to be a close game to the end, and we live in close games and they don't. We're going to know how to operate, and they won't.'"

Back in Michigan, before the St. John's game, Krzyzewski told his friend Moe Mlynski, "I've got to get my guys to show strong faces. They can't back down. They have to look the Vegas players in the eye and show them they're not afraid. We'll be in great shape if we get the game into the final minutes."

UNLV had gone 34-0 with an average margin of victory of 27 points. Make it a tight game in the end, Krzyzewski told his players, and the Rebels will panic. The Rebels will choke. "I want to show you guys something," Krzyzewski told his team as the film started to roll. He did not show his players the entire tape of the '91 final, but enough of it to make his point. He also detailed some changes he planned to make. Coach K said he wanted one of his senior co-captains, six-foot-six role player Greg Koubek, to front UNLV's Larry Johnson, the next number-one overall pick in the NBA draft, and he wanted Laettner to slide off Rebels center George Ackles, a limited offensive player, to provide help.

Coach K also had Gaudet produce highlight films of Duke's most prominent players, just to keep them as confident as possible entering a game nobody gave them a chance to win. The Blue Devils were 10-point underdogs, and Krzyzewski used that betting line to his advantage. He informed his players in advance that he would tell the media that UNLV was virtually unbeatable. Coach K wanted the Rebels, and the rest of the world, to think that Duke was effectively afraid of its opponent, even though he kept privately telling his team, "We're going to beat these guys."

Duke had to pitch a near-perfect game to pull this off. Over the years Krzyzewski had compared the forming of a team to the forming of a fist, something his players at Duke and Army often repeated when talking about their personal and professional lives. Two of Coach K's former West Pointers who became four-star generals said that they used the philosophy in fostering teamwork in the military; one of them, Vincent Brooks, said that he used it to apply pressure on North Korea. Coach K talked about the weakness of the individual's extended fingers when the hand is open, and the incredible power of those fingers when they're clenched into a fist.

Duke needed to hit UNLV with its tightest fist.

Meanwhile, Rebels coach Jerry Tarkanian spent the week swearing that this rematch was no gimme, that Vegas wasn't guaranteed to become the first undefeated champ since Bobby Knight's 1976 Indiana team, and that he didn't have a defender who could adequately cover Laettner. No matter how much he tried to sell his concerns, Tark the Shark couldn't find many buyers. Duke was the team that seemed hopelessly overmatched. Looking for genuine concerns? Bobby Hurley had spent much of the off-season trying to sleep through nightmares of being surrounded by sharks in a swimming pool. Seriously.

On arrival in Indianapolis, the Blue Devils got their first bad bounce of the week when they surveyed their accommodations — at the Holiday Inn–Airport. Krzyzewski wasn't happy. "I'd like for my team to be with our fans downtown, so they can remember it as one of the great events of their lives," he said. "Staying at an airport I don't think is the way to do it." Tarkanian, on the other hand, was taking a "Do Not Disturb" approach to the week. He closed UNLV's practices and kept his players as secluded as possible at the Radisson Plaza by banning autographs and posting security guards on the players' floors. Duke and Vegas were destined to be different in every way.

Krzyzewski had called his friend P. J. Carlesimo for an extra scouting report on the Rebels; Carlesimo's Seton Hall Pirates had just lost to UNLV by a respectable 12-point margin in the regional final. "Are they beatable?" Krzyzewski asked his friend. "Yes, they are," Carlesimo responded. The Seton Hall coach thought that Duke was a better team than it was in 1990. He also thought Krzyzewski ranked right up there with the NBA's Pat Riley as a master motivator.

Coach K kept winking at his players behind closed doors while working the Rebels, and the media, in the public arena. "I'm not sure if we are capable of beating UNLV," he said. "The bad thing is that you get more time to watch them on tape — and the more you become scared of them."

More than 45,000 fans packed the Hoosier Dome on Friday, the day before the Final Four kicked off, to watch the four teams run through an open practice. North Carolina–Kansas was the other semifinal, and the matchup of Dean Smith and his former assistant, Roy Williams, made it intriguing. So did the apocalyptic possibility of North Carolina winning, and then facing Duke in the mother of all NCAA Tournament finals. Then again, since the Blue Devils were widely expected to lose, the only team of the four that was deemed worthy of booing on entry was, of course, the UNLV Runnin' Rebels.

The Tarkanian empire was clearly in its final hours; the entire starting five would not be returning next season, and the university had cut a strange deal with the NCAA that allowed it a chance to defend its title in exchange for a TV-and-postseason ban (for various recruiting violations) in 1991–1992. The Rebels, desperate to go out with a bang and deliver, in the form of an unbeaten season, the ultimate F-U to the NC-2-A, clearly commanded the most attention in Indianapolis, especially on workout Friday.

Bob Hurley Sr., who had won 115 of 120 games coaching his son at St. Anthony, was among the observers of UNLV's practice. He recalled thinking that the Rebels looked like an NBA team out there. He was struck by the immense talents of Johnson, Anderson Hunt, and Greg Anthony. Back at his hotel, Hurley told his wife, "I can't believe how good their practice was." One thing hit him as odd, though, and a bit hopeful. He didn't see anything from Stacey Augmon, who was on his way to becoming a three-time National Association of Basketball Coaches Defensive Player of the Year. "I couldn't find Augmon in that practice," Bob Sr. said.

Duke spent the first five minutes of its practice putting on a dunking exhibition, Krzyzewski's way of flexing those underdog muscles. Laettner was the obvious leading man, averaging about 20 points per game, but the balance of his supporting cast was striking: Hurley, Thomas Hill, Billy McCaffrey, and Grant Hill were all averaging a little more than 11 points per game. Krzyzewski thought this year's team was tougher and less ponderous than the Duke team that had been crushed by Vegas, and there was no question that the chemistry was better. Laettner suggested that he looked at the three departed seniors in an addition-by-subtraction context.

"I think the guys on this team are closer," he said.

Krzyzewski was living up to his promise not to hang the 1990 Final Four banner until all those seniors earned their degrees and kept his ten-year Duke graduation rate of 100 percent. Meanwhile, that team's legacy was his legacy. He hadn't proved he could win the big one, and he would be questioned about it until he won a ring.

Krzyzewski was confident that he had the game plan to silence that line of inquiry forevermore: smother Johnson. Limit turnovers. Keep the Vegas fast break contained. And talk. Krzyzewski always demanded that his players, on defense, lead the nation in talking. Calvin Hill once asked his son Grant why he didn't wear a mouthpiece for protection, and Grant told him he couldn't because it would make it more difficult to talk to his teammates.

Hill was a player Krzyzewski had to work on, if only because he was too selfless for his own good, and for the Blue Devils' own good. Hill announced his greatness to his teammates during one of his first practices, a couple of weeks after his eighteenth birthday dinner with teammates, when the twenty-one-year-old Koubek tried to force him to the baseline. Hill faked to the baseline and went right around him into the lane and dunked on everyone in sight. "And then I knew how special Grant Hill was," Koubek said.

Krzyzewski was concerned that Grant Hill did not know how good Grant Hill was already, as a freshman. He did not want Hill deferring to older players. He did not want him waiting for *his turn*. "Sometimes it takes a little prodding," Krzyzewski said. "We have to tell Grant, 'When you dunk, you're not in the way.'" Coach K enlisted Laettner, Hurley, and others to keep pressing Hill to be assertive and to embrace the fact that he was the most talented player on the floor in almost every game he'd play.

The evening before the UNLV rematch, the approach seemed to work. Calvin and Janet Hill had just arrived at Duke's hotel from the Indianapolis airport, where a Vegas fan with a deep tan had assured them that the Rebels were about to kick the Blue Devils' asses. After the Duke players emerged from Krzyzewski's suite, Grant found his parents in the lobby.

"Coach K says we just need to execute, not beat ourselves, and keep the game close," he told them. "If we keep it close, we'll take over the game near the end. They will make a mistake because they haven't been in close games.

"I'm going to be guarding Augmon, and I'm stronger than him. I'm bigger than him. And they're going to have Larry Johnson on me, and I'm quicker than him. I have the advantage in both matchups."

When Grant left his parents, Calvin Hill couldn't get over how confident his son looked and sounded. He thought to himself, *Larry Johnson is a man. He could have played for the Dallas Cowboys. Stacey Augmon is a man too, and Grant is eighteen years old.*

Calvin turned to his wife. "Either they're smoking something up there," he told her, "or Coach K is the greatest coach in the world. He actually has them convinced they can win."

EVEN AS MIKE KRZYZEWSKI focused all his attention on UNLV, the possibility of meeting North Carolina on Monday night for the national title hovered over the Final Four. Duke-Carolina was hard to explain to those who hadn't lived it. "It's the difference between someone telling you what it's like to have children," said Tar Heels center Eric Montross, "and what it's actually like to have children."

Steve Kirschner, North Carolina's assistant sports information director, was a Connecticut native who was raised on the Red Sox–Yankees rivalry and had worked for a dozen years with a Red Sox affiliate. The fan bases of baseball's blood rivals generally lived far enough apart to hide from one another, he pointed out, but there was no hiding on Tobacco Road. For that reason, Kirschner said, "The worst thing that could ever happen would be if Carolina and Duke play in the national championship game. For the team that loses it would be so bad that it wouldn't be worth it."

The Tar Heels hadn't been to the Final Four since 1982, and Duke fans had no interest in seeing Smith emerge with a second title before Krzyzewski had earned his first. While Duke fans openly cheered for Kansas during the first semifinal, some Duke players watched on TV in their huge locker room. Others watched their personal highlight tapes on Krzyzewski's portable VCR — the tapes Coach K had ordered up to enhance their confidence. Laettner was not interested in any such enhancement. "I don't need to watch any damn tape," he told Krzyzewski.

Near the end of the Kansas–North Carolina semifinal, which Kansas won by six, official Pete Pavia called a second technical foul on Smith that ejected him from the game. Smith lost to both his alma mater and to his former assistant, Roy Williams, whom he congratulated on his way off the floor.

"And as soon as that game was over," Bilas said, "Coach K tore out of [an anteroom] and told everybody, 'It is not okay for us to lose because Carolina lost. It is not okay.' He'd felt a sigh of relief in the locker room, almost audibly, and he wanted that eliminated. He was like, 'Fuck that.'"

And then the Duke Blue Devils took the court to get ready to play the indomitable UNLV Runnin' Rebels. Duke's redshirting freshman, Kenny Blakeney, immediately noticed about a half dozen Rebels "just kind of laying down on the floor, lounging a little bit. I was like, 'These dudes are not taking us seriously.'" During pregame introductions, Thomas Hill thought the UNLV players were carrying themselves nonchalantly, as though they were expecting another blowout. Hill turned to Brian Davis and said, "We got these MFs. We got these dudes because they are taking us lightly. They don't think we can beat them."

Surrounded by their teammates and more than 47,000 fans in the cavernous dome, Laettner and George Ackles took their positions on the Final Four logo at midcourt, the official tossed up the ball, and Ackles beat the Duke center to it, flipping it into the backcourt toward Greg Anthony. Koubek, the first player to ever appear in four Final Fours, contested the Anthony catch and helped create a loose ball that was scooped up by the streaking Grant Hill, who took one quick dribble with his right hand to control the ball before soaring in for an uncontested layup, sending a message only three seconds into the game.

Anderson Hunt and Laettner traded three-pointers, before Hill beat Augmon for a defensive rebound, then beat Johnson down the floor to receive a bounce pass on the run from Hurley and score another layup. Hill had told his father he was stronger than Augmon and quicker than Johnson, and he'd just proven both claims in giving Duke a 7–3 lead that would quickly become a 15–6 lead on a Hill pull-up over Johnson.

"Well, if anyone wondered if Duke could play with UNLV, the answer, early, is yes," Jim Nantz said on the CBS broadcast. Krzyzewski was exploiting Tarkanian's decision to put the slower, thicker Johnson on Hill by having the freshman handle the ball and take some pressure off Hurley. Vegas quickly worked its way into the game, switching back and forth from man-to-man to its amoeba defense, a hybrid of man and zone principles defined by aggressive trapping. But on the other end, the Rebels' best player, Johnson, was showing signs of frustration over the way Duke was defending him — with Koubek fronting and Laettner helping from behind. On a three-point shot from Anthony that made it a 37–37 game, Johnson swung his arm right into Koubek's throat. It hurt like hell, and the Duke senior complained to a ref about it. "But to me," Koubek said, "I knew we were getting to them."

Duke was down only two points at halftime. In the stands, Mickie Krzyzewski had been sitting next to two Kansas players — Mark Randall, who had played for her husband on Team USA over the summer, and Mike Maddox. Mickie told them that she was not afraid of the consequences of losing this game. "At least now we can deal with the Carolina fans," she said.

With seventeen tie scores and twenty-five lead changes, the second half was an incredibly tense experience for both sides. Laettner was hurting the Rebels with his versatility and range, forcing UNLV's big men away from the basket. Hurley was playing a strong and steady game at the point. Grant

Hill was reducing Augmon to the nonfactor that Hurley's father thought he'd been in practice the day before, and the Blue Devils were not surrendering an inch to UNLV's physicality.

Early in the game, after the slender Augmon bounced off the sturdier Grant Hill, Duke assistant Mike Brey said the UNLV senior shot his classmate Anthony a look that said, *Goddamn, that's different from last year.* Near the end of the first half, Hill did nothing to prevent his right shoulder from crashing into Anthony's face, sending the UNLV point guard to the floor. Early in the second half, McCaffrey undercut Hunt as he soared to the basket on the break, forcing him to crash-land on his shoulder: Augmon responded with a retaliatory forearm to the chest. Hurley then hammered Hunt a few minutes later when the Vegas guard had a baseline lane to the basket, leading to a brief skirmish.

This was a new look for the Blue Devils, whose freshman reserve, Marty Clark, said that Krzyzewski had to rein in his team in practice because it competed fiercely for everything. "Nobody backed down, ever," Clark said. "Every day was like a Super Bowl at practice . . . I caught a forearm from Brian Davis and it knocked a tooth out, and I wanted to punch him right in the face. Coach K was a poor guy from Chicago, and he coached like he was poor. He wanted us to play like we were poor, and that's how we rolled."

Davis, recruited by Duke as an afterthought, burned to show that the sport's heavyweight programs had made a big mistake by not making him a priority signing. When he cried after the UNLV loss, he said, it was the first time he'd ever cried after a game. In the closing minutes of the rematch, Davis made a stunning play in his attempt to avoid another round of tears.

With Vegas leading by three, Anthony was in the middle of a hard drive to the goal when Davis intercepted him, squared up to the ball, absorbed the contact, and fell to the floor with the UNLV point guard while the ball dropped through the net. A three-point play would have meant a six-point Vegas lead with 3:51 to play and Anthony still in the game. Instead, official Ted Valentine waved off the basket and called charging on Anthony, fouling him out. Though a George Ackles tip-in of his own miss gave the Rebels their largest lead at 76–71 and created a sense of pending victory, Duke was about to be saved by the one player Mike Krzyzewski related to and lived through more than any he had coached, or would ever coach.

Robert Matthew Hurley.

"Bobby went to a school where the coach once wanted to be Bobby as a player," Hurley's father said.

Coach K had asked his team to watch Hurley's back in case the Rebels tried to humiliate him like they did in Denver, when he was sick. For all of his merciless taunting and big-brothering of Hurley, Laettner was always willing to get in an opponent's face or light him up with a blind pick if he was harassing Hurley. Christian was the only one allowed to mess with Bobby.

The Duke point guard didn't need any teammates to be his bodyguards that night. Krzyzewski had put him in the perfect frame of mind. Hurley had carefully watched his coach in the days leading up to this game, saw that fierce look in Krzyzewski's eye, and decided that Coach K needed to beat the Rebels every bit as much as Hurley needed to beat them.

"So I took on his personality in that game," Hurley said. He knew that if Duke didn't score on the possession following Ackles's basket, the season would be over. After taking his dribble across midcourt, Hurley passed to the right wing, to McCaffrey, then drifted toward the left-center section of the court behind the three-point line and waited. He didn't know if he would see the ball again on that possession, "but I wanted the shot," he said. "I believed I could make the shot."

McCaffrey looked inside for Laettner, who was swallowed up by the amoeba defense, and then fired a perimeter pass back to Hurley, who made the catch, took one step toward the goal without dribbling, and let it fly with 2:17 to go. Swish. Krzyzewski called a time-out, and the dome crowd made it clear that it wanted Duke to pull this off.

The Rebels were rudderless without Anthony at the point; they struggled so much against Duke's suffocating man defense that they committed a shot-clock violation on their next possession. Hill then penetrated off the dribble and dished toward the baseline to the high school player nobody really wanted, Davis, who scored while being fouled by Johnson. His free throw gave Duke a 77–76 lead. On the UNLV sideline, sitting on 599 Division I victories, Tarkanian did not look like a man who believed he was about to celebrate number 600. Johnson got fouled and missed his two free throws with the crowd roaring for him to do just that. But his strange foul-shooting delivery — he paused after lifting the ball above his head — had drawn Thomas Hill into the lane early, handing Johnson a third attempt, which he made, tying the score with 49.9 seconds left.

On the CBS broadcast, as Duke was looking for a shot to take the lead, analyst Billy Packer said, "Jerry Tarkanian, sitting on the bench with a towel on his head like he's on vacation in the Bahamas or something. Mike Krzyzewski, up on the sidelines." Thomas Hill missed a short pull-up, but Grant Hill kept alive the rebound corralled by Laettner, who was fouled by UNLV's Evric Gray with 12.7 seconds left.

During the time-out, Laettner told Krzyzewski, "I got 'em, Coach."

Krzyzewski told his players, "When he makes them, get back on defense, and do not give up a three." *When* he makes them, not *if.* Duke always practiced foul shooting when tired, often after a long series of wind sprints, to best simulate these endgame moments on the line. Laettner coldly sank both foul shots with a trace of a smirk on his face, while Tarkanian chewed his fingernails on the UNLV bench. Time-out, Vegas.

"Duke is twelve seconds away from one of the biggest upsets in Final Four history," Jim Nantz said on the broadcast. Tarkanian sent his players back onto the floor and had Johnson bring the ball upcourt. The nation's best player had made only 5 field goals and scored 13 points, 15 fewer than Laettner, and he had spent part of the night looking exhausted — the result of Krzyzewski's defensive strategy. Now Johnson was crossing midcourt, then breaking free after Ackles set a screen on Grant Hill. Staring at an open three-pointer with 7.5 seconds left, Johnson couldn't pull the trigger. He shot-faked a closing Laettner, who left his feet to contest a jumper that wasn't taken. Johnson passed toward the near hash to Hunt, who had matched his 29 points against last year's Duke team.

Hounded by Hurley, Hunt took two emergency dribbles to his left and released his three-point attempt with less than three seconds to go. Hurley and a charging Laettner jumped to challenge the shot, which bounced hard off the backboard and rim, off the outstretched left hand of Thomas Hill, and into the waiting arms of Hurley as the buzzer sounded and Tarkanian reached for his jacket on the back of his chair. The Duke point guard took two dribbles upcourt, as if he could not believe that the game was over, that his yearlong nightmare had been exorcised, before Grant Hill grabbed him from the rear and told him it was okay to let go.

As Hurley jumped into Hill's arms, Krzyzewski had already started coaching for Monday night's championship game against Kansas, throwing his palms toward the floor and ordering his delirious players to calm down. "It's the only time I ever didn't listen to him," Hurley said. He jumped on senior co-captain Clay Buckley, and rode the reserve center's back toward the tunnel while pumping his fists in the air. Duke had flipped the building upside down. The rollicking crowd would leave behind more tons of trash than the Hoosier Dome cleaning crew had seen since the Rolling Stones hit town three years earlier.

The Blue Devils were rock stars now. "I think they wanted it more," Hunt said in a profound admission. On the way to their postgame presser, Hurley walked with the man who wanted to be Hurley as a player. The Duke point guard had played high school basketball for his father's approval, and now he was playing college basketball for Krzyzewski's approval. Hurley had hated the look he saw on the coach's face after that 30-point loss in Denver, and he needed to make it right.

They looked at each other before arriving in the interview room. "Do you really believe we just did this?" Krzyzewski asked. "They were really freakin' good, weren't they?"

"We were both like, 'Wow, did this really happen?'" Hurley said. "It was a really cool moment for us. To see Coach K look the way he did after that game is why you lace them up."

ON MONDAY NIGHT, as tipoff approached, Krzyzewski knew he had the better team. He also knew what Herb Brooks, the U.S. hockey coach at the 1980 Olympics, knew after his underdog team shocked the world by defeating the Soviet Union in the semis: if the U.S. players were not completely focused on Finland in the final, they would lose the gold medal.

Kansas was Duke's Finland.

After beating UNLV, Krzyzewski had pointed a jabbing finger down at his players in the locker room and shouted, "Stop celebrating. We are not done. This is not what we came here for. We came here to win a championship."

Coach K had so much to navigate that night after the team returned to its hotel, where fans, family members, and players were like Times Square revelers on New Year's Eve. Krzyzewski tried to get everyone to give his players some space, to let them get to their rooms and go to bed, but it was a hard sell when his own wife was playing a game of Quarters with their daughter Debbie and chugging beers with her sister Donna and mother-in-law Emily.

The next day Krzyzewski saw two of his players, Koubek and Clark, wearing Indiana Jones–styled hats; Koubek said they were gifts from a Final Four committee. Coach K did not like the vibe he was getting on the bus ride to practice, or when the Blue Devils arrived at the Hoosier Dome. Duke had a champion's swagger, without the championship. Krzyzewski knew Kansas was good enough to beat his team. Roy Williams had defeated Bobby Knight, Nolan Richardson, and Dean Smith back to back to back to reach the final. He was quite capable of beating Coach K too.

So Krzyzewski jumped all over his players in the locker room. "I don't like your body language," he shouted. "I don't like your attitude. You guys think you've won something, and you haven't won anything. And you won't win tomorrow night."

Ten minutes after storming out of that meeting, Krzyzewski found his players gathered at center court, quietly waiting for him. They were standing close together, standing as one. He was moved by their sudden change in disposition. Krzyzewski thought to himself, *We're going to win it. We're going to win the national championship.*

Grant Hill made him a prophet on Duke's second basket of the game. Laettner had run down a rebound and thrown an outlet pass to Hurley, who took one dribble across midcourt and launched a high lob to the streaking freshman. Somehow, in full flight, Hill caught the ball with his outstretched right hand near the top of the backboard box and slammed it home as his head grazed the bottom of the board. His father, Calvin, missed the remarkable slam because he was busy talking to Krzyzewski's youngest daughter, Jamie. Calvin heard the crowd explode and turned to his wife and asked, "What happened?"

"Grant scored," Janet said.

He sure as hell did.

"Grant jumped higher than I've seen anyone ever jump to get that pass," Williams would say. Hill pointed at Hurley to acknowledge the assist, because that's what Duke basketball players did.

Williams was already seriously concerned about his team after the Jayhawks won the opening tip, only to commit a backcourt violation. *Oh my God,* he thought to himself, *if we're that nervous, this could be a long night.*

His worst fears were confirmed. "It was the kind of game where I never felt like we had a chance," Williams said. "We were just hanging on and hoping something miraculous was going to happen."

Duke took an eight-point lead into halftime, and in the middle of the second half Hurley pushed the lead to 14 with two free throws. A physically drained Laettner was walking up the floor at this point, crawling to the finish line. It had been an endless thirty-nine-game season for him: battling (and completely outplaying) Shaquille O'Neal despite giving away two inches and 60 pounds; getting his head slammed into the court twice by UConn's Rod Sellers, who was responding to a Laettner elbow, in the middle of a scramble for the ball in their Sweet 16 matchup; and dueling (and completely outplaying) Larry Johnson in the semis.

Laettner and Hurley had each played the full forty minutes against Vegas. Only Hurley would do the same against Kansas.

The Jayhawks cut the lead to five with 34.5 seconds left, but a Brian Davis dunk sealed it. With 8.1 seconds left and Duke about to inbound the ball, Billy Packer said on CBS, "And there it is. The first time I've seen Mike Krzyzewski smile. He knows he has that monkey off his back."

Grant Hill grabbed the final rebound at the final horn, with Duke's 72–65 victory frozen forever in lights, and Krzyzewski lost himself in a group hug with his assistants. On the night of April Fool's Day, April 1, 1991, Duke University won its first national title. Krzyzewski headed down to console Williams the way others had once consoled him. "I'm very sick for my team," the Kansas coach said, "but I'm very truthfully happy for you."

"You're going to get yours one of these days," Krzyzewski responded.

Hurley and Hill were among the exhausted Duke players practically passed out on the floor. Krzyzewski accepted a hug from Davis, who shouted in his ear, "We got it for you, baby," and he embraced and kissed his wife and three daughters. Though he conceded that "it feels really good to finally win a game in April," Coach K tried to tell anyone who would listen that this night wasn't about him — it was about the Duke students he'd ordered to play for themselves. "It's never been a monkey on my back," he claimed. "I always tried to keep all that in perspective. Did you see my players, the look on their faces? Did you see my three girls crying?"

This was about everyone in the Duke universe. Trainer Max Crowder, a Duke institution, who had been 0-for-8 at the Final Four. Coach K assistants Tommy Amaker and Jay Bilas, heartbroken members of the 1986 team. Clay Buckley, the senior co-captain and bench player who came out of a family desperately seeking a ring — his father Jay had been a Duke star who lost in two Final Fours in the 1960s. Koubek, the other senior co-captain, who scored the Blue Devils' first five points in the national title game three months after nearly quitting over playing time. McCaffrey, the sophomore guard overshadowed by Hurley who outscored the entire Kansas bench, 16–14, in his last game at Duke. (McCaffrey would transfer to Vanderbilt.) Laettner, who sank all 12 of his foul shots and finished with 18 points and 10 rebounds and one Most Outstanding Player Award. Tom Butters, who made it all possible by taking a big chance on a 9-17 coach from Army.

Some of Krzyzewski's most brilliant work was found in his managing of the Laettner-Hurley relationship. He let the two stars work it out on their own, and in the end that Monday night, after Laettner told Jim Nantz that he did feel fatigued in the Kansas game, he said this on national TV: "I think Bobby did a very good job because he has to handle the ball the whole game, and he didn't sit out once. And he just played a superb game, a lot of assists and not that many turnovers . . . and I'm very happy for Bobby." The camera caught the point guard smiling over the sweet sound of that.

Hurley's nine assists fittingly gave him 289 for the season, breaking his own Duke record by one. The faith Butters had put in Krzyzewski mirrored the faith Krzyzewski put in Hurley. On the first Monday night in April, the Blue Devils were the ones climbing ladders and cutting down the nets, while their coach stood in the lane, with his family, looking up like the proudest father as he basked in everyone's joy.

"It's a family business," Krzyzewski would say. "Those expressions mean a lot more to me than a trophy."

Coach K eventually cut the last available strand, then held the severed net in the air. Emily Krzyzewski had told her son in Denver that he would do better this year, and sure enough, he did. Some of the Columbos from Chicago — Moe Mlynski, Larry "Mondo Twams" Kusch, and Linda Wolczyz Kasprzak and her husband Frank — were in the house, with tears rolling down their cheeks.

They eventually retreated to the Holiday Inn–Airport, where they gathered in Krzyzewski's appropriately unpretentious suite. Mike's big brother Bill passed around a bottle of Jack Daniels to the Columbos. They drank and laughed and told neighborhood stories deep into this glorious night.

The Polish kid from 2039 West Cortez had conquered the world at last. There was nothing left for Mike Krzyzewski to do other than go conquer it again.

9

DUKE-KENTUCKY

THE BLUE DEVILS were one and done. Sean Woods of Kentucky had just made a prayer of a bank shot with 2.1 seconds left in overtime of the NCAA Tournament's East Regional final, and as the Duke players staggered back to their bench, they were thinking about lost opportunities. Their painful trip home. Their next trip to the beach.

They were thinking about everything except a legitimate chance to repeat as national champs.

Mike Krzyzewski saw it in his players' eyes. They were defeated. They were deflated. They were demoralized.

They were done.

It was an indelible fifteen-round heavyweight fight in Philadelphia, and Kentucky, a Rocky-like underdog, had just thrown the decisive punch. The Wildcats were recovering from heavy NCAA sanctions that included a two-year ban from the tournament, for violations committed under deposed coach Eddie Sutton. The mess left Kentucky with a roster plucked from the island of misfit toys. The school hired the unhappy New York Knicks coach, Rick Pitino, and charged him to return the Wildcats to their former glory. And he did.

Or at least he was about to, in 2.1 seconds, with this victory over a Duke team that was 31-2 and might have been 33-0 had Bobby Hurley not broken his foot during its first loss, at North Carolina, and sat out its second, at Wake Forest. Many old-timers who'd gathered in the Spectrum on the night of March 28, 1992, would call this the best college basketball game they had ever seen. Some thought it was the best game they had seen, period, college or pro.

Now, like the UNLV Runnin' Rebels the year before, the Duke players realized that they had just blown their opportunity to become the first team to win consecutive titles since John Wooden's UCLA Bruins won their seventh in a row in 1973. Kentucky's fifth-leading scorer, the six-foot-two Woods, had just lofted an attempt over the six-foot-11 Laettner that CBS analyst Len Elmore called "a terrible shot." A terrible shot that happened to bank in off the glass to give Kentucky a one-point lead and land the Wildcats on the doorstep of the Final Four. "When shots go in like that you say, 'This isn't meant to be,'" Bobby Hurley said.

Krzyzewski saw that resignation on his players' faces, and deep down he understood what they were feeling. Duke had to navigate the full length of the court, 94 feet, and score a basket in two seconds against a defense designed by a thirty-nine-year-old coach, Pitino, who had already led Providence on a miracle run to the 1987 Final Four, turned the New York Knicks into 52-game winners two years after inheriting Hubie Brown's 24-win team, and turned the Kentucky Wildcats into a 29-6 team three years after inheriting Sutton's scandal-scarred 13-19 team.

As a rising Buffalo high school star, Laettner had attended many of the big basketball camps in the East, and at one of those camps he ran into a guest instructor who made quite an impression. "Christian would rave about Rick Pitino all the time," Christopher Laettner said. "He would say, 'You've got to see this guy coach.' I'd never really heard of him, but Rick Pitino was his favorite coach."

Now Krzyzewski had to persuade his players that they could beat Pitino's team, that 2.1 seconds was an eternity for a coach with a plan. Taking their seats for what they all expected to be their final huddle of their season —and of Laettner's remarkable career— the Blue Devils made eye contact with the man who had brought them to this moment. "We are going to win," Mike Krzyzewski told them. "We are going to win."

It had been a hell of a two-year ride to this point, with the Blue Devils in the role of America's most wanted boy band. Krzyzewski told his players that they couldn't accommodate every autograph request, that it was okay to say no, politely. "If you can't sign," he told them, "shake hands while you're moving along. Be cordial. Apologize. Tell 'em to write you in care of the school. But be persistent about your time." The crush had already started in 1991, when Hurley had the managers stuff him into an equipment bag in an attempt to avoid a crowd of admirers — mostly young and female —gathered outside the visitors' locker room at Notre Dame.

The 1991–1992 Blue Devils won the ACC Tournament, drilling the Tar Heels by 20 in the final, before entering the NCAAs as the nation's number-one team and prohibitive favorite. They beat Campbell and Iowa to advance to a Sweet 16 matchup in Philly against Seton Hall that pitted Hurley against his younger brother Danny, a freshman reserve for the Pirates. The occasion called for nonstop reminiscing about life in Jersey City, about being the sons of high school coaching royalty, Bob Sr., the probation officer who nearly single-handedly kept afloat a tiny Catholic school, St. Anthony, while racking up a dizzying number of state titles.

Seton Hall coach P. J. Carlesimo, who coached Bobby on the U.S. gold-medal winning World University Games team, knew the Hurley backstory about as well as Bob Sr. did, so he put Danny on the floor for eighteen minutes — about six minutes more than he usually played — for the sole purpose, one columnist wrote, "of using Danny as a human can of mace to spray into Bobby's eyes." It worked. "I was in a funk," Bobby said. The Duke point guard ended up with more turnovers (six) than points (four), while Danny, who went scoreless, focused on hounding him. When one official asked the Seton Hall freshman to stop hand-checking his opponent, Danny told the ref, "He's my brother. I'll do whatever I want." Laettner threatened to come to Bobby's aid and knock Danny into oblivion with a hard screen, at least until bruising Seton Hall forward Jerry Walker intervened.

Duke won by 12 because Duke had better players, better depth, and a better grasp of how to win games like these. It was a bit of a crazy night all around, as Kentucky beat Massachusetts in the earlier regional semi thanks in part to a surreal technical called on UMass coach John Calipari for leaving the coaching box — this after the Minutemen had cut a 21-point deficit to 2. When the smoke cleared, it was Duke-Kentucky, a repeat of the 1978 national championship game.

They called the Wildcats "the Unforgettables" because they were anchored by long shot kids from small mountain, river, and coal towns in Kentucky who grew up dreaming of playing for UK. Sutton was effectively forced to take them in, if only to keep the locals happy. Seniors Deron Feldhaus (Maysville), John Pelphrey (Paintsville), and Richie Farmer (Manchester) weathered the NCAA storm because they would never leave their old Kentucky home, and also because, Pitino said, "nobody else wanted them. They had no place else to go." Woods, their classmate from Indianapolis, decided to stay. They would all get their jerseys retired in the arena named after the baron of the bluegrass, Adolph Rupp, in tribute to their loyalty, their resilience, and their ability to carry the Wildcats into this epic struggle of wills with the defending champ.

Duke-Kentucky was made possible by the fact that the Wildcats had an otherworldly six-foot-eight sophomore from New York, Jamal Mashburn, who signed up because he wanted to play for the coach of the Knicks. Mashburn was a Laettner-sized talent, and worthy of mention with all the past Kentucky greats. His NBA-ready moves kept the Wildcats in the game after they went down 5 at halftime, and after they went down 12 on Hurley's three-pointer with 11:16 to go. Pitino's famously frenetic full-court pressure defense helped, as did the Wildcats' aim — they shot 67 percent from the field in the second half.

Three minutes after his teammate Hurley's shot, and a few seconds after he was fouled underneath by Kentucky backup center Aminu Timberlake, Laettner nearly ended Duke's season with an egregiously selfish act: stomping his right foot on Timberlake, who was flat on his back on the Spectrum floor. Laettner was assessed only a technical foul for conduct that could have earned his ejection, inspiring postgame commentary on whether his star power, his skin color, and his association with a program often portrayed as pristine kept him in the game.

"That was unbelievably dumb," Krzyzewski told his center.

Kentucky was not rattled either way. A Feldhaus follow off a Pelphrey miss made it 93–93 with thirty-eight seconds left, and Hurley's leaning miss over Woods in the final seconds sent the game and the Spectrum crowd tumbling head over heels into overtime, where the expert punching and counterpunching continued. Pelphrey opened the scoring with a three, and Hurley answered with his own three (after missing one five seconds earlier), with Duke's Brian Davis fouling out in between. Pelphrey hit a tough banker in the lane, and Laettner answered with two free throws while his family watched from the stands; his mother Bonnie wore a white Duke button and shirt carrying her son's name and number and a heavy-duty neck brace made necessary by fusion surgery.

Inside one minute to go, Krzyzewski was pawing at the hair above his forehead. He knew that he was locked inside a classic, with the stakes growing with each possession. With 37.1 seconds to go and only 5 seconds left on the shot clock, Grant Hill threw an inbounds lob to Laettner in a play that was almost a dress rehearsal of what was to come. The Duke center went high to make the catch with his back to the basket, took one dribble, then turned left toward the goal with Mashburn and Pelphrey on him. Laettner left his feet, double-pumped to create room to shoot, and threw up a banker that nearly spun out before dropping in with thirty-two seconds left to make it 100–98.

"Oh . . . my . . . goodness," Verne Lundquist cried on the CBS broadcast. "How did he get the shot off?" But if the Blue Devils thought the first one to 100 would win, Mashburn had other ideas. He got loose on the baseline for a basket while drawing a foul on Antonio Lang that was whistled by veteran crew chief Tim Higgins; Mashburn's three-point play gave Kentucky a one-point lead with 19.6 seconds left.

The officials — Higgins, Charles Range, and Tom Clark — couldn't hear themselves think. This game was getting bigger and bigger and bigger. If a bad call ended up deciding it, Higgins said, "We would have lived with the infamy of that forever. You work your whole life to get there, and if it blows up in your face it's your worst nightmare."

Pitino called time-out and ordered up full-court pressure and a defender, Feldhaus, on the inbounder, Grant Hill. Hurley broke free to receive Hill's pass in the near corner, then quickly found Laettner downcourt, where a strong drive into the lane was met by a Mashburn foul — his fifth. The Kentucky sophomore had fouled out with 28 points and 10 rebounds and a legion of new admirers, leaving the game in the hands of the Wildcat seniors. The Unforgettables.

Laettner sank both free throws. Duke 102, Kentucky 101. Pitino called time-out with 7.8 seconds left, after his team crossed midcourt. With Mashburn out, the Kentucky coach called on his most productive Unforgettable — Woods, who had 19 points and 9 assists while going toe-to-toe with Hurley (22 points, 10 assists). Farmer inbounded to Woods, who dribbled to his right and watched as Pelphrey obliterated Hurley on a barely legal screen. Liberated from the Duke point guard, Woods attacked Laettner with his dribble near the foul line and then launched himself into the air, one-handing the ball over the center's outstretched arms and sending Kentucky's bench and fans into a state of delirium.

Laettner and his teammates immediately signaled for a time-out, wasting not even a tenth of a second; they were coached by a West Point man after all. But the situation was beyond grim. Thomas Hill thought to himself, "Oh man, there's no way we're going to win." Mark Williams, senior team manager, looked down at his classmate and good friend Davis, whose head was sunk low. *I can't believe we're not going to the Final Four in my senior year,* Williams told himself. One of the managers handed Krzyzewski his dry-erase board and a marker.

While an animated Pitino was in his players' faces, gesturing with his hands as he exhorted them to finish the job, Krzyzewski stood calmly beside his assistant and former quarterback, Tommy Amaker, looking toward the court as if he were merely pondering what to order for a late-night snack. Sitting a few rows behind the Duke bench, Calvin Hill locked in on Coach K; Kentucky fans were cheering madly, shocked Duke fans were in tears, and the former NFL running back was marveling at Krzyzewski's composure.

"They've got a play," Calvin Hill told his wife. "I don't know what it is, but it's not over."

The Blue Devils had worked on these endgame full-court situations nearly every day in practice and, in a way, during their second and most recent loss — at Wake Forest a month earlier. Grant Hill was supposed to hit Laettner with a long pass in that game, yet his throw curved toward the sideline and caused his intended receiver to step out of bounds while catching it. Krzyzewski ordered his players to report the following day to the home of Duke football, Wallace Wade Stadium, where the Blue Devils had done intense conditioning work and now expected punishment drills. Instead, Coach K served them ice cream and cake, just to break up the grind. They had gone 10-0 since that day.

Now in the Spectrum, Krzyzewski had shifted into a sitting position to address his players at eye level. Calvin Hill saw Coach K look at his son. "I thought it might be a long alley-oop or something to Grant," he said. It was not.

Duke had one player, above all, who was absolutely born to get the ball on this play.

Laettner had made all 9 of his field-goal attempts, and all 10 of his free throws; he had broken Elvin Hayes's all-time NCAA Tournament scoring record of 358 points during the first half. And of course, Laettner had sent Duke to the Final Four as a sophomore with that buzzer beater against UConn.

"Christian has always thought he was so good, but not off the court," said his mother Bonnie. "Only in games does he think he's the best, and he's so competitive. He brags to his teammates that he'll beat them in different games, and then he'll do it. And he's so happy when he does it."

The scouting report from one preschool teacher said that young Laettner had "too much self-confidence," according to Bonnie. "No one thinks more highly of me than myself," the Duke senior confirmed the day before the Kentucky game. He compared himself to tempestuous tennis champ John McEnroe: "People always look over his competitiveness, and his desire to win because he uses some profane language and might not be able to control himself at times," Laettner said. "People say I have similar qualities."

Krzyzewski now needed Laettner to keep his composure while everybody around him was losing theirs. He also needed a player to put Laettner in position to win it, a teammate who was tall enough to see the floor and throw the inbounds pass over the expected defender, and composed enough to put a long heave on the money under stressful conditions. No wonder he was looking at Grant Hill. "Grant's going to be the best we've ever had here," Laettner had told Krzyzewski during Hill's freshman year.

"If you had Laettner on one team and Grant Hill on the other in a scrimmage, it was going to be Armageddon in our gym," Hurley would say. "Christian was more verbal, and Grant was very poker-faced, but Grant wanted to win as much as or more than Christian did."

Krzyzewski looked directly at Hill, the Blue Devil who had failed to make this play against Wake Forest. "Grant, can you throw the ball 75 feet?" he asked him. "Yes," Hill responded.

Then Krzyzewski turned to Laettner and asked him, "When you come off the baseline, can you catch it?" In his typical smart-ass way, Laettner responded, "Coach, if Grant throws a good pass, I'll catch it." There was no need to ask Laettner if he could make the shot; his body of work spoke for itself. Krzyzewski made Hurley the second option, as a receiver near midcourt. Thomas Hill would flash hard to the basket from the left wing, in pursuit of a potential Laettner deflection, and so would Lang from the right wing, after setting a pick for Hurley.

"We are going to win," Coach K told them again.

When the Blue Devils broke their huddle, their mood had changed. Their slumped shoulders had straightened, and their dead eyes had come alive. Krzyzewski had actually persuaded them to believe in the unbelievable. If Duke's faith in that situation was measured on a scale of 1 to 10, said reserve Marty Clark, it would've been a 2 at the start of the huddle. At the end of the huddle? "Coach K made it feel like an 8," Clark said.

Grant Hill headed to the far baseline, where Higgins waited with the ball, while the rest of the Blue Devils took their places. Laettner planted himself in the deep corner near the Duke bench, slightly bent over with hands on knees. The Kentucky defenders took their positions, and everything seemed in place for the final 2.1 seconds, except for one thing: Pitino did not put a defender on the ball. Mashburn and six-foot-eight sophomore Gimel Martinez had fouled out, and the Kentucky coach did not have another big player he trusted to handle that assignment. Pelphrey and Feldhaus were both six foot seven, but if Pitino put one of them on Hill, it would have forced him to put the other alone on the six-foot-eleven Laettner, who had added 20 to 25 pounds of muscle during his time at Duke.

Unbeknownst to anyone on the Duke side, Pitino had also repeatedly implored Pelphrey and Feldhaus to avoid fouling Laettner. The Kentucky coach might not have realized it, but he had just turned his two seniors into passive bystanders for the final play of this East Regional final.

When he realized that Pitino was leaving him a clear look at the court, Hill couldn't believe his good fortune. "My eyes lit up," he said. Wake Forest had put a six-foot-nine defender on him, and Duke came out the loser when Hill's pass hooked left. This time he would be sure to put no sidespin on the ball. With the crowd buzzing in anticipation, Higgins told Hill that he was allowed to run the baseline if he so desired. The ref would usually warn the defender that if he reached across the baseline, he would be assessed a technical foul; since the last thing Higgins wanted to do at the end of this game was to call a technical, he was happy there was no Kentucky defender there to warn. "It made my job easier," Higgins said. Hill's job too.

The ref blew his whistle and handed the Duke forward the ball. Hill slapped it, took two slide steps to his right as he surveyed the movement down the floor, and then the football player's son threw a baseball pass that seemed to hang in the air forever. It was the kind of Hail Mary that Calvin Hill's former teammate Roger Staubach once threw to Drew Pearson to win a playoff game.

Laettner went up high to grab it just above the foul line, with Pelphrey and Feldhaus behind him offering no real resistance. His back to the basket, Laettner took one dribble to his right. From a distance, Hill thought to himself, *No!!! No, no, don't dribble! We don't have enough time for that!* In the stands, about a dozen rows behind the Duke bench, Laettner's father George was thinking the same thing: *What the heck is Christian doing dribbling?* Only Christian knew exactly what he was doing. He turned back to his left to find that Pelphrey had completely retreated, giving him the space needed to plant his feet and launch his turnaround jumper over Feldhaus, who offered only a soft challenge to the shot.

As Laettner released the ball with three-tenths of a second to go, and as camera lights flashed around him, Krzyzewski remained seated while others jumped up around him. He was holding a white towel. He had refused to throw it into the ring.

Laettner's 17-footer ripped through the net after the buzzer sounded, and only then did Krzyzewski explode out of his seat, his mouth open wide and his arms in the air. He spiked his towel defiantly. He didn't think Woods's shot for Kentucky was worthy of deciding this night, as it had accidentally banked in. Laettner's jumper was worthy on all levels. He had finished 10-for-10 from the floor, 10-for-10 from the line, and 1-for-1 from three-point range — good for 31 points. The perfect player with the perfect box score had made a perfect play to win the perfect game.

Duke 104, Kentucky 103. The Blue Devils' sports information director, Mike Cragg, jumped up from the scorer's table and shouted at the top of his lungs before apologizing to the Kentucky SID, Chris Cameron, who had done the same thing after Woods's shot. Cragg would say decades later that it was the only time in his thirty-year career as a college administrator that he had ever actively cheered a play made by his school's team. "That's what that game did," Cragg said.

Watching at his in-laws' home in Yorktown Heights, New York, Laettner's brother Christopher jumped up and punched a hole through the low ceiling, then rolled on the ground crying. In the Spectrum, Laettner's sister Leanne grabbed their mother Bonnie while she started screaming, "He's mine. He's mine." Under the basket, Antonio Lang had collapsed. Near the Duke sideline, Thomas Hill grabbed the back of his head with both hands and wore a surreal expression of bewilderment on his contorted face. Laettner went charging down the court, toward the Kentucky sideline, where he was tackled and piled on by his teammates. Meanwhile, a number of devastated Wildcats had fallen to the floor. Woods collapsed near the press table and was face-down on the court. When Krzyzewski caught a glimpse of Richie Farmer, the six-foot schoolboy legend and Mr. Kentucky from the eastern coal hills, he immediately jogged over to him. Coach K felt guilty celebrating while Farmer had just pulled himself from the floor, his basketball career over, his Final Four dreams in ruins.

Empathy was so important to Krzyzewski in this moment, even as his wife and daughters were crying tears of joy in the stands. Coach K was touched to see some of his players hugging Kentucky's, trying to ease their pain. The two schools had combined for fifty-one trips to the NCAA Tournaments, and now, nineteen trips to the Final Four. Duke understood that none of this was possible without Kentucky. Pitino and his players would cry many tears in their locker room, and the haunted coach would blame himself over and over for not putting a defender on Hill. But the truth was, the Wildcats were just as responsible as the Blue Devils for this gift to everyone fortunate enough to have seen it.

"You hope someday you're a part of something like this," Krzyzewski said. "I was just standing around afterwards, figuring what a lucky son of a gun I am."

Before he left the Spectrum that night, Krzyzewski needed to pay his respects to Kentucky fans and to the retiring voice of the Wildcats, Cawood Ledford, who was busy thanking the Unforgettables who "brought this basketball program back from the dead" and was just about to sign off after thirty-nine years when he told his listeners that Coach K was suddenly joining him courtside. Krzyzewski called the Kentucky players "absolutely sensational," and said, "I feel bad for them. I hope you believe that."

"I do," Ledford said. Before congratulating the announcer on his legendary career, Krzyzewski said, "I hope we represent this region well when we go to the Final Four."

Krzyzewski called Duke-Kentucky maybe the best game he'd ever been associated with. Most people inside the Spectrum were more definitive than that. The lead official, Tim Higgins, who would ref thousands of games over a thirty-five-year career, including three NCAA finals, was certain that he would never come across another one like it. At the start of his drive home to Ramsey, New Jersey, that night, Higgins told his wife Kathy, "You come once every five years, and you just saw the greatest game ever played."

INDIANA COACH BOBBY KNIGHT walked up to Duke special assistant Colonel Tom Rogers, his former officer representative at West Point, and handed him an envelope to give to Mike Krzyzewski. Inside was a clipping and a note that would represent the beginning of the end of the Knight-Krzyzewski relationship.

The Hoosiers were about to play the Blue Devils in the national semifinals in the Minneapolis Metrodome, where Krzyzewski was making his fifth consecutive trip to the Final Four, and his sixth in seven years. The last man to stop Coach K short of this point in the tournament was his West Point coach and mentor, Knight, who hadn't reached this weekend since 1987, when the Hoosiers knocked out Duke in the Sweet 16.

The Knight-Krzyzewski dynamic was so much simpler then. Knight, the teacher, had proudly worn a GO DUKE button around Dallas during the 1986 Final Four while serving as his student's lead cheerleader. The following March, when they met for the first time, some close Coach K observers thought he was deferential to his former coach, to his team's detriment. Knight had expressed his pride in Krzyzewski's accomplishments and his dismay in having to face him in such an important game.

But by April 1992, Duke had surpassed Indiana as an elite program, and Krzyzewski had surpassed Knight in Final Four trips, 6–5 (though the Indiana coach held a 3–1 lead in national titles and had already been inducted into the Naismith Basketball Hall of Fame). Coach K was being widely portrayed as everything that was right about major college sports, and Knight, increasingly, as everything that was wrong about them. Knight's latest self-inflicted wound was seen in a photograph of him pretending to use a bull-whip on an African American player, Calbert Cheaney; that attempt at humor drew rightful condemnation from all corners. The Hoosiers' coach refused to apologize for his insensitivity, giving Coach K yet another reason to create some distance between his career and Knight's.

Over the years Krzyzewski had explained to recruits, and to media members, that he was his own man, and published quotes from Coach K surfaced here and there that showed him carefully, and respectfully, trying to distinguish his approach from Knight's. On a number of levels, Krzyzewski needed some separation from the Knight Way as he built his own legacy. And yet all of the pregame focus in Minneapolis would revolve around the two coaches, as illustrated in newspaper headlines such as "Krzyzewski Out from Under Shadow of Knight," "Knight-Krzyzewski Matchup a Battle of Mirror Images," and "The General, Coach K Behave Differently."

Even the players couldn't get away from the one head-to-head matchup that jumped off their scouting reports: Krzyzewski, with a 31-7 career NCAA Tournament record was the winning percentage leader, at .816, among all active coaches, while Knight, with a 35-12 record, was second at .745.

Before their Saturday night game, the Duke and Indiana coaches offered no hint of a rupture in their relationship. Krzyzewski called the Blue Devils and Hoosiers his two favorite teams, and Knight said he shared that sentiment. "But I don't think I'm going to wear my Duke button to this one," he quipped. Knight said that his former player "has a side that's very loyal, very understanding. He's a great friend to have because he's going to tell you the truth." Knight also emphasized that Krzyzewski had put his own program together, and that he would have had the same success at Duke "regardless if he would have played for me or not."

Coach K called himself a good friend of Knight's and promised, "We'll be good friends after the game is over."

One newspaper report said that Coach K had "privately bristled" over the constant media references to Knight's enormous impact on his career as far back as 1987. "It was as if Mike owed his whole career to Coach Knight," a Krzyzewski associate had told the *Baltimore Sun*. The paper also quoted Krzyzewski saying of Knight, "I can call him and talk to him as a friend, and I was privileged to learn a lot from him. But by now, I've figured out how to put together my own game plan. I don't call my mother and ask her what to eat for dinner."

It was unclear if Knight ever saw that story, or the recent *Sports Illustrated* piece in which Krzyzewski said: "I value Coach Knight very much. He's been a tremendous influence on me, mostly in good ways. There are also some things I don't do as a result of being influenced by him. But to keep bringing him up doesn't give credit to others who have helped me: my mom, my brother, my wife, my AD, my assistants, my buddies. I've been a head coach for sixteen years and I don't go over every game plan with Coach Knight."

One *SI* story that Knight most certainly did see before Duke-Indiana was a Final Four preview piece that was written by Curry Kirkpatrick and included this paragraph:

In 1987 Indiana beat Duke in the Midwest Regional semifinals, a crucible that a friend of Krzyzewski's describes as the "divorce" between the two coaches, because Krzyzewski wanted so badly to eliminate the notion that he was nothing without Knight's patronage. Since then Coach K has taken every opportunity to outline their many differences while still staying on Knight's good side — wherever that is — undoubtedly a stickier task than teaching dozens of trophy makers how to spell his name.

Krzyzewski wasn't quoted as confirming what his anonymous friend claimed, but Knight took the piece as gospel. He was originally leafing through *Sports Illustrated* to find some tidbit that might help or motivate his players, only to accidentally stumble upon these seventy-nine words that angered him. Knight clipped out the offending paragraph, wrote a note to Krzyzewski, and stuffed both inside an envelope before he boarded the Indiana bus for the ride to the Metrodome and his encounter with Coach K. Knight gave the envelope to Rogers before the game. The colonel would not give it to Krzyzewski until after the Blue Devils and Hoosiers settled things on the floor.

The game was advertised as a battle of motion offenses and man-to-man defenses, with Duke, the nation's number-one team the entire season, holding a clear advantage in talent. But no matter how flawed he was, Knight was a genius of the game — even his worst enemies had to concede that. And he had devised a genius plan that bottled up Christian Laettner in much the same way as Duke had bottled up Larry Johnson a year earlier.

Coming off his perfect game and miracle shot against Kentucky, Laettner had a trying week leading into this game. The Black Coaches Association was among those asking why UConn's Rod Sellers, a Black player, had been suspended for a tournament game for his shot to the Duke center's head the previous March, while Laettner, a white player, hadn't been suspended for stomping Aminu Timberlake. That nobody on the Duke side had a sufficient answer to that perfectly legitimate question had probably taken a toll on the sport's Player of the Year.

Frustrated by Indiana's help defense, Laettner missed five of his six first-half shots. The Hoosiers shot nearly 60 percent from the floor and dominated the boards, yet allowed Duke to cut a 12-point deficit to 5 before halftime. Bobby Hurley kept the Blue Devils in the game, and Krzyzewski challenged the rest of his team to rise to the point guard's level in the final twenty minutes. It was an interesting turn of events, as Coach K had challenged Hurley to elevate his own effort after committing a combined 14 turnovers against Kentucky and Seton Hall.

Duke scored the first 13 points of the second half (and 18 unanswered overall), ignited, in part, by a Knight eruption and technical foul; the Blue Devils took a 50–42 lead and held Indiana scoreless for seven and a half minutes. Indiana was down nine points with less than a minute to play before seldom-used reserve Todd Leary—summoned into action after four Hoosiers had fouled out—suddenly ripped off three three-pointers in twenty-five seconds to give Knight a chance to break Krzyzewski's heart. But with Grant Hill fouled out and Brian Davis down with a sprained ankle, Marty Clark, Duke's own seldom-used reserve, sank five of six foul shots before Indiana's Jamal Meeks missed a potential tying three with sixteen seconds to play. Two Antonio Lang foul shots three seconds later gave Duke a five-point lead before the Hoosiers' Matt Nover sank a three with seven seconds left to make it an 80–78 game.

Yet Knight had no more time-outs left to call. Indiana fouled Cherokee Parks on the inbounds pass with one-tenth of a second to play, effectively ending the game. Parks made his first free throw, missed the second, and Duke was an 81–78 winner. To offset Laettner's season-low eight points, Hurley tied a career-high with 26, including 18 on three-pointers, and badly outplayed his counterpart, Chris Reynolds, who scored 2. (Once upon a time, Krzyzewski had told his targeted recruit, Hurley, that he had Reynolds lined up in case the Jersey City point guard didn't commit to Duke soon enough.)

Indiana finished with more baskets, assists, and rebounds than Duke, but the Blue Devils took 42 foul shots to the Hoosiers' 16; on the season Krzyzewski's team would take 460 more free throws than its opponents and make 197 more than its opponents attempted, a testament to its aggressive offensive style and ability to carry leads into the final minutes. The burgeoning Duke dynasty had turned the foul line into a weapon.

Now all that was left was the handshake between two titanic coaches. Krzyzewski marched purposefully toward the Indiana bench, then slowed down, extended his right hand, and waited for the affectionate exchange of words that normally punctuate a spirited contest between old friends. Only Knight did not break stride when grabbing and releasing Krzyzewski's hand. It was a drive-by handshake, meant to send a clear and cold message. Coach K said a few words as their hands met; the losing coach seemed not to say much of anything at all. Krzyzewski looked shaken as he walked away. And then to ensure that the winning coach got his message, Knight wrapped his left arm around Rogers and pulled him in tight, said something in his right ear, and pointed in Krzyzewski's direction. "The General" and the colonel then walked down the tunnel arm and arm.

Knight attended the postgame press conference with a couple of players, fielded questions about one of his most bitter defeats, and then, while exiting the interview room, congratulated the Duke players waiting behind a curtain, Hurley and Laettner, before making yet another decision on Krzyzewski. Mike was right in front of him, again, hoping this do-over would go better than the on-court drive-by. This time Knight walked right by him without saying a word or shaking his hand.

In his presser, a rattled Krzyzewski was asked about the conspicuous lack of warmth from Knight after the final horn sounded. "He just said, 'Congratulations and good luck.'" the Duke coach said. "That was about all I expected."

As instructed by Knight, Rogers gave the note to Krzyzewski, who all but buckled upon reading it. Yes, Coach K wanted some independence from his college coach. No, he did not want this fight. Krzyzewski never forgot how Knight treated him and his mother after his father died during his senior season at West Point. Coach K brought that up all the time with his friends. In his darkest hour, Krzyzewski had seen Knight's considerable capacity for kindness. And now his old West Point coach was declaring war on him.

As much as Coach K wanted to downplay the whole thing, his pain was obvious. "I've never seen Coach K hurt by anything like that," said his sports information director Mike Cragg. "The colonel gave him the letter, and he was trying to figure what the fuck is going on."

Coach K had tears in his eyes and sure did not look like a man who had just advanced to the national championship game for a third straight year. When Mickie asked what was wrong, Krzyzewski answered, "Knight," and then told her about the note. Knight later said that he pointed out in the letter that he'd always had a great relationship with Krzyzewski, and that, in the event of a Duke victory over Indiana, he would be rooting hard for the Blue Devils to win it all.

But no, the note didn't read quite like a Christmas card. Knight wrote that if Krzyzewski wanted to sever their relationship, that would be easily arranged. "He wrote that you should remember how you fucking got your job," said one prominent friend of both men.

Krzyzewski carried Knight's note with him from the locker room to the team bus to the Radisson South hotel in Bloomington, where the coaching staff met in his room. Coach K was lost in a deep funk. He had just earned a trip to the title game and a rematch with the vaunted Fab Five freshmen of Michigan, after beating his mentor for the first time, and yet he appeared as gutted as he was after losing by 30 to Vegas.

"Mike was crying about that letter, literally in tears about that," said Krzyzewski's former backcourt partner at Army, Jim Oxley, who was in the room along with Mickie. "And how Coach Knight, after all they'd been through, with Mike on the brink of a second straight national title, could choose to be not a friend or a supporter, but he had to do this. Mike was so . . . not pissed off about it, but hurt about it . . . It was just devastating to anybody who was from West Point to see that."

Said another person in the room: "Mike was really shaken, and it took a while for him to snap out of it."

The person who snapped him out of it was Mike Brey, the full-time assistant who was already establishing a reputation as one of the true gentlemen of major college sports. In the middle of a long night of Michigan film study, Brey was one nice guy who wasn't in the mood for Knight's bullshit. He saw that Coach K was "really knocked back" by the handshake and the note, and he felt compelled to act.

"Fuck that," Brey told Krzyzewski. "Fuck Knight. We've got a chance to go back to back, and this is exactly what he wants — for us to be bothered by this, and to let this get in the way of winning another title. I'm tired of this shit. We've got to deal with it on Tuesday."

One member of the Duke program said that Brey's "pep talk" to Krzyzewski "really made a significant difference. Nobody else would have said it like Mike said it, and it worked. Right after that we all kind of moved on."

So the Blue Devils moved on to Monday night, when they would be tested by one of the greatest recruiting classes in college basketball history, knowing that their own superstar player had almost nothing left to give.

THE WOLVERINES HAD still been figuring out who they were, and where they were going, when they lost a fun, trash talk–filled overtime game to Duke in December before a raucous home crowd at Crisler Arena. Michigan erased a 17-point deficit to take a 5-point lead before falling short. Laettner and Hurley had combined for 50 points and 23 made free throws in 26 attempts, while Michigan's most talented freshman, Chris Webber, finished with 27 points, 12 rebounds, and 4 blocks. Three members of Webber's celebrated recruiting class started against Duke, including Jalen Rose, who had 18 points and 6 assists.

"This was kind of a wakeup call for the country," Rose said that day.

Michigan was a good team for most of the season, but not a special one, at least not until it defeated the second-ranked Indiana Hoosiers on March 8, the start of an eight-game winning streak that was punctuated by a Final Four victory over Cincinnati. All five freshmen — Webber, Rose, Juwan Howard, Jimmy King, and Ray Jackson — were now in a starting lineup that was universally known as the Fab Five.

In addition to their extreme talent and their choice of college, the Fab Five had one other thing in common:

"All five of us were pulling for UNLV to smoke Duke and win it all," Rose said of the '91 final.

Much like the UNLV Runnin' Rebels and the Georgetown Hoyas of the 1980s, the Fab Five were embraced by African American fans across the country for their unapologetic, norm-busting pursuit of greatness. The Wolverines wore baggy shorts down to their knees, black socks, and black sneakers, and they carried themselves like decorated seniors. They raged against the system, and no team represented the system — or what was perceived to be the system — like the Duke Blue Devils.

It didn't matter that four of Krzyzewski's top six players were Black, or that Laettner and Hurley came from blue-collar backgrounds, or that Coach K was working-class all the way. Duke was seen as a private-school sanctuary for white privilege.

"I hated Duke and I hated everything Duke stood for," Rose said years later. He was raised in a single-parent home in Detroit, and "schools like Duke didn't recruit players like me. I felt like they only recruited Black players that were Uncle Toms."

On the national championship night of April 6, Duke's African American players were enraged when they heard some of Michigan's Black players calling them that pejorative term — among others, including the n-word — during warm-ups. "It was unfortunate what they were called, the terms used to describe the Duke team," said Calvin Hill, Grant's father. "The Michigan kids were young kids, and they were into the moment, the swag and trying to represent something. But in the process of thinking they were representing Black America, to them anybody who was different was not representing that. My father had migrated from the South, where he had been a sharecropper. Bob Hurley Sr. was a probation officer who probably had more experience with inner-city kids than any guys on the Michigan team . . . But the Fab Five needed to pick a foil."

Hurley wasn't comfortable being part of this highly charged conversation about race, but he was proud that he was, in his words, "very accepted by the African American community" in and around Jersey City because of the respect he'd earned on the playgrounds. He also said: "Grant Hill shouldn't have to defend how he was raised or his family background, and I'm not going to sit back while my teammates are getting destroyed."

Hurley revealed that his 26-point performance against Michigan in December "was largely based on anger," because he knew the Fab Five thought that Duke's white stars were overrated. "Michigan might've had a psychological edge over other teams because of the arrogance and swagger they brought to the floor," Hurley said, "but that didn't affect me or Laettner or Grant Hill or Thomas Hill. Most of us had already seen UNLV, so nothing Michigan did would ever intimidate us. UNLV was by far the best team we ever played . . . We just felt that nothing about Michigan's routine was ever going to shake our confidence. They weren't going to bully us."

But on this championship night, Krzyzewski knew he was coaching a tired team, and a very tired Laettner, who seemed to have needed the season to end after he made the shot against Kentucky. That was partly why Coach K dismissed any talk of a Duke dynasty. "I get a little uncomfortable when people try to put us in the same class with UCLA and when I'm compared to John Wooden," he said. "They won championships all those years. I'm not trying to diminish what we have accomplished, but there's no comparison."

Krzyzewski was more willing to talk about how exhausting the victory over Indiana had been for the Blue Devils, physically and mentally, and how severely limited his senior rock, Brian Davis, was by his ankle injury. Michigan was fresher and bouncier and posed a credible threat to become the first team ever to win a championship with five freshmen in the starting lineup. Krzyzewski warned his players against engaging in a war of words with the Fab Five because they didn't have any energy left to waste. "Don't play their game," he told them. "You are not allowed to talk to Michigan."

As the first half unfolded, that Fab Five threat appeared as real as Laettner's fatigue. The Duke center was running in quicksand and playing even worse than he had in the first half against Indiana. Krzyzewski kept pulling him out of the game for heart-to-hearts on the bench, but neither Coach K's soft touch nor his tough love worked. Laettner's seven turnovers — *seven* — and only two baskets in the first twenty minutes allowed Michigan to get to halftime with a 31–30 lead.

Just as he'd done at halftime of Duke's NCAA Tournament victory over Northeast Louisiana in the Metrodome a year ago, Coach K took out his anger on the chalkboard. He also ripped into Laettner before storming out of the room. The Blue Devils had to gather themselves; the question was how to get their best player back on track. Laettner had recently said that Coach K was the only member of the Duke program to yell at him," because he's the only one not scared to. A lot of times I'll yell at my teammates just so they'll yell at me. I need that sometimes."

And he was going to get it from a most unlikely source: Hurley. After Laettner harassed his point guard for the better part of three years, it was time to even the score. "Bobby just lit him up," Marty Clark said. "It was the most words I've ever heard Bobby say, and he went straight at him."

Sensing that Laettner might need to hear a new voice for the final twenty minutes of his college career, Krzyzewski let his favorite player go. Hurley cursed out Laettner like he'd never cursed out anyone. "Where the fuck are you?" the point guard shouted. "We're playing for a national championship and you're letting us down."

Hurley knew that volume alone wouldn't lift Laettner back into the game. So on Duke's first possession of the second half — a fast break off a Michigan turnover — Hurley passed up a chance to score by drawing Webber away from Laettner and then throwing an over-the-shoulder dish to the trailing Duke center, who gave his team the lead on an uncontested layup. Hurley then immediately found Laettner for an open three-pointer. He wanted only to jump-start his teammate, who would score 14 of Duke's first 24 points of the half and play the final twenty minutes turnover-free.

The Blue Devils held a three-point lead with 6:51 left when Krzyzewski called a time-out and designed a play for Laettner, who dribbled to the right baseline, lost the ball, recovered his own fumble, and hit a scoop shot in traffic on the other side of the basket. The game changed right there. Duke deployed its brand of suffocating defense, holding Michigan to a mere 20 points in the second half. Grant Hill gashed the Fab Five with hard drives to the goal as the defending champs pulled away. Krzyzewski jumped in the air and pumped his fist on a Thomas Hill basket that gave Duke a nine-point lead. The Wolverines finally showed their inexperience in the final minutes, and a reasonably close game turned into a 71–51 coronation.

Duke scored 23 of the final 29 points. "We broke their spirit," Hurley said.

When it was over, Krzyzewski embraced his players on the sideline and waved to family and fans in the crowd. He got a warmer greeting from Michigan coach Steve Fisher after the final horn than Knight had given him forty-eight hours earlier. Soon enough, Coach K was on a ladder to cut down yet another net.

"I'm happy," he said. "This is the greatest year I've ever had as a coach . . .

Put yourself in my position, when the whole year they've been ranked number one and they do the things that they did, and that's why I'm happy."

Duke became the first top-ranked team in America to win the title since North Carolina in 1982. Of greater significance to Tobacco Road fans, Krzyzewski was now ahead of Dean Smith in national championships, 2–1. His powerhouse team had left the fearless Michigan kids in tears.

Months earlier Krzyzewski had ordered his team not to *defend* its 1991 title, but to *pursue* the 1992 title. That pursuit ended with Hurley blasting Laettner (at last) at halftime of the final game, and with Laettner responding just as Hurley, the Final Four's Most Outstanding Player, was running out of gas. Krzyzewski had managed that volatile relationship perfectly over three years. He forced Laettner and Hurley to resolve their differences on their own, building a trust that helped them navigate the turbulence against Michigan.

Hurley would return for his senior season, but this was it for Laettner. At their final Duke press conference together, Krzyzewski — stat sheet in hand — corrected Laettner when he said he had five turnovers in the first half.

"Seven," the coach said.

"No," the center responded. "Five times in the first half."

"Seven," Coach K repeated.

"Oh, really?" Laettner said.

"See?" Krzyzewski said to the gathered reporters. "He doesn't have any eligibility left, so he's talking back now."

They would be paired up one more time as player and coach at the Summer Games in Barcelona. The Olympic movement had turned to NBA megastars after John Thompson and the college kids lost to the Soviet Union and settled for the bronze medal in the 1988 Games in Seoul. Krzyzewski almost certainly would have been named head coach of the '92 team if not for the NBA takeover that led to the appointment of Detroit Pistons coach Chuck Daly, who asked Coach K to serve on his staff. The Americans would be known worldwide as the Dream Team. One roster spot among the Michael Jordans, Magic Johnsons, and Larry Birds was reserved for a college player, and Krzyzewski pushed Laettner hard to make sure he beat out Shaquille O'Neal for that spot.

But as fulfilling as the Dream Team's indelible gold-medal romp would be for both, Krzyzewski was an assistant and Laettner was the last man on the bench. Nothing could replicate what they had shared over four trips to the Final Four, three trips to the title game, and two trips to the champion's podium. This was never more evident than it was at Duke's annual basketball banquet in April, when Laettner addressed his team and its fans for the final time. Before he walked out the door, one of the all-time college basketball greats wanted it on record that a singular figure meant more to him than anyone or anything else.

"I love Duke," he said. "I love Duke. I love Duke.

"But I'd rather play for Coach K than for Duke."

10

BREAKDOWN

IN THE SPRING OF 1993, Jim Valvano was dying of cancer inside Duke University Medical Center, with Mike Krzyzewski constantly at his bedside. Jimmy V had become a TV star after being forced out at NC State, and now that he was no longer fighting Krzyzewski for ACC supremacy, the old rivals had grown close.

They had become like brothers over the previous four or five months, when the monster within Valvano, metastatic adenocarcinoma, was slowly but surely taking him.

Krzyzewski would walk across campus to visit his friend in his room, and the two of them would ask family members, nurses, and staffers to keep out while they swapped stories about their lives and careers and told jokes about Dean Smith. In Duke's first year without Christian Laettner, the Blue Devils lost to the University of California–Berkeley and Jason Kidd in the second round of the NCAA Tournament, leaving Krzyzewski in tears as he said goodbye to seniors Bobby Hurley and Thomas Hill. But Duke's earliest exit from the tournament since 1985 had one benefit: more time for Coach K to spend with Jimmy V.

Krzyzewski and Mickie had flown with Valvano and his wife Pam to New York on March 4 for ESPN's first Excellence in Sports Performance Yearly, or ESPY, awards show. Valvano was being given the first Arthur Ashe Courage and Humanitarian Award. On the plane, he kept filling up the big gold vomit bag his wife had brought for the trip. He was taking a couple dozen Advil a day to temper the pain. Nobody close to the former North Carolina State coach thought that he would make it to the ceremony, but somehow he willed himself there, dressed in a tuxedo, and ordered his ESPN colleague Dick Vitale to find a way to get him on that stage.

Vitale wrapped his right arm around Valvano and guided him up those seven steps to the microphone, and then, as always, it was lights, cameras, action for Jimmy V. He told the emotional crowd to do three things every day—laugh, think, and cry—and then he made every man, woman, and child in the house do all three. Vitale stayed up there, off to Valvano's right, just in case he needed any physical help. Jimmy V quoted Ralph Waldo Emerson, told the audience that Krzyzewski was "a ten times better person than he is a coach," and introduced the motto of his new V Foundation for Cancer Research: "Don't give up. Don't ever give up."

When Valvano was done, Krzyzewski walked up to help Vitale escort him down the steps and back to his seat. Valvano had a little more than seven weeks to live. Coach K was with him nearly every day. He had enjoyed his visits when Valvano was assigned to broadcast Duke games. They both realized that despite their stylistic differences, and despite the fact that Krzyzewski admitted to once having hated Valvano, so much more united them than divided them.

"I know I'm gonna die, but I'm gonna win," Jimmy V told Coach K one day.

"What do you mean?" Krzyzewski responded.

"After I die, when we finally beat cancer, I want to be there," Valvano said.

He deteriorated rapidly in the end. His whole body would spasm as if locked in an epileptic fit when a cancerous tumor pressed on a nerve. "It was heartbreaking to watch," his brother Bob Valvano said. "Mike walked in during the middle of one of those, and I'll never forget the look of shock on his face."

Krzyzewski was the last nonfamily member to see Valvano alive. On April 28, he visited about three hours before his friend suddenly opened his eyes, looked around the room and then at his wife, closed his eyes, and stopped breathing. Pam ran out of the room screaming for a nurse. Her husband was pronounced dead, and before hospital staff removed the body, Bob Valvano stood at the foot of his hero's bed and read Jimmy's favorite poem, "First Fig" by Edna St. Vincent Millay.

> My candle burns at both ends;
>   It will not last the night;
> But ah, my foes, and oh, my friends—
>   It gives a lovely light!

After his last visit, on his walk back to his office, Krzyzewski recalled that Valvano had told him that he regretted not spending more time with his wife and three daughters. "I was really wrong," Jimmy V told him. "Don't screw it up, Mike."

Krzyzewski had two rings, the Dream Team run, and an upcoming chance to win a third national title in Grant Hill's senior season. Coach K had little reason to believe that he was about to confront his own human frailty and a crisis that would bring him to his knees.

MIKE KRZYZEWSKI, wearing an oversized hooded sweatshirt, could barely stand before his team. The Duke Blue Devils in the room would never forget the way he looked:

Frail. Sick. Broken.

"He looked like death," said Jeff Capel, a sophomore guard.

It was the first week of January 1995, and Duke was 9-3 overall. Krzyzewski was only nine months removed from a 76–72 loss to Arkansas in a national championship game that was also Grant Hill's farewell.

The Blue Devils had just lost to Clemson at Cameron Indoor Stadium, and in the postgame press conference one reporter, Steve Politi, took note of how worn out the forty-seven-year-old Krzyzewski seemed and how red his face appeared. Chuck Swenson, the former Duke assistant who had returned from William & Mary to be the Blue Devils' director of basketball operations, also noticed Krzyzewski's face turning beet red while doing some pre-practice stretching with his team. "It scared me," Swenson said. "I had never seen him like that."

Mickie Krzyzewski and others close to the coach described his facial coloring as gray. Chris Collins, a junior guard, thought his coloring was a bit green too. It was hard for the player to look at this great leader he had come to play for. Collins was a Chicago Bulls ball boy when his father Doug was coaching Michael Jordan. Later voted Mr. Basketball in Illinois as a high school star, Collins knew he had to embrace tough coaching because, he said, "I saw the greatest player ever embrace it. So I wanted Coach K to coach me. I wanted him to hold me accountable."

Now the coach was trying to run a team meeting in a crammed lounge area while looking like he'd been run over by a truck. Duke's perpetual source of strength was coming undone, and the Blue Devils didn't know how to react. "I don't think people realize the pressure cooker that players are under when you're at a blue-blood program, where every single game you play . . . the expectations are on you," Collins said. "But you always knew we had Coach K there to be our rock, to be our Superman. And for the very first time for all of us, we saw weakness."

Jim Valvano's death was just the start of a turbulent period for Krzyzew-

ski. In December 1993, Bobby Hurley, a rookie first-round pick of the Sacramento Kings, was nearly killed after a game when a man driving a station wagon without its headlights on broadsided Hurley's SUV in a collision
that ejected the point guard from his vehicle and left him in a drainage
ditch. Hurley would somehow recover from what surgeons described as
catastrophic injuries to return for the 1994–1995 season. Three and a half
months after that accident, Krzyzewski was in Charlotte preparing to lead
his surprising (for a change) Final Four team when he got word that his
middle daughter, sixteen-year-old Lindy, had been mugged outside the
Northgate Mall in Durham. A young man who had motioned that he was
carrying a gun rushed up on her near her Honda Civic, demanded her keys
and purse, and drove away in Lindy's car while she ran inside to inform security. Police arrested a twenty-two-year-old suspect (who was later convicted); there was no evidence that the perpetrator knew the identity of his
victim.

Lindy was rattled but feeling relatively fine by the time she arrived the
following day in Charlotte, where Duke defeated Florida before losing with
valor to a superior Arkansas team. Coach K's off-season then started with
news of academic problems up and down his roster, including four freshmen who would be forced to attend summer school, compelling the Duke
coach to cancel a planned exhibition tour in Australia. "The fact I had to do
it was disappointing, embarrassing, and upsetting to me," Krzyzewski said,
"because I had given my word to a lot of people, especially in Australia." He
expressed frustration that his desire to monitor his players' academic performance was at odds with a policy that restricted the coaches' contact with
professors over that performance. It was an open secret that Krzyzewski
did not have the warmest relationship with Nan Keohane, who had become
president of Duke the previous summer.

When Keohane arrived at Duke after serving as president of Wellesley,
which competed in nonscholarship Division III athletics, she was taken
aback by the significance of men's basketball at the school. "It was a whole
other universe," Keohane said. "I learned as fast as I could what it meant to
preside over such a university."

Krzyzewski made it clear to the new president that he opposed the
school's mandate forcing all freshmen — including the full-scholarship
athletes in revenue sports — to live on East Campus, a bus ride away from
Cameron. Over time, Keohane said, Krzyzewski would be her only head
coach who accepted that fact of Duke life. She also said that Coach K never
made her feel that she was any less of a leader because of her gender. Keohane recognized that he wanted to be taken seriously as an educator, and

she would ask his advice on matters that had nothing to do with how one might counter Dean Smith's playbook.

But when Krzyzewski reviewed the classroom casualties among his players and chose to discuss them for public consumption, he made sure to identify Keohane as one of those who deserved blame.

"No specific person was at fault," he said. "But a lot of us have to share the responsibility for the problem — myself, the president, the players, and a number of others in between . . . I believe we needed some kind of monitoring mechanism to provide players with more support than they've been getting."

Dismayed that his dynastic winning percentage hadn't earned him more administrative backing, encouraged by Mickie to pursue an NBA opportunity, and emboldened by his Dream Team experience and the respect he was granted by Michael Jordan and other NBA icons, Krzyzewski announced in May 1994 that he was "looking at other coaching opportunities." NBA commissioner David Stern wanted him in his league, and a few teams were interested. Among them was the Portland Trail Blazers, who employed a scout and a friend of Krzyzewski's, Keith Drum, formerly of the *Durham Morning Herald,* and who played 10 miles from Nike's Beaverton headquarters. The sneaker giant had given Coach K a $1 million signing bonus (double the amount Dean Smith got to jump from Converse to Nike) and a long-term contract that included stock options and paid him $375,000 a year to put his team's Adidas shoes in the closet for keeps.

"A major setback for us," said Adidas executive Sonny Vaccaro, who had been fired by Nike CEO Phil Knight in 1991, seven years after he'd signed Michael Jordan to his first sneaker deal. "Mike went to my mortal enemy." Krzyzewski said he made the switch to Nike because he felt that "our product wasn't out anywhere, not just in Durham, but nationally."

Krzyzewski pulled back from the Trail Blazers opportunity after a clear-the-air meeting with Keohane and athletic director Tom Butters. He said he didn't see a good enough reason "to leave behind fourteen years of really loving what you do." Coach K began to build a working relationship with Keohane because, well, it made sense to have one. "You want to know the secret to my success?" Krzyzewski asked one of his assistants. "It's always been my ability to collaborate."

He had a great thing going at Duke, yet a miserable summer and fall turned his charmed world in Durham into something else entirely. Krzyzewski suffered what he thought was a left hamstring injury playing racquetball. The condition worsened over time; by the start of practice on October 15, Krzyzewski was in so much pain that he started lying down on the Cameron court while his assistants ran the Blue Devils through drills. On October 19, as part of testing, Dr. Wesley Cook asked Coach K to walk on his toes. When the patient tried doing that with his left foot, it collapsed and turned numb. Cook diagnosed a ruptured disk in his lower back and performed surgery on October 21.

Doctors wanted Coach K off the job for six to twelve weeks, yet Krzyzewski ran a staff meeting at his house two days after he left the hospital and rushed back to practice a week later. "It was a stupid mistake and I paid dearly for it," Krzyzewski said. The Blue Devils were 6-1 when they traveled to Honolulu for the Rainbow Classic in late December, and Krzyzewski spent much of the ten-hour commercial flight from Atlanta in extreme discomfort on the main cabin floor. He made it through a sleepless week on pain pills, leading Duke to two victories in three games. The flight back was no easier than the flight out. Krzyzewski was now trapped in a state of severe exhaustion.

On the night of January 4, 1995, after Duke lost at home to Clemson for the first time in nearly eleven years, some people close to Krzyzewski worried that he might need to quit. Given his run of Final Fours, he had coached many more games over that period than any of his peers. He was also Team USA's head coach in three international competitions from 1987 through 1990, and an assistant coach in '92, while serving on a number of USA Basketball selection committees. He had made countless charitable, professional, and commercial appearances as his brand grew bigger than the university's; granted his full cooperation to a book project; governed his ever-growing basketball camp; and given his time to the board of Jim Valvano's V Foundation for Cancer Research, to Duke Children's Hospital, and to issues concerning the National Association of Basketball Coaches. He had said yes to so many things because he didn't want anyone to think that he had forgotten where he came from.

Dean Smith, who had won his second national title in 1993 to pull into a tie with Krzyzewski, knew this was coming. After Krzyzewski won his first title in '91, Smith wrote him a congratulatory note with this warning attached: "If you think it was bad before, wait 'til now." Nearly four years later, Krzyzewski was physically and mentally fried. He had lost 20 pounds, and his eyes were hollowed out. On returning to coaching, he sat in a special chair, watched practice and even conducted interviews while flat on his back, and leaned against walls and lecterns and anything within reach that would help keep him upright. He didn't walk as much as he staggered about, like a zombie, imprisoned by the stiffness throughout his body. Mickie couldn't take it anymore. She had been married to Mike for more than a quarter-century and had never tempered his maniacal work ethic or stood in the way of his basketball ambitions. She was regarded as Duke's co-head coach, or executive head coach, and was heavily involved in far more than the postseason banquet and the summer basketball camp.

Krzyzewski had left his wife no choice on this one. The night of the Clemson loss, Coach K told her that he would resign the next day. Though he didn't follow through, his body kept insisting that he needed a significant break from coaching. On the morning of January 6, he got up and then quickly returned to bed. He got up again, showered, then returned to bed. He got up a third time, shaved, then returned to bed. He got up a fourth time, dressed, then returned to bed again.

"He looked like he was eighty years old," Mickie said. Scared, she made her way to the kitchen to place a private call to Mike's doctor. She made an appointment for 2:30 p.m. that day, a time that conflicted with the Blue Devils' last practice before they hit the road for a game with Georgia Tech. When Mickie walked back up to the bedroom and told her husband about the appointment, he snapped at her, "I've got to go to practice. We're going to Georgia Tech. I've got to go, I've got to go."

This was Mickie's moment of truth. The people in Mike's professional life — and his doctors — had failed to stop him from damaging himself. "It was almost like everyone in his support system collapsed," she said. Mickie was the last person standing between Krzyzewski and a physical meltdown or nervous breakdown. Or both.

"Mike," she told him, "I've never issued you an ultimatum. This is an ultimatum. It's either basketball or me. If you don't show up at the doctor's office at 2:30, I'll know what you chose."

On her drive to the doctor's, Mickie thought to herself, *Please, God, let him be there.* She pulled into the parking lot, and sure enough, Coach K had made the right choice: he had beaten Mickie to the appointment. Dr. John Feagin, a Class of 1955 West Point graduate who'd served in Vietnam, wasn't about to take any bunk from a Class of '69er. Feagin almost immediately told Krzyzewski that he needed to be hospitalized for his back and extreme fatigue. He allowed the coach to return to Cameron to break the news to his assistants and players that they would face Georgia Tech without him.

Krzyzewski had never missed a practice or a game in his life, and now he had missed one and was about to miss the other. He was not just a West Point man and Army captain taught to overcome all adversity; he was the son of parents who never, ever missed work because of illness. This was not the Emily Krzyzewski way. This was not the William Kross way.

Duke's assistants couldn't believe that the man they saw as an unbreakable machine was breaking down right before their eyes. When healthy, Krzyzewski wore out his assistants after home games with marathon film sessions at his house, ordering Mike Brey or Tommy Amaker to pick up Pizza Hut pies before they sat and reviewed every possession, head to toe, into the morning. The assistants sometimes nodded off during these endless tape reviews while Coach K seemed to maintain the same energy he'd had at halftime hours earlier. Sometimes Brey left Krzyzewski's place so late that he'd pick up the delivered newspaper at the end of the Krzyzewskis' driveway and throw it closer to the house.

"Mike's biggest fear for himself personally is that he will lose his hunger," Mickie said. "He works like a madman to keep it." To anyone who might have been surprised to learn that her husband customarily took a pregame nap, Mickie could offer a disclaimer or two. "It's not a long sleep," she said, "and he wakes up mad."

Now his rage had turned to resignation that he wasn't fit enough to coach the Blue Devils. The players described their meeting with Krzyzewski as stunning and surreal. He had game-planned every detail of every day for them, including his handwritten pre-practice plans that were photocopied and left in a staff assistant's mailbox in case the players wanted to sneak a peek. He had recruited them, developed them, berated them, hugged them, cried with them, laughed with them.

Suddenly he was telling them that they were on their own in Atlanta. "We were out there on the court — this is in practice — and Coach is back there and all the lights are off," Capel recalled. "He said, 'I'm not feeling well. I'm sick. I'm not going to make the trip with you.'" When Krzyzewski said those words, the silence in the room was deafening.

"I'll never forget it," Capel said. "This was, 'Wait a minute. This is the toughest guy, a military guy who accomplished so much. Our leader. The backbone of everything with our program.' It wasn't just the fact that he said he was sick. It was how he looked."

Like death.

KRZYZEWSKI DECIDED THAT Pete Gaudet, who had been with him at Army and was his longest-tenured Duke aide, would serve as the interim head coach until he was cleared by doctors to return. But deep down, Coach K was worried that he might never return. He was forty-seven, Jim Valvano's age at the time of his death, and he had intense back pain, like the former NC State coach. "I thought I had cancer and I was going to die, just like Jimmy had," Krzyzewski told his friend, the author John Feinstein. Back in the hospital for four days starting January 6, he underwent an endless series of tests and scans that showed no signs of cancer or any other serious ill-ness. The doctors told Coach K that rest and physical therapy would allow him to finally heal. Problem was, it was impossible for Krzyzewski to rest while the basketball program he had built into America's finest had started crumbling along with his body.

Gaudet had failed after replacing Krzyzewski at Army, making him a curious choice to temporarily replace Krzyzewski at Duke. He was a fifty-two-year-old advance scout who projected a professorial vibe when teach-ing good big men how to become very good big men. Once earning $75,000 — including about $50,000 to run Krzyzewski's camp — Gaudet had been reduced to what was known as a "restricted earnings coach": he was re-stricted, by a new NCAA rule, to making $16,000 a year while the two full-time assistants per staff allowed by the NCAA (in Duke's case, Brey and Amaker) confronted no such salary cap.

Gaudet landed a part-time position teaching a three-credit coaching class at Duke to supplement his income (while his wife took a job as a sub-stitute teacher) and filed a lawsuit over what he and other coaches regarded as an artificial cap. After the suit was tossed by a North Carolina court, the coaches joined in a class-action antitrust suit against the NCAA.

"I was replacing a legend and making $16,000," Gaudet said. He was sud-denly being asked to fill in for a coach already being compared to John Wooden and leading a relatively thin Duke team through the teeth of its ACC schedule. "I was not given any parameters other than, 'You take the team and see what happens,'" Gaudet said. "I maybe didn't even realize how big it was going to be."

It was not pretty. Gaudet lost his first five games, to ACC opponents, including a double-overtime game with the Virginia Cavaliers, who over-came a 23-point deficit to silence a vocal Cameron crowd energized by the presence of an all-everything Florida recruit named Vince Carter. Dur-ing warm-ups, Carter had stood and waved to the Cameron Crazies who were chanting, "We want Carter." The recruit had spent a couple of hours of his visit with Krzyzewski in the head coach's home at a time when Mickie wasn't allowing her husband to see visitors or even field phone calls from longtime friends.

Any good that visit might have done was canceled out by an incident in the locker room after the game. Chris Collins, who had averaged 10 points and thirty-one minutes for the '94 NCAA finalist, had not been the same player since breaking his foot on the first day of practice. This frustrated his father Doug, the former NBA All-Star and head coach known for his fiery temperament. After his son played only eleven minutes against Virginia and took only one of the team's 61 field-goal attempts, Doug Collins stormed into the Duke locker room and exploded. He berated Gaudet for the way he was using (or not using) his son. "And he got Tommy and me pretty good," Brey said. "Tommy recruited Chris, so he really took it."

Carter was in the locker room at the time of the Collins eruption. "He heard the whole thing," said Johnny Moore, Duke's assistant sports information director. "As Doug left, he made a snide remark to Vince about the fact that he was going to be part of a team with a bunch of shooting guards — good luck." Another witness to the tirade, Bill Brill, a Duke graduate and prominent longtime sportswriter, turned to Moore and said, "Looks like we won't be getting Carter." Two and a half months later, Carter announced his commitment to North Carolina.

Unranked for the first time since December 1986, a period covering 153 Associated Press polls, Duke was blown out at home by North Carolina State to start 0-5 in ACC play for the first time in school history. The losing ate Krzyzewski alive and made him feel guilty. "It was horrible, horrible," Mickie said. "Getting well for him was worse than being sick because he felt he had deserted his men."

Coach K's players were questioning why Gaudet was in the position he was in. "He has always been our big man coach," said senior center Cherokee Parks, one of the three captains. "He was never our Xs and Os guy. Coach G taking over instead of Brey and Amaker never made any sense."

Krzyzewski was so distraught over his condition and the impact of his absence on his team that he offered his resignation to Butters over dinner at the athletic director's home. Coach K was afraid when he made the offer that the AD might actually accept it. "But I knew I needed to say that in order to have the peace of mind going into my rehabilitation," Krzyzewski said. Butters assured him the job would still be his, and only his, whenever he was healthy enough to coach.

The Blue Devils lost at Florida State to make it six defeats in a row, their longest losing streak since Eddie Cameron's team lost seven straight in 1938–1939. Krzyzewski decided that it was time to clarify his status. He met briefly with his assistants that Saturday night, after Duke returned from Tallahassee, giving them a heads-up on what was likely to come the following day. He spent about ninety minutes with the school's sports information director, Mike Cragg, to write up a statement that would be released on Sunday. On January 22, with Mickie by his side, Krzyzewski met with the players to tell them that he would miss the rest of the season.

One of the captains, Kenny Blakeney, said that his coach, looking thin and run-down, cited exhaustion as the principal reason for his extended absence. "If he was a car," Blakeney said, "he'd be running on fumes." The players were stunned: many had assumed that Coach K would miss two games, maybe three, before making a comeback that would inspire a charge toward the NCAA Tournament. Now he was telling them that he would be away for seventeen regular-season games in all, along with a likely ACC Tournament exit that would keep Duke out of the NCAAs for the first time since 1983.

"I feel like I have made good progress in the last couple of weeks, but to return to coaching without a 100 percent time commitment would only hurt the Duke basketball program," Krzyzewski said in his statement. "The indecision of when I would return should be put to rest so the team can move forward. I am confident they will, and the coaching staff and players know I will continue to support them and monitor their progress for the remainder of the year . . . I look forward to coaching basketball at Duke again next season."

After spending those days in the hospital earlier in the month, Coach K was finally showing some improvement at home with his back and his fatigue. Dr. Feagin said that the coach was resting, walking, and undergoing physical therapy. (Krzyzewski was doing some of his walking on Duke's golf course.) "I have no doubt he will return 100 percent healthy in the near future," Feagin said. Butters maintained he was confident that Krzyzewski would be on the bench for the start of the 1995–1996 season. Understanding the weight of the moment, Duke president Nan Keohane also weighed in. "Coach K is a Duke treasure, and we want to take care of our treasures," she said. "We all miss him, and look forward to having him back next year."

The following day, the prominent Raleigh sportswriter Caulton Tudor wrote a column in the *News and Observer* headlined "Coach Needs to Squelch Rumors," calling on Krzyzewski to be more specific in explaining his leave to halt what the writer said was a rumor mill that had been churning nonstop. "Rumors aren't good for anyone," Tudor wrote. Gaudet had also referred to talk of an undisclosed reason for Krzyzewski's sabbatical when he said, "I just did the [coach's] radio show, and I heard the rumors, everything from cancer to leaving coaching."

Krzyzewski's dear friend and teammate from West Point, Jim Oxley, kept calling to check on his guy, but Mickie wouldn't put him through. "She really cut him off," Oxley said. "A lot of people, including myself, thought maybe Mike had some kind of cancer like Valvano had." Mickie eventually assured Oxley that her husband did not have cancer, though Krzyzewski's former backcourt partner and roommate never did get to speak with him during his recovery. One of Coach K's former Army players, a four-star general named Bob Brown, could not get through either. "She was ruthless during that," the general said of Mickie.

Cancer was a popular theory. So was marital discord . . . a severe case of depression . . . a nervous breakdown . . . and even AIDS. Krzyzewski heard it all and joked later that he had compiled a David Letterman Top Ten list of rumors about his forced break from coaching. In part because he wanted to remain invisible for the sake of his team and avoid creating a distraction, Krzyzewski was never moved to make a public statement to quiet the whispers. "Unless you actually show people you're okay, the worst thing you can do is say you don't have AIDS or cancer or marital problems," he would say later. "So you have to indicate you don't have them without actually saying so, without dignifying the rumors."

The Blue Devils did respond to his announcement that he was done for the year by winning a game at Notre Dame, their first victory under Gaudet. A fan sent the interim coach a little trophy to mark the occasion. When the Duke players returned from South Bend, Capel said, they found a handwritten message of congratulations and encouragement from Krzyzewski on the whiteboard in their locker room.

But the feel-good moment was fleeting. Duke lost by two at Maryland, which snapped a fifteen-game losing streak against Krzyzewski's team. The Blue Devils then lost an epic double-overtime game to second-ranked North Carolina in Cameron, first blowing a 12-point second-half lead in regulation, then erasing a 9-point deficit in the final 1:37 of the first overtime. Capel hit an absurd running three-pointer from inside the midcourt line to beat the first-overtime buzzer, turning the place upside down as the Cameron Crazies chanted, "We're not losing." But lose they did. They lost because Carolina dressed Jerry Stackhouse and Rasheed Wallace, who would be the number-three and number-four overall picks in the 1995 NBA draft, just as they'd lost the previous game because Maryland dressed Joe Smith, who would be the number-one overall pick in that draft.

Still, Gaudet was the easiest available target. He had the would-be number-twelve overall pick in Parks and a couple of good young players in Capel and freshman Trajan Langdon, from Anchorage, Alaska, but it was a team in transition that looked a lot more like five individual fingers than Krzyzewski's famous fist.

Duke lost at Clemson, 51–44, giving the Tigers their first season sweep of the Blue Devils since 1977 and earning for themselves their lowest score in a game since 1972. History was haunting Gaudet from gym to gym. The Blue Devils were 0-9 in the conference, their worst ACC start ever. They were beaten to nearly every loose ball, and despite their height advantage, Clemson outrebounded them, 35–20.

During halftime of this Clemson disaster, as Gaudet clinically reviewed his team's mistakes, Brey finally exploded. "Fuck that, Pete, fuck that!" he shouted. "These motherfuckers, we've been holding their hands. Enough!"

Brey and Amaker were growing concerned about what this downward spiral might do to their careers. Krzyzewski had said he looked forward to being back the following season, but he didn't exactly guarantee it. "Tommy, it's probably best for us for it to be a little bit of every man for himself now," Brey told Amaker. "We've got to think of our futures if he doesn't come back."

The assistants and Swenson, the director of basketball operations, ended up in a meeting with Dr. Keith Brodie, the former university president who, as a psychiatrist and teacher, remained a figure of prominence on campus and someone Krzyzewski later called "the best man I've ever known at Duke." Brodie was among the medical professionals who had been working with Krzyzewski; part of his counseling involved showing his patient old tape of himself coaching with passion. "It was more than back pain," Coach K said after watching the video. "I lost emotion. I lost feeling."

Brodie did not put all of the assistants' fears to rest, "but the impression we got from Brodie was . . . that this was Mike's job, and they were not going to take it away from him," Swenson said.

As he started feeling stronger in February, Krzyzewski became a bit more actively involved in the program, though not much changed on the scoreboard. Gaudet finally won an ACC game, at home against Georgia Tech, before losing his next three contests. A victory over Florida State was followed by a blowout nonconference loss at UCLA, and then losses to Maryland and North Carolina to close out the regular season at 2-14 in the ACC.

Krzyzewski was a master of making his players believe in the final, frantic minutes of tense contests. Gaudet had the opposite effect on his team. He was looking more and more haggard with each passing endgame crisis.

"Coach G had that blue shirt on, and he'd be soaking wet," Parks recalled. "He would just be sweating and sweating and sweating. And in Cameron, with the place so loud, he would just be moving his lips and you'd hear no words coming out. You couldn't hear him, and he was just drawing it on the whiteboard."

ACC teams, seeing a weakness in Duke they hadn't seen since the early '80s, attacked with a vengeance. Gaudet was paying for Krzyzewski's ruthless conquests.

After the heartbreaking Maryland game, won by the Terps on Joe Smith's buzzer-beating tip-in, Capel called up Krzyzewski. "I was at wits' end," said the sophomore guard. Coach K told him to grab some food and come over to his house. They would talk, Krzyzewski said later, "the way a coach and player should talk. I missed that. It's not about wins and losses. It's about re-lationships, and I think I was getting away from that."

Capel was more than encouraged by the conversation and by his coach's revived spirit. "I knew he was coming back then," the player said. "It was just a matter of getting through the season."

Krzyzewski asked an old friend, Richard Cardillo, one of Army's basket-ball officer reps, to sit behind the Duke bench during its game at North Car-olina, observe Gaudet and his interaction with the players, and then report back what he heard and saw. Cardillo told Krzyzewski, "I think there's times when [Gaudet] is a good coach, but he spends too much time with the of-ficials. I think you lose sight of what the game's about when you're worried about the officials."

Two days after that game, Coach K launched his comeback at Cam-eron . . . sort of. He appeared before the news media for the first time in more than two months in a peace-in-the-Middle-East-sized press confer-ence that included more than eighty reporters from around the country, national networks, and local TV outlets that interrupted their program-ming to broadcast Krzyzewski live. He was dressed for coaching success in a jacket and tie and looked rejuvenated as he sat at a table on a stage in the south end of the darkened arena, below the two illuminated national cham-pionship banners.

Krzyzewski fielded questions for an hour. Though he described himself as "very scared" over his physical condition, he called some of the rumors about his absence crazy. "I was out because of a bad back," he said. "That was all." He confirmed that he would return for the 1995–1996 season and even left open the possibility that he would rejoin his team in the upcoming NCAA Tournament if Duke somehow won the ACC Tournament and the automatic bid. Krzyzewski chided himself for "trying to go like a twenty-four-year-old" and admitted that he needed to do a lot more delegating in the future to prevent another breakdown. "I'm setting a new list of pri-orities," he said. "My family is at the top, then my team after that, because they're like family." Although he would cut down on his commitments and slash his availability to the local media (much to their dismay), Krzyzewski pledged to remain involved with the Duke Children's Hospital, the V Foun-dation, and the American Cancer Society.

He also pledged to coach the Blue Devils with the same passion that had earned him those seven Final Four trips in nine years. "I'll be as intense," Coach K said. "I wouldn't want to coach again unless I'm as intense. But I plan to be smarter too."

Krzyzewski showed up at practice before Duke played the league's second-worst team, North Carolina State, in the ACC Tournament play-in game in Greensboro for the right to face the league champ, Wake Forest, and its center Tim Duncan. "You could see he had that look back in his eye," Collins said. And then the Blue Devils went out and beat NC State, with Krzyzewski watching back at home. "Just seeing Coach K at practice helped us," Collins said.

Before the Blue Devils faced Wake Forest, Swenson approached the senior team manager, Jeff LaMere, with word that Krzyzewski wanted to speak to the team by phone. The staff had to feed Coach K's call into a microphone in a hotel ballroom. "It was very surreal," LaMere said. "You have this voice coming over the speakers into the meeting room where you're eating your meal. It was the voice of God coming in to guide you, and it would have been tremendous had we won the game."

Krzyzewski's command voice did ignite the Blue Devils, who took a stunning 31–13 lead over the number-one seed in the middle of the first half before reality set in. Wake's Randolph Childress went wild on his way to 40 points. Duke lost by 17 and broke its streak of eleven straight NCAA Tournament appearances. Krzyzewski thanked the coaches and players for losing with dignity. Many of the players felt that they had let down those who came before them, the Hills and Hurleys and Laettners. In his heart of hearts, Coach K was embarrassed by what had become of his team. Duke finished with a 13-18 record, the most losses in school history. Years later, Krzyzewski would tell Cherokee Parks, speaking of the 1994–1995 Blue Devils, "It's like having a hub on a bicycle wheel. If you don't have the hub, the spokes just flap around. I was the hub."

Now things were going to have to change in Durham, and one longtime friendship was going to have to be sacrificed along the way.

PETE GAUDET SCORED a courtroom victory in May when U.S. District Judge Kathryn Vratil did away with the NCAA's restricted-earnings rule. There was only one problem:

Mike Krzyzewski had already fired him.

"Mike said that we needed some new blood around here, there was something lacking," recalled Gaudet, who would stay on at Duke as a teacher.

When Mike Brey left for the head coaching job at Delaware in April, Krzyzewski did not initially give his papal blessing. He told Brey that he shouldn't sell himself short, but Coach K was never happy when coaches left him. "He was Coach Knight-ing me a bit at that point," Brey said.

But he wanted Gaudet out, despite their long-standing friendship. The two men disagreed on the role assigned freshman Steve Wojciechowski, a thick grinder who played the point. Krzyzewski wanted Wojo to play more, and Gaudet not so much. Coaches on the same staff disagree on players' roles all the time, so there was more to it than that.

Krzyzewski did want his staff to get younger and more energetic. He wanted assistants in the age range of Tommy Amaker, who was about to turn thirty. He promoted twenty-eight-year-old grad assistant Quin Snyder, his former point guard, and brought in thirty-one-year-old Tim O'Toole, a highly caffeinated Syracuse assistant who, as a boy, had written Krzyzewski a letter about Army's defense in a game against Iona and a terrible block-charge call made in the Gaels' favor; Coach K had responded three days later with a note and an application to his summer camp, and a relationship was born.

"Our kids believe in them and in their enthusiasm," Krzyzewski said of Snyder and O'Toole. "I'm going to try riding that for a while. I feel very enthusiastic, but I don't want to go to the party alone. Sometimes in the past I've felt I've been a little too much the source of enthusiasm."

Gaudet was perhaps the nation's best professor of the post, but as a lower-energy guy he was voted off the island. (Donna Keane, Krzyzewski's longtime staff assistant, would also leave.) Gaudet wound up stuffed into a tiny office in Card Gym, next door to Cameron. The nameplate on his office carried, not his name, but the word STORAGE. He taught a class on coaching and others on basketball and tennis skills. "He was persona non grata," said one player who adored him.

Duke sports information director Mike Cragg called the NCAA to ask which coach, Krzyzewski or Gaudet, should be assigned the Blue Devils' 4-15 record in Coach K's absence. The NCAA advised the SID that Duke could make whatever decision it wanted to make on wins and losses. Cragg said that he made the call to put the 4-15 on Gaudet's record, and that Krzyzewski was not aware of his decision when it was made.

"I was one of three or four people who knew [Krzyzewski] was not coming back," Cragg said. "If [Krzyzewski] was coaching the team from home or watching tape or calling in directions, it's a debatable issue."

One friend to Krzyzewski and Gaudet, Bob Seigle, a former Army player and a member of the West Point selection committee that hired Krzyzewski, saw the firing as a move shaped by academy training. "Mike learned a lesson at West Point that most guys up there instilled in us," Seigle said. "There's only one commander . . . Mike knew the only way to get his arms around the thing was to take charge of it himself. It was drilled into us in our Army career. You never let the old guy stay."

But Seigle saw no West Point values in the decision to saddle Gaudet with those fifteen losses. "Mike turned over the reins of the team to Pete," Seigle said, "but in my mind he never stopped being the head coach . . . I didn't have any problem with him telling Pete that he couldn't stay. They had to reestablish that there's a new sheriff back in town, but when they decided to stick all the losses on Pete, I thought that was a little hokey."

Gaudet said that he found out the 4-15 record was all his by reading about it in *USA Today*, and that it didn't bother him. Meanwhile, Krzyzewski focused on getting more involved in recruiting and getting to really know the prospects as he used to when he landed those banner-hanging stars. Duke recruits weren't quite what they used to be. The Blue Devils had brought in Joey Beard, a six-foot-ten McDonald's All-American who transferred to Boston University after only one year, and six-foot-ten Canadian Greg Newton, who arrived with Beard in 1993 and stayed at Duke, but whose suspension for reportedly cheating in a computer science class advanced the program's academic woes and made him one of Krzyzewski's least favorite players. (Newton was not a fan of Coach K's either.)

Just as he wanted to hire younger assistants, Krzyzewski wanted to sign tougher recruits, the kind of players who wouldn't allow a program to go from NCAA finalist one year to NCAA doormat the next. That was a priority. So was managing his time by cutting out USA Basketball selection committee and NABC duties and reducing speaking engagements, media sessions, commercial opportunities, and pop-up requests for his attention. "It was time to be like a human being again," Krzyzewski said, "instead of this person who just gets everything done."

Over the summer Krzyzewski spent some time with Mickie in New York and at their Carolina beach house; by the beginning of the fall semester, he declared himself physically and emotionally fit to start the second act of his already historic collegiate career. He also brought in a time management consultant to ensure that he didn't slip back into some bad habits. "I think it's a pivotal year for Duke basketball, for Mike Krzyzewski, for our whole family," Mickie said.

The 1995–1996 Blue Devils were not a talented or deep team, even before sophomore Trajan Langdon was lost for the year with a knee injury and senior forward Tony Moore was dismissed for academic reasons. Five original walk-ons ended up playing for Duke over the course of the season, including three soccer players; Krzyzewski knew early on that he had to do some of the best coaching of his life to keep this team afloat.

On the first official day of practice in October, he couldn't let his players see his doubts about their skill, or his doubts about his own ability to lead them while on the mend. "In our first team meeting he was so excited to be there," O'Toole said. "He knew he had some fragile guys who had just gotten their heads beaten in . . . so he wanted to make sure they knew that, 'Hey, the Rock of Gibraltar just showed up, and every one of you can now get behind me and follow me and I'm not going to let you down.'"

During that first practice, Chris Collins said, everyone had their tongues dragging on the court. "And that wasn't there last year," he recalled. Collins had never seen Krzyzewski as animated and enthusiastic as he was now.

The year started promisingly enough with three victories and a tournament championship at the Great Alaska Shootout, including a 70–64 decision over the General, Bob Knight. Unlike their meeting at the 1992 Final Four, there were no theatrics between Knight and Krzyzewski, just routine interaction between two coaches who acted as if they were mere acquaintances. Before the tournament, Krzyzewski had described the state of his relationship with Knight for *Sports Illustrated*: "It's not as close as it was, because you grow apart running your own programs. But it's good even if our contact isn't as frequent . . . I wish we were closer, and it's a little bit sad, really."

Of greater importance in Alaska, Collins, his foot healthy and his chosen coach back on the sideline, delivered a career-high 30 points and 7 assists in the title-game victory over tenth-ranked Iowa, giving unranked Duke its second straight win over a Top 25 team and reason to believe that this season could signal a return to business as usual in Durham. Ricky Price scored 25 in the final, and Steve Wojciechowski made clutch endgame plays against Indiana and Iowa. Players who had various issues under Gaudet were suddenly whole again under Coach K. The Blue Devils were so moved by an actual winning streak that a couple of them were crying in the locker room. "They're crying for good reasons instead of reasons they cried for last year," Krzyzewski said. They were ranked twelfth in the next Associated Press poll.

But by the time they arrived at North Carolina State's Reynolds Coliseum on January 18, the Blue Devils were back in a 1994–1995 frame of mind. They were 0-4 in the ACC after collapsing against Virginia, and they entered the game in Raleigh having lost eighteen of their last twenty conference games. The players were not the only members of the program who were down on themselves. "I don't even want to coach this team anymore," Krzyzewski told close associates.

"He was really frustrated," said one Duke assistant. "He'd started talking like, 'If we don't get this recruit, I'm not coming back.' He started mentioning ultimatums. 'If we don't get Vince Carter, I'm not going to be back.' There was a point after the back injury, to be honest, when Mike wasn't Mike. Before that he was the most levelheaded, smartest guy in the room. All of a sudden he started making statements that, it wasn't the Mike I know. He'd never say that."

This had been a far more difficult season than Krzyzewski had envisioned. He said that the surprising success in Alaska "created an illusion that our team was better than it was." The reality of the season, O'Toole said, was that Collins, Capel, and Price had to score in bunches for Duke to win games. "And if they didn't," the assistant said, "we had no chance." When they were down late at NC State, Krzyzewski even switched his motion offense to the flex offense — a simplistic exercise in junior-high screening and passing — to get his team untracked.

The Blue Devils were losing by two to the Wolfpack in the closing seconds when Collins decided to break the designed play. He was supposed to execute a dribble handoff to Price, but as the two teammates converged Collins recalled that the last time Duke ran this action, both NC State defenders followed Price. So this time Collins kept the ball on what was effectively a play-action fake, the two defenders jumped Price, and the Duke senior fired an open three-pointer from a few feet behind the arc. The ball hit the rim, bounced straight up, and hung there for what felt like an eternity.

The ball dropped back onto the rim, rattled around, and finally fell through the net to give Duke the lead with 5.5 seconds left. "I think it hit the rim five times," Collins said. NC State's Curtis Marshall raced the length of the floor and put up a final shot that hung on the rim, rolled around it, and dropped harmlessly to the court as the Duke players and coaches jumped for joy.

Krzyzewski was seen after the game crying on the shoulder of his first-born, Debbie. He had needed this one more than any of his players.

It was an extremely emotional time for him. Krzyzewski had earlier learned that his eighty-four-year-old mother Emily had been diagnosed with breast cancer; he missed some practices to fly to Chicago to spend time with her. Coach K was also enduring the stressful final stages of the trial of the suspect who had robbed and carjacked his daughter Lindy in 1994. After the man was convicted and sentenced to eight years in prison, his sister approached Mickie inside Durham Superior Court — with the jurors still seated — and screamed at the top of her lungs, "I'm going to get you," compelling Durham police to monitor the Krzyzewski home and the Duke bench (a plainclothes detective sat behind it during games).

Mickie did her own policing of her husband and his staff during the season, just to make sure the head coach who had broken down in 1994–1995 was surrounded by as much support as possible. "Rightfully so, during every time-out, I'm never looking up . . . and worrying what's going on with X, Y, and Z," O'Toole said. "Mickie would be watching you. Are we supporting Mike? I'd never look up. No winks into the crowd, no TV cameras. She had to have his back, the girls had to have his back, because if they didn't, who did? . . . Mickie was all of our mothers."

Meanwhile, after splitting their conference games following the breakthrough victory in Raleigh, the Blue Devils were barely hanging on at 13-10 overall, and 4-7 in the ACC. Krzyzewski then made his coaching move of the year. He sat down with Collins in the locker room the day before the Virginia game at Cameron on February 14 and acted like he was about to spend considerable time reviewing film with him. "We watched one clip and he turned it off," Collins said. Krzyzewski moved his chair close to his player's and told him, "Listen, you have five conference games left. You're a senior, and you're the heart and soul of this team. You're the captain."

And then Coach K grabbed Collins by the arm. "Listen, in these last six games I want you to go out and play as if you can do no wrong. Play as if nothing is a failure. Shoot when you want to shoot, say what you want to say to a teammate. I'm not going to take you out unless you ask for a sub. I believe in you. I love you. I want you to go down swinging."

Collins said it was the most powerful meeting he ever had with his coach. "I felt like a million bucks," he said. Collins responded like he was worth more. Suddenly, he was a whirling dervish out there, draining jumpers, driving to the goal, making sweet passes, even running down rebounds, scoring 23 against Virginia in a 10-point victory.

Collins scored 12 against NC State before ripping off 27-point games against Florida State, UCLA, and Maryland. Krzyzewski then flew to Chicago for funeral services for Emily Krzyzewski's sister, Aunt Mary, and spending some time with his own stricken mother before returning to Durham for one more tussle with Dean Smith. Collins scored 18 points in the first twenty-five minutes against North Carolina in the final regular-season game of his career, but then suffered another foot injury that helped end Duke's five-game winning streak.

An 18-12 overall record and relatively strong finish to the season (despite the opening-round ACC Tournament loss to Maryland, without Collins) was enough to earn Duke an eighth seed in the NCAA Tournament, a date with Eastern Michigan in the first round, and a chance to review what was advertised as a bridge season. "It has been a helluva bridge," Coach K said.

Truth be told, though Krzyzewski's back felt good, the season turned out to be much harder on him than his wife or other family members anticipated. "It required so much more of Mike," Mickie said. "Coming off last year, we kind of thought that X percent of Mike would be devoted to basketball, and it took up a much larger percent than we hoped it would."

Coach K and his assistants were proud that they made something out of next-to-nothing through sheer physical and emotional effort. They knew they had to recruit more talent to elevate the program back into Final Four contention. This Duke team had no margin for error. As they surveyed the roster minus the injured Trajan Langdon, the coaches all wondered how the hell they squeezed 18 wins out of this group, a fact that made Krzyzewski's quick turnaround all the more impressive.

"He's done as good a coaching job this year as he's done in his life," Mickie said. NBA teams noticed, as they always did, and fresh rumors connected Coach K to a new school close to his hometown, Illinois, as Lou Henson's successor. A year after it seemed he was falling apart and on the verge of walking away, Krzyzewski declared publicly that he wanted to meet with President Keohane and Tom Butters to secure a long-term contract extension.

"I hope there will be an announcement when the season ends about my continuing commitment to Duke — to build the program back to where it has been," he said.

The distance between where Duke basketball had been and where it was now never looked greater than in the opening round of the NCAAs. The Blue Devils could not keep pace with Eastern Michigan's five-foot-five Earl Boykins, who scored 23 in the 75–60 victory. Duke lost in the first round of the NCAAs for the first time since 1955, and yet this would go down as one of Krzyzewski's most important teams ever.

This was the team that stabilized a program in chaos. "I thought it was a great year for us," Krzyzewski said. Duke had taken its first baby step back toward national championship contention, and Krzyzewski would no longer ask himself if he still wanted to coach this team. His world was back in order . . . at least until it was shattered all over again.

EMILY KRZYZEWSKI DIED on Friday, September 6, inside St. Mary of Nazareth Hospital. Mike had flown up on Monday to join his older brother

Bill, the Chicago Fire Department captain, at her bedside. He got to say the goodbyes he didn't get to say to his father twenty-seven years earlier.

Emily was Chicago tough. Krzyzewski told his assistants about the time his mother, then seventy-five, was jumped by three young men after she stepped off a bus. They wanted her purse, and she wouldn't let go of it, inspiring the would-be thieves to give up and run away. According to Tim O'Toole, Krzyzewski said that he told his mother, "Ma, just give them the damn pocketbook," and that Emily shot him a look and responded, "Hey, Michael, your father gave me that pocketbook. It's the only thing I have left from him, and they're going to have to kill me to take it."

Three years before Coach K's mother died, Duke had been in town to play the first two rounds of the NCAAs. Emily Krzyzewski made cookies for them on that trip, because that's what she did.

Krzyzewski talked about his mom nonstop, and called her after every single game. She watched or listened to all of his games while sitting in the West Point rocking chair that her son had gifted her. One visitor to her home, Jimmy Oxley, Mike's old Army backcourt partner, said the handles of the rocking chair were worn black from all the nervous rubbing Emily did during those games.

When she wasn't asleep in the final days of her life, Emily did some laughing and crying with her boys. She always had a fondness for laughing; it was her go-to move. Her generosity of spirit was no less present than Mike's intensity. "She was as happy a person as I've ever been around," Coach K said.

Emily kept a handwritten journal of every game her son coached over twenty-one seasons at Army and Duke, including the name of every opponent and every score, the date of the game, and a *W* or an *L* to signify a win or a loss. Krzyzewski had no idea that his mother was keeping score of his professional life at home. He cried again when his brother sent him that steno pad and Emily's rosary beads after her death.

Funny, but even after her son led Duke to all those Final Fours, Emily forever worried that he was one losing streak away from getting fired. She couldn't get over how a cleaning lady and an elevator operator, both without a high school diploma, could have raised one of America's most recognizable men. One day while sitting on the porch with her son, Emily asked Mike, "How did this all happen?" The fame. The fortune. The whole world at his feet.

"Because of you," Krzyzewski told her.

"C'mon, c'mon," Emily responded.

"Mom, if I could do as well in what I do with the resources I have as you did with what you had, I'd be unbelievable. Mom, you did better than me. I'll never be that good."

Father Francis Rog, Mike's geometry teacher and father confessor at Weber High, presided over the Funeral Mass at St. Helen. The family asked that donations be made to the V Foundation in lieu of flowers. Emily was buried at St. Adalbert Cemetery in Niles, Illinois, next to her husband William, whose original tombstone carried the name Kross before Emily had it replaced with a tombstone bearing the name Krzyzewski. Emily's tombstone was graced by the image of the Virgin Mary, William's by the image of Jesus Christ.

A devastated Coach K returned to Duke as his mother's son. He carried her rosary in his shirt pocket during games and prayed for her in the small hours of the night. "The bus that you drive, make sure it's the right one," Emily had told her younger son in his schoolboy days. "Make sure that you only let good people on it."

Mike Krzyzewski had already driven his bus to places an immigrant's daughter couldn't fathom. It was time to steer it back onto a championship course.

11

AGONY

H<small>E WAS BACK</small> in the national championship game, back where he belonged, and there was a feeling that order had been restored to college basketball. Four years after the sport cut him in half, Mike Krzyzewski had returned with a vengeance. His mighty Blue Devils were ready once again to rule the world.

Only this Duke program was not your older brother's Duke program. The Blue Devils were dominant, yes, entering this 1999 NCAA final matchup against the University of Connecticut with a 37-1 record and old-timers debating where they stood among the all-time great teams.

The one loss had been to Cincinnati in November at the Great Alaska Shootout (a homecoming event for Trajan Langdon), right after Duke beat a Fresno State team coached by Krzyzewski's old friend Jerry Tarkanian. When talking to his team before the game, Coach K accidentally referred to Fresno as "the Runnin' Rebels" more than once. In the Cincinnati game, the Bearcats needed to execute a perfect full-court play in the closing seconds to beat Duke. It was a close replica of the Hill-to-Laettner play, with a twist: near the foul line, Kenyon Martin rose up to catch Ryan Fletcher's long baseball pass and then redirected it to a teammate racing alone down the right side, Melvin Levett, who dunked to give Cincinnati a two-point lead. Duke somehow pulled off a more miraculous play with one second left, throwing its own baseball pass to six-foot-eight center Elton Brand; the sophomore tipped it to classmate William Avery, who banked in a shot that would have forced overtime had officials not correctly ruled that it came after the buzzer.

That's how close the Blue Devils came to showing up at Tropicana Field in St. Petersburg with a 38-0 record and a chance to be the first unbeaten champion since the 1976 Indiana Hoosiers. And yet, as often as this Duke team was being compared to the early '90s Duke powerhouse, so much had changed about the program, the players, and the head coach managing both. The younger assistants Krzyzewski brought in after the dreadful 1994–1995 season had some fresh ideas that they imposed on their older boss.

"We had to try to change the image and say, 'Hey, we are preppies no more,'" said one of those assistants, Tim O'Toole.

Mickie Krzyzewski was largely behind one change — to occasionally keep the blue and white in the closet and put Duke players in black uniforms on the road, to add an edge to the team's image. Mickie put her stamp on just about everything, from running the annual postseason banquet, producing video tributes to departing seniors, picking a theme (and supervising the photo shoots) for the annual team poster, and dining with job applicants and recruits at the Washington Duke Inn. She sometimes shared lunch with coaches and recruits in the on-campus Oak Room and made her feelings known about whether or not the prospects were Duke material.

She also continued to oversee her husband's schedule, making sure he didn't overdo it; if that meant some prominent national writers accustomed to extra access to Coach K left Durham disappointed, so be it. "She's Mama Goose, brother," said one player. "She ran the show, bro, no doubt about it. Players knew really quick upon meeting her who wore the pants in that household."

Example: Elton Brand was preparing to do a photo shoot as a Playboy All-American — at least until he received word that Mickie did not appreciate what *Playboy* stood for. "Once I heard that," Brand was, "no way I was taking that picture." So if Mickie wanted Duke's uniforms to make a more forceful statement on certain nights, that's what was going to happen. One player described those black unis as a powerful source of energy. "It was like, 'Hey, man, how do we get people buying our gear so Duke was cool?'" O'Toole said. "Years ago the cool teams were UNLV and Georgetown. But no, we are Duke. We're going to get the best of the best. We are preppies no more. We want to be great."

Tweaking team uniforms would only go so far. To return to dominance, Duke needed to change the way it recruited. Some members of the program thought that Krzyzewski had tried too hard to replicate his Christian Laettner and Bobby Hurley teams, forgetting that Laettner and Hurley were once-in-a-generation players. Big men such as Greg Newton, Joey Beard, and Taymon Domzalski struggled, and point guard Steve Wojciechowski did not perform at the Hurley level; Duke had gotten too white in a sport where the vast majority of outstanding players were Black.

Krzyzewski's assistants talked privately about race, but not publicly. For the record, they talked about opening up the process and pursuing high school players who didn't necessarily come from traditional Duke backgrounds, an approach that was not met by administration resistance. University president Nan Keohane had been a nontraditional student at Wellesley, an ultra-elite Northeastern institution for women not used to embracing middle-class girls from small Arkansas high schools. Keohane believed that Krzyzewski would not push to admit a student-athlete who was incapable of doing the work at Duke, as it wasn't in anyone's interest for a recruit to flunk out. Christoph Guttentag, the university's director of undergraduate admissions, watched this process closely every year to ensure that every recruited ballplayer had a legitimate chance to earn a degree.

"The whole landscape was changing," O'Toole said. "Let's not pigeonhole ourselves. We're going to recruit everybody we thought could help Coach K try to dominate college basketball again."

This new approach was spearheaded by one particularly charismatic figure: Quin Snyder. "As avant-garde an out-of-the-box thinker as you'd ever meet," O'Toole said. "A genius."

On the surface, Snyder was a Duke graduate out of central casting. As an undergrad, he double-majored in political science and philosophy, and he now owned a law degree, an MBA, and a cool head of Leonardo DiCaprio hair. Snyder started Blue Planet, a newsletter to send out to recruits, and Aladdin, a life-after-Duke network for players to support one another. In the early days of everyday internet use, once computers were finally added to the basketball offices, Snyder used technology to transform Krzyzewski's mom-and-pop operation into a modern business. With the help of staffers and managers, he used proprietary desktop software to add eye-grabbing visuals to recruiting materials and to establish a spreadsheet that helped identify the prospects who best fit Duke basketball.

The basketball program came a long way with technology in a short period of time. Assistants started tracking the performances and the comings and goings of their top recruits on newspaper websites and communicated with them and their coaches by email.

"We got ahead of some ACC and big-time schools," O'Toole said. "We knew we had to, because we were in last place."

Snyder and O'Toole pushed Krzyzewski to expand his reach in the perpetual hunt for talent by strengthening relationships with AAU coaches and assorted middlemen. A native of White Plains, New York, O'Toole had played for the Riverside Church program run by Ernie Lorch. Elton Brand, a top Duke target from Peekskill, New York, had played AAU ball for Lorch and a Syracuse coach named Mickey Walker, who ran a traveling team of former collegians known as the Upstate All-Stars that competed against Division I schools for a fee.

Walker said that the typical major college program paid him about $10,000 per exhibition, and that Duke paid him that amount. It was all legal — under NCAA law — when O'Toole helped Duke schedule a series of games over three years with the Upstate All-Stars while recruiting Walker's former player, Brand, but the approximately $30,000 arrangement caught the attention of rival schools. Duke beat Upstate by 11 in 1996, by 54 the following year, and by 53 the year after that, when Upstate was known as Team Fokus. Brand contributed a combined 41 points and 20 rebounds for the Blue Devils in those last two games.

"I wasn't as close to Elton at that point; he wasn't playing for me anymore," Walker said. "I don't think I had much to do with Elton going to Duke." Walker did say that he had a good relationship with Krzyzewski, O'Toole, Snyder, and other Duke assistants.

O'Toole left Durham after two years to work for another departing Duke assistant, Tommy Amaker, who had become the new head coach at Seton Hall. Former Blue Devils Johnny Dawkins and David Henderson filled the staff void in 1997, when Snyder was promoted to associate head coach. "Quin would push things as close to the line as he could," said one Duke athletics official, "and it made Coach K uncomfortable . . . I don't know about any breaking of rules at Duke, but he was aware of people you had to call. You had to call handlers, and Coach K didn't want to deal with that BS."

Krzyzewski usually fell in love with his point guards, and Snyder was no exception. He had fought through migraines while playing for Coach K, and theirs was described by many as a father-son type of relationship.

"But Quin always had a thousand plays he wanted Coach K to run," the official said, "and they would butt heads sometimes . . . They're both very stubborn in their approach, and they're both super-smart. Quin had a savant mentality with Xs and Os, and he would be frustrated and feel, 'I think I have a better concept.' Quin is an amazing guy, a super guy, and he was anxious to be a head coach because he had a million ideas."

The Blue Devils were fascinated by Snyder's relationship with Krzyzewski. During one NCAA Tournament game, Coach K yelled at Snyder for not delivering a message to Brand, and then lit into him during halftime for not getting him the first-half stats sooner, making the assistant jump, one columnist planted behind the bench wrote, "as if someone had set off a cherry bomb at his feet."

"I saw tension between them," one player said. "I think I saw jealousy from K to Quin. K snapped at Quin more than any coach or any player combined, and when he did it, it felt personal. It wasn't, 'Do your fucking job.' It was, 'Stop thinking of the next thing, Quin, and do your job.' That's what was profound to me."

Snyder looked at the game more analytically than did Krzyzewski, who was never considered by his peers to be a master strategist, especially on the offensive side of the ball. Staffers would say that Snyder explained the game in detailed ways they never heard Coach K explain it, and that he was more in tune with the development of the individual player, physically and mentally, while his boss forever focused on team-first values.

During stressful times in Shane Battier's freshman year, Snyder took the forward to his office to breathe together with him silently. Battier said Snyder had so many ideas "just shooting out of all parts of his body. His brain works so fast, he doesn't have time to write 'em all down."

Krzyzewski believed in giving his assistants plenty of leeway, in allowing them to learn from their own mistakes. He invited his staff to push innovative ideas. "But you really have to go to bat for them; he'll fight it," said one staffer close to Coach K.

Snyder was not afraid of that fight. He had the benefit of knowing that the Krzyzewski women — Mickie and daughters Debbie, Lindy, and Jamie — were all big fans of his. While other assistants arrived early for the daily 10 a.m. staff meeting, honoring the boss's West Point ethos, Snyder would march in a minute or two late with a smile on his face, a breakfast sandwich in one hand and a giant Starbucks cup in the other, and think nothing of it. Quin was the brilliant absent-minded professor who was constantly losing his cell phone and Duke ID, but he had a lot of balls. "And he was a master of attacking the gray areas," said one Duke assistant coach.

For a long time, scarred by the calls for his firing in the early days, Krzyzewski wanted nothing to do with Duke boosters; Snyder loosened that position and connected him with a Duke graduate and Snyder mentor, Morgan Stanley CEO John Mack. When Krzyzewski complained to aides that the AD who replaced the retired Tom Butters in 1998, Joe Alleva — Coach K's racquetball partner — was too tight on funding, Snyder was a strong voice in pursuing alternative revenue sources such as the Legacy Fund, a fundraising organization that was established by Duke sports information director Mike Cragg and consisted of partners who donated a minimum of $1 million to support the basketball program. Krzyzewski saw the Legacy Fund as a means of building a new practice facility and sustaining the program beyond his own coaching days.

But Snyder's value to Krzyzewski was best measured on the recruiting trail, where he was helped by staffers Lee Rashman and Anne Wilson. One prime example was Snyder's work on a gregarious six-foot-six forward named Chris Carrawell, who was raised by a single mother in a north St. Louis neighborhood that did not fit the profile of a Duke training ground. "When it rained outside it would rain in my house," Carrawell said. "We didn't have a kitchen table. My mom and my sisters and brothers, we slept in one room, with no TV. They slept on one mattress with no springs, and I slept on another mattress with my sister. You got bars on the windows, and on our front door were bars. You had to have bars. The little shit you did have, you wouldn't have if you didn't have bars."

Carrawell's uncle Maurice credited Snyder for winning over his nephew by focusing on the post-basketball value of a Duke degree. Carrawell was floored by the whole process. "You don't have a guy from the inner city who gets recruited by Coach K and Duke University," he said. "We were on welfare. We had gangs, drugs, it was fuckin' tough. And I had an opportunity to go to Duke. Are you kidding me?"

Carrawell called his mother Joanne a superhero for shepherding her family through the turbulence. Joanne, a longtime postal worker, wanted Chris to go to Duke because Krzyzewski promised her that her son would graduate; that was all she wanted to hear. And Duke wanted Chris Carrawell, who had battled through major shoulder injuries, because it needed to toughen up a Charmin soft roster.

Along with Coach K's first transfer, Roshown McLeod from St. John's, Carrawell raised the intensity of Duke practices to a place, O'Toole said, "where people were fighting every day for their lives." Carrawell also helped persuade other recruits from challenging backgrounds that the Blue Devils were now a viable option for them.

"I hosted Elton Brand, who was raised by a single mom," Carrawell said. "He sees me at Duke and he's like, 'Maybe I can do this.' Will Avery comes from a single-parent household. Duke hadn't had those guys."

Brand said that Carrawell's presence and his stories about inner-city St. Louis were difference-makers for him. On his visit, he said, the university "did not feel like the elitist, preppy, or I'm-better-than-you Duke." The fact that Coach K gave a shot to a kid like Carrawell made Brand feel at ease in Durham.

"Chris, for Duke, was a marginal student," Krzyzewski said. "But he's not a marginal person . . . A lot of students here were not aware of Chris's world.

He's given all the people a different view. He's gotten a street education and a Duke education, and he's shown he can be successful in both cultures."

Carrawell became one of the most significant players in the program's history, as his presence helped Duke land the monster recruiting class that followed and included four Parade All-Americans (Brand, Chris Burgess, Battier, and Avery). Duke's Fab Four. "All of a sudden C-Well gave Duke a lot of street cred," said the six-foot-eight Battier, the son of a Black father and white mother from a tree-lined Detroit suburb who was more representative of the traditional Duke recruit. "It opened up a whole new silo of recruits from tougher parts of urban areas." With the Duke student body being predominantly white and upper-class, one coach noted that many African American athletes spent their social time at North Carolina Central, the historically Black university just three and a half miles away. "Chris was the main guy who bridged those worlds for us," the coach said.

Though he missed six weeks of his freshman season with a broken foot, Brand was planning to enter the 1998 NBA draft. He thought he would be a top-twenty pick, and that was good enough for him. He discussed his plans with Krzyzewski, who argued that another college season would make the center a top-five pick and land him on the cover of magazines and in the Final Four. Coach K explained that NBA franchises invest so much more in top-five draft choices than in later first-rounders, and besides, wouldn't it be nice to reach the national semifinals after the Blue Devils closed the 1997–1998 season by blowing a 17-point second-half lead to Kentucky in the Elite Eight?

The Wildcats' Wayne Turner blew past Steve Wojciechowski, the National Association of Basketball Coaches Defensive Player of the Year, in the game's defining moments, and the ending reminded everyone who watched it of the 1992 Duke-Kentucky classic. The Blue Devils inbounded the ball from their own end with 4.5 seconds left (instead of 2.1 seconds). Battier threw a short pass to William Avery (instead of Grant Hill's baseball pass to Christian Laettner). And Avery, who said he had "all the images of Laettner's shot playing in my head," launched a buzzer-beating runner that slammed off the backboard (instead of Laettner's perfect buzzer-beating swish).

Brand delivered a disappointing performance — four points and two rebounds before fouling out — in what he thought would be his final game at Duke, at least until he had that meeting with Krzyzewski, who successfully recruited him back to school for his sophomore season. And then Brand had to tell his mother Daisy, who had raised him by herself in public housing in Peekskill; Elton had never known his father.

Mike Krzyzewski (standing, third from left), his best friend Dennis "Moe" Mlynski (standing to Krzyzewski's immediate left), and the rest of the Columbos were a gang in name only. *Courtesy: Dennis Mlynski*

At Weber High, Mike Krzyzewski was the two-time leading scorer of the Chicago Catholic League. *Courtesy: Doug Ternik, Chicago Catholic League*

Mike Krzyzewski, West Point man, was born to play the point guard position. *Courtesy: Army Athletic Association/U.S. Army Photo*

At the academy, Mike Krzyzewski would play for the man who had the greatest influence on his basketball career, Army coach Bob Knight. *Courtesy: Army Athletic Association/U.S. Army Photo*

Bob Knight did not want Mike Krzyzewski to shoot at Army, even though Mike had good form on his jumper. *Courtesy: Army Athletic Association/U.S. Army Photo*

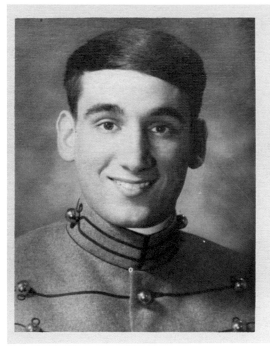

MICHAEL WILLIAM KRZYZEWSKI
Chicago, Illinois   E—3

Krzyzewski, pronounced Kriz-il-lon-ski or some other variation, has made a name for himself amongst the rest of the cream. Whether on the basketball court or in the phone booth Mick has shown his spirit and endurance. His humble manner and dynamic personality has made him the leader of the Sesumarongi, a backwards tribe but all around us. In all seriousness, we are confident that Mike's success in the future will rank with such notables as Durante, DeBergerac and Pinocchio.

Basketball 4, 3, 2, Captain 1; Fine Arts Forum 3, 2, 1; KDET 3; Behavioral Science Club 2; 1969 Class Committee 2, 1.

They made fun of Mike Krzyzewski's name, and his nose, next to his 1969 Army yearbook photo. *Courtesy: Army Athletic Association/U.S. Army Photo*

Mike Krzyzewski was only twenty-eight when he was named a Division I head coach at West Point. *Courtesy: Army Athletic Association/U.S. Army Photo*

Mike Krzyzewski and his Army staff, including future West Point head coach and Duke University interim head coach Pete Gaudet (far left). *Courtesy: Army Athletic Association/U.S. Army Photo*

Even as a young Division I coach, Mike Krzyzewski could work the sideline with the best of them. *Courtesy: Army Athletic Association/U.S. Army Photo*

Gary Winton was the powerful West Point force who helped land Mike Krzyzewski in the big time. *Courtesy: Army Athletic Association/U.S. Army Photo*

Hired at Duke in 1980, Mike Krzyzewski felt compelled to spell his name for reporters at his introductory press conference. *Getty Images/Bettmann*

After surviving the difficult early years at Duke that almost got him fired, Mike Krzyzewski climbed the ladder of March Madness success. *Richard Mackson/Getty Images*

North Carolina legend Dean Smith and Duke's Coach K engaged in one of the greatest rivalries in college sports history. *Bob Donnan/Getty Images*

Coach K had to manage the complicated relationship between stars Christian Laettner (behind Krzyzewski) and Bobby Hurley (second from right, front) on the way to winning back-to-back national titles. *Manny Millan/Getty Images*

Mike Krzyzewski built his Duke dynasty on the competitive rage within. *Sipa USA/Alamy Live News*

On the bumpy road to Olympic gold, Coach K had a lot of work to do to build trust with a skeptical LeBron James. *Reuters/Lucy Nicholson/ Alamy Stock Photo*

LeBron James told Coach K to "fix" Kobe Bryant at the Olympics. Mission accomplished. *Reuters/Gustau Nacarino/Alamy Stock Photo*

Love at first sight. Coach K and the Blue Devils were always a match made in heaven. *Reuters/ Mark Blinch/Alamy Stock Photo*

Coach K broke his mentor's wins record at Madison Square Garden. "Boy, you've done pretty good for a kid who couldn't shoot," Knight said. *Reuters/ Mike Segar/Alamy Stock Photo*

Coach K and the team at the White House with President Obama after Duke won its fifth national title in 2015. *UPI/Pat Benic/Alamy Stock Photo*

Krzyzewski and his Core Four: daughter Lindy, wife Mickie, and daughters Jamie and Debbie. *Streeter Lecka/ Getty Images*

Mike Krzyzewski, a decorated West Point man for life. *Courtesy: Army Athletic Association/U.S. Army Photo*

The three Army coaches who led teams to gold-medal finishes in the Olympics, including Jack Riley, the legendary hockey coach, who won in 1960, standing between Bob Knight (left) and Mike Krzyzewski. *Courtesy: Army Athletic Association/U.S. Army Photo*

A masked Mike and Mickie Krzyzewski getting ready to ride off into the sunset, after Coach K announced he would retire at the end of the 2021–2022 season. *Grant Halverson/Getty Images*

"You're going to leave me here?" Daisy asked her son.

These were the questions from parents that Duke's star players of the past never had to answer.

"I trust Coach, Mom," Brand replied. "I trust his advice."

Brand wasn't so sure about that advice after Krzyzewski benched him for a couple of December games for inconsistent play, replacing him with the bulked-up six-foot-ten Chris Burgess. Coach K thought that Brand was too busy reading stories that described him as a strong national Player of the Year candidate. "It was a 'Go take another picture for ESPN and get out of my gym' type of thing," Brand said. "I needed to grow up."

The sophomore center did win Player of the Year, while leading a group that included his roommate, fifth-year senior Trajan Langdon, Carrawell, his classmates Avery and Battier, and his freshman teammate and fellow NBA prospect Corey Maggette to Duke's third straight ACC regular-season title. The Blue Devils won thirty-two games in a row, including a bruising Final Four victory over Michigan State that landed them in the final against Connecticut, which Duke had eliminated from the tournament in 1990 and '91. On this night inside the domed Tropicana Field, Duke, once known as the white school with the white program and the white stars, fielded a team with only players of color in the top six of its rotation, including several from difficult single-parent backgrounds.

With five or six NBA prospects, the Blue Devils had more talent now than they did when they won back-to-back championships. "The last time I checked," Snyder said, "the '92 team, a few of those guys were still in the [NBA], but there was a realization that we needed better athletes. What does Duke do best? Defend. And to defend, we needed better athletes."

Krzyzewski was in pain again near the end of 1998–1999, hobbling here and there with more than a slight grimace, and needed hip replacement surgery. But over the course of the season he coached those Blue Devils with the same passion he showed in the dynasty years. Players recalled one riveting halftime speech that wasn't exactly a speech, but a man in his early fifties with an early sixties body demonstrating to his players how he played the game at West Point and how they needed to play it at Duke.

Coach K was furious that day that the Blue Devils weren't diving for loose balls. So in the middle of his cramped locker room, with players seated on both sides of him, a coach known for smashing chalkboards and berating underperforming players rolled a basketball on the floor as if it were a bowling ball. "And two of us reached for it," said walk-on Jay Heaps. "The next thing you know, Coach dove on the loose ball and tore it out of our arms and said, 'That's what I'm fuckin' talking about. We've got to fuckin' dive on loose balls.' It was awesome, a really powerful moment."

Some speechless Blue Devils looked at Krzyzewski on the ground as if he had finally lost his mind. "He starts wrestling around with the ball for like five to ten seconds," said Heaps's teammate Justin Caldbeck, "and at the end of it we did our, 'One, two, three, go,' with him on the ground. He could not get up . . . When we went out for the second half, he was absolutely still on the ground. I recall the senior managers helping him up."

A fired-up Duke won that day, easily, because the Blue Devils won almost every game easily. They routinely beat ACC teams by 20, 30, even 40 points. They had five future first-round picks among their top six players, and the sixth, Carrawell, was good enough to be named ACC Player of the Year and to be drafted in the second round. They had the next number-one overall pick in Brand, one of the nation's best shooters in Langdon, one of the best point guards in Avery, and one of the most explosive freshmen in Maggette. They also had a sophomore, Battier, whom Krzyzewski would call the most complete player he'd ever coached.

Battier at Duke was like Bill Bradley at Princeton — a perfect pairing of athlete and school. Battier listened to Beethoven, quoted Albert Schweitzer, read C. S. Lewis, and landed an internship on Wall Street. Oh, and he made sure his teammates made it to their classes on time.

To a man, the Blue Devils thought Battier might someday become president of the United States. "You know in the movies where somebody gets hit in the head, it opens up the head, and it's really a robot?" Krzyzewski would say. "We won't open up Shane's head. We might find he's a robot and we've broken NCAA rules."

He was almost always the first Blue Devil in the gym, jumping rope as hard as he could so he'd be sweating buckets before practice even started. Much like a young Grant Hill, Battier's only flaw was his willingness — if not eagerness — to defer to others, to wait his turn. Krzyzewski had to work on that. And yet when humble Mr. Battier studied Duke's opponents during pregame warmups, he could see in their eyes and body language that they knew they were in for a long night.

"We'd inevitably put a 16–4 run on, or a 12–2 run, and the game would be over," Battier said. "You could see teams say, 'We can't beat this team,' and they would move on. I'll never forget Coach K telling us, 'Make it okay to lose to Duke. Make it okay.' And we made it okay. The only way to do that is to jump on a team early and don't let them up and move on, and both parties go home satisfied."

The Blue Devils blew the roof off their building when they went on those runs. The Cameron Crazies — with their faces and bodies painted blue and white — would stomp and chant and reach out to nearly touch opposing players while advising the poor, crushed reporters sitting courtside that they needed to fix those dangling participles on their laptop screens.

On the road, Duke's players motivated one another by setting goals for sending a dissatisfied home crowd to the parking lots. "There was nothing better than those fans leaving with eight minutes to go in the game to beat the traffic rush," Battier said. "That was our motivation. That's what we enjoyed."

The Blue Devils won eighteen of their nineteen ACC games by double-figure margins. They defeated Virginia three times by a combined 129 points. The Cavaliers' first-year coach in 1998–1999, Pete Gillen, would square off with Krzyzewski for seven years and endure enough blowout losses to say, "The ultimate snub came with two minutes left in the game, and the Cameron crowd yelling, 'Go to hell, Carolina, go to hell.' They gave up on us because they were beating us so badly."

A leader of Division I programs for two decades, Gillen called Cameron the toughest place he'd ever coached. He could hardly hear himself think during games, and the suffocating proximity of the screaming fans caused him to sweat right through his clothes. Krzyzewski also made Cameron the most forbidding stop on the schedule. Gillen raved about his leadership, his recruiting ability, his commitment to defense, and his talent for motivating young athletes. Like many opposing coaches, Gillen did not see Krzyzewski as a creative teacher of offense, despite Duke's precise execution in critical endgame situations (see Laettner versus Kentucky, 1992).

"He might be the greatest coach ever by the time he's done," Gillen said years later, "but he isn't a great X and O guy … When you watch him, you wouldn't say, 'I've got to have that play.' He was good, but that's not his strength. He's off the charts in everything but Xs and Os."

Given the number of top recruits he signed, Krzyzewski didn't need to be Stephen Hawking with his motion offense, not when he was at a Vince Lombardi level as a motivator. That skill was on display when he decided it was time to end Wake Forest's nine-game winning streak against Duke — including a five-game winning streak at Cameron — that ran from 1993 to 1997. Wake's coach, Dave Odom, had the advantage of dressing six-foot-eleven Tim Duncan during that stretch. He also had the audacity (in Krzyzewski's mind) to start incorporating how-to-beat-Coach-K lessons into his presentations at clinics. "That enraged Coach K," said one of his assistants.

Odom's philosophy, in his words, was to "look at what Mike's teams did best and attack that. I didn't coach away from that, or around it. We tried to go right at their strength." Knowing ball denial was a big part of Duke's defensive game plan, Odom worked tirelessly with his team on ways to get the ball where it needed to go. The Wake coach also thought it was important for Duncan and other frontcourt players to catch the ball in the low post, and he worked on ways to stop the Blue Devils from pushing them out of position. Odom instructed the Demon Deacons to attack the middle of the Duke defense; he believed that the Blue Devils wanted to funnel opponents to the outside. "And defensively," Odom said, "we tried to play as they did, and be as tough at the three-point circle on in, as they were."

Krzyzewski was always searching for real or imagined slights to motivate himself and his team. Already angry at Odom for spreading the gospel of Duke destruction, Coach K grew angrier at Duncan in January 1997 when the center had the audacity (again, in Krzyzewski's mind) to sit cross-legged on Duke's court, like a kid at a campfire, before finishing with 26 points, 14 rebounds, 4 blocks, and 3 assists in Wake's 81–69 victory.

After that game, Coach K instructed his director of basketball operations, Jeff LaMere, to find the VHS clip of Duncan sitting on the Cameron floor. "He played that clip for the team," LaMere said, "and said something to them about the disrespect Tim Duncan showed. He said, 'We'll never lose to this team again.'"

Duke beat the second-ranked Demon Deacons a few weeks later, 73–68, its first road win over a team ranked in the nation's top two in nine years. Krzyzewski went with a small lineup and put the six-foot-six Carrawell, then a freshman, on Duncan, who scored 26 points on 11-for-13 shooting but couldn't get a shot off in the final 5:14. Krzyzewski told his staff beforehand that Duncan could score 50 points against his defensive alignment, but decided against double-teaming him for this reason: the senior center was too nice of a young man to keep shooting and would pass the ball to keep his teammates involved.

Once the Blue Devils had defeated Duncan, they ran off fourteen consecutive victories over Wake. Before a few of them, Krzyzewski went back to that clip of a sitting Duncan.

BY THE 1998–1999 SEASON, Krzyzewski was back to being the undisputed king of the ACC. Odom was no longer a nemesis, and Dean Smith was no longer a rival. At sixty-six, saying he could no longer bring the requisite enthusiasm to the job, Smith had retired in the fall of 1997 as the winningest Division I coach of all time. Over the years, Krzyzewski had gained a greater appreciation for his bitter rival, and for everything he had built in

Chapel Hill. Now Krzyzewski understood what it took, and what it meant, to run *the* program in all of college basketball.

Coach K was in the middle of a seven-year contract with terms that Duke, as a private school, declined to disclose, other than to acknowledge that its most recognizable employee was making a lot more than ol' Eddie Cameron's $7,500 a year. Krzyzewski was actually making $521,500 in salary in 1999, though his Nike deal, radio and TV deals, endorsements, and summer camp money put his take in the millions. He had hired Michael Jordan's superagent, David Falk, to represent him. As much as Krzyzewski had reduced his availability to the media, his brand was still growing.

But he never strayed far from who he was, or where he came from. He treated team managers as fully invested members of the program, and every season he made sure to introduce the custodial staff to his players to make certain they knew the staffers' names, respected their work in the facility, and appreciated their significance to the team's daily culture. (If Krzyzewski spilled a cup of soda in or around the gym, he would grab a towel, drop to his hands and knees, and clean it up; he was the son of a cleaning lady, after all.) When signing autographs for hundreds of people at his summer basketball camp, Coach K was also in the habit of looking each person in the eye before carefully writing a perfectly legible signature. He would tell his players, "When you put your signature on something, that's lasting."

Krzyzewski's signature was all over everything his team did. His practices were still run like military exercises, with each drill scheduled to the minute and every deflection, charge, and screen charted to measure a player's efficiency. Coach K didn't like to use a whistle in practices because, he said, "I want my players to listen for the sound of my voice." Team huddles were moved to different parts of the stadium to give his players a new look, to keep every day as fresh as possible. The Blue Devils treated every small-picture detail with big-picture urgency.

They rolled through the ACC Tournament and the first four rounds of the NCAAs, before surviving their Big Ten football game of a semifinal with Michigan State. And then it was on to the UConn Huskies and Jim Calhoun, a bare-knuckle brawler from greater Boston who was making his first trip to the national semis. The UConn coach called Krzyzewski "the coach of our generation." Calhoun's Northeastern team had beaten Krzyzewski's Army team two decades earlier, on a near-halfcourt shot by Perry Moss. Coach K had broken Calhoun's heart a couple of times since.

The Huskies approached this game the way the 1991 Blue Devils approached their rematch with UNLV. UConn had fearless perimeter players in Rip Hamilton and Khalid El-Amin and a senior guard, Ricky Moore, who might have been the best defensive player in the country. Moore and Duke's Avery were raised on Hazel Street in the dilapidated Sand Hills section of Augusta, Georgia, where they won a state championship for Westside High. Moore was two years older than Avery, who grew up wanting to wear his mentor's number. The UConn guard was used to being the superior player, and Calhoun thought that gave his side one of many advantages.

"We were tougher than them," he said. "And I told our kids before the game, 'Over the next forty-eight hours, they're not going to get tougher than us.'"

Calhoun told his players that they would practice hard Sunday for the full hour that the NCAA allowed before Monday night's game, and that Duke was choosing to skip practice and rest up because it didn't believe UConn was good enough to win. "That was a 100 percent made-up thing by me," Calhoun said. "But in those captured moments you create a narrative."

The Huskies felt completely disrespected as 9.5-point underdogs; they were 33-2, winners of the Big East, and the former top-ranked team in America. Even the Duke players couldn't believe the way the media portrayed the Blue Devils as certain champions waiting to be crowned.

Deep down, some of those players knew there was something slightly amiss about this Duke juggernaut. "We would go to restaurants sometimes, and you [could] just tell the players didn't click together," said one Blue Devil. "And it was sad. Really sad, frankly. I don't know what drove that. Elton, Corey, and Will were a clique, the NBA clique. Shane wasn't a part of that . . . But those three guys sat at their own table all the time. Elton was a really nice guy, and so were the others, but that was a problem."

A member of the Duke program agreed with this player's assessment and wondered why Krzyzewski didn't do more to address it. "The five fingers weren't working as a fist," the official said. Some inside the program came to believe that a few Blue Devils might have been more concerned with being named Final Four Most Outstanding Player than with winning the tournament. That mentality wasn't going to work against the hungry Huskies, who were not enjoying the movie-star treatment being afforded their opponents at their beachfront resort.

A year after being underwhelmed by their accommodations at the Sandpiper, and after being appalled (along with most everyone else) by the leaking mess that was Tropicana Field, the site of their regional final loss to Kentucky, the Blue Devils decided to go in style. Though the NCAA Final Four guide listed Duke's hotel as the Doubletree near the Tampa airport, Krzyzewski rewarded his kids with a booking at the Don CeSar, a pink paradise that had pampered several U.S. presidents, Babe Ruth, F. Scott Fitzgerald, and Liz Taylor. The Duke contingent was surrounded by media as it arrived by bus, and one photographer accidentally bumped into Mickie Krzyzewski, who pointed a finger in the man's eye and warned, "Don't ever bump me again." The staff at the resort made certain that was the first and last indignity the Blue Devils suffered over their five-day stay.

As soon as they were done with their Sunday media obligations at the Trop, Krzyzewski gathered his tired and sore players in the locker room to tell them he was canceling practice and sending them back to the Don Ce-Sar to collect their playbooks and perhaps spend a little time in the spa or on the beach. A Monday night victory celebration was being planned. One player said the word was that Kevin Costner, Bill Cosby, and Leonardo DiCaprio might make appearances.

The Blue Devils had to play the championship game first before advancing to their own party. A limping Krzyzewski was in quite a bit of pain as he approached surgery on the degenerative condition in his left hip. He insisted that he was doing fine, that he was enjoying coaching more than he ever had. His family said he was happy, and why wouldn't he be?

Life was good on and off the court. Married nearly thirty years, Mike and Mickie were loving their big new house right near Duke Forest, hidden away from civilization, 11.5 acres of peace and quiet and privacy. They were loving their two Labradors, named Cameron and Defense, and enjoyed taking walks with them through the woods. Mike cherished his time as an amateur gardener and may have set a world record for flowers planted by a Columbo.

He had watched his oldest daughter Debbie get married two years earlier. ("He never let go of my hand that day," Debbie said.) His middle daughter, Lindy, was about to graduate magna cum laude from Wake Forest, and his youngest, Jamie, was playing point guard (what else?) at Durham Academy. Krzyzewski was spending more time at Jamie's games and more time at home, where he could complete the same work he used to do in the office and eat more dinners with his wife and girls. From his deathbed, Jim Valvano had reminded Krzyzewski to put his family ahead of his craft, and the Duke coach kept a *Sports Illustrated* profile of Valvano on his nightstand, with his friend's lessons highlighted.

That didn't mean basketball and winning were any less important to him, whether his bum hip cooperated or not.

"Oh, he's still driven," Mickie said. "The word 'pain' still isn't in his vocabulary. When I ask him how [the hip] feels, he'll say, 'It's a little tight today.' He's still so stoic. He won't admit weakness. He's afraid if he lets his guard down and deals with his feelings, he might not be able to bounce back from it."

Before Duke and Connecticut took the floor on the night of March 29, 1999, the UConn guard, El-Amin, told the national CBS audience that the Huskies "plan to shock the world." The teams then played a game that really shouldn't have been a shock to anyone. Like the Duke team of eight years earlier, the Huskies had great players, and a great coach, and a great desire to finally break through and win a title.

The Huskies and Blue Devils went back and forth in front of a charged dome crowd of 41,340, with Duke unable to contain Rip Hamilton and UConn unable to contain Trajan Langdon. Inside, the Huskies perfectly executed their game plan to slow down Brand, double-teaming him when necessary and holding him to a manageable 8 shots and 15 points. As Calhoun predicted, the matchup of Augusta guards, Moore versus Avery, tilted heavily in favor of the older UConn player. "Coach, he's not that tough," Moore had told Calhoun. "Ricky, you can attack this kid," Calhoun responded. "He's just a kid." Avery missed 9 of 12 field-goal attempts, while Moore made 6 of 10 and grabbed 8 rebounds.

UConn's goal was to make it anyone's game in the final minutes — the same goal Duke had against UNLV in '91. "I told my kids, 'Down the stretch they will fold,'" Calhoun said.

And down the stretch they came. UConn was up, 75–74, when El-Amin shot an airball on a spinning pull-up in traffic. Carrawell gathered the miss and passed it to Avery, who gave it right back to the junior forward. "Duke with a basket to take the lead and win the game," Jim Nantz said on CBS. Carrawell dribbled down the left side and, with fifteen seconds to go, gave the ball to Langdon, whom Krzyzewski had called the best shooter he had ever coached. As the only holdover from the 1994–1995 disaster, and as the kid Coach K called "The Bridge" for leading the program back into contention, Langdon was the right choice to take the ultimate shot.

He faced off against Moore above the left hash, and, surprisingly, Krzyzewski decided against calling a time-out to set up the final play. "Wow, Trajan Langdon with the ball, he's going up against a great defender. What's he doing here?" analyst Billy Packer said on the broadcast. Three times Langdon dribbled between his legs before executing a final crossover dribble on the UConn defender, driving left with seconds to play, and then spinning toward the lane as Moore quickly moved his feet to stay in front of him. Bothered by the defense, Langdon took an extra step before throwing up an awkward leaner that bounced out while the whistle blew repeatedly. Traveling. UConn ball.

Krzyzewski called time-out with 5.4 seconds left. Up in the stands, an anguished Mickie lowered her head while Debbie, seated to her left, buried her head in her hands before dabbing at her tears. When play resumed, Duke immediately fouled El-Amin, and Krzyzewski called over his players to remind them of the plan they had discussed during the time-out. El-Amin then stepped to the line and drained his first free throw to give the Huskies a two-point lead, compelling a seated Coach K to lower his head and wipe his brow.

El-Amin sank the second to make it 77–74 before Battier grabbed the ball and looked to make the inbound pass. Avery was the most sensible receiver in this situation, with five seconds to go, as he was the point guard and the fastest Blue Devil with the ball. But starting from the three-point line, Avery did not break free from his defender. Langdon came toward the ball and received the pass as he was heading toward the wrong baseline, starting the play with a mistake.

Langdon headed up the left side of the floor with Avery in front of him, and after the fifth-year senior from Alaska crossed midcourt with two seconds to play, three Huskies converged on him. Langdon lost the ball, tripped, and fell to the court as the UConn players and coaches jumped into one another's arms. Knowing the unbearable pain of defeat, Calhoun quickly separated himself from the jubilation and headed for Krzyzewski, who gave him a warm hug and a couple of pats on the back before telling him, "It's your turn." That was how you were supposed to handle these moments, in case Bobby Knight was keeping score at home.

Krzyzewski then found Avery on the court and pulled him in tight. The point guard buried his head in his coach's left shoulder. "I thought we were beaten tonight," Krzyzewski said later. "We didn't lose."

He maintained that he wasn't sorry about finishing second, that he coached for relationships, not rings. Krzyzewski said that he wanted to win or lose with Langdon, his best perimeter player, and that he didn't call time-out on Duke's penultimate possession because his team had the momentum (off the El-Amin airball) and he didn't want to give the Huskies a chance to regroup.

"Anybody expects me to be down about this game, they don't understand me," Krzyzewski said. "I'm not gonna be down about this game because it would take away from my experience with this group."

Two members of the Duke basketball program said that Krzyzewski was angry at Avery on the final play for not making a proper cut to get the ball. "He said that Will fucked up because Will didn't have attention to detail," one player said. "He said that it cost us not only the championship, but it cost Trajan too. He was forced into a bad situation, and now he has to live with the memory of it."

Krzyzewski would have to live with the memory of it too. "That's the most crushed I've ever seen Mike," Calhoun said. "That was his best team. His best team that ever lost."

One Duke team member cited the selection of the Don CeSar as a tactical error, compounded by Krzyzewski's decision to give his players some free resort time the day before the title game. "We went into that game too cocky," that team member said. A second team member said, "At that point in the year we were really being treated like rock stars. We'd show up places and the lobby would be packed, and girls were around, and Tampa is kind of a distracting place."

Carrawell said that distractions had nothing to do with the final outcome, that team chemistry was solid all year, and that the Michigan State game took a lot out of Duke. "And Rip Hamilton was a monster," Carrawell said. "He busted my ass." (One player thought Coach K should have tried a zone defense to neutralize Hamilton's curls off screens.) Battier said the Blue Devils took the Huskies quite seriously, but since it was later in the year, they just weren't as sharp as they'd been when dominating the ACC.

Either way, there was a lot of crying at the Don CeSar in the hours after UConn won the title, and no victory bash like the one promised on the hotel flyers that carried the words, "NCAA Champions. Duke Blue Devils."

Duke was 0-2 in elimination games in the Trop over two years, but this loss hurt so much more than the first one. "We all just wanted to get out of there," Battier said. "We wanted to get the hell out of Tampa."

Only things in Durham were about to get worse. The Duke program would be thrown back into chaos, though its leader would discover later that the pain was very much worth the gain.

12

ECSTASY

THE RECOVERY STARTED in Mike Krzyzewski's home in the early spring of 1999. Coach K had already known that he was losing sophomore Elton Brand, who would be the number-one overall pick in the NBA draft and the very first player to leave Duke early to turn pro.

But he did not expect Brand's classmate, William Avery, and freshman Corey Maggette to turn pro with him, nor did he anticipate that Chris Burgess, who had been rated higher than Brand coming out of high school, would decide to transfer, or that Burgess's father would publicly blast Krzyzewski on their way out the door. Quin Snyder would also leave to take the head coaching job at Missouri. Though Krzyzewski knew that Snyder's promotion to the big chair was coming sooner rather than later, this was a really bad time to lose a valuable program asset.

So junior Chris Carrawell and sophomores Shane Battier and Nate James paid a surprise visit to the coach's remote compound near Duke Forest. When Mickie answered the door, she was surprised to see the three players before her. Unannounced visits were not part of the Krzyzewski protocol in the post–back surgery/burnout era, but Mickie knew her husband needed a lift. She let them in.

Krzyzewski was on his back in the days after his April 4 hip replacement surgery, literally and figuratively. He was having trouble sleeping, but over the state of his team, not the state of his hip. Players leaving early for the pros? Yeah, Coach K should have seen that coming. High school phenoms Kevin Garnett, Kobe Bryant, and Tracy McGrady didn't even attend college, instead entering the 1995, '96, and '97 drafts, respectively, to start the clock on the money-making portion of their careers as soon as possible. College freshmen and sophomores were also making the jump, putting the four-year Christian Laettner, Bobby Hurley, and Grant Hill model in serious danger at Duke.

"It was inevitable that this would happen in our program," Krzyzewski said after Brand announced he was leaving Durham after two seasons.

Losing Brand was, in Coach K's mind, the price of doing business in the modern game. Losing Avery and Maggette was an entirely different proposition. Once again, it felt like Krzyzewski's program was coming undone.

So his three visitors assured the coach that they were staying right by his side. "The kingdom has not fallen," they told him. Their reassurance, and their concern for his well-being, moved Krzyzewski to tears. "I'm going to be ready to fuckin' coach you guys," he told them.

Following the devastating loss to Connecticut, April had been one long series of April Fool's Days stacked on top of one another. By mid-month, Krzyzewski's surgery and rehab were followed by Brand's expected defection, which was immediately followed by Avery's surprising defection, angering the coach; Krzyzewski did not think the point guard was ready to pursue his dream of playing in the NBA. Avery and his mother, Terry Simonton, met with the coach at his home, and one published report claimed that the Krzyzewski told Simonton, "Your son is going to fuck up my program."

Simonton denied that Coach K ever yelled or cursed at her. "Nobody's going to get in my face and say that," Simonton said. "Trust me, if that was said to me you would have known . . . I feel like my son played as good as anyone else for two years, and if it's his decision to leave school early, then that's his decision. He gave Coach K and the university everything he could give them."

When Snyder and Johnny Dawkins had started recruiting Avery at Westside High in Augusta, Georgia, Krzyzewski never thought the prospect would elevate his grades to a point where he could attend Duke. Avery improved his grades at Oak Hill Academy, a Virginia boarding school and basketball factory, though one Krzyzewski aide who had seen his transcript acknowledged that it was still "a stretch" for Duke to admit him.

Now, after taking a chance on Avery, Coach K felt betrayed that his point guard was bailing after two years. In stark contrast to his public support of Brand's decision, which he called "absolutely a no-brainer," Krzyzewski released a statement on Avery that read, "I am not in favor of William's decision at this time. We have done extensive research into the NBA for William and my conclusion was that entering the draft now would not be in his best interests. However, everyone is entitled to make their own decisions. I certainly wish him the ultimate success in his future endeavors."

It was stunning for a multimillionaire coach to publicly rebuke a player this way, especially a player who was raised in relative poverty. Krzyzewski was trying to navigate the new world of major college basketball, and he was struggling. Avery said he was trying to help his unemployed mother, who had suffered a back injury, and his sick grandmother, who he said was potentially facing two leg amputations. He confirmed his mother's account that Krzyzewski did not yell at them in their meeting at his home, but he said that the coach was clearly upset over his choice. Avery was not offered the Cameron Indoor Stadium news conference afforded Brand; he was left to conduct his presser at May Park Community Center in Augusta.

"He wanted to set me up really well," said Avery, who would reestablish a relationship with Coach K and, years later, return to Duke to work toward earning his degree. "I think he thought I deferred at times to Trajan and Elton, and he wanted me to come back and have a chance to be the guy. He knew if I'd done that and continued to work hard and improve like I did from freshman to sophomore year, I would be a special player." (The fourteenth pick in the NBA draft, Avery would start only one game in three seasons with the Minnesota Timberwolves before playing eight years overseas.)

Krzyzewski took another hit a week later when Burgess, an all-everything player in high school, announced that he was transferring for a chance to find the stardom that had eluded him as Brand's backup at Duke. Burgess's father, Ken, told reporter Pat Forde that Krzyzewski had blatantly lied to the family about what his son's role would be with the Blue Devils. "He's petty and he's dishonest," said Ken Burgess, who claimed that Krzyzewski granted most-favored-nation status to players such as Shane Battier and Steve Wojciechowski, to the detriment of the team.

Chris Burgess recoiled at some of his father's comments and later said that Krzyzewski coached him the same way he coached Battier and Brand. After Burgess struggled in his freshman season, Krzyzewski called him into his office and said, "You need to be chocolate and vanilla and have a go-to move and a counter. You're not thirty-one flavors. I want you to run your own race and stop comparing yourself to other top freshmen in the country. You're doing great."

It was clear Elton Brand was simply a better player than Chris Burgess. Many years after joining Billy McCaffrey, Joey Beard, and Mike Chappell as significant Krzyzewski transfers, Burgess would say, "I love my dad, but he was just frustrated and wanted what was best for his kids and he was speaking on his own behalf . . . Thank goodness there wasn't social media back then."

The same might have been said about Krzyzewski's decision to play

Maggette only eleven minutes against UConn in the championship game. The freshman started only three games — a testament to Duke's remarkable talent — yet averaged 10.6 points in 17.7 minutes of playing time. Maggette's was the final defection, announced in May, and the decision so unnerved Krzyzewski that he didn't make a statement on it. As Maggette was preparing to bolt Duke, athletic director Joe Alleva said, "It's just a different world, it has changed enormously. We're a victim of the environment."

Nobody in college basketball wept for Duke, not after four Blue Devils went in the top fourteen picks of the NBA draft — Brand (number one), Langdon (number eleven), Maggette (number thirteen), and Avery (number fourteen) — and not after Coach K brought in a recruiting class that included four McDonald's All-Americans, led by a playmaker, Jason Williams, who was far more talented than Avery. Like Bobby Hurley, Williams was a highly skilled Catholic school point guard from Jersey who grew up a North Carolina fan. Unlike Hurley, Williams was told by Dean Smith's successor, Bill Guthridge, that he wasn't a fit for the Tar Heels, leaving him intent on playing for Rutgers — at least until he took a visit to Cameron Indoor Stadium that he didn't even want to take.

The recruit was awed by the retired jerseys and banners in the rafters and by the two national championship trophies — with clipped game nets hanging from them — resting on a cabinet in Krzyzewski's old cubbyhole tucked away in a back corner of the gym. Williams was also struck by how small Coach K's office was despite his extra-large résumé.

Among three new starters, Williams would help Krzyzewski win his fifth ACC Coach of the Year award in the 1999–2000 season. For the third straight year, Duke either went 15-1 or 16-0 in the league. Carlos Boozer, the six-foot-nine freshman, was a solid replacement for Brand, and Coach K's second elite recruit from Alaska; another freshman, Mike Dunleavy, son of the longtime NBA coach and player, showed promise coming off the bench. But the team was driven by the veteran forwards, Battier and Carrawell, the latter winning their friendly intramural battle for ACC Player of the Year.

Carrawell had overcome a lot of doubts about his Duke worthiness to help the Blue Devils win four consecutive ACC regular-season titles. But when Coach K needed to make a point with his team, he often used Carrawell to make it. "He was on my ass all the time," Carrawell said. "He wasn't yelling at the stars, so he yelled at me. I could take it."

With one exception: the St. John's game at Cameron on February 26, 2000, when the best and worst parts of playing for Coach K were on full display. The best? Before the game, Krzyzewski and Battier had implored Duke students to refrain from mocking St. John's guard Erick Barkley, who had been hounded by the NCAA over a swap of cars with a family friend (you can't make this stuff up) and over the source of a relatively small prep-school tuition payment made on his behalf. Known for raining down clever chants and vulgar put-downs on visiting players, the Cameron Crazies were so welcoming to Barkley (they cheered for him and chanted, "Stop the witch hunt," during warm-ups) that he became the first opponent ever to write a letter of thanks to the Duke student newspaper.

The worst? After the game, outraged by Carrawell's decision-making on the last possession of St. John's 83–82 overtime victory, Krzyzewski ripped into his senior captain like he had never ripped into anyone. Coach K had designed the last play in the final five seconds for Battier, who was supposed to come off a screen and take the pass from Boozer. But on the court the inbounds passer, Carrawell, called an audible and instructed the center to get the ball back to him. Boozer listened, and against Coach K's orders, Carrawell put up a difficult 17-foot shot against two St. John's defenders and watched it bounce off the rim, ending Duke's streak of sixty-four straight victories over unranked teams.

Krzyzewski couldn't believe what he had just witnessed. On what felt like a 100-degree day inside Cameron, Coach K was angry enough that his Blue Devils had just lost to a nonconference team on their home court for only the third time in 129 such games since 1983. Carrawell's decision to create his own play on the fly elevated Krzyzewski's blood pressure to Defcon 1 levels.

On the one hand, Coach K was only honoring the West Point way of following orders at all times, remaining disciplined, and paying full attention to the smallest details. On the other hand, Krzyzewski said he didn't want programmed athletes on the floor. "One of the most consistent messages from Coach K was, 'You've got to be instinctual. Don't be a robot,'" Battier said. Carrawell, senior captain, had thought he saw something in the St. John's defense, and then acted on instinct.

That didn't matter when Krzyzewski addressed his losing team in the locker room. In defeat, Coach K was an unpleasant human being to be around. Sometimes he would walk past his own players in the hallway without even acknowledging them.

"After the game Coach K was pretty heated at C-Well, shockingly heated at C-Well," Battier said. "We all felt bad. He was trying to make a play. It wasn't insubordination by any means."

Players who heard this profane tirade would be talking about it twenty years later. "When you ask guys, 'What's the worst thing you ever saw Coach K do?' half of them reference this," said one player, who described Carrawell as "bawling." Another player said that Krzyzewski seemed more hurt than angry, and that his volcanic response reached a level the team hadn't seen before.

"He went too far," Carrawell said years later. "I didn't run the play. I took the shot, and I missed it . . . As a senior, as a captain, I was wrong. But I was pissed off [at Krzyzewski]. That's the only time where I thought it could have been handled differently.

"I didn't do what Coach wanted, and he got mad, and I thought he went too far. But at the end of the day . . . I would play for Coach K a million times out of a million. The dude is a competitor, man. If you're in the fox-hole, you want to be in the foxhole with him. I'd run through a brick wall for him."

Krzyzewski's aides knew that this episode needed careful follow-up attention. "The assistants discussed it as a staff — how do you fix this?" said one Duke staffer. Carrawell and Krzyzewski moved past the incident, as much as they could, and the Blue Devils won their next five games, including the ACC title game and the first two rounds of the NCAA Tournament. Carrawell scored 21 against North Carolina in his Cameron farewell, punctuated by a warm embrace with his coach. With five seconds left in Duke's Sweet 16 loss to Florida in the NCAAs, Krzyzewski took out Carrawell, he said, "as just my way of saying thanks. There's only going to be one overall winner in the tournament, but all these kids can be winners if they have the careers Chris did."

Carrawell had helped give Coach K four regular-season ACC championships and two ACC Tournament titles, including one of each right after four Duke players were selected in the first round of the 1999 NBA draft. So C-Well was angry and hurt when he was picked in the second round, forty-first overall, in the 2000 draft. How could forty players be picked ahead of a first-team All-American after he did what he did for Duke?

He knew that his shoulder surgeries had hurt his draft stock, but C-Well also thought that something else, or someone else, was the cause of his plunge. "I blamed him at the time for that," Carrawell said, "for not getting in the first round." *Him.* Krzyzewski. "I was really pissed at Duke for that, and at him in particular," C-Well continued. "Look, man, I did everything for the program, but it wasn't in the cards . . . You point fingers like, 'Man, shit, Coach K didn't do enough. I should've went with this [agent].' That was a tough pill to swallow when you're twenty-two."

Carrawell wasn't the first Duke player to blame Krzyzewski for not getting picked in the first round, and for not securing an NBA career because of it; Thomas Hill, from the Blue Devils' two title teams, was known to feel that Coach K didn't do enough to promote his pro potential to executives and scouts. Krzyzewski certainly had some influence with NBA decision-makers, but expecting him to create a market where one didn't naturally exist was probably asking for too much.

Two weeks after the 2000 draft, Coach K had a more forbidding concern to deal with when his first one-and-done player, Corey Maggette, admitted that before he had enrolled at Duke he had received $2,000 from his Kansas City–based and Nike-backed summer coach, Myron Piggie, a former crack cocaine dealer who had been indicted on federal charges of defrauding universities by making illegal payments to prospects they had signed. Nike, a Duke business partner, had reportedly signed Piggie's grassroots team, the CMH 76ers, to a $425,000 sponsorship deal, including $250,000 over five years for Piggie. By taking money from him, Maggette had forfeited his right to play college basketball. By playing Maggette in 1998–1999, Duke faced the possibility that its title-game appearance and some or all of its thirty-seven victories that season could be vacated, and that some of the $375,000 it earned in the tournament would need to be returned.

Of greater consequence, Mike Krzyzewski's supposedly spotless program could vacate its standing as college basketball's shining city on a largely corrupt hill. Coach K said that he was never aware of Maggette's connection to Piggie while the freshman forward was playing at Duke. "We've cooperated fully with the NCAA since it was brought to our attention," said Krzyzewski, who declined further comment.

Three college players paid by Piggie — UCLA's JaRon Rush, Missouri's Kareem Rush (JaRon's brother, who played for Quin Snyder), and Oklahoma State's Andre Williams — received significant suspensions, while Maggette was in no position to be benched for a violation of his amateur status now that he was playing in the NBA. Would the NCAA actually punish its signature program?

Krzyzewski was not certain where the case was heading. Of course, nothing makes a coach and a school more untouchable than winning. And entering the 2000–2001 season, Coach K thought he had a team that was good enough to finish what his 1999 team could not.

IT SURE LOOKED like the 2000–2001 season was over before it was over. Carlos Boozer broke the third metatarsal bone in his right foot during a loss to Maryland in late February. When word of the fracture reached Mike Krzyzewski, he immediately thought second-ranked Duke was dead. Looking into his players' eyes, he realized that they thought second-ranked Duke was dead too.

During Boozer's early days in Durham, Krzyzewski told the center that he was a talented kid, but that he was slow doing everything. Slow when he walked on campus, slow when he got dressed for practice, slow when he was chewing gum. Boozer explained that was how he grew up in Alaska, just taking his time. "Coach, when I have to run, I'll run for you," the center said. Boozer had run enough for the Blue Devils to make himself a vital part of their machine.

"Devastating," Mike Dunleavy called his injury. Krzyzewski and his staff stayed up until 4 a.m. trying to figure out how to replace a starting center averaging 13.9 points and 6.5 rebounds a game. Coach K now had three of his former guards as assistants in Johnny Dawkins, Steve Wojciechowski, and Chris Collins, along with director of basketball operations Jeff LaMere and academic and recruiting coordinator Mike Schrage, son of Krzyzewski's former Army teammate Dan Schrage. Collins was one who wasn't afraid to walk up to the board and write something down when he was frustrated with some of Coach K's Xs and Os; Krzyzewski didn't reprimand him for it, as he'd have done with Quin Snyder, said one Duke source. They all grabbed a few hours of sleep and returned to the office at 9 a.m. to work throughout the day on a revised approach to winning basketball.

The bleary-eyed Blue Devils reported to practice at 6 a.m. the following day to begin preparing for their regular-season finale against the Tar Heels in Chapel Hill, and the session was an exercise in despair and doubt. Krzyzewski was good for kicking his team out of practice once or twice a year, and this indifferent and sloppy showing afforded him the perfect opportunity to send his team a message.

Those kick-outs were often manufactured, but this one was legit. "You guys are bullshit," he shouted, according to Battier. "I don't want to coach you. You're feeling sorry for yourselves. Come back when you stop feeling sorry for yourselves and when you want to work and win." The players retreated to their locker room, and Battier, senior captain, presided over a team meeting that turned emotional. He referenced fellow seniors Nate James and walk-ons Ryan Caldbeck and J. D. Simpson. "I started to cry," Battier said.

He also started to kick the door, the wall, and the trash can. "You guys don't understand," Battier shouted, directing his rage at the underclassmen. "This is it for us. This is it. We don't have time. We could go to Carolina and get blown out, and lose in the ACC Tournament in Atlanta, and get upset by a fifteen or sixteen seed in the NCAA Tournament, and then I'm done. But we're not going down like that."

One of the sport's most dignified statesmen, Battier suddenly shifted into Terminator mode. "I was throwing chairs in the locker room," he said.

The Blue Devils did indeed return to the gym in a better frame of mind, and Krzyzewski rewarded them by disclosing his reinvention plan. He said he was going to tweak the starting lineup and alter Duke's pace of play.

"And if you believe in my plan for us," he said, "we will win the national championship."

Then Krzyzewski lowered his voice and repeated his message, with a little twist. "If you motherfuckers . . . listen to me . . . we're going to win a national championship."

Krzyzewski persisted. "He went down the line to a man," Battier recalled, "and said, 'Do you believe in me? Do you believe in my plans? Do you believe in this team?' We all had to say yes."

The Blue Devils showed up in Chapel Hill on Sunday, March 4, with most of America expecting them to lose to the fourth-ranked Tar Heels. Krzyzewski did not have his name on Duke's arena when he walked into the Dean Dome, but he did now own a claim on Cameron's home floor, officially named Coach K Court after the Blue Devils defeated Villanova in November to give their coach his five-hundredth victory at Duke.

Nearly four months later, Krzyzewski had a chance to beat Dean Smith's former team, coached by Smith's former player, Matt Doherty, and win at least a share of a fifth consecutive regular-season ACC title. To do that, Krzyzewski planned to play faster than Duke had ever played before. He moved freshman Chris Duhon into the starting lineup next to Jason Williams to give the Blue Devils two point guards in the backcourt and liberate the electric Williams from some ball-handling responsibilities so he could fire away. Krzyzewski also replaced Boozer with six-foot-eleven sophomore Casey Sanders, a big man who was not nearly the same offensive threat but one capable of running the floor all day and night.

Nate James, fifth-year senior, had to accept a new role as sixth man, and that was asking him to accept a lot. He didn't love the downsized assignment, especially in favor of a freshman, but in grand Duke fashion he took one for the team. Duhon's speed was necessary for what Krzyzewski wanted to accomplish — a Blue Devil reinvention. "We are going to try to shoot fifty threes against North Carolina," he told his team. "J-Will, I want you to shoot fifteen threes this game. Shane, I want you to shoot fifteen threes this game. If we miss, keep shooting. Keep shooting."

The visitors launched thirty-eight threes, making fourteen, as they ruined North Carolina's Senior Day much as Maryland had ruined Duke's

Senior Night five days earlier. In the middle of the second half, with Duke holding a big lead, Doherty effectively surrendered to Krzyzewski's desired pace when he benched his two biggest starters, six-foot-eleven Kris Lang and seven-foot center Brendan Haywood, who had welcomed Sanders to the game's opening tip with a bemused, you're-really-playing-this-guy-against-me look. Haywood spent much of the game trying to catch his breath, and that only emboldened his opponent.

"Coach K said you should never allow your opponent to see you sweat, ever," Battier said. "We were never allowed to grab our shorts . . . We always had to have a look of invincibility. You never want to have your opponent see that Duke is tired, Duke doubts themselves, Duke is fatigued. No, we wanted them to look at us like we're not human."

Battier was good for 25 points, 11 rebounds, 5 blocks, 4 assists, and the kind of nonstop talking on defense that made him sound, Coach K proudly pointed out, like a play-by-play announcer. Williams delivered 33 points and 9 assists while Duhon, in his first start, managed 15 points and 4 assists in thirty-six turnover-free minutes. "It was one of the best game plans I've ever seen put together," Battier said of Duke 95, North Carolina 81.

Done tormenting Carolina with their playground style, the Blue Devils ran off the court shouting, "Five in a row," as they represented the first ACC team ever to win at least a share of five straight regular-season championships. They ripped through the ACC Tournament, winning it for the third straight time despite a comical hiccup before the opener — packing for the trip to Atlanta, Duke's managers had forgotten the team's white jerseys, its designated color to wear against NC State, which was scheduled to wear red. Krzyzewski asked for, and received, permission from Wolfpack coach Herb Sendek to wear the black jerseys that were packed. The managers actually had to buy Duke T-shirts in the concourse concession stands so the players would have something to warm up in.

"I was like, 'We're dead,'" said Nick Arison, son of Miami Heat owner Micky Arison and one of about ten Duke managers on that trip. "But it was incredible seeing how Coach K handled it. He said, 'We're going to make it work. This is not a big deal. This is not an excuse.' It was all about making the best of the situation and trying to keep moving forward."

Krzyzewski never erupted on the managers, though he did meet with them in Durham after the Blue Devils beat North Carolina by 26 points to earn their third straight ACC Tournament title. The message was simple: that can never, ever happen again. Meanwhile, Williams emerged from the Carolina blowout with a sprained ankle that wasn't expected to be a problem in the NCAA Tournament, where Duke hoped to get Boozer back at some point.

As the tournament's number-one seed, charged to play its first two games only 54 miles from home in the Greensboro Coliseum, Duke made quick work of Monmouth before matching up with Missouri and its second-year head coach Quin Snyder. The Tigers were a ninth seed with a 20-12 record, but Krzyzewski still didn't want to play them. Snyder said that his former coach had shaped his life more than anyone other than his parents. "I love Quin," Krzyzewski said. "My daughters and my wife all feel like Quin is a part of our family. He kind of grew up with us . . . Why would you want to compete against someone you love?"

The two coaches embraced before the game while a battery of photographers closed hard around them. Krzyzewski was emotional; it was the first time he'd faced a former player as a head coach. But everyone knew he didn't want to lose a sudden-death game to Snyder any more than Bob Knight wanted to lose one to him. Coach K beat the counterpart he jokingly called the "good-looking guy with long hair," 94–81, to win what his players were calling a two-game tournament.

That was how Krzyzewski always wanted them to look at the subregional and regional competitions that made up the first four rounds of the NCAAs. Don't look at the entire bracket. Focus only on your four-team site each week. By beating Monmouth and Missouri, the Blue Devils had essentially won the Greensboro Invitational. The following week, they defeated UCLA and USC in the Southern Cal Classic — even though it was staged in Philadelphia. Boozer returned in Philly to score three points off the bench. He would be a much bigger factor at the Final Four in Minneapolis, where Duke would face a Maryland team that had given it hell all season.

The Blue Devils had barely survived Maryland in the ACC Tournament, prevailing on a last-second James tip-in, and the two teams had split their two regular-season games. The Terrapins ruined the Cameron farewells of Battier and James a month after watching a 10-point lead disintegrate inside the final 60 seconds, thanks to the greatness of Williams, who was angered by the "overrated" chant from the Cole Field House crowd. What would go down as the Miracle Minute inspired Duke's victory in overtime, to which some Maryland fans responded by throwing debris at the Duke parents' section. Three of the players' mothers were hit by thrown objects; Boozer's mother Renee was struck in the head by a plastic bottle. No, these programs did not like each other.

Duke arrived at Krzyzewski's ninth Final Four as the most prolific three-point shooting team ever, a fun fact given the coach's former opposition to the three-point rule. The Blue Devils were running and trapping and launching threes; Williams was on his way to scoring more points in a single season (841) than any Duke player before him, while Battier was collecting national Player of the Year awards and earning the NABC Defensive Player of the Year award for a third straight time.

But Maryland was a tough team with particularly tough guards in Juan Dixon and Steve Blake. Beating the Terrapins a third time in one season wouldn't be easy, a truth that was never more apparent than in the first half in the Metrodome. Maryland was tearing apart the Blue Devils before more than 45,000 witnesses. They held a 34–17 lead with 7:55 left in the half, and the five values that represented the five fingers of Coach K's famous fist — communication, trust, collective responsibility, caring, and pride — were nowhere to be found on the Duke side.

Krzyzewski always seemed to know exactly what to say in these situations. Before the Miracle Minute unfolded in Cole Field House during the regular season, Coach K had told his team, "We're going to win this game," exactly what he had said in 1992 before beating Kentucky. But a guarantee of victory this time around, when the Blue Devils were down big in the first half, would have sounded absurd. And Krzyzewski did have a history in the Metrodome of wiping out chalkboards, so it seemed likely that he was going to tee off on something, or someone, in this Final Four huddle.

Jeff LaMere was kneeling next to his boss, waiting for him to blister his team. "I thought it was going to be, 'What the fuck are you doing? Pull your heads out of your asses,'" LaMere said. "I had a backup clipboard ready in case he slammed the first one. We always had backup clipboards and backup pens; that was my manager training."

Instead, the Duke coach shocked his players by relaxing them. By telling them that the Terrapins weren't about to keep making everything for forty minutes, and that the Blue Devils weren't about to keep missing everything for forty minutes either. Krzyzewski ordered his players to look him in the eye and then told them, "Look, just play the way we play. You're losing by so much, you can't play any worse. So what are you worried about? That we're going to lose by 40? We're already losing by 20, so will you just play?"

Coach K thought his team had "played young" for the first twelve minutes. The Blue Devils were nervous, and he wanted them to leave that huddle relaxed. Over the last four years, including the postseason tournament, Duke had won seventy of seventy-six games against ACC opponents. The program was built on resilience, on finding a way, and when Maryland pushed the lead to 22, Duke started to find a way.

Nate James made a three-pointer to cut the deficit to 19 with 6:37 left in the half, and suddenly his teammates felt a surge of confidence. "That shot relaxed us," Battier recalled. "Then we said, 'It's okay for us to win this game.' Mike Dunleavy, the six-foot-nine sophomore, elevated high above the rim to tap in a Battier miss to cut it to 18. Duke kept chipping away, cutting the Maryland lead to eight in the final seconds before allowing Dixon an open look on a three-pointer that gave him 16 points for the half and gave his team a double-figure cushion.

As the Blue Devils ran into their locker room, Battier shouted at the top of his lungs, "We're going to win this fuckin' game." The players responded to their captain, then grew still as they took their seats. The locker room fell as silent as a church confessional booth at midnight. Krzyzewski was red-hot over that Dixon three, but again, he projected an even-tempered disposition to his team. He calmly told the Blue Devils that they needed to follow their instincts, play defense, and just be who they had been all year. He also told them that they were not to run any plays in the second half, that they were to attack with a purpose within the guidelines of his motion offense.

Soon enough, with Boozer back to being Boozer in the second half, Duke-Maryland became anybody's game. "Because of the Miracle Minute, and because in Atlanta we made a last-second shot to beat Maryland, we knew Maryland doubted whether they were better than us," Battier said. "In their heart of hearts, I don't think they knew if they could beat us . . . I remember [Maryland coach] Gary Williams with his jacket off, sweating through his shirt, and their players yelling at each other. We said, 'We've got these guys exactly where we want them.'"

When it got close, assistant Johnny Dawkins advised Krzyzewski to tell his players to stop gambling on defense, that it wasn't necessary any longer. Coach K thought it was the best suggestion of the night. Duke finally took the lead, 73–72, on Williams's first three-point make after eight misses, and then took the lead again on a Williams crossover and drive past his nemesis, Blake, a dogged lateral defender. Nate James, whom Krzyzewski had harshly criticized (as a source of motivation) for his Philly failures, contributed a huge tip-in with four minutes to play that gave Duke a 90–77 lead and reminded everyone of his tap to beat Maryland in the ACC Tournament.

James hounded Dixon in the second half, holding him to three points. Battier was brilliant on both ends, especially on the defensive end, where he finished with 4 blocks along with his 25 points and 8 rebounds. Williams contributed 23 points, and Boozer 19 on 7-of-8 shooting from the field as the Blue Devils completed the biggest second-half comeback in Final Four history. They outscored Maryland, 78–45, over the final twenty-seven minutes, leaving the Terrapins in tatters at the end of the school's first trip to the national semis.

"This team has a lot of heart," Krzyzewski said.

It was clear that he thought it had more heart, or at least better chemistry, than the '99 team. In the lead-up to Monday night's championship game against a powerful Arizona team, Coach K conceded that the looming NBA defections had fractured Duke's focus during its failed bid to win the national title two years earlier.

"There were probably some distractions there," he said. "And there's probably a tendency to think we didn't need each other as much, not malicious or anything. Whereas this team has been in so many close games, so many situations, they know they need each other. We're better prepared to be in this game. I don't think we're more talented than that team, but we're more prepared to be in this game than we were in 1999."

One Duke player said Krzyzewski did address with the team the problems he identified with the '99 group. "And we came together in '01 ten times better than the '99 team," the player said. "The '01 team was willing to have hard conversations with each other. That team had genuine love and respect for each other. It doesn't mean we always got along. Shane and Jason a lot of times didn't get along, but they would confront it more than the '99 team . . . They didn't let that shit bottle up. In '99, it bottled up."

Back when the players were preparing for the annual preseason Blue-White scrimmage, Coach K spotted what he thought might be friction between Williams and Battier, arguably the nation's two best players, when Battier ignored his open teammate on the perimeter to take a forced shot. Krzyzewski asked them why they weren't passing to each other, inspiring a conversation between the players that ended in a shared commitment to working together toward a championship.

COACH K CARRIED an interesting roster into the 2001 title game. It included big man Matt Christensen, who had arrived in Durham in 1995 and, after missing three consecutive seasons (two as a missionary in Germany for the Church of Jesus Christ of Latter-day Saints), still had another year of eligibility remaining for 2001–2002. It also included Krzyzewski's nephew, sophomore walk-on Andy Borman, a scholarship soccer player and the son of Mickie's sister Donna and the grandson of Frank Borman, the first commanding astronaut (of the Apollo 8 crew) to fly around the moon.

Andre Buckner, five-foot-ten grinder, was a late, emergency addition in recruiting after William Avery announced he was leaving for the NBA. As a member of the blue team, the Duke backups who competed against the starters in white, Buckner was a defensive-minded player who once caught Coach K's eye by repeatedly dribbling into trouble in the corners. "You can't keep burying yourself in the fuckin' corner like a little fuckin' mole," Krzyzewski shouted at him. Dahntay Jones, an athletic transfer from Rutgers, gave Krzyzewski the Jersey toughness he craved in practice by pushing Battier to the limit. Freshman Reggie Love, a scholarship football player, added some necessary speed. Senior walk-on Ryan Caldbeck, who started out as a freshman manager, said he spent much of his time hoping Coach K would yell at him, "because he yells at people he thinks are great." After noticing Caldbeck's father sitting in the stands during one practice, Krzyzewski went out of his way to praise Ryan on a particular play so his dad could hear it. "That was worth a 25-point game to me," Caldbeck said.

In the end, the Blue Devils were defined by two stars comparable to the cornerstones of the New York Yankees dynasty: Williams was Mariano Rivera, the indomitable closer. Battier was Derek Jeter, the team's heartbeat and a model representative of his sport.

"He played the game the right way all the time," Love said. "I was never confused about [whose team it was]. It was Shane's team."

The senior captain thought this team was hungrier than the '99 team. He thought it showed uncommon resolve in overcoming the Boozer injury and the 22-point Maryland lead. "It felt like a team of destiny," Battier said. "When I left the hotel, I felt like, 'This is our time.' I didn't feel like it was our time in '99. I never had that feeling in '99 that 'this is our moment. This is our night.'"

On April 2, 2001, Arizona just happened to be the available opponent. "We felt like we were invincible," Boozer said. Everyone at Duke wanted this one, especially the university president, Nan Keohane, who had taken over after the Blue Devils won their back-to-back titles in the Laettner-Hurley-Hill years. She once heard someone at her alma mater, Wellesley, ask her in a dismayed tone, "Do you really have to go to all the games?" Keohane responded, "I beg your pardon. I can't believe you asked that question." She loved basketball, and she loved the idea of Krzyzewski's team winning it all on her watch.

It was all going to work out. Duke was not losing Shane Battier's last college game, not after what went down in '99, and not after Krzyzewski had asked the deferential sophomore then to start looking in a mirror and telling himself he could be the best player in the game.

Coach K played that same game with himself. He sometimes looked in his own mirror to get motivated before speaking engagements, telling himself, "You're going to be good. This is going to go well. You're going to be strong." Krzyzewski performed this little drill with his mirror, he said, so he could see himself showing "a strong face."

Krzyzewski had a very strong face as he watched his team beat Arizona, 82–72, to win his third championship ring. Mike Dunleavy, who had struggled against Maryland, made three consecutive threes in forty-five second-half seconds to give Duke a 10-point lead, and Battier blocked a Jason Gardner layup and threw a no-look, behind-the-back, falling-out-of-bounds pass to start a fast break that CBS analyst Billy Packer called the play of the tournament.

Coach K had made a critical adjustment at halftime, while presiding over his usual intermission routine — meet with the players, meet with the staff, then meet with the players again before taking the floor. He told the Blue Devils he would start Boozer in place of Sanders for the final twenty minutes, and then he asked Sanders in front of his teammates to confirm that he would accept this move. Sanders did as he was asked, and Boozer finished with 12 points, 12 rebounds, and 2 blocks. The great Duke teams always made individual sacrifices for the benefit of the whole.

Arizona fans and even the Maryland fans who had stuck around ranted about the officiating afterward, especially about a noncall involving Williams in the first half, when he ended up on Gardner's back in pursuit of a loose ball and somehow didn't get whistled for his third foul. Fans were claiming that Duke got all the calls, just like the Yankees, or the Celtics, or the Lakers, and they were citing the stat sheet as strong circumstantial evidence. The Blue Devils took 301 more free throws than their opponents in 2000–2001 despite launching more than 1,000 three-pointers. How in the world was that possible?

"I think in any sport there's a tendency at times to blame something that shouldn't be blamed," Krzyzewski had said. Funny how things worked out. Coach K once caused a Tobacco Road shitstorm by crying that there was a double standard in the ACC, that Dean Smith's North Carolina got the benefit of every doubt. And now the Blue Devils had become the Tar Heels, and Mike Krzyzewski had become Dean Smith.

In the final seconds, young Duhon had the presence of mind to hand the ball to Williams. The freshman had recalled the sophomore telling him it was his dream to someday throw the ball toward the ceiling of a big arena after winning a ring, and heave it toward the Metrodome ceiling he did. Krzyzewski jumped into a group hug with his assistants, including three former Duke guards — Johnny Dawkins, Chris Collins, and Steve Wojciechowski — who had failed to win it all as players.

The 2001 team had taken the same Greensboro-Philadelphia-Minneapolis journey to the title that the 1992 team had taken. Dunleavy played the game of his life in scoring 21, and Battier delivered 18 points, 11 rebounds, 6 assists, 2 blocks, and 0 turnovers in forty minutes. Krzyzewski wrapped his captain in a warm embrace and told him he loved him. "I'd never seen Coach that happy," Battier said.

Krzyzewski kissed Mickie and daughters Lindy and Jamie in their group family hug. His oldest, Debbie, who was back home after giving birth to her second son, Michael, was on a cell phone, and Krzyzewski told her she was part of that group hug. Coach K, fifty-four-year-old grandfather, had tied Bob Knight with three titles, leaving him behind only Wooden (ten) and Adolph Rupp (four) on the all-time Division I list. The Blue Devils had won an NCAA record 133 games (against 15 losses) in Battier's four years, punctuated by a month their coach called the most enjoyable of his career.

"To give him his third championship and separate him from the pack that had won two is the best way that I could go out," Battier said. "It's my going-away present to him. Coach is the best. He's a mentor. He's a friend. He's a coach. He's a brother. I am the luckiest person to have the relationship with him for the last four years. And I know that he'll be one of my most valuable friends for the rest of my life."

On the jubilant bus ride away from the Metrodome, someone was blasting the Bee Gees song "Stayin' Alive" while the Duke coach went up and down the aisle performing John Travolta's *Saturday Night Fever* moves, to his team's delight. Finally, Mike Krzyzewski was all the way back. Once again, he was the last man standing — and the last man dancing.

BOB KNIGHT WAS onstage preparing to present Mike Krzyzewski for induction into the Naismith Memorial Basketball Hall of Fame, and at one point Krzyzewski had been certain he didn't want Knight there. A relationship that had started to unravel at the 1992 Final Four, with Knight's drive-by handshake and bitter note, was still in need of major reconstructive surgery.

A year after meeting in Alaska without incident, Krzyzewski and Knight met again in the 1996 Preseason NIT at Madison Square Garden. The teams had been invited beforehand to Tavern on the Green in Central Park, and according to a member of Duke's traveling party, Knight put on a show when he was returning to his table after saying a few words about the event. "He walked right by our team and stared us down," the person said. "You forget how big of a guy he is. I remember he looked right in our eyes, trying to intimidate us. It was like looking a shark in the eye."

On game night, the Indiana coach didn't want to look the Duke coach in the eye, at least not when it came time to have a cordial pregame chat. The president of the NIT, Frank McLaughlin, was sitting in his courtside seat when a man approached with word that Knight wanted to see him in the locker room area. *Oh shit,* McLaughlin said to himself, *now I've got to deal with a real problem here.* The Hoosiers were warming up on the Garden floor, all their assistants were on the bench, and Krzyzewski was out there waiting to shake hands with Knight and exchange small talk.

"I go back there, and Knight just wanted to bullshit," McLaughlin said. "This was when they weren't getting along, and if Mike is honest with you he'll say he was very nervous about it. I'm standing in the back bullshitting with Knight, and all of a sudden he hears the horn and says, 'Okay, I've got to go.' Mike was just standing there waiting for him to come out. It was very cold."

Krzyzewski was waiting near the Indiana bench, waiting and waiting, until Knight finally arrived, only to turn away from his former Army point guard to talk to his horse racing buddy, trainer D. Wayne Lukas, compelling the flustered Duke coach to return to his bench. Krzyzewski would later tell author John Feinstein, "That's the period on the end of the sentence. I tried. It's been almost five years. Enough. I'm done."

On the flight back to Durham after Indiana's 85–69 victory, Krzyzewski told Mickie, "I will never let that happen again." One player who observed their conversation said, "I know Coach K was hurt by that moment with Bob Knight . . . Mickie was helping him process that. I didn't hear their exact words on the plane, but I know that's what that was about. Mickie was there to make sure she helped him through it."

Nearly five years later, Krzyzewski needed a presenter for his Naismith induction. He didn't want to ask Knight to do the honors because Knight might say no, or he might deliver an angry lecture Krzyzewski didn't want to hear before saying yes, or he might embarrass the inductee during his presentation. "Mike didn't want to set himself up to be shit on," one of his associates said.

Knight had been fired by Indiana president Myles Brand the previous September for "uncivil, defiant, and unacceptable" conduct, with "gross insubordination" tossed in for good measure. After CNN/*SI* aired a tape showing Knight choking an Indiana player, Neil Reed, in a 1997 practice, he'd been suspended, fined, and reinstated under a zero-tolerance policy that he quickly violated. Game, set, match.

Knight was hired by Texas Tech, but he was still toxic and unpredictable and still holding some kind of grudge against the Duke coach. Krzyzewski sought the counsel of those he trusted, including Mickie. Colonel Tom Rogers, a friend to both, tried to act as a human bridge back to peaceful times. As it turned out, a Knight mentor and Krzyzewski friend, Pete Newell, helped bring the two men together. When Coach K was debating whether to give in and ask Knight, according to a Krzyzewski associate, "Newell said, 'No, you call Bob right now and fix this.'" Krzyzewski collected himself and made the phone call. He told his old coach he would have never made the Hall of Fame without him, asked the question he needed to ask, and then held his breath.

"Mike," Knight told him, "it's not just something I should do. It's something I want to do."

So Knight was up there in Springfield, Massachusetts, on the night of October 5, 2001, three and a half weeks after the 9/11 terrorist attacks. He was wearing a gray suit and looking about seven feet tall. He was closing hard on his sixty-first birthday, and his hair was almost snow-white. The General spoke for eight minutes and forty-one seconds, and it was a command performance. Good Bobby, not Bad Bobby. He spoke of the 9/11 age presenting a challenge unlike any America had faced since the Civil War, and he asked everyone in the audience who had served in any branch of the military to please stand and accept the crowd's gratitude, a thoughtful, moving gesture.

When the two coaches sat next to each other earlier in the day to answer reporters' questions, Knight said he always got a kick out of his former player and frequent target saying that he thought his first name at West Point was "GoddamnitMike." Knight said that his former player could have done anything he wanted if he hadn't gone into coaching, and that the integrity of his basketball program was more important than his 606-223 career record at Duke and Army, his nine Final Four trips, his seven title-game appearances, and his three rings.

The press availability went smoothly, but that was merely the morning shootaround. The game wouldn't start until Knight took the podium and started going who knows where with his speech. Sitting in the front row, Mickie kept her left hand on her husband's right shoulder, as if bracing him for impact. "I think perhaps if I did anything to help Mike along the way," Knight told the crowd, "it was showing him a hell of a lot of things not to do. I think that he learned well in that regard from some of the things I've done over the years." It was a good start.

Knight praised Krzyzewski for proving that you can win high-major college basketball games with good students who know how to represent their university, and for assembling and leading teams "that are a model for every team that plays basketball at any level in the United States." Knight started to choke up as he headed for home, as did Krzyzewski, whose face tightened into a knot while Mickie held onto him with both hands. The two greats looked at each other, their feud temporarily forgotten. Knight then moved to induct his old point guard through the chairman of the Hall of Fame by saying, "I'd like to give Dave Gavitt a graduate of the United States Military Academy, a former Army officer, and the best coach that I've ever had a team play against. Mike, would you come up here?"

Mickie had turned to her right toward her daughters, as if she were stunned by Knight's graciousness. Krzyzewski walked up to the stage with Debbie, Lindy, and Jamie and was officially welcomed into the Hall by Gavitt before he kissed his girls and then walked into the arms of Knight, who patted Krzyzewski five times on the back. And then the new Hall of Famer walked to the microphone with his new Hall of Fame ring in a small box. He was sniffling, wiping away tears, and exhaling with exaggeration, before he turned to Knight and told him that he was the only person in his life he'd ever called "Coach," and that he felt "there's really no greater honor for me than having you be the person who presented me tonight."

Krzyzewski introduced his big brother Bill, a captain in the Chicago Fire Department, and asked all his former Duke and Army players in the audience to stand. He gave a shout-out to the Columbos and to his best friend from that group, Moe Mlynski. He recalled his high school coach, Al Ostrowski, and his demand that Mike shoot the ball whenever he wanted, and he joked about how he would've put his life in danger at West Point had he ignored Knight's demand that he never, ever shoot.

Coach K talked about his mother Emily, the central figure in his youth. He recalled staying in her apartment on a recruiting trip to Chicago a decade earlier, when Emily had served him sandwiches and soup and ice cream that was already stirred up, just the way Mike liked it. She silently watched her son eat and waited for him to finish. That's the way it was during mealtime in those days. "You didn't bother the man," Krzyzewski said. When Mike was free to be bothered, his mother asked him a question similar to the one she asked one day on his North Carolina porch.

"Why is it you?" Emily said.

"What?" her son responded.

"Why is it you? How are you the coach of the national championship team?"

The cleaning lady and daughter of Polish immigrants wanted and expected something better for Mike, but she never expected this. "There was always a limit on your dreams," Krzyzewski said.

Near the end of his induction speech, Krzyzewski described Mickie as the most important person in his life, his partner, and the one person he wanted in the front car of his train. He called his wife over to the podium, pulled her in tight, and prepared to leave the stage with her arm in arm.

One moment in Krzyzewski's speech was more profound than any other. A reporter had asked the Duke coach about his induction, "How do you feel about going in and becoming immortal?"

Krzyzewski started to respond that he had never considered himself immortal, but caught himself. That word "immortal" had triggered something. It made him think of his father.

"I didn't know my dad very well," Krzyzewski said. Nobody did, outside of Emily. William Krzyzewski, the elevator operator who would open a small restaurant and bar, was too busy providing for his younger son to get to know him. He changed his surname to help his two boys navigate a world that often wasn't kind to the families of immigrants. "My dad always went by Kross just so he would get jobs, so we could eat," Krzyzewski told his audience.

Man, how badly Coach K wished William Kross was up on the stage with the rest of his family. He might not have been surprised that his son was being recognized among the all-time greats in his chosen profession, Krzyzewski said, "but he would have been amazed that somebody with the name Krzyzewski would make it." Soon enough the inductee lowered his head, grabbed his ring box, and held it with both hands as a tremor came across his face. "So I'm glad my dad's in the Hall of Fame with me," Krzyzewski said through a quivering voice, prompting the crowd to honor the moment with loud, extended applause.

So this night wasn't about Mickie, or Emily, or the girls, or the Columbos, or even the estranged mentor. For a change, this night belonged to one earnest, distant, and seemingly immortal man. Goddamnit, that was William Krzyzewski's son going into the Hall of Fame.

13

GOLD

Duke got all the calls. That's what just about everyone outside of Durham, North Carolina, was saying. As sure as Mike Krzyzewski once said it about Dean Smith's Tar Heels, people were saying it about Coach K's Blue Devils. And not just when it came to a referee's whistle.

While Duke was preparing to face Connecticut at the 2004 Final Four in San Antonio, the NCAA revealed that the school would not be penalized for playing Corey Maggette during the 1998–1999 season despite the fact that Maggette had taken $2,000 from his Kansas City–based AAU coach Myron Piggie before he attended college. That $2,000 had rendered Maggette ineligible to play at Duke, putting in jeopardy the thirty-seven victories he played in and the Blue Devils' runner-up standing after their title-game loss to UConn.

And yet the NCAA decided — all this time later — that Duke did not deserve to have its relatively pristine reputation tarnished. "After a lengthy investigation," said David Price, the governing body's vice president of enforcement, "we came to the conclusion that there was insufficient evidence to determine the institution knew or should have known" about Piggie's payments to Maggette. Duke's internal investigation, led by former FBI agent and audit department member Paul Stirrup, reached the same verdict. Chris Kennedy, Duke's compliance director and a longtime athletics official at the school, wrote the argument for the NCAA that neither Maggette nor the Blue Devils deserved to be punished.

"The crux of it was that Corey was young, and that in the AAU basketball world sixteen-, seventeen-, eighteen-year-old kids don't always understand where the line is between permissible and impermissible," Kennedy said. "Everyone knows you're not supposed to get a car, but did Corey know that $2,000 wasn't okay beyond all the other stuff he was getting? Probably not."

Kennedy argued that Krzyzewski and his assistants were not heavily recruiting Maggette at the time of the violation. "Our coaches document their observations with every phone call and visit," he said, "and it was clear he wasn't the primary focus of their recruiting . . . We weren't looking closely at him, and we had no way of knowing what he was receiving. We were thinking more about other kids at the time."

Said Krzyzewski of the investigators: "They did it properly. I thought it was never an issue, so I never paid that much attention to it."

But at the time of Piggie's 2000 indictment on seven felony (and four misdemeanor) charges, including defrauding Duke and three other universities by paying high school basketball stars (who later signed with those schools) to compete in summer and AAU tournaments for his team, an NCAA spokesperson said, "We will have to determine if Duke, in fact, had an ineligible player in the NCAA Tournament." Duke did, in fact, have an ineligible player in the NCAA Tournament, and yet nothing was done about it.

The indictment charged that Piggie used the players to obtain payments from a local businessman, sports agents, and Nike, which provided him with a $425,000 consulting and travel team contract and nearly $160,000 in property and money. Three of the four players who attended college after being paid by Piggie were suspended; the lone exception was Maggette, who had already left Duke and was finishing up his rookie NBA season with the Orlando Magic. Piggie would serve thirty-seven months in prison for charges related to the scheme. According to court documents connected to his 2002 appeal, Piggie "realized at least $677,760 in income through his scheme." The documents reported that Duke was "subject to the forfeiture of its second place finish in the 1999 NCAA Tournament and the loss of $226,814.51 in tournament revenue." By using the ineligible Maggette in competition, the documents said, "the validity of Duke's entire 1998–1999 season was called into question."

But the university and its basketball program didn't lose anything as a result of the case; in fact, Piggie would occasionally send Duke court-mandated restitution checks from prison in the amount of $30 or $32 toward the $12,704.39 it cost the school to investigate the Maggette matter.

Numerous major figures in the sport were stunned by the NCAA's decision to effectively clear Duke and pointed to other cases of schools vacating victories and Final Four appearances and returning postseason tournament revenue when rule-breaking was confirmed after the fact.

In 1997, Massachusetts became the sixth Division I school forced to vacate a Final Four appearance for violating NCAA rules. Though head coach John Calipari was not directly tied to violations, and though NCAA officials did not find that UMass was aware that star center Marcus Camby had received improper gifts from agents, the school had its first trip to the national semifinals wiped out. The NCAA's Bill Saum explained that UMass was penalized because "they still received the benefit of a competitive advantage by competing with the ineligible student-athlete."

So did Duke.

The entire Fab Five era at Michigan was vaporized by the discovery that prominent players had taken money from a booster. Years later, one of Krzyzewski's best friends, Syracuse coach Jim Boeheim, lost 108 victories from his then-total of 966 because of various infractions in his program. One such infraction reportedly involved forward Terrence Roberts and money he was paid by a local YMCA. "I lost forty-five games for $300," Boeheim said. "A guy got $300 and paid it back, but they said he didn't do it the right way, so the forty-five games he played in that you won, we're taking away . . . I'd like to have those wins, but that's the way it is."

Asked if Krzyzewski, the only man ahead of him on the all-time Division I victories list, should have lost the thirty-seven victories that Maggette participated in, Boeheim said, "I don't know. Every ruling is different. A committee can say nobody knew, so we're not going to punish you. Or they can say, on the same case, that you should have known, and so we're going to take [the victories]. That's what they can do. They can do it either way."

Asked if he felt that a school such as Syracuse would have lost those thirty-seven victories by playing Maggette, Boeheim said, "I don't know. There's no way of knowing that . . . I've heard the double-standard thing many, many times [about Duke] from many, many people. I think the thing with the NCAA is, if they investigated anybody hard, really hard, going deep, they're going to find something."

Did the NCAA want to investigate Duke as thoroughly as it would Jerry Tarkanian's programs and the other usual suspects? Was the governing body guilty — as some coaches believed — of selective prosecution?

On April 3, 2003, Josh Peter of the *Times-Picayune* of New Orleans reported that the mother of Duke's Chris Duhon and the father of Duke's Carlos Boozer were hired by Krzyzewski associates after they moved to Durham. The pharmaceutical company head who hired Carlos Boozer Sr., Robert Ingram, told the newspaper that he was proud of his friendship with Krzyzewski, but that he had never discussed the hire with the Duke coach.

(Boozer Sr. denied to the newspaper that Duke played any part in securing him employment.) Peter reported that Duhon's mother, Vivian Harper, filled a job opening at a money management firm that was never posted, and that, according to a former company executive, she "started at a higher salary than other account specialists and got a significant raise in her first few months on the job." Harper declined comment in the report. Chris Kennedy told the newspaper that Harper was the most diligent of the Duke parents when it came to potential NCAA violations. The compliance director would say years later, "She called all the time with compliance questions. I do remember when they moved to Durham, we didn't even recommend the realtor because we thought that might be an extra benefit.

"In both [the Duhon and Boozer] cases, we're not going to tell somebody you can't apply to this job because it's associated with Duke, because the owner or employer went to Duke or is a Duke fan. We're just not going to help."

The NCAA conducted no meaningful inquiry into the *Times-Picayune* report. "If they go after Duke," said one former Division I head coach with ties to Krzyzewski, "it makes the whole thing look corrupt." It appeared the only reporter or columnist who followed up the report at the Final Four was the *Boston Globe*'s Bob Ryan, who wrote:

> Coach K? Say it isn't so! . . . Duke always wants you to think it takes the highest road possible. Remember when Coach K refused to hang an early championship banner in Cameron because Phil Henderson and Alaa Abdelnaby had left school without degrees? Seems like a long time ago . . . The world has changed, and Mike Krzyzewski has been forced to react by lowering his standards. Every kid Krzyzewski goes after now is just one more spoiled AAU pup with a ridiculous entitlement mentality. He'll never see another Grant Hill or Shane Battier if he lives to be 500.

Carlos Boozer Jr., who played three seasons for the Blue Devils before turning pro, later denied that he or any family members ever received any improper inducement from a Duke coach, associate, or third party acting in the school's interest. "Coach K said, 'Everything you get from Duke, you're going to have to earn, on the court and in the classroom,'" recalled Boozer, who said that this no-frills approach appealed to him.

Boozer said that one school that didn't speak directly to him but made a pitch to his parents "offered to buy them an $800,000 house, and $300,000 in cold, hard cash. My parents were like, 'No.' On the spot they said, 'No.' I had a person tell me directly at the time, 'Either an Expedition or a Lincoln Navigator. An expensive SUV, and a two-bedroom apartment, and $5,000 in cash a month.' And I wouldn't have to go to class . . . I didn't want that.

"You see a top-five player in the country going to a football school, you know what happened. I'm not going to name names, but you know what happened. We have a joke in the NBA [about players like that]: 'He took a pay cut to go to the league.' I was one of the guys in that situation. People were trying to buy my services. My mom and dad taught me the right way at an early age."

Many Duke players told similar tales of rejecting the easy life inside a morally bankrupt program for the West Point values of Krzyzewski's own little academy in Durham. Elton Brand said that he had turned down offers of cars and money from different places, and the convenience of a luxury lodge (with an in-house chef) near the basketball arena from one major program where, he said, the players were already treated as semipros. He chose Duke despite the fact that there would be no perks (legal or otherwise); that freshmen weren't allowed cars on the grounds; that he would live in a dorm with all other freshmen on East Campus, away from the main West Campus; and that he would have to take early morning buses for classes and workouts.

"My mindset was education," Brand said.

But so much money was at stake for the nation's top recruits, and so many agents, financial advisors, sneaker reps, summer coaches, workout coaches, and assorted handlers were often making a play for that money, that it was hard to see how any major college program could remain 100 percent clean. "It is almost impossible to do this job without cheating," said one major college head coach with ties to Krzyzewski. "I'm trying, but it's very hard." The head coach said that many elite prospects already had deals with agents before they stepped on a college campus, and that he knew to stay away from a recruit if that kid's list of finalists included mostly schools known to cheat to get their man.

"I've lost a kid for $100,000," the coach said.

A second major college head coach, this one from the South, said it had become impossible for a Division I staff to monitor everyone their players and recruits were associating with. "Did things happen at virtually every school, Duke included, that the head coaches definitely would not have wanted to happen? I would say that's true," said the coach, who had won hundreds of Division I games and had competed against Krzyzewski. "I'd say it happened to me, things I didn't know that maybe I found out about five years later. Fortunately, I never had an NCAA problem.

"You think when you hear these things involving Duke, 'Well, now there has to be some sort of investigation.' And then somebody finds a sinkhole somewhere and flushes it."

One highly respected recruiting analyst said that the practice of finding ways to help parents move close to campus and secure employment was "incredibly common" among schools. Said Boeheim: "Can you argue, 'I didn't know my friend was doing this?' You can, you can. And I'm sure [investigators] went in and said, 'How did you get this job?' And they said, 'Well, I read about it and I went over there and I applied and they gave me the job.' And the guy that hired him said, 'Mike [Krzyzewski] didn't tell me that. I just felt like they would be good.' It happens all the time."

The recruiting analyst pointed out that what the NCAA enforcement officials knew about such practices and what they could prove about them were two entirely different things. The same went for Nike and Adidas pouring money into certain prospects' summer basketball programs for future considerations, or for the kind of paid exhibition games that Duke played against Mickey Walker's team of ex-college players. UConn paid a $25,000 appearance fee to an AAU program that included elite Baltimore recruit Rudy Gay, who then signed with the Huskies, much to the dismay of Maryland coach Gary Williams. The same also went for the kind of package deals that schools made to land a recruit — giving an assistant's job to his high school or summer coach, or even to a family member. While coaching Kansas, Larry Brown landed Danny Manning after hiring his father Ed. The Jayhawks won the national title four years later.

"At the highest level, everyone cheats," the recruiting analyst said. "It comes down to, are you going a little over the speed limit, or are you outright paying people? In my mind, at that highest level, everyone is breaking NCAA rules, but not everyone is outright paying players."

One Duke athletics official recalled Krzyzewski specifically advising Elton Brand to never take money from anyone, especially agents. "You have too much to lose," Coach K told Brand. The official said that Krzyzewski was proactive in talking to his players about the dangers of associating with unscrupulous third parties. The school appointed a committee to counsel athletes on matters involving agents.

But as the Blue Devils kept winning, and kept signing big-time recruits, questions kept coming up. One member of the program during the late 1990s said that he wondered why family members of players often moved to Durham, and how they could travel to all the away games, and why team members often ended up driving luxury cars. "At a team meal or an event you had to drive to," said the program member, "you'd see a caravan of expensive cars, like in a movie when someone important has an escort of eight or nine SUVs in a row. It was like that." A Duke athletics official from the same time period said it wasn't uncommon to see a player "roll up in a bling'd-up Escalade." Though neither Duke source believed that Krzyzewski or any Blue Devil assistant or staffer had anything to do with providing the cars, both wondered if players were receiving improper benefits from agents or financial advisors looking to cash in later on professional contracts. (The NCAA did not allow student-athletes to borrow against future earnings.)

Duke's Chris Kennedy said that his compliance office was never made aware of an issue involving players driving luxury cars. "I would have been the one to look into it," Kennedy said. When it came to the underbelly of the recruiting game, the compliance director had earlier conceded that it was "impossible to know everything that's going on out there."

One veteran Blue Devil from the late 1990s said that teammates had told him they'd rejected up to $100,000 from other schools to sign, but that he had never heard any tales of Duke impropriety. "There certainly were one or two guys driving around nice cars," he said. "I never asked about it. My impression was that stuff never went through Duke . . . Coaches would tell us to stay away from people, to keep it clean. But I could walk into a Foot Locker in Durham and get whatever I want. Nobody's wearing face masks in basketball, so people know us. There's only twelve on a team."

Another veteran Blue Devil who was part of a Final Four run in the 2000s maintained that he almost never saw team members driving luxury vehicles, and that some players from lower-income backgrounds needed to borrow gas money to get around. "Some of them really had nothing," said the veteran player, who knew of fellow recruits on the AAU circuit who received offers of cars, cash, clothes, travel allowances, jobs for parents, and family relocation to houses near campus from other schools. The veteran player said that he did believe agents had made relatively small, but improper, payments to Duke teammates in need.

"We're talking clothes, PlayStation, the electric bill; they came from nothing," said the player, who added that the only basketball-related perk provided him over four years at Duke was the ability to call someone to fix a campus parking ticket.

"Coach K is one of the most genuine human beings I've met," he said. "He practices what he preaches at the highest level. I believe the Duke program is run that way. All I saw in my experience at Duke was, we all ate the same food and lived in the same dorms with everyone else. I saw what cars people were driving, and everything was exactly the way it should be —

aboveboard. I lived in a twelve-by-twelve dorm room with two roommates, and we all slept on twin beds and had to take a bus to 6 a.m. conditioning. There were no special privileges for players."

And sometimes not for parents either. To make her son's weekday games, Dahntay Jones's mother Joanne, an information technology manager at Johnson & Johnson in New Jersey, used up all of her vacation time and personal time to leave company headquarters in the early afternoon to race to Newark International Airport to catch a flight to Raleigh-Durham to make the nighttime tipoff at Duke. She would then take the 6 a.m. flight back the next day and be at Johnson & Johnson by 8:30. Her husband joined her for weekend games. They never requested, nor were offered, help in finding jobs in Durham.

One longtime major college coach with multiple NCAA Tournament appearances agreed with popular public opinion — and with the official NCAA infractions record — that Krzyzewski had never knowingly violated rules. "Coach K would live in the gray area, but would never go to the side where he flat-out cheated," the coach said. "There's a certain amount of honor going back to his upbringing. I think he would go right up to the line, but he wouldn't cross it."

While Krzyzewski was still being held up in most corners of major college athletics as one of the sport's last incorruptible figures, the Coach K assistant who spearheaded Duke's philosophical change in recruiting to an aggressive, more open-minded approach with the AAU community was running into serious trouble at Missouri. Quin Snyder was named by the NCAA in seventeen allegations of rule-breaking between 1999 and 2003, including recruiting violations, improper gifts and meals provided to players, and a failure, the governing body said, "at all times to maintain an environment of NCAA rules compliance" among his basketball staff.

Snyder believed that he would weather the NCAA storm, and that the vast web of relationships he had established, from the grass roots through the pros, would ultimately elevate Missouri to the same championship level as Duke. Meanwhile, despite undergoing a second hip replacement surgery, his old boss, Krzyzewski, was still going strong in Durham, following up the 2001 title with two trips to the Sweet 16 and his tenth trip to the Final Four.

The run to the 2004 Final Four with sharpshooting sophomore J. J. Redick, the one-and-done freshman forward Luol Deng, sophomore big man Shelden Williams, and the senior Duhon proved to be more painful than the rib injury Duhon was playing through. The Blue Devils held an eight-point lead over Connecticut with 2:48 left in the semifinal when Deng took a three-pointer that probably would've sealed it. He missed, UConn's

Rashad Anderson made a three, and, with Williams fouled out, Duke fell apart in the deciding sequences, taking bad shots and allowing the Huskies to score a dozen straight points. Duhon's running three-pointer to beat the buzzer made the final score 79–78 and, if nothing else, made those who bet on the underdog Blue Devils (getting two or three points) feel like winners.

UConn had the better team; it would place two players — Emeka Okafor and Ben Gordon — among the top three picks in the 2004 NBA draft. But after watching his three guards (Duhon, Redick, and Daniel Ewing) shoot 13-for-37, and Williams shoot 1-for-9 while foul trouble limited him to nineteen minutes, Krzyzewski was tormented by the missed opportunity, and by the wasted chance to avenge his '99 loss to Jim Calhoun. Ignoring the fact that the officials whistled the six-foot-ten Okafor for two fouls in the game's first four minutes, sending the center to the bench for the rest of the half, Krzyzewski yelled at one ref near game's end, "You cheated us."

For once, college basketball fans around the country thought, Coach K did not get all the calls in a big spot. But that was okay. He was about to get the biggest call of his professional life.

ON THE NIGHT of June 6, 2005, Jerry Colangelo stood inside a ballroom above the National Italian American Sports Hall of Fame and looked out on some of the more iconic figures in basketball history. Michael Jordan. Dean Smith. Larry Bird. John Thompson. Oscar Robertson. Chuck Daly. Clyde Drexler. Chris Mullin. Jerry West. Jordan had pulled up to the Chicago museum in a dark green Bentley valued at $160,000. Of course he did.

They served rigatoni and meatballs and fried calamari, but the main item on the menu that night was basketball: USA Basketball, to be exact, and how to fix the international embarrassment it had become. After barely surviving Lithuania in the 2000 Olympic semis, the Americans finished sixth — *sixth* — in the 2002 world championship tournament in Indianapolis, where head coach George Karl blamed his team's lack of competitive fire in three losses on "the money and greed of the NBA." Two years later, when some stars declined to travel to Greece, Team USA failed to win Olympic gold with NBA players for the first time, losing by 19 to Puerto Rico in the opener on the way to a bronze-medal finish that infuriated the NBA commissioner, David Stern.

It was clear early on that head coach Larry Brown hated his young and inexperienced team. He suspended Allen Iverson, Amar'e Stoudemire, and LeBron James for showing up late to a meeting before an exhibition game against Puerto Rico. After Stephon Marbury made a critical comment to a reporter during an exhibition stop in Serbia, Brown was so enraged that he told his assistant, North Carolina coach Roy Williams, that he was seriously considering sending the point guard home.

During the tournament, Stern called a reporter in Athens to rip Brown for failing to give the nineteen-year-old James more playing time, for whining about the limited time he had to mold the team into a cohesive unit, and for blaming the selection committee for not giving him the players he needed to prevail. "This was a team that was put together by everyone, including the coaching staff," Stern said at a press conference he called at halftime of the semifinal loss to Argentina. "And this is a great team. So I don't buy the, 'Well, I'd like to have this, I'd like to have that' . . . It's not about who didn't come. You take your team to the gym and you play what you've got and then you either win or you lose."

Roy Williams thought his fellow North Carolina graduate shouldered too much of the blame. "It wasn't Larry Brown's fault," Williams said. "It was David Stern and all the NBA people making us take those guys who were not ready. They were just thinking about marketing with LeBron and Carmelo [Anthony] . . . That woke up the USA that we can't do this with these kids that young."

It wasn't just the youngsters who had trouble adjusting. Tim Duncan, six-time NBA All-Star, could barely take five steps on the court before being whistled for a foul. "FIBA sucks," Duncan concluded. Watching with disgust, said a USA Basketball source, "Stern was like, 'Why are we doing this? Let's get out of the Olympics." His deputy commissioner, Russ Granik, was among those who argued that the process merely needed an overhaul with someone in the role of overlord. That someone would be Jerry Colangelo, former Phoenix Suns owner and Arizona Diamondbacks CEO. A four-time NBA Executive of the Year who beat George Steinbrenner's dynastic Yankees in the 2001 World Series, Colangelo was home recovering from prostate cancer surgery when Granik called and asked if he would take over USA Basketball.

Colangelo soon accepted on two conditions: (1) full autonomy in picking the players and the coaches, to hell with any committee; and (2) what amounted to an unlimited budget. Stern was fine with the first condition, and not so fine with the second. When Colangelo assured the commissioner that he could raise the necessary money to run the program the way he wanted it run, they had a deal.

"I came to the conclusion that we had lost the respect of the world basketball community not just by finishing third, but in how we conducted ourselves," Colangelo said. "It was really bad, and people were saying a lot of nasty things about our players, and about USA Basketball. It was certainly evident to me that we had to change the culture. And to me the best way to change the culture was to start showing respect to the world basketball community, and only then could we earn back their respect."

Colangelo invited former Olympic coaches and players to his summit in June — the same week as the NBA's pre-draft camp in Chicago — to discuss the best way to build a winning international culture. The three coaches who couldn't make it were Pete Newell, who was recovering from cancer surgery; Bob Knight, who was on one of his fishing trips; and Larry Brown, who was busy leading the Detroit Pistons to a Game 7 Eastern Conference victory over the Miami Heat. Colangelo was not happy that his friend Knight didn't reserve room for this special event in the middle of his fishing and hunting schedule.

There were more than thirty dignitaries in the room, and Colangelo wanted to hear potential solutions from all of them. The mood was serious, yet casual. Colangelo had a big screen at his disposal, and microphones were being passed around the room.

Jordan was drinking a beer while sitting next to Mullin, a recovering alcoholic, who was drinking water. They had been Olympic teammates in 1984 (as college kids) and 1992 (as NBA stars). "When I played in '84, it was a privilege," Mullin told the group. "But when NBA players started playing in '92, it became more of a commitment. We have to get it back to being a privilege and not a commitment."

At some point Colangelo steered his audience into a give-and-take on talent. "We didn't have our best players in Greece, and we had four young guys who hadn't earned it who were put on the roster — LeBron, Carmelo Anthony, Dwyane Wade, and Amar'e Stoudemire," he said. "I always had the old-fashioned idea that you have to earn it."

Colangelo reminded the players and coaches that while he had great admiration for them, he would be the one to make the final call on the team. He directed their attention to the names of dozens of players listed on the screen, young men who would be asked to make a three-year commitment to the program, including the 2006 world championship in Japan and the 2008 Summer Games in Beijing. Colangelo also had posted names of college and NBA candidates to serve as head coach of the team. Just about everyone was in agreement that college coaches should be seriously considered for the job.

"There's only one college coach up there who could get the job done, and I know he can get the job done," Dean Smith announced to his fellow guests. "And that's Coach K." The room fell silent. Smith and Krzyzewski had been bitter rivals. In fact, when the Lakers and Kobe Bryant had vainly

tried their damnedest to persuade Coach K to leave Durham for Los Angeles over the summer, Smith wanted it known publicly that the Lakers had
first reached out to his protégé, Roy Williams, who wasn't interested in leaving Chapel Hill after only one season in Smith's old chair.

And yet here was Smith, with backup support from Jordan, declaring
that Krzyzewski was the man to recapture the gold. More conversation ensued about the other candidates. "And then I passed out some ballots," Colangelo said. The top two coaches in the poll were the same two coaches at
the top of Colangelo's list before the meeting started.

Mike Krzyzewski of the United States Military Academy. Gregg Popovich of the United States Air Force Academy.

Colangelo left the meeting knowing that he needed to meet individually
with the top NBA players, and that he needed to call two academy graduates about the possibility of coaching them. Krzyzewski was always going
to be the easier call for Colangelo; Colangelo first met Coach K while he
was working for Knight at Indiana, and over the years the two would talk
about the ethnic working-class Chicago neighborhoods where they both
grew up.

By contrast, the former Phoenix owner viewed Popovich, a two-time
NBA champ, as strictly a Western Conference adversary. "It wasn't buddy-
buddy," Colangelo said. When they spoke on the phone, Colangelo sensed
that Popovich was still hurt and bitter over the way Athens went down.
People close to the 2004 version of Team USA thought that Popovich did
everything he could to save Brown's sinking ship; his presence had been
one of the few positives in what was largely a toxic experience. The Spurs
coach made it clear that things would have to be dramatically different for
the Americans to win the gold with him in charge. "And unless you know
Popovich really well," Colangelo said, "you're really taken aback sometimes
by his responses . . . I just didn't feel it from Pop."

He did feel it from Krzyzewski, in a big way. "Coach K almost jumped
through the phone when I called," Colangelo said. Krzyzewski had assumed
that once NBA megastars supplanted the NCAA's best at the Olympics in
'92, college coaches would never again be serious candidates for the job. He
couldn't believe that he was back in the game.

They met in July at a restaurant in Las Vegas for two or three hours,
talking basketball in their red velvet chairs. It couldn't have gone better.
"We were joined at the hip," Colangelo said. There would be no need for a
sit-down with Popovich, who later became enraged by Colangelo's public
analysis of Pop's enthusiasm, or lack thereof, for the vacant Olympic job.
The Spurs coach reportedly wrote a letter to Colangelo to tell him to stop

suggesting to reporters that he didn't have a burning desire to coach Team USA.

"It turned out to be a real issue between him and me," Colangelo conceded.

But Krzyzewski's confirmation of his preliminary acceptance, after talking to Mickie, was all that really mattered. Nobody in the know thought that Coach K would turn down a chance to fill Brown's small shoes and coach the world's best players on the world's biggest stage, the Olympics. Then again, Krzyzewski did turn down $40 million from the Lakers and a chance to coach Kobe Bryant.

Life was good — really, really good — for Coach K, who was protected for eternity by the lifetime contract he had signed with Duke after his 2001 title. He was repped by the Washington Speakers Bureau and banking $50,000 for every corporate speech he made (about thirty a year) while enjoying the cachet of having an ethics center carry his name (The Fuqua/Coach K Center on Leadership and Ethics) and his new status as executive-in-residence at the Fuqua School of Business. Krzyzewski had used his business savvy to knock new Duke president Richard Brodhead back on his heels via his $40 million dance with the Lakers, compelling Brodhead to join a pro-Krzyzewski student rally, grab a bullhorn, and chant, "Coach K, please stay!" Not only did he stay, but he announced at his press conference that, for his thirty-fifth wedding anniversary, he had renewed his vows to Mickie in Duke Chapel before their youngest daughter Jamie married former West Point basketball star Chris Spatola.

The view from Krzyzewski's relatively new and lavish sixth-floor tower office off the corner of Cameron, overlooking Krzyzewskiville, kept looking better and better; the son of an elevator operator required guests to run a fingerprint scan to open his private elevator doors. Coach K was going to get that new $15.2 million, 56,000-square-foot practice facility he had been pushing for. He was also going to open a $7 million community center named after his late mother, Emily, to provide educational programs for underserved youths. Krzyzewski would help send to distinguished universities high school students who were the first from their families to attend college. It would be a hell of a tribute to his mom.

At fifty-eight, Krzyzewski was in good health five months after collapsing to the court during a time-out in a victory over Georgia Tech, an alarming scene that brought Mickie racing out of the stands. After Coach K was helped to his feet, he gave his players instructions and coached the balance of the game. He swore later that his fall was merely a case of lightheadedness caused by rising out of his chair too suddenly, and doctors determined there was nothing wrong with him. Coach K finished the season without incident. With his second-round victory over Mississippi State in March, his sixty-sixth career NCAA Tournament victory, Krzyzewski passed Dean Smith as the most prolific tournament winner of all time,

Now he needed to honor Smith's prediction that he was the one and only college coach who could lead the NBA's finest back to the gold-medal stand.

BEFORE HE STARTED coaching Team USA, Krzyzewski was drawn into what would become an infamous legal case universally known as the Duke Lacrosse Scandal. A young African American woman working as an exotic dancer at an off-campus party hosted by the school's lacrosse team in March had accused three white team members of raping and beating her in a bathroom at the house. Duke soon canceled the rest of the lacrosse season and forced out the lacrosse coach, Mike Pressler, before three players were indicted on first-degree charges of forcible rape, sexual offense, and kidnapping.

These allegations of heinous criminal acts brought renewed attention to the divide between a student body largely comprised of privileged white students — many from the Northeast — and the African American community in Durham. As events unfolded over the first three months of the case, Krzyzewski remained silent. He offered some counsel to university leaders, including the president, Richard Brodhead, and privately offered support to Pressler.

Many were calling on Krzyzewski, the instantly recognizable face of the university, to say something, anything, for the record about a case that had become a blockbuster story. Even the man who had hired him, retired AD Tom Butters, expressed surprise that Coach K didn't issue a public comment given the gravity of the situation. "There are times," Butters said, "when you have to put your ass on the line . . . He is so powerful, and he is not one to be shy about his views. I would have thought he would anguish in his silence."

People wanted Krzyzewski to solve it, fix the problem for the university. That's what Coach K did. He solved things and fixed things.

But he couldn't solve or fix this. "He no doubt recognizes that in a case fraught with class and racial implications," wrote *New York Times* columnist Harvey Araton, "the last thing he needs — despite some calls from within the Duke and Durham, N.C., communities for him to be heard — is to risk being misinterpreted as a cheerleader for either side."

Araton described Krzyzewski as a point guard who now understood how to recognize and avoid a backcourt trap. "The last time he stepped into a volatile ideological debate," the columnist wrote, "playing host to a fundraiser in 2002 for the Republican Senate candidate Elizabeth Dole at a university-owned facility, Krzyzewski was criticized around the state, and even the Duke student newspaper was aghast." Araton argued that Coach K wasn't about to join the voices calling the national media's coverage of the accused players and the school unfair when he was pursuing Black recruits for Duke and "preparing famous N.B.A. players, almost all African American, for the 2008 Summer Olympics." (Though a Republican, Krzyzewski later called his former player, Barack Obama aide Reggie Love, after the 2008 presidential election to tell him that he'd voted for the Democrat over Republican challenger John McCain.)

Krzyzewski finally ended his silence in June, explaining that he needed to remember his place at the school. "I am the basketball coach," he said. "I'm not the president, I'm not the athletic director, and I'm not on the board of trustees and don't want to be. What I've tried to do behind the scenes is say, 'We're with you. We'll see what happens, and whatever happened if you did it, you should be punished.' Giving support doesn't mean you're choosing sides. Giving support is what a university should do . . . because we're in the kid business."

Krzyzewski later said that he wasn't completely engaged with the case because, in part, he was trying to better learn the international game for the sake of USA Basketball. "I had tunnel vision into that," he said. Krzyzewski had no idea where the Duke Lacrosse Scandal was heading. He had no idea that all charges against the three lacrosse players eventually would be dismissed, and that the case would come to be defined by a prosecutor running amok and by overheated media commentary that gave the accuser a benefit of the doubt that the attorney general later ruled she didn't deserve. All Krzyzewski knew at the time was that over the next two and a half months he would be allowed to escape the responsibility of a crisis manager and lose himself in his first love — basketball.

HE WAS SITTING inside the Saitama Super Arena outside of Tokyo on September 1, 2006, wearing a white Nike golf shirt graced by the "USA" logo on his left breast. He had in his starting lineup LeBron James, one of the most talented young players in NBA history, and Elton Brand, his former center from Duke. What could be better than that?

Krzyzewski had just won the ACC regular-season and tournament titles. He had also finished converting J. J. Redick from the puffy party boy he blamed for the 2004 Final Four defeat, according to author Seth Davis, into a sleek terminator who became the ACC's all-time leading scorer and the

NCAA's all-time three-point shooter and who led Duke to the number-one overall ranking before its Sweet 16 loss to LSU.

After evaluating talent at high school camps and starting the training of Team USA in Las Vegas, Krzyzewski had coached in exhibition games in China and South Korea before arriving in Japan and landing where he was in this moment: on the sideline leading his 7-0 Americans against the 7-0 Greeks in the world championship semifinals. Along with his good friend, Syracuse coach Jim Boeheim, Krzyzewski's staff included Phoenix Suns coach Mike D'Antoni, Portland Trail Blazers coach Nate McMillan, and former Houston Rockets and Los Angeles Lakers coach Rudy Tomjanovich, who served as director of scouting. The team had two NBA doctors, two NBA trainers, and, of course, one NBA managing director in Colangelo.

Despite all that NBA support, there were lingering questions about whether a college coach's methods would be accepted by some of the league's best players. Krzyzewski had told his team that, despite his West Point background, he was never one to have many rules. Though he preferred the flexibility of judging situations on a case-by-case basis, he did tell the players that he wanted them dressed appropriately when out and about, and that he didn't want them wearing headphones in public. (Krzyzewski felt that headphones sent a detached and dismissive message.)

Player attire was one of the many complaints about the 2004 American team; some players wore T-shirts and long shorts to a formal function in Belgrade. Colangelo hired a tailor to design custom clothes for the team members in line with David Stern's relatively new NBA dress code.

And yet one day while Coach K and his staff were watching a game not involving the U.S. team, Colangelo said, "Here come Carmelo [Anthony], LeBron [James], and [Dwyane] Wade dressed inappropriately, in strapped undershirts, with headphones on. There are 200 or so media people there. We saw this unfolding, and there go the cameras, and that's going to be all over the world, not just in the Sapporo newspaper. I was really upset about that."

Colangelo and Krzyzewski arranged for a meeting with the three players at the team hotel, and surprisingly enough, the players pushed back. "LeBron said, 'Man, we didn't do things like that in Cleveland,'" Colangelo recalled. "I said, 'I know that. You get everything you want.' Wade said something like, 'You don't have to be that strict. We're grown men.' I said, 'I'll tell you what, we'll do what Pat Riley does in Miami.' The point was, we weren't asking for much, and they had it much more difficult with NBA teams as far as rules. That was the only time we had any conversation with anything regarding rules."

Colangelo did most of the talking in the meeting, assuming the role of bad cop, while Krzyzewski offered quiet support. "Mike always handles confrontation terrifically," the managing director said. "He has a way of bringing things down, and not bringing things to a boil." Going forward, there didn't seem to be anything like the major team chemistry issues there had been in Athens. The Americans did surrender 100 points to Puerto Rico in the tournament opener, and they did trail Italy by 12 in the second half of the fourth game, but nobody expected a serious threat from Greece, despite its 2005 European championship, when the two 7-0 teams met in the semifinals. Even the 2004 U.S. team had beaten Greece, despite its home-court advantage in Athens.

Through the first thirteen and a half minutes of the forty-minute game, the United States held a 33-21 lead, even without the services of the NBA's scoring champ, Kobe Bryant, who had to skip the tournament in favor of surgery on his right knee. Krzyzewski had more than enough scoring at his disposal with James, Anthony, and Wade, the reigning NBA Finals MVP. Defense? Krzyzewski was known as one of the best defensive minds in the game, on any level, in any country. Defense wasn't going to be a problem for the U.S. team . . . until it became one.

The Greeks had been playing together for three years, and they always knew their chemistry was their most valuable asset against an American All-Star team that had just been pieced together. Chemistry, precision, and execution. Their coach, Panagiotis Yannakis, decided to use those assets in the one play — the high pick-and-roll — they ran over and over and over again to dismantle their more talented opponents.

From down 12 in the middle of the second quarter to up 14 in the middle of the third, Greece was staging a pick-and-roll clinic without a single NBA veteran on its side. The massive six-foot-ten center known as "Baby Shaq," Sofoklis Schortsanitis — built like a combination of Shaquille O'Neal and Karl Malone — kept setting screens and diving hard to the basket, giving Greece an endless series of barely contested layups and uncontested three-pointers. "They ran like one play the whole game," Wade said incredulously.

Yes they did, and the great Coach K never came up with an adjustment to stop it. He looked stricken on the bench, the color drained from his face. In the closing minutes, the United States was desperate enough to need Kirk Hinrich to hit a pair of three-pointers to keep the game somewhat within reach. But an Anthony airball with twenty-four seconds left and the United States down four, and a missed James three with ten seconds left and the United States down six, sealed the biggest upset in Japan since Buster Douglas knocked out Mike Tyson in the Tokyo Dome in 1990.

"Greece has stunned the United States of America!" shouted the FIBA announcer as Krzyzewski rose from his seat to head down to the winners' side. "Theo Papaloukas kicks the ball up in the stands!" When Yannakis freed himself from a jubilant group embrace, the Greek coach and Krzyzewski hugged and patted each other on the back. The Greek fans were waving flags and jumping up and down as the players wrapped their arms around one another and danced in a circle under the final score that read, Greece 101, USA 95. Anthony was the one American player who stood on the court and watched the celebration, his face a brew of anguish and despair.

"It was a nightmare unraveling before my eyes," Colangelo said.

The managing director was sitting in a corner near the American bench. As a devastated Krzyzewski dragged himself off the floor, he made eye contact with Colangelo and said, "I'm sorry." Now Krzyzewski knew the pain that Larry Brown felt, and that George Karl felt before him. Only Brown and Karl were not graduates of the United States Military Academy, nor were they appointed specifically to clean up someone else's mess.

Krzyzewski felt as though he had let down his country. "The worst day of my life in coaching," he said many years later.

"Coach K is used to being in control and used to having all the answers, and he didn't have them," said one of the American players, Shane Battier, his former Duke star. "He's used to pushing buttons at Duke and things working out, but he couldn't find that button for that team, and I think that hurt him the most . . . At Duke he had a different type of guy who doesn't mind being coached hard. Some players on that [USA] team had never been coached hard a day in their life, and that was evident."

On the bus ride away from the arena, sheer silence prevailed. According to a Duke assistant, Krzyzewski would watch the tape of the Greece defeat "about 100 times." To his credit, before the long flight home, Coach K did lead the Americans to a bronze-medal victory over a strong Argentina team, ensuring that the United States didn't leave Japan without something to show for its work.

Before the Americans left the arena following their semifinal defeat, which cost them a shot at the automatic 2008 Olympic berth awarded the world champ, USA Basketball CEO Jim Tooley was walking to the locker room when he heard Carmelo Anthony say, "Man, now we have to go qualify next year in Venezuela." It didn't matter then that the FIBA Americas qualifying tournament would later be moved from Venezuela to Las Vegas (over the host nation missing a payment), or that Anthony's comment might have reflected the kind of American arrogance that had put the team in this position in the first place.

What Tooley heard was a star American player who had scored 27 points in defeat, and who had watched the Greeks celebrate, thinking a big-picture thought out loud. Carmelo Anthony was already focusing on a different road to the gold-medal stand in Beijing.

"To me," Tooley said, "that meant Coach K had gotten to him that this was a long-term proposition. We lost, but we had created a program."

KRZYZEWSKI'S MOTIVATIONAL TECHNIQUES at Duke were never going to work with the NBA's best. Elton Brand said that Coach K once challenged a teammate to a fight. "I think he would have won," Brand said. He meant Coach K, not the teammate.

"Sometimes there are confrontations with Coach where the next step would be a punch in the face," said one Duke starter. "But what are we going to do, get in a fight with a sixty-year-old man? We'd kill the guy."

Krzyzewski had verbally destroyed a procession of disappointing players; he wasn't even afraid to berate a Blue Devil in front of a large group of guests at practice. He once sat down a talented but oft-injured center, Shavlik Randolph, and told him, "My greatest gift I have as a coach and as a leader is my ability to get angry. But I'm able to harness that anger and channel it into producing positive results."

Coach K once responded to back-to-back ACC road losses by shredding his players in the locker room at 4 a.m., after an all-night ride from Virginia Tech. "You motherfuckers don't deserve to wear the Duke jersey," he screamed. "My previous teams would have kicked your ass. You don't deserve to have 'Duke' across your chest. Get the fuck out of my sight." A couple of hours later, Krzyzewski's team managers summoned the players back to the gym, where they found that all their belongings, including their jerseys and their locker nameplates, had been thrown into a huge pile in the middle of the locker room. After the players picked through the pile, got dressed, and took the floor for practice, Coach K told them, "Take your fucking jerseys off." They still didn't deserve to wear the Duke name, so they would scrimmage in pinnies against skins.

Krzyzewski once severely blistered Jason Williams for not running a designed play in a loss at Virginia, and for supposedly spending too much time thinking about his certain jump to the NBA. Williams shouted back and approached Coach K while punching a fist into his palm. One person in the room, Williams's teammate Reggie Love, later compared the tension and awkwardness of the moment to a 2007 argument he witnessed between rival Democrat candidates Barack Obama and Hillary Clinton on the tarmac at Reagan National Airport.

But then again, after Williams suffered his near-fatal, career-ending motorcycle accident as a member of the Chicago Bulls, Krzyzewski was standing at his bedside when he woke up in the hospital. Williams's agent, Bill Duffy, said that he'd never seen a coach more involved in a player's recovery and post-op medical care. "He was all over it like his own son," Duffy said.

Duke players over the years formed a fraternity they called "the brotherhood," and the common denominator in that brotherhood was Krzyzewski. They gathered and shared stories about his methods of motivation, sometimes laughing in the retelling, sometimes wincing.

Wanting to send a message to his players in an indifferent practice, Coach K once went to flip over a big trash can. Problem was, the trash can was heavier than a post-hip-replacement Krzyzewski expected it to be, leaving him in a Greco-Roman wrestling match with the damn thing as he tried to flip it over. When the trash can finally fell to the court, only a couple of pieces of tissue paper and an empty Gatorade bottle came spilling out. Krzyzewski kicked his players out of practice, and they couldn't stop laughing as soon as they got out of his sight.

The Duke coach was not above pulling high schoolish stunts to fire up his players, like storming into the darkened locker room as if he were Mel Gibson's William Wallace in *Braveheart,* pulling out his West Point saber. and screaming as he drove it into a pot of dirt that he destroyed on impact, sending his players into a frenzy before they kicked some poor opponent's ass. "I remember thinking to myself, *This guy just put his sword through concrete*," said Duke forward Lee Melchionni. "We went nuts." Another one of Krzyzewski's *Braveheart* stunts was storming the locker room and throwing a flaming arrow he held, all but burning down the building, at least until the managers put out the flame with wet bath towels.

Mickie Krzyzewski helped her husband carry out his motivational tactics. As Coach K's chief advisor, she always knew which Blue Devils were in a good place, and which ones needed a boost. Mickie would tell him that he should sit down with a certain player because she thought something was bothering him, and sure enough, when Coach K met with the player, the issue came tumbling out. She would walk over to a player at a team meal on the road and whisper a few words of advice or reassurance. One day when Coach K was preparing to run an unforgiving practice, Mickie asked a male manager to enter the locker room to make sure the team members were all decent. After getting the all-clear, Mickie walked in and said, "All right, guys, listen up. You're going to have a rough one today. I need you to know that you're going to get through it, and I need you to know that he loves you. But you guys are going to have a rough one, so buckle up and be prepared."

On the college level, the Krzyzewski Way worked. He was the best communicator and motivator in the business. "He's the best handler of players, of getting them to buy in," Boeheim said. "The best at the psychology of coaching."

Or, to be exact, the psychology of Division I college coaching. As he began preparing Team USA — it was being called "the Redeem Team" — for the 2008 Summer Games in Beijing, Krzyzewski knew that if he pulled some of his Duke stunts with these players, the results would be disastrous. "When I'm coaching the Duke team," he would say, "I'm trying to help them cross bridges they'd never crossed before. They need to adapt to me. When I'm coaching our national team, they've crossed some bridges. They haven't won an Olympic gold medal, but we need to adapt to each other."

That was evident during an exhibition game against Lithuania in Seoul before the 2006 world championship tournament in Japan. Krzyzewski ripped into Orlando Magic center Dwight Howard, who had skipped college and become the number-one overall pick in the 2004 NBA draft, for the way he was (or wasn't) defending the pick-and-roll. "It wasn't personal," Shane Battier said, "but this is the way Coach K is. You could tell Dwight Howard was not used to having many people talk to him like this. The look on Dwight's face was, *Who the hell are you?* Dwight didn't say anything, but that was the look on his face. *Who . . . are . . . you?*

"Coach K has awareness, so he saw the look on Dwight's face and immediately said to himself, *Oh my gosh, I can't do this. I can't treat these guys this way.* Dwight didn't do what Coach K wanted in the second half because I think he was mad at him, but Coach K found a valuable lesson there. 'I can't push buttons with these guys that work with Duke guys.'"

So at the start of his Las Vegas training camp on July 20, 2008, before entering his first Redeem Team meeting on the road to Beijing, Krzyzewski gave considerable thought to what buttons might work with his gathered pros. After missing the 2004 Olympics because of sexual assault charges brought against him in Colorado — charges that were ultimately dropped when his accuser declined to testify — Kobe Bryant was playing this time. Bryant was going to play at Duke if he played at any college, and he'd wanted Krzyzewski to be his Lakers coach. Kobe had a good relationship with Mickie and was kind to Coach K's grandchildren. So people close to Team USA were not concerned about the Kobe–Coach K dynamic, especially after Bryant showed up in Las Vegas two days early, knocked on Krzyzewski's door, and asked to guard every opponent's best perimeter player with the promise that he'd destroy those players.

It was Krzyzewski's relationship with LeBron James, who also had never played for a college coach, that people worried about. The headphones tiff in Japan didn't hurt much, but it didn't help either. Nor did the fact that James had lost a big international competition with Krzyzewski, just as he had lost one with Larry Brown.

Over two consecutive summers, Krzyzewski had traveled to Akron, Ohio, where James was raised by a single mother who gave birth to him when she was sixteen, just to get to know the Cleveland Cavaliers' homegrown juggernaut. Coach K spoke at a function for James's corporate sponsors and dined with the player and his closest friends and advisors in 2007, then met with him again the following summer while recruiting high school talent at James's skills camp. In the gym, after Coach K told him he needed his leadership, LeBron responded, "You can ask me to do anything, and I'll do it."

They had stayed in touch — James called with congratulations after Krzyzewski nailed down his 800th career victory — and there were signs that the relationship was only improving with time, starting with Coach K's decision in the 2006 bronze-medal game against Argentina to move James to point guard. LeBron had responded with 22 points, 7 assists, and 3 turnovers in his new role and called it "a great adjustment by Coach."

But when it was time to open training camp in Las Vegas in '08, said one Team USA staffer, "there were guys who were still very skeptical of Coach K for a number of reasons." Shane Battier, a member of the '06 team who would not play in Beijing, explained that he was "absolutely sure NBA players were skeptical of Coach K" in the early USA Basketball years, "especially the guys who didn't play in college . . . In the pros it's different. Coaches are more Xs and Os based. There's not a lot of personal development. You get along with your coach, yeah, maybe get a beer. But you don't get taught life lessons from an NBA coach, and that's Coach K's biggest strength."

Was LeBron James really going to embrace the same life lessons Krzyzewski handed down to nineteen-year-old college kids? James was still finding his voice as a player, and according to one Team USA source, "he didn't always steer the team in the right direction. LeBron had to learn to be a killer. LeBron was a showman, and Kobe was an assassin."

It went without saying that Coach K preferred assassins, or at least strong team leaders with a singular focus. Before the Americans' first training camp meeting at the Wynn resort in Las Vegas, Krzyzewski pulled James aside and told him, "I'm going to ask the players for their thoughts and feelings, and I need you to say a few words."

"No problem," James responded. "I've got you covered."

Coach K had similar individual chats with Bryant, Wade, and Jason Kidd, a player deeply respected by James who sat next to LeBron in nearly every meeting. All three addressed the room as they sat behind tables in a classroomlike setting while looking at an image of the Olympic gold medal on the big screen before them. (Krzyzewski wanted that image visible in every meeting he held.) Coach K had folders handed out to the players that included a picture of the gold medal, an image of the Olympic bracket, an itinerary, and a blank page titled "Standards." Jim Delany, longtime Big Ten commissioner and a USA Basketball executive, called what followed "the essence of leadership" and one of the more impressive team meetings he'd ever witnessed.

"Coach K said, 'I want to go around this room and I want to hear from each one of you as to the standards to govern this group, and you guys are going to define the standards of what you'll accomplish here. Once you establish the standards, I as the coach will make sure you live up to those standards,'" Delany recalled. "It was brilliant . . . It was a simple, well-thought-out, and respectful way to communicate with the best players in the world so they could come together and win a gold medal.

"A lot of people spoke from the heart in many ways. Kobe said, 'Coach, I'll do anything you want. If you want me to take the last shot, I'll do it. If you want me to guard the best player, I'll do it. You tell me what you want, I'll do it for you.'"

Bryant spoke specifically of playing defense and rebounding and doing all the grind-it-out things international players didn't think the Americans ever wanted to do. Kidd, the ultimate distributor at the point, spoke about respecting one another and the need to show up on time. Wade spoke of how the players needed to show full commitment to one another. Other players and coaches weighed in with their own thoughts, and with confirmation of Coach K's statement that trust and communication would be among the standards required to win gold.

But about forty-five minutes into the meeting in this hotel conference room, James still hadn't said a word. Krzyzewski later told confidants that he was getting nervous, afraid that LeBron was going to leave him hanging in front of the team. "We were close to ending the meeting," Coach K said, "and this motherfucker didn't speak up. I needed him to talk."

One Krzyzewski associate in the room said it was clear that the Team USA coach was trying to extend the meeting simply to give James an opportunity to finally address his teammates. "Kobe was great," the associate said, "and it was that period where Kobe was at the height of his powers. But he was at the height of his powers because he was Kobe. Everybody in that room knew the best player in the league then and for the next decade was LeBron James. Everybody was waiting for LeBron to say something.

"He was leaning back in his chair, still this air left over from the first two summers . . . He was reluctant. He knew the power he'd be extending Coach K. A great power struggle in sports was going on in that room."

Another staffer in the room thought that LeBron was apprehensive about speaking because he hadn't won a championship yet, in the NBA or in international competition. That staffer thought James was afraid of saying the wrong thing with no trophies to back it up.

Coach K was running out of time and patience. He had gathered the standards he sought from his players, including collective responsibility, poise, unselfishness, and pride, and now he was searching for an exit ramp. Krzyzewski was wearing his 1992 Dream Team ring, and he told his players he would never again wear it, that he wanted to replace it with a 2008 ring, and that such a ring would represent a journey they'd remember for the rest of their lives. He was ready to give up on James and end the meeting.

"If we leave that room and LeBron hasn't said anything," the associate said, "that's not good. We waited and waited, and all of a sudden LeBron spoke. And he spoke eloquently, beautifully."

The conference room turned quiet, and one coach present said that "everyone in the room exhaled when LeBron finally spoke . . . LeBron was not very trusting of male figures and coaches, and Coach K just wore him down and established a trust. That meeting was so emotional and empowering that I think LeBron was like, 'All right, I've got to plant my flag here.'"

James started talking about the United States needing to be "a no-excuse team." He looked around the room, saw all the talent any basketball player could ask for, and announced that the failure to win the gold would be theirs and theirs alone. "During the season, when we're with our teams, how many times do we complain?" he said. "How many times do we say, 'I wish I had Chris Paul in the backcourt,' or, 'I wish I had Dwight Howard with me,' or, 'I wish I had Jason Kidd with me.' Well, guess what? I've got Dwight Howard. I've got Jason Kidd. Everyone is right here in this room. Everyone is here. This is what we always wanted. There are no fucking excuses."

It felt like a moment, a big one, and Krzyzewski immediately sensed it. He had just scored his first victory with his 2008 Olympic team, and before officially ending the meeting, he needed only to add these two words:

"Amen, brother."

MIKE KRZYZEWSKI WAS in a good place with his Olympic team entering its final exhibition game against Australia in Shanghai. Though he felt that the scene in Las Vegas had been too noisy and loose for the serious work he was trying to get done, Coach K believed he had pushed the right human buttons with his players. The first speaker to appear before the Redeem Team was his former Army player, Bob Brown, on his way to becoming a four-star general. Brown was joined by three soldiers who had been severely wounded in combat in Iraq and yet remained in the Army to continue serving their country. The players grew emotional when listening to their stories. One captain, Scott Smiley, was permanently blinded by shrapnel when he took out an incoming suicide car to save his fellow soldiers' lives. "I wanted to bring in wounded warriors to teach the players selfless service," Brown said.

Coach K had a big-screen TV rolled out onto the court before his first practice to show his players their new fight song — Marvin Gaye singing the national anthem, his moving, soulful rendition delivered at the 1983 NBA All-Star Game in Los Angeles. Krzyzewski told them they would hear this rendition before every game, and after they won the gold medal. The song would be played before practices too, and during stretching. The team loved it.

Krzyzewski also invited in Doug Collins, a member of the haunted 1972 Olympic team that suffered the ultimate in controversial last-second defeats at the hands of the Soviet Union in Munich. With three seconds to play and the Soviets holding a 49–48 lead, a fast-breaking Collins was undercut by a Soviet player who sent him crashing into the basket stanchion. Dazed, Collins somehow made the two most pressure-packed free throws in the history of American basketball (the United States had never lost a game in Olympic basketball competition), only to have two bizarre refereeing decisions grant the Soviets three cracks at an improbable full-length-of-the-court victory. The third time was the charm. Collins gave a tear-filled speech about what was taken from him in Munich, and what the Americans should now take from others in Beijing.

Collins's son Chris, the former Duke star, was in the room for his father's pep talk. Krzyzewski had a number of Duke assistants and staffers on this Olympic journey — including Collins, fellow Duke assistant Steve Wojciechowski, former Duke assistant and current Stanford head coach Johnny Dawkins, and Coach K's son-in-law Chris Spatola, who had served in the Army in Iraq and now worked as the Blue Devils director of basketball operations.

Even as he was trying to establish the strongest possible rapport with the pros, Krzyzewski felt most comfortable with his college advocates at his side. One NBA member of the 2006 world championship staff who wasn't part of the 2008 run was Team USA's director of scouting, Rudy Tomjanovich, who had won two titles as coach of the Houston Rockets and had led the Americans to a gold-medal finish in the 2000 Olympics in Sydney. Rudy T was widely respected, but some on Coach K's staff were uncomfortable with how often his voice was heard in meetings. Tony Ronzone of the Detroit Pistons, who was more familiar with the international game, was brought in to evaluate the opposing talent.

The world basketball community had more or less caught up to the United States — that much was clear. Krzyzewski was hired to figure out how to reopen the gap. He had heard that Larry Brown rarely met with his players outside of the gym in Athens; Krzyzewski made sure he was in near-constant contact with his. He tried to make individual contact with four to six players before or after every practice, from thirty seconds to a few minutes, just to maintain a personal connection. He ran quick meetings with players in conference rooms before they boarded the bus to practice.

He did that, according to assistant Nate McMillan, because NBA stars are accustomed to slapping on their headphones and heading to the back of the bus to create space between themselves and the coaching staff. "Coach K wasn't used to that," McMillan said. So if Krzyzewski's NBA players were going to enter and exit their buses through middle doors to avoid passing the coaches seated in the front, the meetings ensured that the Team USA coach still got his quality time with them.

Krzyzewski listened to his players if, for instance, they thought it was a bad idea on a particular day to practice twice, of if they wanted to focus on their individual NBA conditioning routines. "A spa day," he called those days when he let the players do their own thing. Coach K was concerned that players sometimes did stretching exercises when he was addressing the team, but his NBA assistants assured him that they were listening and that he shouldn't feel slighted.

And yet, on one particular ride to a scheduled shootaround, coaches heard LeBron James complaining that he didn't find the extra session necessary. There had already been a moment in practice when James turned his back on Krzyzewski as the coach was addressing him, compelling Coach K to say firmly, "Look at me. We need to have eye-to-eye contact." Now he was griping audibly on the bus. "If you lose LeBron, you lose the whole enterprise," said one Team USA staffer. "You can't have LeBron doing that. They get off the bus and Coach K pulls him aside immediately and says, 'Look, you have to trust that I'll never ask you to do something I don't feel is important. I'm not going to wear you guys out, or put you in a bad situation. You have to trust that we're doing this for the right reasons.' Along the way I always thought to myself, *That's probably the first time LeBron James has been talked to that way.*"

But all in all, the Americans arrived for their final Olympic tune-up, against the Aussies, looking like a unified group that was honoring the standards it had established with Coach K. He was able to connect with his team, according to one of his bench players, Carlos Boozer, partly because he was not carrying any NBA baggage into the arena. "He had no alliance with the Bulls or Lakers or Spurs," Boozer said. "There was no old beef with a player. He's a college coach, not an NBA coach. He didn't knock you out of the NBA playoffs. He didn't trade you, or cut your best friend. At times I'm sure people were like, 'What the fuck is going on?' But it was a brilliant move by Jerry Colangelo to hire him."

McMillan maintained that Krzyzewski was never intimidated by the NBA players in his midst because he "was a star in his own right. He had an ego too." But still, Krzyzewski knew that he couldn't berate the pros like he would his Blue Devils on scholarship, not that they gave him much reason to. His fellow assistant, Jim Boeheim, said that only one player was ever late for a Coach K practice or meeting — Dwyane Wade, by five minutes. "Mike just called him out, and Dwyane said it would never happen again," Boeheim recalled. "And it never happened again."

Boeheim said that the pros quickly took to Krzyzewski's approach because they were desperate to achieve their one and only Redeem Team objective. Bryant, for one, enjoyed how Krzyzewski coached him. A lot of players, including Carmelo Anthony, were surprised that Bryant accepted the invitation to play for Team USA, given his standing around the league as a lone wolf. In that first team meeting in Las Vegas, Bryant sat at a table by himself, removed from his teammates, right behind the coaching staff. "It looked kind of weird," said McMillan. Over time, Kobe felt reinvigorated by the unique challenge before him. NBA players are motivated by money; they are professionals, after all. Kobe had been a pro for ten years and appreciated the fact that Coach K was motivating him in a way that had nothing to do with money.

But standards are standards. Suddenly, on the night of August 5, Bryant wasn't meeting the team's standards. He took a few loose shots in the second half against Australia — enough to draw the attention of his teammates. The United States won the game, 87–76, but looked exceedingly beatable in doing so. The Americans were eager to get on with the Olympic tournament, and Kobe, apparently bored, seemed to be increasing the degree of difficulty on some attempts.

"Everyone knew it," said one Team USA staffer. "They know when another player is being selfish. Players can police themselves, but in this instance, as

LeBron was coming out of the game, he said to Mike, 'Yo, Coach, you'd better fix that motherfucker,' as he walks by. He was talking about Kobe."

The Redeem Team was supposed to be all about accountability, and this was LeBron holding Coach K and Kobe accountable at the same time. Krzyzewski told LeBron that he would talk to Kobe and asked Cleveland's franchise player to trust him. The coaching staff met through the night, which wasn't a big deal to Coach K, who often pulled all-nighters watching tape before catching up on sleep during the day. This time they talked only about how to handle Kobe Bryant.

The next morning, before leaving Shanghai, Krzyzewski asked Bryant, who was coming off his fourth NBA title with the Lakers, for a private meeting. "Coach was nervous," said one of his staffers. "He knew he had to do it."

Coach K pulled out a laptop and sat with Bryant in a room, one on one. He showed Kobe a few examples of questionable shots and pointed out his teammates standing around and watching him on some drives to the basket. "Look at these shots," Krzyzewski told him. "They're bullshit shots." Coach K added, "There has to be more movement," and then held his breath, waiting for Bryant's response.

According to a team source, Bryant just looked right at him and said, "I got it, Coach. I got it. Don't worry about it. Sorry about that.'"

Krzyzewski told James that he'd followed up and confronted Bryant, and that Kobe was back on board with the program. "In the end," said one Team USA staffer, "Kobe, LeBron, and Coach K all did what they had to do.

"It made going to Beijing a lot easier."

RUDY FERNANDEZ HAD just made a three-pointer for Spain to cut the United States lead to two with 8:13 left in the gold-medal game when Krzyzewski called time-out. Wukesong Arena erupted with Spaniards cheering and dancing in the stands and the sounds of all those in the building who wanted to be present for the biggest upset in Olympic basketball history.

Yes, America's NBA players had been beaten three times in Athens, but that team didn't have Kobe Bryant and an all-grown-up LeBron James, Dwyane Wade, and Carmelo Anthony. Losing in Athens was an embarrassment. Losing in Beijing would be a catastrophe.

Coach K's team had blown out both the hosting Chinese and, in a revenge match, the Greeks. They had become the kind of overwhelming fan favorite in NBA-obsessed China that Brown's team was most certainly not in Athens, where anti-American sentiment seemed to be the rule, not the exception. Krzyzewski's only unforced error came in response to a foreign journalist's question about whether the U.S. team's endless series of dunks represented poor sportsmanship.

Taken aback by the implication, Krzyzewski explained that the Americans were merely playing hard, not showing off. "Maybe it's a difference in our languages," he said, glaring at the reporter who asked the question. "Maybe in your language 'playing hard' means 'showing off.'"

Yet now Krzyzewski was eight minutes away from forever being remembered the way his friend and old Bob Knight mentor, Hank Iba, was remembered for losing to the Soviets in the debacle of 1972. Coach K would go down as Coach L. So in this time-out, after holding a considerable (but not comfortable) lead for much of the game, Krzyzewski felt more pressure than he ever did against North Carolina or UNLV. He realized that his players felt the same pressure, so he didn't diagram a series of sets he wanted them to run. He told them he just wanted them to relax and go play.

"We got it," Bryant responded.

The Americans had proven in this tournament, with the help of Toronto Raptors center Chris Bosh, that they could defend the pick-and-roll play the Greeks had used to eliminate them in 2006 in Tokyo. Bosh had become a more significant figure because Krzyzewski was growing angrier and angrier as he watched film of Dwight Howard not doing what he was being asked to do defensively. "Coach K finally says, 'That's it, I'm going to pull [Howard] aside and have it out with him,'" said one Team USA source. "Jim Boeheim told him, 'Don't worry about it. Just don't play him. Play Bosh. Otherwise it will become a much bigger thing' . . . Boeheim was good for Coach K in that way. He convinced him to avoid escalating things."

Defense wins championships, they say, and Bosh was the smarter and better defender. But this final was a wide-open offensive game, and Krzyzewski needed points. He needed one player to carry him, one player who had the extreme belief in himself to come out of that huddle and bend the game — and the Spaniards — to his will. That player was not going to be LeBron, who had yet to win anything in Cleveland. It had to be Kobe, whom one Team USA staffer called "a godlike figure to everybody on that team." Krzyzewski had once dreamed of coaching him at Duke, of watching young Bryant soar over the Tar Heels like a young Michael Jordan had soared over the Blue Devils.

Now Coach K was about to get his chance. The living legend who didn't win him a national championship was going to do his damnedest to win him an international one.

Right out of the time-out, with Spanish fans waving flags in the stands,

Bryant got the ball on the right wing, in front of the U.S. bench, and drove hard into the lane. He made the kind of contested, double-pump leaner that might have drawn another rebuke under different circumstances. Instead, Krzyzewski and his assistants exhaled, knowing it was no longer a one-possession game.

Half a minute later, Bryant was back on the right wing when he again dribbled into the paint, drawing four Spaniards — *four* — before kicking it to Deron Williams, who sank the three-pointer to make it 96–89. On the next U.S. possession, Bryant headed to the same side of the court and rose up for a shot before getting stripped and recovering his own fumble. He launched another drive toward the goal, this time drawing two or three defenders, before passing to Dwight Howard for a dunk and his team-high sixth assist, giving the Americans a nine-point lead. After Spain went down the floor and cut its deficit to six, Bryant responded with a three-pointer from the deep left corner to make it 101–92 with six minutes to go.

Kobe had been missing shots throughout the tournament that he'd normally make. "But when we needed them for the gold medal," McMillan said, "he made them." The proud Spaniards weren't giving up, and after a nasty Fernandez dunk on Howard, Pau Gasol's jumper made it a five-point game with 3:31 left. In the stands, Mickie Krzyzewski was squeezing Chris Spatola's hand so tightly that he thought it might fall off. Just as the crowd was buzzing again with anticipation of an upset, Bryant drilled another three-pointer while being hit by Fernandez, who fouled out. Acting as a pro wrestling heel, Kobe put a finger to his lips to shush the crowd, then completed the four-point play to hand the Americans a 108–99 lead with 3:10 to go.

Beaten by 37 points by the United States in pool play, Spain showed its incredible heart by scoring the next 5 points, leaving a nervous Krzyzewski to bury his chin in his left hand at the end of the bench. LeBron, who had willingly let Bryant take over, found Dwyane Wade wide open on the left wing; Wade buried the three to make it 111–104, with 2:04 left. After Carlos Jimenez missed a three with ninety-five seconds left, James came down with a man-sized rebound, Bryant hit a runner in the lane that sealed it, and Krzyzewski slapped his hands together and stepped eagerly onto the court.

Coach K had gotten emotional during the pregame playing of the national anthem, thinking of his parents and how hard they had worked to build his American dream. He was getting emotional again as the clock wound down and the American fans chanted, "U-S-A . . . U-S-A." Bryant sank two technical foul shots before the U.S. called time-out with 26.1 seconds remaining, leading by 10. The celebration was under way.

With 3.8 seconds left and Spain about to inbound the ball, down 118–107,

Krzyzewski, holding a towel, hugged his assistants one by one. It had been a hell of a game, the highest-scoring game in Olympic history — 225 points in forty minutes. Forced to go without the injured Jose Calderon of the Toronto Raptors, Spain played a seventeen-year-old, Ricky Rubio, for twenty-nine minutes and yet had no trouble scoring against an American defense that had limited its opponents to 75 points per game. The difference was that Bryant scored 13 of his 20 points in the fourth quarter, Wade contributed 27 off the bench, and the Americans made 70 percent of their two-point field-goal attempts. Back home, it was a shame that this performance unfolded in the small hours of the night on the East Coast.

As the final seconds ticked off the clock, Deron Williams walked up behind Krzyzewski and jolted him in the back. LeBron and his teammates headed over to Doug Collins, who had been working the game for NBC, to embrace him and let him feel like a full part of this gold-medal experience. Krzyzewski made eye contact with Jerry Colangelo, and this time, unlike in Athens, he didn't have to say, "I'm sorry."

Bruce Springsteen's "Born in the USA" was blaring on the arena speakers. When Coach K caught up with Colangelo, he kissed him on the cheek, then clapped near the sideline as his players danced together in a circle on the court. NBA megastars were acting like the small-town high school underdogs in *Hoosiers*. They had been a likable group that was a credit to their country. Krzyzewski probably didn't get enough praise for the tone he set with the Olympic refs, never blasting them the way he would have in Durham.

The U.S. players locked arms and climbed up to the gold-medal platform as one, then held their hands over their hearts during the anthem. With tears in their eyes, players kissed their medals. Bryant, who was positively revered by the Chinese fans (teammate Carlos Boozer saw a young woman faint when Kobe passed her while arriving fashionably late to watch Michael Phelps swim), told reporters, "Everybody wants to talk about NBA players being selfish and arrogant and individuals. But what you saw today was a team bonding and facing adversity and coming out with a big win."

Given the man who delivered it, and the stakes involved, that quote represented the greatest compliment Coach K had received since he took the Team USA job.

Wade had already thanked Krzyzewski for believing in his ability to fight through shoulder and knee injuries enough to help the team — the Americans, as it turned out, wouldn't have won gold without Wade coming off the bench. In the locker room, Coach K walked around thanking and hugging every player, while Deron Williams emptied a bottle of water on his head. LeBron James shouted, "That's what you call homework paying off right there." The Americans decided that all twelve players should attend the postgame press conference, a sign of their all-for-one, one-for-all approach. Another sign was more conspicuous—the players gathered around their leader at midcourt.

People are often surprised to hear that Olympic coaches aren't awarded medals, but they aren't. So a dozen NBA stars put their gold medals around the college guy's neck and posed with him for a snapshot.

Mike Krzyzewski was beaming in the photo, and for good reason.

"This has been the greatest experience of my life," he said.

14

LEAVING KNIGHT BEHIND

*M*ISS IT.

Mike Krzyzewski mouthed those words to his center, Brian Zoubek, while the senior was on the foul line with 3.6 seconds left in the 2010 national championship game and Duke holding a two-point lead over Butler.

Miss it?

Miss it.

A mountain of a young man at seven foot one, 260 pounds, Zoubek was the rare Krzyzewski player allowed to wear a beard. Coach K, a West Point man, didn't do beards, but when Zoubek grew one to look tougher, Coach K accepted it as long as he played tougher, kept the thing neatly trimmed, and did as he was told.

Now Zoubek, having made the first of two free throws, had been told by his coach to cut against the grain of any competitor's instinct. He had been fouled down the other end after rebounding Gordon Hayward's fadeaway baseline miss, which he had contested and altered, a shot that would have given Butler the lead. As a four-year player whose college career had been diminished by injuries, and as a free-throw shooter who was making only 55 percent of his attempts, Zoubek could have had a lot on his mind as he made the long and lonely walk to the foul line inside Lucas Oil Stadium. But on the eve of his twenty-second birthday, he was clearheaded and focused on the task in front of him.

Zoubek was thinking only about making his first free throw, and then his second, which would have given Duke a three-point lead. Krzyzewski always liked having one or two New Jersey kids on his team — Bobby Hurley of Jersey City and Jason Williams of Plainfield had helped him win his three national titles — and Zoubek, from Haddonfield, was one of two Garden State starters on this one; the other, Lance Thomas, was from Scotch Plains. The big man seemingly spent half his early years in Durham in a surgeon's office or on crutches, and when he was relatively healthy he didn't get to play much. Zoubek could have transferred to another Division I school in search of more minutes on the floor. He decided instead to stay and fight.

In the championship game against Butler, Zoubek had played the final nine minutes while burdened with four fouls. It felt appropriate that this long-term Duke survivor was the one taking the last shots his graduating class would ever take.

That class included Thomas, star guard Jon Scheyer, and Gerald Henderson, who would turn pro after his junior year. During their freshman season of 2006–2007, Krzyzewski responded to a three-game ACC losing streak by cramming his team into his old office downstairs for a truth-telling film session. Disappointed in his upperclassmen after a six-point loss to North Carolina at Cameron, Coach K stopped the tape after a while and told his veterans, "Listen, the freshman class that we have now, they're going to win a national championship before they leave here. They're fighters. They believe in what they're doing."

And yet that class struggled to live up to the Duke standard. In '07, the freshman Blue Devils finished seventh in the ACC, lost in the first round of the ACC Tournament, and lost in the first round of the NCAA Tournament. In '08, the sophomore Blue Devils lost in the second round of the ACC Tournament and lost in the second round of the NCAA Tournament. In '09, the junior Blue Devils won the conference tourney, but got blown out by Villanova in the Sweet 16.

It was Krzyzewski's first college season after winning gold in Beijing. Many wondered if Coach K was spreading himself too thin between his USA Basketball and Duke commitments. "Everyone had that concern," Zoubek said, in part because all of the players and staffers knew that Krzyzewski, now in his sixties, was incapable of doing anything at less than full speed. But Zoubek was among those who agreed with Coach K's stated claim that USA Basketball had made him a better all-around coach. Working with NBA megastars such as Kobe Bryant and LeBron James had made him a bit more player-friendly than in the past.

"I think there was a transition of how tough he was on us and how old-school he was the first couple of years to the end," Zoubek said. Not that Krzyzewski sacrificed anything when it came to precise execution of every minute of every practice in preparation for games. This was an approach applied equally from the top players down to the team managers, who were sometimes interviewed by six members of the program — at the same time — before being hired for one of ten or more positions on staff.

Forty-five minutes before practices started, managers made the Gatorade and put out the protein bars, whistles, stat sheets, jump ropes, and mats for stretching. When Coach K stopped a practice drill to make a point, the managers were stationed around the court with basketballs in their hands, ready to make an immediate chest pass — with the Nike swoosh facing the potential receiver — whenever Krzyzewski ordered the drill to resume. On the road, during meetings in hotels, one manager was always stationed outside a back entrance to make sure no guest or employee accidentally walked in. Managers helped airport crews load and unload gear in late-night snow and freezing rain, and they often earned loud ovations from the coaches and players when boarding the bus soaking wet. "We were part of the family as much as everyone else," said manager Jenny Kelemen, who, after attending Harvard Business School and interacting with countless CEOs, called Krzyzewski "the single best communicator I've been around my entire life."

Coach K could empower a five-foot-four woman to feel entirely comfortable and confident in a male-dominated land of giants, just as he could empower his 2009–2010 team — devoid of star power and eye-catching physical talent — to believe it could overcome past disappointments. Krzyzewski could empower his seniors to believe that they could make good on his prediction from three seasons earlier and win the whole thing.

Over the years, Duke players are separated into two groups. Like players for the New York Yankees, Boston Celtics, and Los Angeles Lakers, they are in either group 1 — those who won championship rings — or group 2 — those who failed to win championship rings. At Duke basketball functions and reunions, the guys with the rings are treated a little bit differently than the guys without the rings, by Coach K and everyone else. If you are a sought-after recruit who signs with the Blue Devils, the expectation is clear — win a title or live with the consequences of falling short.

"Whether you think it's fair or not," Scheyer said, "it's how I felt 100 percent. If I left Duke without winning that championship, knowing what we'd been through, I 100 percent would have looked at my career as a disappointment. I know that's not right, but that's how my mind worked."

And now Zoubek was on the foul line trying to ensure that his Blue Devils wouldn't spend the rest of their lives regretting a lost opportunity in Indianapolis, where their coach had won his first title in 1991. The senior center took three dribbles, studied the center of the basket, and calmly sank the first free throw to make it 61–59 before punctuating the moment with a fist pump. Zoubek then wiped his mouth with his jersey, exhaled, and prepared himself to put away America's darlings, the Butler Bulldogs, a long-shot mid-major with a thirty-three-year-old coach, Brad Stevens, who didn't look a day older than seventeen. Butler was playing fifteen minutes away from its home field house, where the inspiration for the movie *Hoosiers*, Milan High (enrollment 161), defeated Muncie Central (enrollment 1,662) in the final seconds to win the 1954 Indiana state title.

As the underdog playing in its hometown, Butler was the people's choice to win this game. Sometimes it felt like 69,000 of the 70,000-plus fans in the place were pulling for the Bulldogs to extend their winning streak to twenty-six games and finish off one of the more improbable stories in NCAA history. Duke was the ultimate heavyweight, and very few people ever root for one of those. Three days earlier, the *Indianapolis Star* had published on the front page of its sports section an illustration of Krzyzewski with devil horns and a target on his head next to a story headlined, "Despising Duke," before the newspaper pulled the edition (after more than 20,000 copies went out) and apologized to the Duke coach, who wasn't in a terribly forgiving mood.

"It was just juvenile," Krzyzewski said. "My seven grandkids didn't enjoy looking at it. 'That's not Papi' . . . If we're going to be despised or hated by anybody because we go to school and we want to win, you know what, that's your problem."

Zoubek was now Butler's problem. He was about to take the ball for a second free throw that was likely to prevent a *Hoosiers* sequel when he heard his teammate, Scheyer, tell him to look at Coach K. The center shot a quick look to the bench, where Krzyzewski told him to intentionally miss his foul shot, much to his assistants' chagrin. Chris Collins was among the sideline voices opposed to the strategy, but Krzyzewski wasn't looking for a vote. This was his executive decision.

Once again, Zoubek lowered his head and dribbled the ball three times before rising up to deliver his shot. Only this time he fired an overhead line drive that bounded hard and high off the back of the rim and into the arms of a leaping Hayward, who was about to become a top-ten pick in the NBA draft. Zoubek rushed up to body him, but the Butler forward escaped to his right with three seconds to go and started racing upcourt with Duke junior Kyle Singler approaching to offer resistance. As Singler closed on Hayward, Butler's burly six-foot-eight forward, Matt Howard, set a vicious blind (and moving) screen on him that probably would have been called a foul had it not come with 1.2 seconds left in a championship game. Singler crumpled to the floor as a liberated Hayward picked up his dribble on the run, planted his left foot on the midcourt line, and launched his body into the air as he let the ball fly just before the horn sounded.

Duke's Nolan Smith was concerned about fouling Hayward, so he didn't seriously contest the release. To the players on the floor, it felt like the ball was hanging up there for ten interminable seconds. The Bulldogs thought this was exactly how the fairy tale was supposed to end — with a wild prayer of a shot to beat almighty Duke. As the ball approached the basket, a number of Blue Devils players and staffers thought the damn thing was going in. "I still wake up in night sweats every once in a while thinking about it," recalled Zoubek.

Collins recalled thinking that the ball was in the air for a minute, and that with every revolution it seemed to be tracking the goal. "They were a team of destiny the whole tournament," said the Duke assistant, "and you thought for a split second that destiny was going to win out." His staffmate Chris Spatola said the Hayward heave looked awfully good from his angle on the Duke bench. "We were seen as the evil empire," Spatola said, "and Butler was so storybook. So I thought, 'This thing is going down.'"

Krzyzewski had decided to live or die with this play because the Bulldogs didn't have any time-outs left. He wanted them to have to make a long shot off a mad scramble, down two, rather than have the benefit of a more organized play off an inbounds pass, down three. With four fouls on Zoubek and Thomas, and with the enormous crowd trying to will Butler to victory, Coach K was also concerned about his chances of winning in overtime. He wanted the game settled in regulation.

But by picking the two-point lead and the scramble over the three-point lead (had Zoubek made his second foul shot) and the inbounds pass, Krzyzewski put a potential defeat in play. Butler's shot in Coach K's preferred scenario would almost certainly be a three-pointer, and if it happened to go in, the Blue Devils would suffer their most heartbreaking loss ever. That would have been a hell of a way for this team to go out. Krzyzewski had started three seniors and two juniors; it was a group that had seen it all and weathered more than its share of adversity. Coach K knew the game was changing, and that this might be the last upperclassmen-centric Duke team to compete for a championship. The one-and-done phenomenon of top prospects leaving school for the pros after one season was about to hit Durham harder than Matt Howard had just hit Kyle Singler.

Time stood still as Hayward's Hail Mary seemingly plunged from the roof. The ball banked against the glass, hit the rim, and bounced away as Jim Nantz shouted on CBS, "Ohhhhh, it almost went in . . . almost went in." The crowd shouted along with him. Stevens, the Butler coach, dropped to his knees in disbelief, his arms still folded across his chest. People everywhere grabbed their heads with both hands, unable to fully process, or accept, what they had just witnessed. Krzyzewski jumped into his assistants' arms, and his players piled on top of one another. Soon enough, confetti fell from the rafters. Coach K would call this the toughest and the best of his eight NCAA final matchups.

So much was riding on this night for the Duke coach. He hadn't reached the Final Four since the UConn loss in 2004, and in that time Roy Williams, who took over at North Carolina in 2003, led the Tar Heels to two national titles and ripped off a string of significant victories over the Blue Devils. (His 2009 graduating class led by Tyler Hansbrough and Danny Green went 4-0 in Cameron Indoor Stadium, starting with one of Williams's greatest regular-season moments ever: the epic 2006 victory over the top-ranked Blue Devils in J. J. Redick's final home game.) Krzyzewski needed to prove that he could still win big at Duke while committing to USA Basketball, and that he wasn't longing to make the NBA his full-time passion. (He declared that day he had no interest in the New Jersey Nets, who were reportedly ready to offer him between $12 million and $15 million per year to run their team.)

About that strategy on the final play? "What the hell, it worked," Krzyzewski said. "There are many things that you do during a ball game. Whatever the consequences are, you take it."

After being handed the championship trophy, Coach K said, "I still can't believe we won." His fourth title tied him with Kentucky's Adolph Rupp for second-most of all-time, behind John Wooden's ten. Number four also put him one ahead of Bob Knight.

"He's been my coach, my mentor, and now he's one of my best friends," Krzyzewski claimed that weekend in Indianapolis. "So he's had a profound influence on me throughout my professional and personal life."

But the truth was, as Coach K closed in on his old coach's NCAA career record for victories, that relationship was again careening toward a solid brick wall.

MIKE KRZYZEWSKI and Bob Knight were locked in a warm embrace, their hands around each other's necks courtside at Madison Square Garden on November 15, 2011, when the Duke coach broke his old Army coach's all-time Division I record with his 903rd victory, a five-point win over Michigan State.

It was a great moment for college basketball, and for Duke, its signature program, and a legion of former Krzyzewski players were in the crowd to witness it. After he shook hands with Michigan State coach Tom Izzo, Coach K headed back toward his bench before crossing the court and making a beeline for a certain ESPN analyst. The sixty-four-year-old Krzyzewski told Knight, seventy-one, that he loved him. Knight responded, "Boy, you've done pretty good for a kid who couldn't shoot."

Coach K would say in his postgame news conference, "I took that to mean I think he loves me too."

Krzyzewski told media members what he was expected to tell them — that he wouldn't have been in this position without Knight's guidance, and that he was proud to have studied under the very best. But Krzyzewski was upset about Knight's comment and found it inappropriate for the occasion. "Why does he keep saying that?" he asked a member of Duke's traveling party. "I could shoot. He just didn't let me."

The Duke staff also noticed that Knight was wearing a green sweater that night — green being Michigan State's color. Maybe it was coincidence, maybe not. Either way, Knight told associates that he was in no mood to celebrate a former protégé he believed to be ungrateful and, worse yet, disloyal.

"The biggest word that Bob looks for in relationships is loyalty," said former Notre Dame coach Digger Phelps, Knight's longtime friend. "And if you violate that, you're going to violate Knight, and that's how he is."

Krzyzewski's violation, in Knight's mind, was not accepting his offer to scout international opponents for Team USA. That was clear in conversations between Knight, who had stopped coaching at Texas Tech in the middle of the 2007–2008 season (handing off the job to his son, Pat), and a friend who spoke with the coach nearly every day for years.

Krzyzewski had been genuinely touched the year before the 2008 Olympics when Knight told him, "Just remember, Mike, you are as good as they are," a piece of advice that gave Coach K confidence when dealing with the NBA stars he was charged to lead. But Knight told friends that when he made an offer to scout for his Olympic team, Krzyzewski did not even return his call. "The Olympic deal was a big thing for Bob," said one Knight associate, "and he was really looking forward to doing some scouting. He never heard back from Mike, and he was clearly offended.

"The thing about Coach [Knight] . . . he has like the heart of gold on one side. So Coach K would come to him and go, 'Can I be a student assistant?' Yes. 'Can I go to the Pan Am Games with you?' Yes. [Knight] goes, 'Every time I talked to Mike, it was like he wanted something. I was doing something for him. I was taking him to the Olympics. I was taking him here. I did more shit for him, and I'm not going to say he wasn't good at what he did. But every single one of those things was literally a favor to him."

A few decades later, the associate said, Knight wanted Krzyzewski to act in kind. "Knight said, 'You know what, Mike, if you want, I'll go over there with you. I'll scout the other teams. I'll do this, do that, and we can talk about the other team before the games.' And he never got back to him, which was literally the worst thing he could've done . . . Coach said he did more shit for [Krzyzewski] than he did for his own kids, or as much."

Some Coach K friends thought that the Team USA coach was afraid Knight might cause an international incident while representing the program and the United States. That was hardly an irrational fear, but no matter: Knight was not the forgive-and-forget type, and Krzyzewski was not exactly alone on his shit list. "That list is forever," the associate said. So was the list of coaches who owed him, Knight felt, a debt of gratitude, including a certain former New York Giants assistant looking for his big break through Cleveland Browns owner Art Modell, who had received a recommendation from the Indiana Hoosiers coach. "I got fuckin' [Bill] Belichick his fuckin' Browns job," Knight said.

But Knight's resentment of Krzyzewski was in a league of its own. At some point, Krzyzewski called his former coach to ask him to serve as a radio voice for some Duke event, a request that left Knight angry and incredulous. "He dug all the skeletons out," said a Knight friend. "It was, 'No, but I wouldn't have minded going to Russia, and I wouldn't have minded scouting these people, and I wouldn't have minded going to Italy. But if you think I'm going to sit on the sideline at some fuckin' game and call the radio for you . . .'" Knight told the friend he would never again take a call from Krzyzewski.

Knight also railed against Coach K for accepting USA Basketball's offer to coach again in the 2012 Olympics in London, where he overcame a lack of size to survive another close encounter with Spain in the gold-medal game. (Krzyzewski would also accept USA Basketball's offer to go for a three-peat in Rio de Janeiro in 2016.)

"Oh, he went crazy," said a Knight associate. "He was like, 'You do it once. It's the United States of America. I did it in 1984, I got done with it, I won the gold, and now, goddamn it, now it's someone else's turn. You don't do it more than once, and I told fuckin' Mike that. You do it once. What about [Gregg] Popovich? What about this person, what about that person? . . . You should do it once, and then you should pass it to the next guy. It's not his until he's fuckin' ninety years old.' He went crazy over that. Crazy. Crazy."

So back in New York in 2011, on a historic night in college basketball, it came as no surprise that Knight was telling friends he didn't want to be working the game in the Garden. Nonetheless, before Duke beat Michigan State to make Krzyzewski the sport's most prolific winner, Knight released a statement through ESPN:

> After reading about Roger Bannister and the Four Minute Mile, I thought it would be neat to be the first coach to win 900 games. Once I reached that, I was hoping Mike would be the first person to surpass it. I also think it is neat for a coach and his former player to have the opportunity to win this many games while each one was coaching at nearly the same time. He made great contributions to our Army team as a player, and has been a great example as a coach of how to do things the right way. There is no one I respect more for the way he went about coaching and following the rules than Mike. The history of college basketball has had no better coach than Mike Krzyzewski.

Knight genuinely believed that Krzyzewski was an excellent coach. And he genuinely respected his former protégé far more than he had respected John Wooden, whom he saw as an unworthy beneficiary of rule-breaking conduct within his program. But the first part of Knight's statement bothered some who were close to Coach K. Just as he had told others that he cared only about being the first man to 900 victories, Knight made sure to point out for the record that he had beaten Krzyzewski to that benchmark. It seemed yet another unnecessary jab from someone who couldn't handle being supplanted by a onetime subordinate.

A few years later, after everything Knight had done for him professionally — and personally after the death of his father — Coach K would decide to give his old coach one last chance. He would regret that choice.

DEAN SMITH WAS EIGHTY-THREE when he died in Chapel Hill on the evening of February 7, 2015. He had suffered from dementia, a devastating development for family and friends who knew the iconic coach to have one of the sharpest minds and memories around. Krzyzewski had grown closer to Smith after his rival retired, though they never became close friends. Coach K had seen him for the final time seventeen months earlier, after the Duke coach had come across Smith's daughter on the beach while, unbeknownst to each other, both old coaches were vacationing on North Carolina's Figure Eight Island. Smith was in a wheelchair, looking quite frail. Mickie Krzyzewski told author John Feinstein, "I didn't think he recognized us at all or, as [Smith's wife] Linnea had said, was really even aware that we were there. But Mike, being Mike, he was doing his mind-over-matter thing. So he just kept talking to him as if it was twenty years ago."

Krzyzewski whispered into Smith's ear, "Coach, I love you," as he left. Coach K broke Smith's record of 422 ACC victories three days before the Tar Heels coach died.

"We have lost a man who cannot be replaced," Krzyzewski said after Smith's death. "He was one of a kind and the sport of basketball lost one of its true pillars. Dean possessed one of the greatest basketball minds and was a magnificent teacher and tactician. While building an elite program at North Carolina, he was clearly ahead of his time in dealing with social issues. However, his greatest gift was his unique ability to teach what it takes to become a good man. That was easy for him to do because he was a great man himself. All of his players benefited greatly from his basketball teachings, but even more from his ability to help mold men of integrity, honor and purpose. Those teachings, specifically, will live forever in those he touched. We offer our deepest sympathies — and gratitude for sharing his incredible life with us for so long — to Linnea, his children and the entire North Carolina family."

Before Duke and North Carolina met in Cameron eleven days after Smith died, Tar Heels coach Roy Williams called Krzyzewski with an idea — each team should start the game in Smith's cherished four-corners offense and let the shot clock run out for an intentional violation. Coach K didn't love it and countered with an idea of his own: North Carolina and Duke players and coaches should come together at midcourt before the game and kneel in a moment of silence. Williams signed off on it and ended up locking arms with Krzyzewski as they honored Williams's mentor.

Krzyzewski had a different relationship with Williams than he'd had with Smith. Coach K had already proved himself — the Hall of Fame induction, the two national titles, including one at Williams's expense — by the time the former Carolina assistant had left Kansas for Chapel Hill. Krzyzewski had to fight Smith for every Tobacco Road inch just to compete in Smith's backyard. After landing Harrison Barnes in 2009, Williams said, he went on to lose countless head-to-head recruiting battles to Krzyzewski without scoring a major victory.

Though Krzyzewski now owned four national titles, Williams was still ahead, 2–1, since returning to Carolina, and don't believe for a second that both men didn't think about that. A year after beating Butler with a veteran team in 2010, Krzyzewski dove headfirst into the one-and-done waters in pursuit of his next championship. He had tried to sign John Wall, who played his one-and-done year at Kentucky in 2009–2010, before landing Kyrie Irving for the following season in a move that announced a seismic shift in the Duke program.

Irving had attended a barbecue at Krzyzewski's house on his visit and was so comfortable with Coach K's family and the Duke players that he fell asleep on a chair in the basement, signaling to the people in the room that he would definitely be a Blue Devil. "We had a philosophical discussion before Kyrie," said Chris Spatola, "and decided we needed to start going after these guys. John Calipari had started doing it and had good teams, so we talked about it. We said, 'Okay, either we have to compete against these guys, or try to get these guys.' Wall came in on a visit. We didn't get him, but that shift in philosophy was in motion."

A genius ball handler whose talent blew away players and coaches alike in practice, Irving suffered a serious toe injury in his eighth college game, against Butler, at a time when Krzyzewski thought the 2010–2011 Blue Devils were as good as, if not better than, his 1992 title team. Irving wasn't ready to return until the NCAA Tournament in March, and Coach K asked his captains, Nolan Smith and Kyle Singler, if they were okay with an Irving re-entry at such a delicate time. They approved, of course, though Irving's ball-dominant presence did naturally have an impact on team chemistry, and especially on his good friend and road roommate, Smith, who struggled while the freshman star scored 28 in Duke's Sweet 16 loss to Arizona. Irving gave Krzyzewski eleven games before becoming the number-one overall pick in the NBA draft.

The following season, Austin Rivers, son of Boston Celtics coach Doc Rivers, played in all of Duke's thirty-four games but shot only 5-for-14 in the second-seeded Blue Devils' shocking first-round NCAA Tournament loss to fifteenth-seeded Lehigh. Two seasons later, Krzyzewski suited up Jabari Parker, who would be the number-two overall pick in the 2014 draft after one year in Durham. That season was interrupted by tragedy — Krzyzewski's only sibling, his older brother Bill, died the day after Christmas at age seventy-one, after undergoing cancer surgery. Big Bill, the gentle giant, was a retired captain from the Chicago Fire Department Local 2, where he had worked for nearly four decades. He was his younger brother's kindly bodyguard throughout their youth, and Mike was gutted over losing him.

After Duke split its first four ACC games, Krzyzewski said that his brother's death had profoundly impacted him and his ability to do his job. "I got knocked back right after Christmas," he said. "And I've been knocked back for a few weeks. It's on me, not on my team . . . The head coach is going to do a better job."

Duke suffered another stunning loss in the first round of the NCAAs, this time falling to fourteenth-seeded Mercer, which fielded an entire cast of seniors who would never have been recruited by Coach K. Mercer's Jakob Gollon, a twenty-four-year-old sixth-year senior, scored 20 points, while Parker, who had just turned nineteen, managed only 14 on 4-of-14 shooting. "We're playing against grown men," Krzyzewski said at halftime. Those grown men denied the Blue Devils even one NCAA victory in the abbreviated "Jabari Parker era."

Coach K was determined to stay the course with these high school All-Americans who arrived in Durham with designs on making an immediate jump to the NBA. "The Olympic experience fed into this full force," Spatola said. "I remember [Krzyzewski] saying at one point, 'I just want to coach great talent.' The Olympic experience fed the proliferation of one-and-done for him, because he wanted to coach those special guys.

"He became much more invested in the outcome than the process. He was willing to forgo the process because he wanted to coach pros . . . The thing that disappoints me is that Coach K did two things better than anyone in his profession. One was man-to-man defense, and Duke teams in this one-and-done era were not good defensively. It takes time. And the other thing is relationships. Nobody does relationships better than Coach K, and now he was trying to do it in a year."

Krzyzewski took things to a new extreme in 2014–2015, bringing in *three* one-and-done freshmen — the number-one prospect in America (six-foot-eleven Jahlil Okafor), the number-one point guard in America (Tyus Jones), and a top-fifteen player (Justise Winslow) — along with another freshman (Grayson Allen) who was a top-forty player and a future pro. Krzyzewski had gotten a grand total of two NCAA Tournament victories out of his three most recent one-and-dones in Irving (two), Rivers (zero), and Parker (zero), and yet he was still going all in on the elite prospects who were sure to leave him after a single season. The Olympic experiences had indeed changed him. Coach K wanted to coach only the best of the best.

Many competing coaches were upset over the Duke jackpot and Krzyzewski's clear advantage in recruiting as head coach of USA Basketball's signature team. Okafor, Jones, and Winslow all came up through the governing body's junior system and teamed with a previous Duke signee out of the system, Parker, to win the FIBA Boys Under-17 world championship in 2012. Their multiple years in the USA Basketball program gave Krzyzewski invaluable access that his competitors did not have, access he used to assemble a recruiting class to die for.

USA Basketball itself had grown into a more substantial force in the recruiting process. Every year at its Colorado Springs base, USA Basketball gathered the nation's top prospects, regardless of whether those prospects played for teams sponsored by Nike or Adidas. Their family members mingled in the Marriott lobby to discuss who was going where and what rules-breaking school was offering which package to which recruit. In this environment, Coach K was seen as a law-abiding overlord promoting the Duke brotherhood, the network that was said to bond former Blue Devils for life. Krzyzewski was prioritizing the team, the benefits of the brotherhood, and offering a roadmap to the pros; Kentucky's Calipari was prioritizing the individual and selling the fastest path to NBA fame and fortune.

By hiring Coach K for multiple Olympic cycles, USA Basketball was notarizing not only Krzyzewski himself but his sales presentation to the best high school players in America.

"Over twelve years of him being with USA Basketball," Roy Williams said, "a lot of coaches would call me or see me and say, 'Why do they let him do that? He's getting such an advantage.' Sure enough, that person who told me that was recruiting against Mike on something, and it was a great advantage for Mike. He can say to kids, 'I did this with LeBron. I did this with Kevin Durant.' But I wanted our Olympic team to be the best, and for twelve years he gave away half his summer to do those kinds of things. It was an advantage. He could see kids in advance that none of the other coaches could see. And he paid a pretty darn high price to do that.

"Coaches would call, and I'd say, 'Why are you calling me?' An amazing number of coaches. Am I supposed to cure it? . . . This is the way I like to say it too. Everybody can pick out a reason for losing. And sometimes you pick out a reason without looking in the mirror. [Duke] beat a lot of people. They didn't win the national championship every year, but they got a lot of players that other people wanted. You still have to play on game night."

Steve Alford, the new coach at UCLA, was white-hot over the fact that he couldn't watch his son Bryce in USA Basketball's 2013 training camp for its FIBA Under-19 team, while Krzyzewski had access to that team. The University of Florida's Billy Donovan was the coach of the 2013 U.S. team that included high schoolers Okafor and Winslow and Duke's Rasheed Sulaimon; he wasn't happy when Coach K arrived at his Colorado Springs camp to speak to his players and show them a video of his Olympic team. Krzyzewski was not afraid to push the envelope on his access to the junior players in the USA Basketball system who hadn't announced their college commitments yet. At one of the governing body's fantasy camps in Las Vegas, the senior national coach held a conversation with Okafor while Calipari, who was working the camp, was standing three feet away. Krzyzewski's advantage, said one Olympic team source, "was definitely an advantage that went over the line a couple of times."

Coach K's staffers secured taped testimonials from some of the Olympic team's biggest stars, including LeBron James, who praised Krzyzewski's emphasis on team basketball in one video. "I love the way he treats his players on and off the court," James said. "It's kind of a family-oriented atmosphere." In one clip, the words, "Why did you consider Duke?" appeared on the screen before LeBron reappeared to say, "Duke is one of those colleges that's going to help you become a better player and a better person, because of this history they have, and Coach K speaks for himself."

Never mind that James didn't seriously consider Duke or any other college before entering the NBA draft. The video, which signed off with a Duke basketball logo, was the kind of marketing tool that could be persuasive in recruiting.

In a column following Team USA's 2014 World Cup of Basketball gold-medal rout, *Yahoo!Sports* NBA insider Adrian Wojnarowski wrote of that advantage under the headline, "NBA Needs to Pull Stars from USA Basketball, Which Is Showcasing Only Duke's Coach." Wojnarowski described USA Basketball as an organization that "has been co-opted into a Krzyzewski leverage play for the Duke Blue Devils." Wojnarowski wrote that Coach K needed USA Basketball to keep feeding him recruits the likes of Parker, Okafor, Winslow, and Jones. "Why sit in the steamy summer-circuit AAU gyms trying to make eye contact with 16 year olds, when you can use the media to write about all the close, personal relationships you've developed with LeBron and Kobe, 'Melo and Durant?" read his *Yahoo!Sports* column. "Hey kids, Krzyzewski even texts them during the season — maybe sometimes right after he texts you!"

Krzyzewski maintained that he'd made only two trips in nine years to watch junior players in the USA Basketball system, and that any advantage he'd gained in recruiting was directly tied to the scoreboard. "I would think an accomplishment advantage is more of what it is," he said. "If I didn't [win], it wouldn't be an advantage to be the USA coach. If Kobe Bryant said, 'I didn't get along with Coach K,' would that be an advantage? When people win and do something really good, other people see it. But you didn't get a free pass just because you're the U.S. coach."

Advantages, advantages, advantages. When people complained about Duke basketball, they always talked about advantages. Advantages in recruiting. Advantages with the refs. And advantages with the NCAA, like the one some coaches believed Duke benefited from in the case of Lance Thomas. A starter on the 2010 national title team, Thomas was sued by a

New York jeweler for buying nearly $100,000 in jewelry in December 2009 and failing to pay the balance of his bill beyond his $30,000 down payment. If Thomas had received an improper benefit in the form of the $30,000, or in the credit initially extended to him (student-athletes were not allowed to accept loans based on future earnings potential), while competing for Duke during that 2009–2010 season, the NCAA could strip the Blue Devils of their championship for using an ineligible player.

But in April 2013, Duke released a statement saying that the NCAA and the school had found no evidence of a rules violation in the case, "based on the information available." Neither Thomas nor representatives of the jeweler, Rafaello & Co., agreed to speak to NCAA investigators. In the university statement, associate athletic director Jon Jackson said that "both the NCAA and Duke consider the matter closed." At the time of that announcement, according to the *Raleigh News and Observer,* Krzyzewski had spoken only once about the case, when preseason practice started in 2012 — a month after the lawsuit had been made public and then almost immediately settled confidentially between the two parties.

"Before anything was made public, they started working together to go through a process of seeing what happened," Krzyzewski said of the NCAA and Duke at the time. "I have complete trust and confidence in all the parties involved and am very proud of our compliance record over the thirty-three years that we've been here."

Another prominent head coach who competed against Krzyzewski pointed out that Duke was the party that made the announcement about the NCAA's decision in the Thomas case, not the NCAA, and that the statement made it seem as though the two parties were functioning as one. "Mike is big enough," said this coach, "to make anything in the Southern District of New York office disappear . . . If it were me, it would have been a full-fledged NCAA investigation. If it were Calipari, it would have been a five-year show cause. But at Duke these things never seem to go anywhere."

Sonny Vaccaro, the former Nike and Adidas marketing executive who ran high school all-star games and showcase camps for nearly fifty years, said that Duke's announcement about the Thomas case marked the first time he'd seen a university speak on the NCAA's behalf to close an inquiry. "Never in my lifetime," Vaccaro said. "I don't know how dual opinions arrived at the same time saying the same words. I didn't know the NCAA shared a public release . . . I can only remember this happening with Duke."

Chris Kennedy, Duke's compliance director and senior deputy director of athletics, had heard complaints like these a million times, accusations "that Duke gets away with stuff because we're Duke," he said. "I don't think we get away with stuff. You have to place that in a much broader context of how we've handled accusations and violations over the years."

Kennedy said that his office understood NCAA rules "insofar as they can be understood at all," and that Duke officials realized the importance of precedent and how to apply it to an argument. "And when we do something wrong," he said, "we always admit it, even when there's no way for the NCAA to find out. We're going to self-report. We have a reputation of reporting violations when we discover them and levying appropriate punishment."

The compliance director declined to identify players punished by the NCAA after the school self-reported violations. One source said that a member of Duke's 2001 national title team, Matt Christensen, had been suspended four games after the school informed the NCAA that he had unwittingly broken a rule (and an absurd one at that) by competing in two games in a Utah summer league while attending summer school at Brigham Young University.

Kennedy maintained that Duke opponents were never shy about contacting the NCAA with reports of alleged Blue Devil wrongdoing. "There are accusations all the time," he said. "There are always accusations. You can leave an anonymous voicemail on the NCAA line, and they respond to it. 'It was reported to us that Mike Krzyzewski was at a tournament during a dead period.' No, he was tending to his garden at the time during the dead period, and we have the phone records to prove it."

As much as Duke officials tried to blow holes through the notion that the Blue Devils were protected by the NCAA police, suspicions to the contrary persisted. One head coach pointed to a 2011 case involving a six-foot-seven recruit from Tennessee named Alex Poythress, who told CBSSports.com that he'd been offered a scholarship by Krzyzewski during a summer tournament — an NCAA no-no. Duke said it would look into the claim, and nothing ever came of it. Poythress ended up playing at Kentucky. "It came down to a definition of what is 'during,'" Kennedy said. "It was a Bill Clinton case. When the kid was released from the tournament, I think there was a gray area there."

One prominent head coach said that Krzyzewski had long enjoyed a pipeline directly to the top of the NCAA's leadership; he had a particularly strong relationship with former NCAA president Myles Brand. "Things at Duke have a tendency to go away," said the head coach, who maintained that Krzyzewski leveraged his pristine reputation in recruiting prospects who had run into eligibility issues.

Whether or not Duke's above-reproach reputation in NCAA circles was a significant asset, Krzyzewski was having no trouble persuading elite prospects to play at least a season in Durham. He was getting considerable help from his former player and current assistant, Jeff Capel, the son of a college head coach and NBA assistant. Capel was fired as head coach at Oklahoma when his program cratered two years after he led the 2008–2009 Sooners to the Elite Eight and a 30-6 record; the NCAA later found major violations in Capel's program that involved an assistant coach, impermissible benefits, and a player who should've been ineligible for competition because he accepted those benefits — in this case, money from a financial advisor. The NCAA vacated Oklahoma's thirteen victories in 2009–2010, and though he wasn't implicated in the wrongdoing, Capel was left in need of an image makeover. Enter Coach K.

A thoughtful and engaging talker, Capel was a gifted recruiter who had the kind of connections and credibility with the very best high school players that the other Duke assistants, the lifers, didn't have, the kind that kept the one-and-done assembly line rolling. After he helped Krzyzewski land Jabari Parker, Capel said, "I remember we texted Kyrie Irving and thanked him, because he was the guy who opened the door."

That door was blown off its hinges by Okafor, Jones, and Winslow, who arrived in Durham in 2014 with the objective of winning it all and then bolting for the NBA. After Krzyzewski won the FIBA World Cup in Spain, he was watching a team workout with Capel when the assistant leaned into him and said, "Holy shit, we've got a chance to be really good." The three star freshmen combined with senior guard Quinn Cook to lead the Blue Devils to a 14-0 start, including an impressive neutral-floor victory over Michigan State and a more impressive road victory over the number-two team in the country.

"When we won at Wisconsin," Capel recalled, "I said, 'These young guys are different. They aren't afraid. They actually like this pressure.'"

The Duke program had to deal with two unusual departures during the season. First, former five-star recruit Semi Ojeleye transferred over a lack of playing time. According to a story his mother told the *Boston Herald* about a meeting she had with Krzyzewski, Coach K exploded out of his chair when she asked about her son's prospects for time on the floor.

"He shouted at me," Joy Ojeleye recalled. "He said, 'Am I lying? Am I lying?' Just like that. My oldest son [Victor, who was also in the meeting] said, 'Coach, she didn't say you were lying, she was only asking a question.' . . . Victor, for the first time, he felt so humiliated, so bad and ashamed I was treated like that." Semi Ojeleye transferred to Southern Methodist University and played effectively enough in one season (averaging 19 points and 7 rebounds) to become a second-round pick of the Boston Celtics.

Then, on January 29, 2015, Rasheed Sulaimon was dismissed from the team, marking the first time Krzyzewski had removed a player from his program in his thirty-five years at Duke. In a statement, Coach K maintained that the junior guard "had been unable to consistently live up to the standards required to be a member of our program" and that the "privilege" of representing Duke mandated that a player conduct himself "in a certain manner. After Rasheed repeatedly struggled to meet the necessary obligations, it became apparent that it was time to dismiss him from the program."

The Duke student newspaper, *The Chronicle,* later reported that two female students had accused Sulaimon of sexual assault, and that Krzyzewski and his staff were made aware of the allegations in March 2014, ten months before the dismissal. The alleged victims did not file complaints with the university or the police, the school never substantiated the claims in its investigation, and Sulaimon, who transferred to Maryland, denied that he was involved in any misconduct. It was unclear if the allegations played any role in Sulaimon's ouster from the team.

It was clear that the departure of a second player from the team in six weeks wasn't going to derail these Blue Devils. Two days after Sulaimon's dismissal, a Duke comeback toppled 19-0 Virginia and ended the Cavaliers' twenty-one-game home winning streak. "We were going through a chaotic time," said Capel. "For us to win that game, in the fashion in which we won it, you felt the whole time that this group is really, really special. You have these unbelievably talented freshmen who are incredibly humble, and you have this senior in Quinn who's on a magical journey and is the unquestioned leader and heart and soul of the team, and then the guys in the middle who were the glue to everything . . . Wow, we never had another team like that."

That team had delivered Krzyzewski his 1,000th career victory the previous Sunday, in Madison Square Garden, where signs referred to Coach K as "COACH 1K." St. John's held a 10-point lead, with 8:36 to play, before Duke ripped off an 18-2 run that sealed it. Krzyzewski had experienced some memorable moments in the Garden as an Army player. Outside of Cameron Indoor Stadium, it was the perfect place for him to surpass Knight in 2011 and to become the first coach to clear the 1,000-game hurdle in Division I. (The achievement even earned Krzyzewski a plaque in a pregame ceremony in Chapel Hill, of all places, at the Duke-Carolina regular-season finale in March.)

Speaking of his players, Coach K said, "It was beautiful, really, to see them fight today and win . . . I'm glad it's over." Yes, the chase for 1,000 victories was over. But the pursuit of something even more meaningful, a fifth national title, was just beginning.

MIKE KRZYZEWSKI WAS in his ninth national championship game (after tying John Wooden with his twelfth Final Four appearance), and it looked like he was going home a loser. Wisconsin had a nine-point lead with a little more than thirteen minutes to play in Indianapolis, where Krzyzewski had won two of his previous four titles. The young Blue Devils, sitting around their coach during a time-out, appeared ready to accept their fate at the hands of the older Badgers, who had learned plenty from their December loss at home to this very team.

"We were dead in the water," Coach K said, "and then Grayson put us on his back."

Grayson Allen, an edgy, athletic, slam-dunking guard from Jacksonville, was still the least heralded of the freshmen recruits. Krzyzewski's team had been whittled down to eight players, and Allen was number eight. He didn't even play in the earlier victory over Wisconsin, and he averaged fewer than nine minutes of playing time during the regular season. But when Duke broke from its time-out, he lit a fuse that blew up the game's dynamic, starting with a three-pointer and then a steal on the defensive end that led to a Wisconsin foul on the diving, tumbling Allen; he rose from the court and directed a couple of primal screams toward his bench.

Suddenly Duke had life. On the next possession, after the Blue Devils secured an offensive rebound, Allen took the ball on the left wing and exploded past Wisconsin star Sam Dekker, rising high for a layup and drawing another foul. CBS cut to a live scene of bedlam inside a packed Cameron Indoor Stadium. "A new star is born," analyst Bill Raftery said on the broadcast. On his Lucas Oil Stadium sideline, elevated above the team bench, Krzyzewski rose from his stool and gave an emphatic swing of his right arm, Tiger Woods style. Allen made the free throw and, after Wisconsin's Nigel Hayes sank a three-pointer, made two more to keep it a four-point game.

If this had been a baseball game, Allen could be described as the setup guy who steadied his wobbly team before handing the ball to the closer, classmate Tyus Jones, who had put away Wisconsin in December. A high school sensation from Minnesota, Jones had agreed to an arrangement with Okafor, out of Chicago, that they would take college visits together and eventually commit to the same program. Krzyzewski was the lucky beneficiary of the package deal.

Jones had worked that morning with Duke assistant Jon Scheyer on shooting off ball screens, and the work paid off. He drained a pull-up jumper while getting fouled and completed the three-point play to cut the deficit to one. After Okafor picked up his fourth foul and went to the bench with 9:18 left and the Badgers up four, Jones went back to work, nailing another pull-up to make it a 54–54 game with 7:03 left. Allen gave Duke the lead on another aggressive drive to his right, but Wisconsin was too good and too mentally strong to fold; two nights earlier the Badgers had eliminated Calipari's 38-0 Kentucky team, which was riding its own class of one-and-dones. So nobody was surprised that Wisconsin recovered to regain the lead on Frank Kaminsky and Dekker layups. And nobody was surprised that Jones came off an Amile Jefferson screen and buried a top-of-the-key three with 4:06 left to recapture the lead. At that stage, Jones and Allen had scored 24 of Duke's 28 second-half points.

Okafor returned to the floor in the closing minutes. Out of a time-out, after it appeared that Winslow had stepped on the baseline with the ball without drawing an official's whistle, Okafor took the pass and executed a spin move on Kaminsky. Though the Wisconsin seven-footer had outplayed Okafor all night, this time Kaminsky got the worst of the exchange. He tried to intentionally foul Okafor by wrapping his arms around him, but the Duke center powered through the hold and banked in his shot to give the Blue Devils a 61–58 lead with 3:14 left.

Coach K's signature defense smothered the Badgers on the next possession, forcing a shot-clock violation, and then Okafor scored off a missed Winslow layup to push the lead to five. Wisconsin's Bronson Koenig missed a left-handed layup on the other end, leading to a scramble for the loose ball that, replays showed, appeared to go out of bounds off of Winslow's fingertip. But the same refs who originally ruled that the ball had gone off the Badgers looked at those replays and decided that the evidence wasn't strong enough to overturn, handing possession to the Blue Devils and setting off a fresh round of Duke-gets-all-the-calls fury on Twitter.

Not that it made Wisconsin feel any better, but the following day the NCAA's supervisor of officials conceded that the officials had erred in giving the ball to Duke. Jones was the obvious choice to capitalize on this break. With 1:24 to play, he dribbled to his right again and rose up and drained a three-pointer that extended the lead to 66–58. Wisconsin rallied one last time and cut its deficit to three, but Jones made two foul shots with thirty-five seconds left for the final score, 68–63, that gave Krzyzewski his fifth national championship and put him alone in second all-time behind Wooden's ten.

At the final horn, Coach K embraced his assistants with a look of sheer exhilaration on his face. His players ended up in their customary national-title dogpile, while Kaminsky and other Badgers were doubled over in agony. Duke had outscored Wisconsin by 14 points over the last thirteen minutes and made 16 of 20 free throws to the Badgers' 6 of 10 — inspiring a louder social media outcry over the officiating that ignored how much more assertive Duke was in attacking the basket in the second half. (Allen finished with 16 points in twenty-one minutes.)

"There was more body contact in this game than any game we played all year," Wisconsin coach Bo Ryan told CBS afterward, "and I just feel sorry for my guys that all of a sudden a game was like that. They're struggling with that a little bit . . . It's just a shame that it had to be played that way."

Ryan also said in his postgame press conference, "We don't do rent-a-player. You know what I mean?" Krzyzewski was angered by that remark, particularly by Ryan's use of the word "rent," which could have implied that Duke was doing something illegal to land its top-rated recruits. Coach K was more interested in talking about the character and poise of his freshmen, who scored 60 of Duke's 68 points. "This group has really been like brothers from the beginning in July," he said. "They have not posed any problems for me . . . It's really been an amazing group of kids to work with."

Now sixty-eight, Krzyzewski worried after winning the World Cup in September that he would run out of gas in the season's final weeks. He didn't. "I think I'm as energized now as I've ever been at the end of the year," he said. Coach K credited the passion of his young players and the leadership of his veterans, especially Quinn Cook, for allowing him to live in their moment and to get more joy out of their first title than he got out of his fifth. "I've never had a group that has had this chemistry, and the brotherhood that this group has had," Krzyzewski said.

When it was all over, he picked up his grandkids and hugged them one by one. He climbed a ladder under one basket and clipped the final strands of the net, then waved the net to the crowd. The final word on the accomplishment — and on the winning coach — belonged to the senior guard who had averaged 15.3 points per game and who had immediately embraced the freshmen as full-fledged members of the team. Quinn Cook was only fourteen when his father unexpectedly died after suffering a heart attack during a surgical procedure. Asked what it was like to be on the championship stage next to his coach, during the annual playing of "One Shining Moment" that wrapped a ribbon around the tournament, Cook replied:

"Surreal. Something that we've all dreamed of. Growing up watching Duke, watching Coach K win championships, celebrating with his great players. To be next to Coach, he's been like a father to me over these last four years. To have his arm around me and hugging me while we're watching 'One Shining Moment' was probably the best feeling in my life . . . I'm just blessed that Coach thought I was good enough to come to Duke."

MIKE KRZYZEWSKI DOES NOT always get back what he gives.

"People have no idea what a great man he is, and how much he does to help people," Jeff Capel said.

"If he hears a coach is on the hot seat, he calls them or texts them and asks, 'What can I do to help?' If a guy loses a job, Coach helps him. Players that reach out for help, even at other schools, it's unbelievable the amount of stuff he does privately for people. There are so many requests. He's a guy to this day who still firmly believes in handwritten notes. He gets back to everyone. And if a coach wins a championship, or wins something, one of the first to call is Coach K."

But not a lot of people are as quick to congratulate Krzyzewski for being Krzyzewski.

"I was with him when he broke Coach Knight's record," Capel said, "and the amount of people that did not reach out to him then, or when he won 1,000 games, or when we won the championship in 2015, or when he won the Olympic gold medals . . . it's jealousy.

"I know it hurts him. It did hurt him."

The slights that hurt Krzyzewski the most, however, were generated by the man who had taught him the college game, Bob Knight, who was being honored in September 2015 at Pinehurst, North Carolina. His former Army players were gathering there to celebrate the fiftieth anniversary of his first college team and victory. Unaware that Knight was so angry about several perceived slights, Coach K decided to join his former teammates for the reunion.

"And it was a disaster," said Krzyzewski's former Army teammate John Mikula.

Knight was such a volatile personality, even on occasions designed to celebrate his life, that nobody had any idea what they were walking into when arriving at a Knight-centric function. Dick Simmons, the accomplished Army player whom Knight used to call "Alice," or "Mary Alice" — because he wasn't physical enough for the coach's liking — once walked into a reunion of former Knight players in Bloomington, Indiana, and heard the coach blurt into a microphone, "Here comes the biggest pussy to ever play college basketball." Simmons had been a company commander in Vietnam.

Krzyzewski did not tell friends he was concerned about how he would be greeted by Knight at the Pinehurst event. According to people in the hotel ballroom where the event took place, Knight was holding court with friends at his table when his former point guard approached. "Mike came in and said, 'How are you doing, Coach?'" recalled Jim Oxley, Krzyzewski's close friend and old backcourt partner. "And [Knight] barely even hesitated and continued with his story, that kind of thing. That was the start of it."

Oxley recalled that Krzyzewski had come in for the whole day. "It just didn't turn out good, and it really wasn't because Mike wasn't being totally gracious, because he was," Oxley said. "He wasn't trying to steal the spotlight, he never does. He didn't sit with Knight at his table because Knight was there with all his guys. He sat with me and a couple of other guys. It just didn't turn out good . . . That was one of many straws that broke the camel's back. I remember Mike walking out of there saying, 'That's it. I'll never do this again.'"

Mikula's version of the interaction went like this: "Knight was sitting in a corner table with [former Army coach] Tates Locke, and I think [former Army assistant] Don DeVoe was there, and Mike went over to him and got down on a knee just to see him eye to eye, and everyone else kind of continued their conversations. Mike got up, walked away, and went over and stood outside the room and said, 'That's the last fucking time. That's it.'"

Two former Army players said that Knight had taken ill that weekend, and that his behavior might have been affected by his condition. A third, Dennis Shantz, said that he wasn't comfortable with a speech that Knight made at the event "because it was in mixed company and he used the same sort of language he would use in the locker room." Bob Seigle, who played for Knight and who later helped Krzyzewski land the head coaching job at Army, had his son and daughter with him and called the speech "cringeworthy." Whatever it was that aggravated his former coach, Seigle said, "That night at Pinehurst was tough for everybody."

But toughest for Krzyzewski.

"There was a general feeling of a disconnect," Oxley said. "Mike was involved with the Olympics then, and Knight might have said something derogatory about Jerry Colangelo to Mike, and Mike thought a lot of Jerry and what he did for the Olympics. It was a combination of things, but I think in general Knight didn't even acknowledge Mike when he came into the room."

The friction that night, and other nights, made it beyond awkward for the players and coaches who had relationships with, and respect for, both Knight and Krzyzewski. Most blamed Knight for the damage done, and many felt that he simply couldn't handle the fact that he had been surpassed in every way by one of his former players and assistants. Coach K broke his former mentor's records in part because he adapted with the times and tweaked his methods to become more user-friendly—adjustments that Knight never made.

Some mutual friends attempted to serve as mediators between the two iconic coaches; others didn't bother trying because they knew it would be fruitless. Asked if he had ever tried to make peace between his former coach and Krzyzewski, former Indiana point guard Quinn Buckner said, incredulously, "Are you crazy? These are two very strong-minded men. That would definitely fall on deaf ears."

DeVoe, a Division I head coach at five schools over thirty-one years, was among those with West Point connections who thought that Knight was the one—and the only one—who should have borne the burden of repairing the relationship. "As far as I'm concerned, Mike has always reached out to Coach Knight and given him credit, where most coaches and players do not do that," DeVoe said. "I think Mike has done everything he can to show his appreciation for what Coach Knight has done for him, and it's up to Coach Knight to be mature enough, in my opinion, to acknowledge that. I heard Mike say, 'I love you,' to Coach Knight, and I don't think that would ever be in Coach Knight's repertoire to ever say the same to Mike."

Coach K was still telling people a year later that he would never again speak to Knight. When he ran into Mikula and some other old West Point grads at the December 2016 funeral for Colonel Tom Rogers, the man who had handed Coach K that divisive note from Knight at the 1992 Final Four, Krzyzewski said of Knight, "I'll have nothing more to do with him. But if you guys need anything, call me."

In the past, when Knight had done him wrong, Krzyzewski would tell Mickie and others close to him that he was done with his former coach. He would talk about the incidents, and about how Knight was being so unfair to him, working through the problems out loud. And then, usually, Krzyzewski would try to fix what was broken.

This time was different. "The Pinehurst one was never talked about," said Chris Spatola, Coach K's son-in-law. "It never came up again with family. That was it. It was clear-cut. He finally said, 'Okay, that's the end of that.'

"He was finally done with Coach Knight."

15

LAST STAND

THE DUKE COACHES gathered in their downstairs conference room after a blowout victory over Pitt for one of the most important TV shows they would ever watch. Zion Williamson, an outsize high school star best described as a Mack truck on a pogo stick, was ready to announce where he would play his one-and-done season of college ball.

Mike Krzyzewski had already landed a dream recruiting class with ESPN 100's number-one-ranked prospect, RJ Barrett, and number-three Cam Reddish, along with seventeenth-ranked Tre Jones. He didn't necessarily need Williamson, rated behind Barrett at number two, but he still very much wanted him. At six foot six and 272 pounds, Williamson had an explosive athleticism around the basket never before seen in a young player so big, and his gym-shaking dunks had earned him more than a million followers on Instagram.

Coach K wasn't optimistic about his chances of signing Williamson, who grew up in Spartanburg, South Carolina, about a seventy-minute drive from Clemson University, the presumed favorite. North Carolina coach Roy Williams thought he had a better shot at Williamson than Krzyzewski did. "Thursday night, I was the last coach to go into Zion's home before he made the announcement on Saturday," Williams said. "I left there and I thought we were going to get him . . . I thought, 'If not us, Brad Brownell and Clemson will probably get him.'"

Outside of Clemson, North Carolina, and Duke, Williamson's final six included South Carolina, Kansas, and Kentucky. When Krzyzewski and his four former players-turned-assistants — Jeff Capel, Nate James, Jon Scheyer, and Nolan Smith — met to watch Zion's big reveal, Scheyer said, the coaches were completely in the dark about his decision. The staff had made multiple visits to see Williamson. "But he wouldn't respond to you a lot," Scheyer said. "So with that, and knowing we've already got Barrett and Reddish, you can think the writing is on the wall. The Williamsons are very private . . . and some guys don't want to play with other really good players.

"Generally you have somewhat of a feel right before they call you. Since I've been a coach, that was the only time when we truly had no idea. None. No indication. Nothing. It put us through more stress beforehand."

On Williamson's official visit to Duke, Smith noticed that the recruit was very intelligent, and very comfortable in his own skin. "Coach K said, 'You get to mix your brand with my brand,' and that really excited Zion," Smith said. "It was, 'Let's make a big splash together. How can we make a big splash? Let's mix the Zion brand with the Duke brand and let's throw in the Coach K brand and make a big splash.'"

The Coach K brand was pretty powerful. Krzyzewski had won more than 1,000 games at Duke alone; no other Division I men's coach had ever reached 1,000 victories overall, never mind at one school. And yet Coach K was not the Duke coach who established the strongest connection with the Williamson family. That was longtime assistant Nate James, a member of the 2001 national championship team. He'd made a lot of drives and flights to South Carolina and built a particularly good relationship with Zion's mother, Sharonda Sampson.

"I knew what his mom wanted, and I knew what Zion wanted," James said. "He wanted to be part of something special. Zion didn't want to be the man; he had that in high school for four years. He had to carry his team each and every night, and he didn't want that . . . I heard the noise. I heard he was a lock here or there. Until his mom Sharonda told me, 'He's not coming,' I'm not going to hear that. We all know when Mom wants something, it's going to happen. And Mom really believed in Coach K."

On the big night at his high school — also his mother's birthday — Zion came dressed in jacket and tie. He wore a silver cross around his neck, and a large gold watch on his left wrist. He sat at a table, flanked by his mother and stepfather, Lee Anderson, and started reading from his prepared script. As he thanked his family members and former coaches and teachers for their support, and then wished his mother a happy birthday and thanked her for being "my rock, my ride-or-die girl," the tension grew in the Duke conference room. "Nerve-racking," was how Smith described it. Sharonda Sampson had told her son, "You've got to be happy in life. You only get to go down this journey one time, so you have to be happy. And I don't want you to do anything for me. I don't want you to do anything for your fans. I want you to do it for Zion, what's in Zion's heart. I know you'll do the right thing."

Early in Williamson's speech, he mentioned that at age five he'd told his mother that his dream was to someday play college basketball and be the best in the country. Those words stirred something in Scheyer, who knew that Williamson had also said that, as a kid, he'd harbored a dream of playing at Duke. "I remember looking around the room and thinking, 'We've got a shot,'" Scheyer said.

Finally, the moment of truth had arrived. Williamson said, "In the fall of 2018, I will continue my basketball journey at . . ." He paused, lowered his head, and reached into the unseen bag that contained the school cap of his choice. He grabbed the cap and kept it hidden as he looked up, smiled, and leaned into his microphone.

"I will be joining the brotherhood of Duke University," he said. As the audience let out a rousing cheer, Williamson put on the familiar bright blue cap with the white letter *D* and hugged his mom.

Krzyzewski and his assistants jumped and roared in unison as if they had just witnessed a buzzer-beating shot to win an NCAA Tournament game. "We got up," Scheyer said, "and we tackled Nate James."

As much as he enjoyed the moment, James didn't want to be singled out. Duke wins and loses as a team, you know. He also happened to be the least surprised person in the room. "I knew it wasn't going to be Clemson," he said. "He did not want to be the guy. He wanted to win a national championship. He wanted to be part of a contender and didn't want to carry that load . . . He wanted to be pushed and challenged, not the one doing the pushing. With him it was like, 'Wow, RJ and Cam are going to make me better every day, and Jones is going to help me and teach me some things' . . . He wanted to play for Coach, and with some good guys. It was not a shock."

Williamson revealed that he hadn't been 100 percent sure about his decision until he woke up that morning, after scoring 34 for Spartanburg Day School the night before. He explained that the Duke brotherhood matched up with what he was looking for. "I'm all about family," he said. He said that he took his mother's advice and followed his heart, which was telling him he belonged in Durham.

"Coach K is just the most legendary coach that ever coached college basketball," Williamson said. "I can learn a lot from him."

When Krzyzewski visited his house, Williamson said, the Duke coach had emphasized that he wasn't interested in only helping him improve over the course of one season. Coach K had spoken about "how he could build Zion as a brand on and off the court," Williamson said, "for the next twenty years and the rest of my life."

That word "brand" was thrown around an awful lot in this recruitment, and all around major college athletics, which the NCAA ludicrously maintained was still an amateur enterprise. But as he identified the school he had picked to serve as his temporary bridge to the NBA, Williamson made it clear that he was not concerned about NCAA ideals.

"This is a business decision," he said.

Big business.

PRESIDENT OBAMA, Spike Lee, and Ken Griffey Jr. were among the A-listers in the house to watch the latest chapter of the rivalry, the top-ranked Blue Devils against the eighth-ranked Tar Heels, as both teams started preparing for the 2019 edition of March Madness. Roy Williams was a couple of years removed from his third national title. Mike Krzyzewski was two and a half years removed from his third and final Olympic triumph in Rio, where the Americans (barely) made it to the gold-medal stand without the services of Kobe Bryant and LeBron James. The coaches and their programs were still very much at the top of the sport.

But really, President Obama was there to see college basketball's ultimate larger-than-life figure — Zion Williamson, who had grown into a six-foot-seven, 285-pound acrobat in the air. Zion's Blue Devils were bigger than Michigan's Fab Five, if only because the social media age had made that possible. Krzyzewski followed his players on Twitter via a burner account, just to track their comings and goings in case someone's tweets needed to be tempered. Frankly, it was going to be hard to temper anything about this group.

Just as The Game got started, all hell broke loose inside Cameron Indoor Stadium. Williamson took the ball on the left wing, dribbled toward the foul line, and then tried to plant his left foot to execute a spin move on the Tar Heels' Luke Maye. Only that foot slid out from underneath the Duke freshman, leaving him in a full leg split. Williamson crumpled to the court, grimaced in pain, and grabbed his right knee while the Tar Heels took off for a fast-break basket.

Thirty-six seconds into the game, the building turned almost silent as everybody stopped and held their breath. A seemingly indestructible force was in a heap, and those national championship dreams were down there with him. Suddenly the focus shifted away from the athlete and toward the sneaker he'd been wearing on his left foot.

"His shoe broke," President Obama said as he pointed toward Williamson from behind the Duke bench.

The Nike shoe broke.

Actually, "broke" was putting it kindly. Williamson shredded the Nike PG 2.5 sneaker (a signature shoe for Oklahoma City Thunder star Paul George) with the force of his attempted plant, and there it was on the national broadcast, the separated white shoe and blue sole dangling from the injured athlete's ankle while his exposed foot rested on the court.

"His shoe blew apart," said an incredulous ESPN analyst, Jay Bilas, the former Duke player. "I've never seen anything like that."

Williamson was helped to his feet by a teammate before he bent over and, with a measure of disgust, picked up a very expensive shoe that now looked like a piece of roadside trash. While shocked Cameron Crazies wearing blue-and-white face paint held their hands over their mouths, he hobbled off the floor, left his tattered shoe under his chair, and headed to the locker room. Emotionally as flat as that sneaker, the rest of the Blue Devils lost by 16 points.

Not that anyone cared afterward about the score. Krzyzewski told the media that Williamson had been diagnosed with a mild knee sprain, that the knee was stable, and that he did not know how long he would be sidelined. Immediately on social media, the whole enterprise of major college athletics was called into question. Again.

Why in the world was Williamson effectively forced to play a season of college ball — and to accept the inherent risks to his career ambitions — when he was clearly ready to play professionally? (The NBA had long stopped allowing high school stars to make the jump straight to the league.) Why were all the credentialed coaches, administrators, officials, broadcasters, and reporters gathered for this event allowed to be paid, while the main attraction of the event was not allowed to profit beyond his scholarship and related school costs?

Why could people sell game tickets on the secondary market for more than $2,500 while the participants received no cut of the gate, concessions, or parking? Why could ESPN package and sell this broadcast by using Williamson in promos while the player wasn't allowed to make money on his name, image, and likeness? And why was Nike free to use Williamson as a human billboard while compensating his coach and his school, but not his family?

Utah Jazz star Donovan Mitchell tweeted, "Again, let's remember all the money that went into this game . . . and these players get none of it . . . and now Zion gets hurt . . . something has to change @NCAA." Commentators, NBA players, and fans started advising the Duke freshman to sit out the rest of the season and prepare for the NBA draft even if he recovered in time to return. Though a reasonable take under the circumstances, Williamson loved his teammates, his coaches, and his school, and he wasn't about to surrender his dream of being the next great Duke player to win a national title.

Zion was going to bounce back, that wasn't a question. But would Nike?

"Wouldn't have happened in the Pumas," tweeted the Nike rival, before a Puma official deleted it. Nike released a statement that read, "We are obviously concerned and want to wish Zion a speedy recovery. The quality and performance of our products are of utmost importance. While this is an isolated occurrence, we are working to identify the issue." The statement didn't quite ease investor concerns. One *Newsweek* headline the following morning said it all: "Nike Shoe Blowout: $1.12 Billion Wiped Off Swoosh Brand's Stock after Zion Williamson's Injury."

Nike sent representatives to China to oversee the design and manufacturing of a stronger sneaker. The whole incident turned another spotlight on the relationship between Nike and Duke and Coach K. The school had signed a new twelve-year licensing deal with the shoe company in 2015 for all of its varsity teams, and as a private institution, it was under no obligation to release the terms. Nike had a ton invested in Duke and Krzyzewski, and through its sponsorship of USA Basketball had done everything it could to elevate Coach K as a man every basketball star should want to play for.

Starting with the high school basketball stars searching for the right big-time schools to enhance their NBA stock. In March 2018, *The Oregonian* reported that the family of Duke freshman Marvin Bagley III, once the nation's top high school recruit, might have benefited financially from Nike's sponsorship of Bagley's AAU team, which was coached by the prospect's father, Marvin Bagley Jr. The report stated that Bagley Jr. and his wife had declared bankruptcy in 2008, three years before their home was sold in a trustee's sale; shortly after Nike began funding the summer team, the family moved into a house in a gated Southern California subdivision where similarly sized homes were selling for $750,000 to $1.5 million and renting for $2,500 to $7,500 a month.

Sneaker companies had long backed AAU teams in order to build relationships with elite high school players, to subtly (or not so subtly) steer them to college programs and coaches they sponsored, and to increase the odds of signing them to lucrative deals after they turned pro. The shoe giants' practice of funding these teams while they were being run by the prospects' parents or other family members had long been viewed as a transparent means of flouting a system of amateur athletics that was hopelessly broken.

That system was about to be put on trial by the United States government.

In September 2017, federal prosecutors in New York announced that they had arrested and charged four Division I college assistants, three Adidas representatives, and three men described in the complaint as "athlete advisors" as a result of an ongoing FBI probe into corruption in college basketball. The government alleged that assistants from Arizona (Book Richardson), Auburn (Chuck Person), Oklahoma State (Lamont Evans), and Southern California (Tony Bland) took cash bribes from the advisors "in exchange for using their influence over college players under their control to pressure and direct those players and their families to retain the services of the advisors paying the bribes." The government also alleged that a senior executive at Adidas, James Gatto, was "working in connection with corrupt advisors, funneled bribe payments to high school-aged players and their families to secure those players' commitments to attend universities sponsored by [Adidas], rather than universities sponsored by rival athletic apparel companies."

Acting Manhattan U.S. attorney Joon H. Kim would say, "The picture of college basketball painted by the charges is not a pretty one — coaches at some of the nation's top programs taking cash bribes, managers and advisors circling blue-chip prospects like coyotes, and employees of a global sportswear company funneling cash to families of high school recruits." The allegations against Adidas included the payment of $100,000 funneled to a prospect for his commitment to an Adidas-backed college program; the prospect and program would be identified as Bruce Bowen and Louisville, coached by Rick Pitino.

In October 2018, Gatto and Merl Code Jr. of Adidas and Christian Dawkins, an aspiring player agent, were found guilty of wire fraud. Prosecutors made their case that the Adidas-sponsored universities had been defrauded in the scheme because they unwittingly granted athletic scholarships to prospects who were no longer eligible to play. To most longtime observers of big-time college basketball, the idea that the very universities aggressively recruiting the prospects to enhance their visibility and financial bottom line could be defined as victims was laughable.

So was the idea that the conduct had been anything but college basketball business as usual for decades. One ESPN columnist wrote:

Nobody familiar with the game's underbelly needed the FBI investigation into black-ops bribery and fraud and subsequent convictions of relative small-timers to know that college basketball, or the ideal of college basketball, has long been as much of a sham as the idea that the bad guys here defrauded the benefiting schools. One person with extensive knowledge of the federal probe was asked recently how many top 40 prospects he believes arrive on campus without a handler, a family member, a summer coach, or the player himself having already accepted money from an unauthorized source. "None of them," the person said. "By the time they get to college, these kids are not amateurs in any way."

Executives inside Nike and Under Armour were not unhappy that Adidas was drawing all the federal scrutiny, given that the shoe company strategy of establishing relationships with, and funding the summer teams of, America's finest high school players while guiding them toward business partners at major colleges was hardly an Adidas-only game plan. At Nike-backed Duke, Krzyzewski was asked for his reaction to the convictions in New York.

"I think it's minute," he claimed. "It's a blip. It's not what's happening." Only that was exactly what was happening. The following day, a transcript of a phone call the FBI had taped between Code and Kansas assistant Kurtis Townsend was read in federal court: the Adidas official was telling the Kansas assistant of Zion Williamson, or Williamson's stepfather, "I know what he's asking for. He's asking for opportunities from an occupational perspective, he's asking for cash in the pocket and he's asking for housing for him and his family." Townsend responded, "I've got to just try to work and figure out a way because if that's what it takes to get him here for ten months, we're going to have to do it some way."

Nobody familiar with the underbelly of major college recruiting was stunned by this transcript. And as *Yahoo!Sports* columnist Dan Wetzel wrote, "If K.U. was indeed willing to do this and Zion Williamson actually signed with Duke, then what were the Blue Devils, or their interests (boosters, affiliated agents, Nike) willing to do?" A fascinating question, and one the game's governing body had no enthusiasm for exploring. "Does anyone out there believe the NCAA is really, truly going to investigate Duke?" Wetzel wrote. "And not some cursory, rubber-stamp, we-found-nothing-now-please-enjoy-the-NCAA-tournament-starring-Zion-Williamson attempt, presented by all of the commercials starring Mike Krzyzewski?"

Coach K later tried to explain what he meant when he called the corruption case "a blip," but he said what he said and he certainly knew better when he said it. Krzyzewski knew that many of the top high school players and the people close to them had been outright paid by third parties with a potential financial stake in their future. Duke even had its own documented case from the past — Corey Maggette, a significant contributor to the 1999 NCAA finalist. Two decades later, shoe giants Nike and Adidas were maneuvering for the right to sign a generational talent, Zion Williamson — who returned to the Blue Devils for the ACC Tournament, demonstrating to the world that he had never had any intention of skipping the rest of the season, if healthy.

Williamson led Duke to the ACC Tournament title, delivering 31 points and 11 rebounds in thirty-five minutes in a classic one-point victory over North Carolina in the semis. "The guy that's been hurt came back and put on his Superman jersey again and was incredible," Roy Williams said. "It's such a blend of strength and power and quickness that we couldn't stop him getting the basketball inside and going to the basket."

With a healthy and driven Williamson and a cast of freshman stars, Duke was expected to win the whole thing again. Zion was ultra-likable, and invested enough in his team to risk another injury for the greater cause. If any one-and-done college player deserved his One Shining Moment on the championship stage, it was Williamson. Now it was on Coach K to lead him there.

MICHIGAN STATE WAS HOLDING a 68–66 lead over Duke with 8.4 seconds left in the East Regional final. Krzyzewski, it seemed, had one clear responsibility as he talked to his players and diagrammed a play:

Get the ball to the most dynamic player in the sport.

"I like Zion Williamson having the ball in his hands," said CBS analyst Grant Hill, the former Duke star. "We talked about at the elbow, making a quick-move decision. I think some misdirection to get it to him because they've had trouble getting him the ball, a bunch of turnovers off of doing that."

In 1992, Hill had been on the passing end of college basketball's greatest play, Christian Laettner's shot to beat Kentucky, drawn up by none other than Coach K. And yet despite that forever moment, and despite the five national titles and three Olympic gold-medal finishes, Krzyzewski was not known as the world's greatest offensive strategist. If major college coaches had to pick a peer to come up with a creative way of getting his best player the ball in the final, frantic seconds of a sudden-death game, Coach K would not even come close to winning that vote.

But then again, if his peers were asked to simply name the best coach in college basketball, Krzyzewski would win that vote in a landslide, which was a hell of a thing. In the summer of 2017, Coach K had knee replacement surgery—his sixth surgery over a span of fifteen months. Krzyzewski had four surgeries, including ankle and hernia procedures and his first knee replacement, before coaching the 2016 Olympic team in Rio. In January 2017, he missed seven games after undergoing surgery on a herniated disc in his back. Going strong despite having both of his knees and hips replaced, Krzyzewski still looked young and vibrant, with that trademark jet-black hair that he swore he didn't maintain through artificial means (though some of his friends suspected otherwise).

He was rejuvenated by these precocious kids and by no longer having to defend Grayson Allen's habit of tripping opponents or his own unwillingness to severely punish him for his misdeeds. Allen had graduated into the NBA, and the freshmen who had taken over the team were actually more talented than Allen's freshmen classmates in 2015.

The 2018–2019 Blue Devils opened the season by blowing out Kentucky, 118–84, John Calipari's most lopsided defeat as the Wildcats' coach. And now here they were, Zion & Co., potentially on the brink of a Final Four appearance that would be Coach K's thirteenth, breaking a tie with John Wooden for the all-time record. All Krzyzewski needed—on the forty-fourth anniversary of Wooden's final game and tenth national title at UCLA—was a play for Williamson in the final seconds, and then Duke could then take its chances in overtime.

Krzyzewski's motion offense had evolved into a five-out motion offense, which positioned all players on the perimeter, opening up lanes for aggressive slashing to the basket. The Blue Devils had won thirty-two of thirty-seven games but had barely survived Central Florida—coached by Johnny Dawkins—in the second round of the NCAAs when two potential winning UCF shots fell off the rim in the final seconds. They barely survived their Sweet 16 matchup with Virginia Tech when Hokies coach Buzz Williams ran a great, multiple-screen inbounds play with 1.1 seconds left, getting one of his players a point-blank chance to tie—off a lob pass—that he didn't convert.

Could Krzyzewski come up with a similar play against Michigan State? Williamson had given Duke a 66–63 lead on a powerful drive with 1:40 left, before a Spartans basket cut the lead to one. On the ensuing Blue Devils' possession, Barrett plowed into the lane and threw up a brick that crashed off the backboard and into Michigan State's hands. Tom Izzo, already a Naismith Memorial Basketball Hall of Famer himself, drew up a play during a time-out with 43.6 seconds to go. With a record of 1-11 against Krzyzewski, Izzo was desperate for the damn thing to work. And sure enough, his brilliant junior playmaker, Cassius Winston, threw a pass to the right elbow to Xavier Tillman, then set a down screen on Williamson so Kenny Goins could pop out behind the three-point line. While Tre Jones chased after Winston, Tillman hit an open Goins, who sank the shot over a late-closing Williamson to give Michigan State the 68–66 lead with 34.3 seconds left.

"What a play called by Tom Izzo in that time-out," Grant Hill said on the air. Now Hill's former coach had to match it after Barrett took a pass from Williamson (Krzyzewski had initially decided against calling time-out) and fired up a three-pointer that barely hit the front of the rim. Duke lucked out in the mad scramble for the rebound — the ball went out of bounds off Michigan State with those 8.4 seconds to go — and Krzyzewski huddled up with his players. It was time to go to Zion, who led all scorers with 24 points.

Jones inbounded the ball from behind the baseline, tucked dangerously close to the sideline corner. Duke was almost certainly going to call a play to the basket, as it ranked 328th in the country in three-point shooting. *Three hundred and twenty-eighth.* Krzyzewski had failed to surround Williamson with the kind of perimeter shooters who would have made Duke impossible to guard, so someone would likely take the inbound pass and slash to the goal. And that someone turned out to be Barrett, who had arrived in Durham as the nation's number-one recruit but who clearly was not the equal of his bigger, stronger teammate. Barrett ran out toward the corner to receive the ball after Williamson traded places with him down low, and then the six-seven forward barreled into the lane and drew enough contact to get the whistle with 5.2 seconds left. Problem was, Barrett was shooting 66 percent from the foul line.

He was too strong on his first attempt, forcing Krzyzewski to do what he did with Brian Zoubek in the 2010 championship game — order him to miss the second attempt. But just Barrett's luck, after he fired his line-drive free throw, it bounced high off the back rim and through the net, cutting the deficit to one. That was the bad news. The worse news? The Blue Devils had only three team fouls to their name in the second half, meaning that as long as Michigan State could keep successfully inbounding the ball after intentional Duke fouls, time would virtually expire before the Spartans went to the line.

Duke fouled on the first inbounds pass, with 4.7 seconds to play. On

Michigan State's second attempt, Winston took the pass on the run, streaking down the sideline and avoiding the Duke defenders trying to hit him. With Williamson chasing in vain, Winston dribbled toward midcourt and heaved the ball in the air as the horn sounded and a dazed Izzo turned to his aides, trying to recall what it felt like to actually beat Coach K.

Krzyzewski graciously congratulated an opponent he had immense respect for, while his freshmen struggled to accept this unfathomable end. Jones was doubled over, crying into his jersey. Zion had a piece of his jersey in his mouth as he tried to walk off the pain. If he was upset over the fact that his friend Barrett had taken Duke's last three shots, he certainly didn't say so for public consumption.

"I regret nothing about this," Williamson said in a locker room full of weeping young men. "Even if the one-and-done rule wasn't there, this is an experience I don't think you can get anywhere else . . . It's been an incredible ride."

In his press conference, Krzyzewski looked and sounded shaken. He praised Winston and said the Spartans "played older than we did." Coach K thought Izzo and his team were most worthy of advancing, a truth about an opponent that always made defeat more bearable to him.

Before he left his presser and walked away from his final day coaching Zion and friends, Krzyzewski thanked reporters for their coverage of the season. "It's been a remarkable year for these young men," he said. "I'm not sure another group will have it, a year with all of this. And my guys were terrific in representing themselves and representing their program and representing a great university."

Williamson would be the first overall pick in the NBA draft, Barrett the third, and Cam Reddish the tenth. Krzyzewski knew it was going to be a whole new world for him, as a coach, after that group.

He had no idea.

CELEBRITY ATTORNEY MICHAEL AVENATTI, known for representing porn star Stormy Daniels in her lawsuits against President Donald Trump, sent out multiple tweets in April 2019 suggesting that Nike had effectively paid Zion Williamson's mother in order to persuade her son to attend Duke.

Avenatti claimed to have information from his client, Gary Franklin, coach of the California Supreme team of the Nike Elite Youth Basketball League, that the shoe company had funneled money to the families and handlers of recruits to persuade them to attend what he called "Nike colleges." The attorney was facing federal extortion charges, accused of trying to extort $22.5 million from the shoe company in exchange for his silence on the alleged payouts and for a job conducting an internal investigation of Nike practices. In a separate federal case in California, prosecutors had charged Avenatti with embezzling more than $1 million of a client's money.

In a motion to dismiss the Nike case, filed in U.S. District Court, Southern District of New York, Avenatti cited purported electronic communications of February 2017 between the shoe company's Elite Youth Basketball League executives and its recruiting coordinator as alleged proof that Nike had arranged for concealed payments to Williamson, fellow top high school prospects, and their families and associates.

Nike released a statement saying that it would not respond to "the allegations of an individual facing federal charges of fraud and extortion," and that it would continue to cooperate with the government's investigation into grassroots basketball. Nike had earlier said that it "believes in ethical and fair play, both in business and sports." Duke athletic director Kevin White told the student newspaper *The Chronicle* that the school was "looking into" Avenatti's allegations and remained committed to NCAA compliance. "With regard to men's basketball," White said, "all recruits and their families are thoroughly vetted by Duke in collaboration with the NCAA through the Eligibility Center's amateurism certification process."

Ten months later, Avenatti was convicted of the extortion charges. Zion Williamson's former marketing rep, Gina Ford, would later allege in court filings that the former Duke star — who had sued her to terminate their agreement so that he could sign with Creative Artists Agency — should have been ruled "permanently ineligible" to play college ball because of public information suggesting that Williamson and his family were "receiving monies, benefits and/or other prohibited benefits" before he enrolled at Duke. Ford cited text messages between Nike officials allegedly discussing financial offerings to Williamson, who had severed ties with Ford on the grounds that her Florida-based Prime Sports Marketing Company was not certified by the National Basketball Players Association and was not a registered athlete agent in North Carolina and Florida.

Ford sued Williamson for $100 million. She claimed that the recruit and his family had lived in a South Carolina house valued at around $153,000, with a rental cost of $895 a month, before committing to Duke. After the family moved to Durham, Ford claimed, the Williamsons were living in a home owned by a Duke graduate valued at around $950,000, with monthly rent listed at $4,995. (The five-bedroom, six-bathroom brick custom home would be sold in June 2021 for $867,786, according to the listing realtor.)

In an earlier stage of their legal battle, Ford had also asked Williamson to admit that his mother and stepfather had "demanded and received gifts, money and/or other benefits from persons acting on behalf of Duke University (directly and/or indirectly) to influence you to attend Duke University to play basketball."

Williamson's attorney, Jeffrey S. Klein, called Ford's allegations "baseless," "shameful," and "predatory." After its own five-month investigation into the allegations surrounding Williamson, Duke released a statement saying, "As soon as Duke was made aware of any allegation that might have affection Zion Williamson's eligibility, we conducted a thorough and objective investigation which was directed by individuals outside the athletics department. We found no evidence to support any allegation. Zion thrived as both a student and an athlete at Duke, and always conducted himself with integrity and purpose."

Chris Kennedy, Duke's compliance director and senior deputy director of athletics, later added that "there were explanations for all the accusations that didn't rise to the level of a violation," including the house in question, without detailing those explanations. One source said the university found that the owner of the house had a long history of supporting student-athletes at Spartanburg Day School, including Williamson, leading the NCAA to determine that the arrangement did not run afoul of its rules. Kennedy would call Williamson "the greatest kid in the world."

Duke was at the top of Nike's pecking order, ahead of Kentucky, Oregon, and Arizona — that much was clear. But any school that signed Williamson was likely to face scrutiny afterward — he was that big of a teen celebrity. A Duke source said that the university reviews the financial records of each top recruit to ensure that there are no transactions inconsistent with his family's employment status and financial standing. One source confirmed that Duke reviewed the Williamsons' bank records before Zion enrolled. Of course, if any family is determined to hide an account, the university isn't in position to do much about that. "We don't have subpoena power," one school official said. "We can't be confident we see everything, but we try."

Krzyzewski's chief rival, Roy Williams, had no issue with Duke's signing of Williamson, even though he was among the many who were surprised, and later impacted, by the Blue Devils' photo-finish victory in the Zion derby. "There's not been one second that I thought he chose Duke for any reason other than he wanted to play at Duke," Williams said. "That's what it was, and I never had any time in my life that I said, 'Oh, they cheated or did this or did that.' Whenever Duke beat us on a player, they just did a better job recruiting him than we did."

Coach K's lieutenants were sensitive to the notion that their boss ran a program bolstered by willful ignorance, given his constant reminders to staffers that they should never, ever break NCAA rules in pursuit of a prospect.

"I remember sitting in meetings with Coach K," said one longtime Duke assistant, "and this is not bullshit. This is the God's honest truth. Any time a kid's recruitment or visit came up, anything related to recruiting, he would always look us all dead in the eye and say, 'We need to make sure we're doing this the right way, the way it's supposed to be done.' And we're like, 'Coach, everybody is doing this. We can get away with this. People are looking the other way on this.' But he was emphatic on it. He was maniacal about being compliant.

"So any time a question came up, I knew there was nothing to it, just because he was so dogged. He reached a level in his career that he was not going to jeopardize for one recruit. That came right out of his mouth. 'We've been doing this for so long, why would we risk this for such and such?' So when questions about Zion came up, never for one second did I say, 'Hmmm, maybe there is something there.'"

Krzyzewski told his coaches, according to this assistant, that if they attended a tournament during a recruiting dead period and ended up using a urinal next to a prospect's father, they shouldn't even say hello.

In the end, Zion Williamson won his lawsuit against Gina Ford and fended off the allegations made by Michael Avenatti, who, while facing trials in several federal cases, reportedly ended up in solitary confinement in a Manhattan jail cell that once housed Mexican drug lord Joaquin "El Chapo" Guzman. Avenatti was ultimately sentenced to two and a half years in prison for attempting to extort Nike.

And after one year at Nike's top school, Duke, Williamson signed with Nike's Jordan Brand for $75 million over five years.

THE NIGHT OF JANUARY 28, 2020, Mike Krzyzewski was screaming and gesturing at his student body, acting crazier than the Cameron Crazies. They had been chanting, "Jeff Capel, sit with us," at the Pittsburgh head coach and former Duke player, and Krzyzewski responded by repeatedly shouting "shut up" at the students. At the end of the first half, he crossed the court and screamed at the stunned Crazies, "He's one of us," while pounding his chest.

It was a bizarre scene. Krzyzewski clearly misunderstood the nature of the student chant, which was meant to assure the enemy coach that they considered him one of their own. Afterward, Coach K apologized for the outburst . . . or at least attempted to apologize.

"I don't know if I made a mistake on that," he said, "but I've never heard another coach's name yelled out in the middle of the first half when we're in a war with the team . . . I thought it was personal . . . I apologize to the students for that."

But Krzyzewski also said about the chant, "You shouldn't say that . . . In the middle of the first half and an ACC game, this isn't some cutesy little thing. I'm not going to say, 'Will you please tell me exactly what you're doing?' So it's a mistake on my part, but I'd rather make the mistake and protect my guy . . . Let's think of a different cheer — like 'Defense!'"

Krzyzewski had reason to be emotional on this night. Like the rest of America, he was still reeling from the shocking death of Kobe Bryant, his daughter Gianna, and seven others in a helicopter crash in Calabasas, California.

"I coached [Bryant] on three teams," Krzyzewski said. "He was my leader. We had special moments, private and public. He was amazing with my grandkids. It's been bad. It's been bad. I have been very emotional about it, not publicly." That emotion likely helped trigger Coach K's response to what he misinterpreted as a disrespectful act by Duke students, which is more than understandable.

It's just that Krzyzewski had a history at Duke of struggling with apologies; he couldn't simply say, "I was wrong," without quickly adding, "But you were wrong too." Though he was in a job that often demanded that he be critical of others, Krzyzewski was not particularly good at accepting criticism.

Five weeks after his Capel eruption, Krzyzewski was appearing on the Duke postgame radio show when he addressed recent criticism of his Blue Devils, who had lost three of their previous four ACC games. "I mean, you can question my coaching and what the hell — and then when you do question it . . . just come into Cameron and look up in the ceiling, and then find out if you should question that." For those close to Krzyzewski, it was a cringe-inducing boast.

Coach K is often gracious in defeat in his postgame press conferences, as well as in later reflections on the coaches and players who figured out ways to beat his program. But he struggles with accepting losses in the handshake line, where, in victory, he often consoles his losing counterparts with shoulder or chest pats. Even Krzyzewski's dear friend Jim Boeheim conceded as much about the Duke coach. "No, he's not great," Boeheim said. "A lot of guys aren't good in the handshake line."

After Zion Williamson got hurt and Duke lost to North Carolina in 2019, Krzyzewski pulled a drive-by on Roy Williams as the Tar Heels' coach was trying to tell him, "I hope Zion is okay." After a 2020 loss to North Carolina State, Krzyzewski blew off Wolfpack coach Kevin Keatts in the handshake line. (Coach K tried to explain that Keatts had warned him that the crowd was about to storm the court, but video showed the Duke coach completely ignoring his counterpart.)

Years earlier, after Virginia Tech shocked the Blue Devils in Cameron in overtime, Krzyzewski grabbed one of the Hokies' celebrating players, Xabian Dowdell, and told him, "Act like you've been there before." Dowdell hadn't been there before. The Blue Devils had broken Virginia Tech's heart the previous season on Sean Dockery's 40-foot, buzzer-beating heave, and they had beaten the Hokies in Cameron by 35 the season before that.

Dowdell's coach, Seth Greenberg, had great respect for Krzyzewski, who had said kind things about the Hokies. But Greenberg was furious that Coach K made that remark to his player, especially after the Blue Devils had acted like Times Square revelers on New Year's Eve after the Dockery shot. "Mike's shoulder pats are strictly for losses, yours," Greenberg said. "If Mike beats you, you're going to get the handshake and the shoulder pat." And if he doesn't, you might get what Oregon's Dillon Brooks got in the 2016 NCAA Tournament — a lecture on how to comport yourself at the end of a big victory.

The Ducks were about to finish off the Blue Devils, 79–68, when Brooks decided to try to make the final score 82–68. He launched a very deep three-pointer in the closing seconds to avoid a shot-clock violation, and wouldn't you know it, the ball went in, much to Krzyzewski's dismay. On the handshake line afterward, Coach K stopped the Oregon star and told him, "You're too good of a player to do that . . . You're too good of a player." Brooks repeatedly told Krzyzewski he was sorry, even though the Oregon coach, Dana Altman, had instructed him to take the shot.

Brooks shared with reporters what Coach K had told him, and then added that the living legend was right. "I need to respect Duke," he said. As it turned out, Krzyzewski didn't know about Brooks's disclosure when he was first asked about their exchange during his postgame presser. "Yeah, I just congratulated him," Krzyzewski said. "He's a terrific player. He's a terrific player." He went on to talk more about Brooks's positionless skill before praising one of his teammates, never referencing his rebuke of Brooks.

Seven questions later, a reporter circled back to the handshake line. The brief Q&A went like this:

Q: Apparently after the game Dillon said that you told him that he was too good of a player to be showing off at the end like that . . .

A: I didn't say that.

Q: He said of you that you were right.

A: You can say whatever you want. Dillon Brooks is a hell of a player. I said, "You're a terrific player." And you can take whatever he said and then go with it, all right?

Krzyzewski then thanked reporters for their coverage and exited stage left. He figured that was that, time to prepare for the off-season. But then TV replays surfaced with a microphone picking up the Coach K–Brooks conversation. The audio confirmed that Krzyzewski had indeed told Brooks what the Oregon player said he'd told him. Coach K had little choice but to release a statement saying that he had, in his words, "reacted incorrectly" to a reporter's question about Brooks. Krzyzewski said that he called Altman and apologized for speaking to his player. "It is not my place to talk to another team's player and doing so took the focus away from the terrific game that Dillon played."

Much like a player who needs to work on his post moves, Krzyzewski needed to work on his losing handshake decorum. But as the 2019–2020 season was winding down, he wouldn't have the opportunity to repair that flaw in his approach. There wouldn't be any more handshakes, because there wouldn't be any more games.

MIKE KRZYZEWSKI HAD two plagues to confront — the Covid-19 pandemic and racism. Like the rest of college basketball, Duke never finished its 2019–2020 season, never played a game in the conference or NCAA tournaments. The shutdown gave Krzyzewski a lot of time to think about things that had nothing to do with the balance of power in the ACC. A lot of time to think about the separate-but-unequal realities defining America.

George Floyd, a forty-six-year-old Black man, was murdered under the knee of a white Minneapolis police officer, Derek Chauvin, on May 25 after saying, "I can't breathe," more than twenty times. As protests swept across the country and the globe in response to a seemingly endless series of killings of unarmed African American men and women, the Duke brotherhood of players and ex-players held regular Zoom calls to discuss the crisis and their response to it.

"We had over 200 guys on these calls," said Duke assistant Nolan Smith. "The first call Coach got on, I said, 'Guys, Coach just wants to listen.'" The conversations sometimes lasted ninety minutes or two hours. Krzyzewski mostly listened before deciding he needed to say something publicly. He didn't want to put out a written statement; he knew that he needed to do more, and that his message had to come from the heart.

"I told Coach, 'Look, hey, don't come up with something generic,'" said another Duke assistant, Nate James. "We all talked about that leading up to the moment, when things were coming out from various people, pro coaches, whoever. Don't make it generic. People will take that as a sign of disrespect in a lot of ways. It was, 'Look, don't feed us some bullcrap. Say what needs to be said and address some real issues.'"

Krzyzewski focused on the simple yet profound statement "Black lives matter," and thought about how that statement had somehow divided people. "And then he was like, 'Boom, I've got it figured out. I want to do a video. I know exactly what I've got to say,'" Smith recalled. "He was crazy emotional. He asked me if I could sit in with him while he was giving the statement."

Krzyzewski was sweating as he appeared for the taping in the players' lounge, as if he had worked himself into a lather preparing for such an important moment. Coach K spoke with an obscured Duke logo in the background, but he made it a point not to wear Duke gear for the video. "He wanted to be Coach K, America's coach and America's human being," Smith said. So Krzyzewski wore a U.S. Olympic Team shirt with the symbol of the nation's flag stitched to the left breast and left sleeve.

Smith was in the room when Krzyzewski gave his speech. "It wasn't a script," the assistant said. "It was almost like he wanted to talk to me. He wanted to talk to someone. He just talked."

Looking straight into the camera, Krzyzewski talked on the video for two minutes and forty-seven seconds. And this is what the most successful and recognizable figure in the history of college basketball said:

Black lives matter. Say it. Can't you say it? Black lives matter. We should be saying it every day. It's not political, this is not a political statement. It's a human rights statement. It's a fairness statement. Over the last couple of months, I have had an opportunity to see more, to listen more, to think more, and to understand at a deeper level. So have you. Yeah, so have you. And do we not see the problem, the disease, the plague, that has been with our country for four centuries? Do we not see systemic racism and social injustice? Come on, we all see that, it's manifested in so many ways. Criminal justice, the killings that we have seen and that we haven't seen. And the denial of economic opportunities for our Black community. Educational opportunities, health care, it's manifested in so many ways, and has been there for four centuries. You know, we see that, and what do we do when we

see it? We talk, all right, but we turn the other way. We don't solve the problem. The problem will not be solved. And no problem is solved unless you
acknowledge the problem. Acknowledge it. If you acknowledge it, you have
the duty to solve it. We as a country have the duty to solve this problem.
When I was a cadet at West Point — and the prayer is still there — there's
a cadet prayer. In the cadet prayer, one of the segments of the prayer says,
"Lord, help me choose the harder right. Help me choose the harder right
instead of the easier wrong." We as a country have chosen the easier wrong
for four centuries. It is time to choose the harder right. It is time to end systemic racism and social injustice. It's time. Black lives matter.

When the taping was done, Krzyzewski turned to Smith and asked,
"How was that?" The assistant told him it was perfect. "I just wanted to talk
to the camera," Coach K said. "I wanted to talk to America." The video was
circulated on June 26, and Smith started receiving texts not just from his
fellow former Duke players but also from young men who had competed
for North Carolina, Georgetown, you name it.

"We knew Coach felt that way," Nate James said, "and a lot of people who
believe what he felt and what he said, they don't always get the opportunity
to express it. But he did it. He actually let the world know how he felt . . .
and that showed anyone who ever put on a uniform for him, that he had our
backs. It is different out here for Black men, and for people who you look
up to like Coach K, when they have our back and let us know he's with us,
it just solidified what we already knew. We were just very proud of him for
doing that."

FAMILY. MIKE KRZYZEWSKI was always talking about family. On his final
Zoom conference call with reporters of the 2020–2021 season, Krzyzewski
interrupted a question from columnist Jim Sumner to express his condo-
lences over the recent passing of the writer's ninety-three-year-old father
Ernest, an Army veteran and a Yankees fan born the year Babe Ruth hit
sixty home runs. He asked Sumner how he was holding up.

"God bless your family," Coach K said. "I hope you comfort one another . . . I forgot your question. I was concerned about you, and I'm
seventy-four. So, what game did we just play?"

Duke had just beaten a solid Louisville team by 14 points to advance to
the ACC Tournament quarterfinals in a Greensboro Coliseum left empty
by the Covid-19 pandemic. It had been a miserable season on all fronts; the
victory gave the Blue Devils a 13-11 record and kept them barely alive for an
NCAA Tournament berth. As the tenth seed, its lowest ACC Tournament

seed ever, Duke would have to upset Florida State and then perhaps win the semifinal to secure an at-large berth and avoid missing the NCAAs for the first time since 1995.

Assuming the Blue Devils' Covid-19 tests kept coming back negative.

On the Zoom call, the camera appeared to be six inches from his face. Krzyzewski looked like a disembodied head. He sounded like a coach who felt that his team had finally figured it out in the nick of time. He talked about using the defense he called "Eleven" against Louisville, a switching man-to-man he'd used with past teams, and he seemed pleased and a bit surprised that it actually worked with this one.

But as he got up to leave his Zoom holding cell and exit the call, Krzyzewski moved the conversation back to family. "Again, Jim, our thoughts and prayers are with you, okay?" he said.

Coach K had spent a lifetime turning his basketball program into a family operation, honoring a bygone promise he had made to Mickie when taking the West Point job in 1975. His oldest daughter, Debbie, had been a fundraiser since 2002 and was now an assistant director of athletics and director of the Legacy Fund. Lindy, who had earned her master's in clinical psychology at Pepperdine, was working as a team counselor. Jamie, the youngest, was an author who served on the board of directors of the Emily K Center and had written two books with her father.

Mickie was not as involved in the program as she used to be, but she was still a chief advisor — and a concerned fan when it came to a certain Blue Devil at the bottom of the roster, Debbie's son Michael Savarino. "The first time a grandmother has given me a hard time about playing time," Krzyzewski said.

Mickie hadn't only influenced many of her husband's basketball decisions over the years; she had moved him a bit to the left of his long-standing Republican views, a shift also inspired by his antipathy toward President Trump, whom he described as "the only person in our country who's not accountable to anybody." An angry Krzyzewski later called for the prosecution of everyone involved in the January 2021 attack on the U.S. Capitol. "People say that's not who we are — that is who we are right now," he said. "It is who we are. We need to change who we are. We need to get back to the basic principles that have founded this country."

Krzyzewski made that call after returning from a quarantine that forced him to miss Duke's victory over Boston College; his daughter Debbie and seventeen-year-old granddaughter Emmie had tested positive for the Covid-19 virus and had taken ill. "It's not going away," Krzyzewski said after coaching the Blue Devils to a victory over Wake Forest. "They are doing okay but not great. My heart goes out to everyone out there who has a family member or they are fighting this. It's serious. We've had 16,000 people die the last four days. I'm just happy that we have such a good medical center and medical people to take care of us."

Coach K had continued to test negative for the virus through the morning of the Wake Forest game, when staff from Duke's testing partner, Mako Medical, arrived at his home at 5:45 a.m. to collect a sample that came back negative after 8:30 a.m. and liberated him to coach that night.

The pandemic took a heavy personal and professional toll on Coach K. In December, after suffering uncharacteristic home losses to nonconference opponents Michigan State and Illinois, Krzyzewski questioned the wisdom of playing on through a pandemic that was still killing and hospitalizing Americans at a terrifying rate. Concerned about the safety and the mental and physical health of players and staff, he felt it was time "to assess where we're at. We're just plowing through this.

"People are saying the next six weeks are going to be the worst. To me, it's already pretty bad. On the other side of it, there are these vaccines that are coming out. By the end of the month, 20 million vaccine shots will be given. By the end of January or in February, another 100 million. Should we not reassess that? See just what would be best?"

The entire season was an unholy mess for Krzyzewski, who endured three separate three-game losing streaks in the conference. The Blue Devils suddenly looked like all the ACC teams they used to beat. They were undisciplined and unable to execute in the closing minutes of tight games. An increasingly frustrated Krzyzewski watched the whole thing devolve while wearing his mask, about the only thing that could keep his profane temper in check.

The season was best captured by an off-the-court exchange on January 23, following a road loss to Louisville. A student reporter from *The Chronicle* asked the coach how the team planned to move forward after its third straight loss.

"Why don't we just evaluate the game," Krzyzewski sniped. "I'm not into what our next step forward is right now. We just finished a hard-fought game. I don't know when . . . What's your major?"

Coach K waited a moment for a response from the student reporter, Jake Piazza, before asking again.

"What's your major at Duke?"

Awkward silence again.

"What's your hardest class?"

"Econ," Piazza said.

"Okay," Krzyzewski continued. "So say you just had the toughest econ test in the world, and when you walked out, somebody asked you, 'What's your next step?' You see what I mean? Does that . . . you have some empathy. Just give us time to evaluate this game and then we'll figure out just like we always try to do, what the next step will be. The next step is obviously to prepare for Georgia Tech. How we prepare for them, that's what we're going to have to figure out."

As the exchange went viral, Krzyzewski was roasted for his lack of grace in defeat, and for taking out his frustrations on a Duke student reporter, though not as loudly and profanely as he'd taken out his frustrations on the *Chronicle* sports staff more than thirty years earlier. Piazza would write in *The Chronicle* that Coach K called him with what sounded like a genuine apology, though the reporter noted that the call was short. All these years later, Krzyzewski still had trouble saying he was sorry.

After Krzyzewski received his second Pfizer vaccination shot in early February, he said, he got "knocked back" for six or seven hours the following day, then was good to go the rest of the season. Probably underpaid at a reported $7 million a pop — given what he had meant over the years to Duke fundraising, Duke applications, Duke branding, Duke everything — Krzyzewski really had to earn his money just to keep the Blue Devils afloat. They had played one of their best games of the year against Louisville in the conference tournament and felt good about their chances of upsetting Florida State and possibly earning an NCAA bid.

And then the news: a Duke walk-on had tested positive for Covid-19, and that was that. Contact tracing protocols forced the Blue Devils to withdraw from the ACC Tournament and ended their season.

Krzyzewski put his stamp on it with this statement: "While our season was different than any other that I can remember, I loved the 2020–21 Duke Basketball team and was honored to be their coach. We have not asked more of any team in our history, and they deserve enormous credit for handling everything like the outstanding young men they are . . . As many safeguards as we implemented, no one is immune to this terrible virus."

The coming off-season would hurt. Krzyzewski would lose his top two players, underclassmen Matthew Hurt and DJ Steward, who declared for the NBA draft, following the in-season departure of Jalen Johnson, who was expected to be a lottery pick. And just like every other major college team, the Blue Devils would also lose some players through the transfer portal. Of greater consequence, seven-foot center Mark Williams, who had 23 points and 19 rebounds against Louisville, decided to return to play with another heralded Krzyzewski recruiting class headlined by six-foot-nine Paolo Banchero of Seattle, rated as the number-two prospect in America.

But the most important Duke returnee was obvious — a veteran point guard who would turn seventy-five years old in February. Krzyzewski was not about to retire after a season from hell. His heart was still very much in the pursuit of a sixth national title, and yet at the same time, after forty-one years at Duke, that heart was telling him that he was actually in alignment with his young players.

Coach K was ready to tell the world he had finally become a one-and-done.

WEARING A MASK, a blue suit, and a Duke button on his left lapel, his hair not quite as black as it used to be, Mike Krzyzewski appeared from behind a dark curtain inside Cameron Indoor Stadium while holding Mickie's hand.

At his introductory press conference in 1980, when he jokingly thanked the one person who clapped when he approached the podium, the new coach had felt compelled to spell his name for reporters. Now his retirement press conference was being broadcast on national TV and taking place on a basketball court named after him.

Krzyzewski hugged Mickie, stepped up to the podium, and removed his mask while family members in the audience danced to "Everytime We Touch." Coach K briefly pumped his arms to the music, then clapped along with the non-journalists in the crowd while social media lit up with comments about how bizarre it was that the seventy-four-year-old began his farewell presser with a Cascada dance tune from 2006. Those Twitter users were not familiar with the Cameron Crazies' pregame tradition of warming up to that song.

Coach K took his seat and nodded and pointed at his daughters, their husbands, and his ten grandchildren. He had been talking with Mickie about this for years, and the two finally agreed on a recent vacation in Las Vegas that he should coach one more season at Duke — his forty-second — and then never coach again. Krzyzewski held a Zoom call with his three daughters in April. "It wasn't to ask them what they thought," said one Duke source. "It was telling them, 'Here's the plan.' The decision was already made."

Not everyone was in favor of an announcement like this one, which would naturally set up Duke's 2021–2022 season as a running celebration of all things Krzyzewski. Chris Spatola thought a farewell tour, or victory tour, would take a lot out of his father-in-law while he was trying to lead the Blue Devils to another championship. Krzyzewski countered that he couldn't in good faith keep his decision a secret while he was recruiting the next class of prospects.

On April 12, a couple of days after informing his daughters, Coach K informed assistants Jon Scheyer, Chris Carrawell, and Nolan Smith in the conference room outside his sixth-floor office. Carrawell, who was about to be promoted to associate head coach, was not surprised by the news. He was happy for Krzyzewski and glad that the coach had chosen not to end his career with the miserable season just completed.

"We've got the next head coach in this room," Carrawell blurted. Krzyzewski seemed to be caught off guard by the comment, and so did the man Carrawell was talking about — Scheyer. "I shoot from the hip," Carrawell said. "Sometimes it works, sometimes it doesn't." It seemed to work this time. Krzyzewski looked at Scheyer and asked, "What do you think about what C-Well just said? Would you want to do that?" Scheyer responded that he would. "I think you'd be terrific," Coach K said.

Carrawell thought that Scheyer, who is white, would succeed in part "because he's proven he can recruit African American kids, and maintain relationships with them." Scheyer had helped Duke win a national title as a player (2010) and as an assistant (2015). Better yet, he was from the Chicago area, and like Krzyzewski when he was hired by Duke, Scheyer was thirty-three years old. Coach K wanted this to happen. He wanted Scheyer to replace him.

Jon Jackson, deputy director of athletics and Krzyzewski's senior communications aide, ran a search committee that included university officials Chris Kennedy, Troy Austin, and incoming athletic director Nina King. The committee worked in concert with an outside search firm, Collegiate Sports Associates. But as the search unfolded and candidates were interviewed by Zoom, it became clear that the Duke administration, led by President Vincent Price, wanted to hire Harvard coach Tommy Amaker, Krzyzewski's former player and assistant. Sources maintained that Duke informed Amaker the job was his if he wanted it.

It seemed a no-brainer for the former Michigan and Seton Hall coach who had been about as close to Krzyzewski as any member of the Duke family, and who, after fourteen years in the Ivy League, might not get another crack at the big time. But there was a problem, a big one: Coach K did not want Amaker to get the job.

Krzyzewski embraced the West Point article of faith that identified "continuity of excellence" as an essential part of a succession plan. That continuity was easier to find in Scheyer, who had been on the Blue Devils' staff since 2014, than in the fifty-five-year-old Amaker, who had left Duke in 1997. Control was everything to Krzyzewski, who planned to remain in his office in retirement as a school ambassador and de facto coach emeritus while two of his daughters continued working in the department. Coach K would have some control through Scheyer, who had never been a head coach and owed his mentor everything, and not so much through Amaker, who had his own way of running a program and had been gone from Durham for a quarter century.

So Krzyzewski arranged a Zoom call with the Harvard coach and had what a source described as "a very difficult conversation" with him. Amaker mistakenly thought he would receive his mentor's blessing. Coach K explained that if he left Harvard and joined the Duke staff for the 2021–2022 season as the appointed successor-in-waiting, he would force the demotion of another Blue Devils assistant and create an awkward dynamic with Scheyer. "Mike had to explain to Tommy why he couldn't be the guy," said one Duke source. "He can be Don Corleone when he needs to be."

Amaker was heartbroken, according to someone close to him. He had a great situation at Harvard, where he had built the premier Ivy League program and where his wife, Dr. Stephanie Pinder-Amaker, worked as an assistant professor at the university's medical school and as a senior executive at McLean Hospital. But still, this was Duke. This was Amaker's school. This was the biggest college basketball job in the country. This was succeeding a legend among legends.

Amaker could have said the hell with it and taken the job against Krzyzewski's wishes, but he ultimately decided that would be a mistake. "How was Tommy going to feel if Coach K was walking into his practice every other day?" asked one source close to the situation. Though Duke had made Nina King only the third African American female athletic director in a Power Five conference, the university missed an opportunity to hire a highly qualified Black candidate for its most visible position, a truth not lost on some former Black players.

But by announcing his retirement in advance, Krzyzewski had all but ensured his preferred candidate would get the nod. "Mike is the ultimate orchestrator," said one source close to him. "He wakes up in the morning trying to figure out ways to stay ahead of you. Sometimes Coach K has to eat his young, and Tommy Amaker just got eaten."

So on June 1, Scheyer got the call from King that changed his life and officially marked the beginning of the end of the Coach K era.

It was actually a perfect time for Krzyzewski to call it a career. College basketball had become a free-for-all with early NBA departures, a mass exodus shaped by the 1,600 players in the transfer portal, and the reality of the G League, overseas leagues, and a new option, Overtime Elite, offering high-paying alternatives for high school stars. Pressured by laws in more than a dozen states freeing college athletes to make paid sponsorship and marketing deals, the NCAA was on the verge of allowing athletes to be compensated for their names, images, and likenesses. Lord knows how much stress Krzyzewski would have felt trying to keep track of the professional deals his amateur players were making.

Coach K had also expressed frustration to friends about riding the pandemic roller coaster in 2020–2021 — showing up at the office every morning without knowing who would be available for practice or whether the scheduled opponent that night would be cleared to play.

People close to Krzyzewski had been waiting for (and dreading) this decision in recent years, which became public knowledge on June 2 when *Stadium*'s college basketball insider Jeff Goodman — his finger shaking as he pressed the Send button on a tweet he knew would rock the sports world — broke the news on Twitter that the coach would retire after one last go.

Before Krzyzewski spoke at his news conference, there were prepared remarks from Vincent Price, the retiring Kevin White, and his replacement, King, who mentioned a Coach K contribution that never appeared in a box score. "The thousands of people that Coach has corresponded with over the years," she said. "People in moments of need, fans celebrating a wedding, children battling heartbreaking disease, and so many others. Never once did he seek attention or thanks for participating in these moments."

For friends and strangers alike, in times of tragedy and triumph, Krzyzewski had been a handwritten-letter machine. Nobody could ever take that away from him.

When it was time for him to speak at his own farewell party, Coach K talked about missing the music and the people of Cameron. He acknowledged the players in attendance and predicted that Scheyer would be an "incredible" replacement. He spoke of the family atmosphere he had instilled at Duke and called himself a lucky man.

Sitting in a large chair that had the look of a throne, Krzyzewski then narrated his own life story, starting with his mentors at Weber High in Chicago, Coach Al Ostrowski and Father Francis Rog, and working his way back to his parents. He got emotional when he thanked God for giving him Emily and William, the laborers who didn't need a high school education to provide a strong, encouraging upbringing for their sons Big Bill and Mike. Coach K called West Point "the greatest leadership school in the world," and his Army coach Bob Knight "one of the greatest coaches in the world."

Krzyzewski turned emotional again when he talked about the late Duke AD who had hired him against the odds, Tom Butters, and about the late Duke president Keith Brodie, whom he called "the best person I've ever known" in more than four decades at Duke, and a leader who "believed in me in one of my darkest hours" — when Krzyzewski nearly quit coaching after his breakdown in 1995. He thanked Jerry Colangelo for hiring him to coach Team USA and called the 2006 loss to Greece "the worst day of my life in coaching. The worst day. I wanted to end it, that's it." Krzyzewski won eighty-eight of eighty-nine Team USA games for Colangelo.

Coach K maintained that he wasn't stepping down for health reasons, or because of the pandemic, the relatively dreadful season he had just completed, or the chaotic happenings in the sport. "I have been in it forty-six years," he said, "and you mean the game has never changed? . . . The reason we are doing this is because Mickie and I have decided the journey is going to be over in a year and we are going to go after it as hard as we possibly can." Krzyzewski would later say he wanted to spend time watching his grandchildren play sports and "win in Ninja."

But first, he couldn't wait to coach his final team. "A message to our students," the one and only said before departing the stage. "Come back in August, man, and we're going to be ready. You be ready, and let's see what happens. Let's see what the hell happens."

Krzyzewski walked down to the court to hug and kiss Mickie, and soon enough they were off to savor the first day of the rest of their lives.

Coach K had faced extraordinary challenges during the pandemic, but then again, so did a lot of coaches who ended up with better records than he did. Deep down, as an honest West Point man, Krzyzewski knew he did not do a good job in his forty-first season at Duke.

The protocols didn't help him, no question about that. Why? Krzyzewski always talked about the need to show a strong face. How could he possibly show one behind his goddamn mask?

Thank God the pandemic had retreated and the mask was expected to be unnecessary. Coach K carried into the final year of his coaching life 1,170 victories, 12 Final Four appearances, five national titles, and absolutely no excuses.

This would be his last season and his last stand. And more than ever, the Duke Blue Devils were ready for their head basketball coach, Michael William Krzyzewski, to show his strongest face.

ACKNOWLEDGMENTS

This work was informed by a number of outstanding books that preceded it, including John Feinstein's *The Legends Club* and *A March to Madness*, Gene Wojciechowski's *The Last Great Game*, Mike Krzyzewski and Donald T. Phillips's *Leading with the Heart*, Krzyzewski and Jamie K. Spatola's *The Gold Standard*, Gregg Doyel's *Building the Duke Dynasty*, Barry Jacobs's *Coach K's Little Blue Book*, and Seth Davis's *Getting to Us*. Other invaluable resources included the Duke student newspaper, *The Chronicle*, which has covered Coach K in a fair, professional, and thorough manner for more than four decades, and the *Raleigh News and Observer*, the *Charlotte Observer*, the *Durham Morning Herald/Herald-Sun*, the *Greensboro News and Record*, the *Winston-Salem Journal*, the *Chicago Tribune*, and the Associated Press.

Two industry titans, Jack McCallum and J. A. Adande, provided a most useful roadmap with their podcast *The Dream Team Tapes*, as did Dana O'Neil with her definitive account of Coach K's youth — "Do You Know Mike Krzyzewski?" — for ESPN.com. Other accomplished journalists whose coverage offered an education on Krzyzewski, Duke, and major college basketball include Chip Alexander, Rick Bonnell, Bill Brill, A. J. Carr, Charles Chandler, Art Chansky, Luciana Chavez, Al Featherston, Scott Fowler, Jeff Goodman, Ron Green Sr., Ron Green Jr., Dane Huffman, Andy Katz, Larry Keech, Tim Layden, Don Markus, Malcolm Moran, Skip Myslenski, Jim O'Connell, Steve Politi, William C. Rhoden, Jim Sumner, Barry Svrluga, Joe Tiede, Caulton Tudor, Daniel Wallach, Dick "Hoops" Weiss, Steve Wiseman, and Alexander Wolff.

Some longtime friends and distinguished authors were kind enough to lend a hand or two during the process, most notably Wojciechowski, Davis, Adrian Wojnarowski, Tom Konchalski, and Larry "The Scout" Pearlstein.

Jim McLaughlin and Murray Bauer were most supportive, as always. A special thanks to the family of Joe McGuinness for trusting me with their story.

Among the many lifelong Krzyzewski friends from the old neighborhood who made this book possible, Dennis "Moe" Mlynski was a true franchise player. Chico Kurzawski, football star, also came up big. So many West Point players and coaches deserve credit for shaping this biography with their memories and insight, including Dr. Jim Oxley, Dick Simmons, Tom Miller, Pat Harris, General Bob Brown, Scott Easton, and Marty Coyne. On the Duke side, the ultra-thoughtful Jay Bilas, Chris Carrawell, Chris Spatola, Chuck Swenson, and Pete Gaudet, out of the goodness of their hearts, were most patient. Bobby Hurley, Billy King, Shane Battier, Elton Brand, Carlos Boozer, Nate James, Lee Melchionni, Nolan Smith, and Jon Scheyer were among the scores of players and coaches who did more than chip in. At North Carolina, Steve Kirschner and Roy Williams were gracious in giving their time for a bio on their chief rival. At USA Basketball, Craig Miller, Sean Ford, and Syracuse coach Jim Boeheim were very helpful in detailing Coach K's gold-medal triumphs. Others whose insight contributed to the narrative include Nicholas Dienes, Paul and Vivian Kolpak, Dick Quinn, Steve Vacendak, and Dennis Wrobel.

Jon Jackson, Duke deputy director of athletics and Coach K's chief communications rep, facilitated some interviews for this book when he was under no obligation to do so, and it was greatly appreciated. Johnny Moore, a longtime Duke sports information and marketing executive, was a reliable historian and precise storyteller. Meg Ellis and Mady Salvani were a big help at West Point.

My literary agent, David Black, has somehow shepherded me through five books, more proof that he is the best in the country at what he does. At Mariner Books, the terrific Deb Brody made the manuscript better and pushed it into the end zone, and Megan Wilson was brilliant, yet again, in promoting the book. Jeff Neuman was asked to cut 30,000-plus words from the original document without diminishing it, and amazingly enough he pulled it off, while making really smart suggestions along the way. Cynthia Buck, copy editor, cared just as much about the words as I did, and that meant a ton. I am indebted to Emma Peters for carrying my exhausted self in the end.

Finally, my wife Tracey and son Kyle were the perfect copilots on this long journey to publication. They are the best teammates and friends a husband and father could ever ask for. I have no idea what I would do without them.

NOTES

I spoke with more than 250 people exclusively for this book, and those interviews — along with more than 100 others I conducted over the years with major college basketball figures — served as the foundation of the narrative. Mike Krzyzewski did not agree to be interviewed for this project, though he did not discourage his closest friends and generations of Duke and West Point coaches and players from speaking with me, which I greatly appreciated. Some quotes attributed to Krzyzewski and prominent Duke players were pulled from press conferences that I attended, and others from press conference transcripts posted by ASAPSports.com. The following is a chapter-by-chapter summary of additional sources that made important contributions.

CHAPTER 1. COLUMBO

Josef Pituch, U.S. Department of Labor, Bureau of Naturalization, "Certificate of Arrival & Declaration of Intention," 1906; "Petition for Citizenship," 1923–1929.

Emily and William Krzyzewski, U.S. Census, 1940.

William Kross, U.S. World War II draft card, honorable discharge, January 16, 1946.

Mike Krzyzewski, Naismith Memorial Basketball Hall of Fame induction speech, October 5, 2001.

Seth Davis, *Getting to Us: How Great Coaches Make Great Teams* (New York: Penguin Press, 2018).

Bryan Strickland, "B.D.: Before Duke," *Durham Herald-Sun,* October 1, 2001.

Dana O'Neil, "Do You Know Mike Krzyzewski?," *ESPN.com,* January 22, 2015.

Skip Myslenski, "For Coach K, Best Values, and Cookies, Are Homemade," *Chicago Tribune,* November 26, 1989.

"Kurzawski Senior Class President," *Weber News,* October 2, 1964.

Timothy J. Gilfoyle, "Sporting Heroes: Interviews with Mike Krzyzewski and Jerry Colangelo," Loyola University eCommons, 2014.

"Hail to the Champs!" *Weber News,* March 5, 1965.

"Weber Upset in Catholic Semi-Finals," *The News* (Chicago), March 17, 1965.

Mike Krzyzewski, Duke University commencement speech, May 15, 2016.

Gregg Doyel, *Coach K: Building the Duke Dynasty: The Story of Mike Krzyzewski and the Winning Tradition at Duke University* (Lenexa, KS: Addax Publishing, 1999).

Mike Krzyzewski, with Jamie K. Spatola, *Beyond Basketball: Coach K's Keywords for Success* (New York: Warner Business Books, 2006).

Barry Jacobs, *Coach K's Little Blue Book: Lessons from College Basketball's Best Coach* (New York: Total/Sports Illustrated, 2000).

CHAPTER 2. COACH KNIGHT

Mike Krzyzewski, with Donald T. Phillips, *Leading with the Heart: Coach K's Successful Strategies for Basketball, Business, and Life* (New York: Grand Central Publishing, 2001).

Jack Isenhour, *Same Knight, Different Channel: Basketball Legend Bob Knight at West Point and Today* (Washington, DC: Potomac Books, 2003).

Timothy J. Gilfoyle, "Sporting Heroes: Interviews with Mike Krzyzewski and Jerry Colangelo," Loyola University eCommons, 2014.

John Feinstein, *A March to Madness: The View from the Floor in the Atlantic Coast Conference* (Boston: Little, Brown, 1998).

Larry Keech, "Double Trouble: Coach Mike Krzyzewski Gets Back into the Game," *Greensboro (NC) News and Record,* March 26, 1999.

"The Sounds Scene," *Chicago Tribune,* August 11, 1967.

Ron Green, "Hurley Not a Bad Guy — He Made a Mistake in Judgment," *Orlando Sentinel/Charlotte Observer,* May 10, 1992.

Nick Martin, "Mrs. Coach K: Q&A with Carol 'Mickie' Krzyzewski," *The Chronicle* (Duke University), January 25, 2015.

Bob Knight, with Bob Hammel, *Knight: My Story* (New York: Thomas Dunne Books, 2002).

William Kross [Krzyzewski] obituary, *Chicago Tribune,* March 4, 1969.

Jacobs, *Coach K's Little Blue Book.*

Dee Wedemeyer, "West Point Weddings," Associated Press, June 11, 1969.

CHAPTER 3. HOOSIERS

Ed Zieralski, "Altitude Factor May Be Tied to Attitude," *San Diego Union-Tribune,* March 30, 1990.

"Fort Carson Cagers Clinch Crown in 5th Army Meet," *Colorado Springs Gazette-Telegraph,* February 6, 1970.

Bill Walton, *Back from the Dead: Searching for the Sound, Shining the Light, and Throwing It Down* (New York: Simon & Schuster, 2017).

Doyel, *Coach K: Building the Duke Dynasty.*

Krzyzewski, with Phillips, *Leading with the Heart.*

Davis, *Getting to Us.*

Charles Chandler, "Profile: Mike Krzyzewski — He Approaches the Game of Basketball the Way He Does Life: With Feeling," *Charlotte Observer,* November 17, 1991.

Ken Denlinger, "At Duke Success Is the Signature," *Washington Post,* April 26, 1992.

Larry Keech, "Double Trouble: Coach Mike Krzyzewski Gets Back into the Game," *Greensboro (NC) News and Record,* March 26, 1999.

CHAPTER 4. COACH K

"Matt Brown Debuts at West Point," *York (PA) Dispatch,* November 29, 1975.

Al DeSantis, "Army Recruiting Pleases Mike K.," *Middleton (NY) Times Herald-Record,* July 1, 1976.

Don Fillion, "Army Stuns Seminoles in Opener," *Burlington (VT) Free Press,* December 30, 1976.

Leni Muscarella, "Army Snaps Tournament Jinx 50–49," *Middletown (NY) Times Herald-Record,* December 31, 1976.

James H. Jackson, "Army Cagers Thwart Spirited Navy Comeback to Notch 54–53 Victory," *Baltimore Sun,* February 27, 1977.

Jack Wilkinson, "Army, St. John's Advance," *New York Daily News,* March 3, 1978.

Jack Wilkinson, "St. John's Champs: Nips Army, 65–63, for Metro Title," *New York Daily News,* March 5, 1978.

Jack Wilkinson, "Army, Rutgers, Fairfield Only Area Teams in NIT," *New York Daily News,* March 6, 1978.

Ian O'Connor, "The First Time That Bobby Knight Got Away," *Gannett Newspapers* (Westchester, NY), March 20, 2001.

Milton Richman, "How Guilty Is Bobby Knight?," United Press International, August 24, 1979.

Jacobs, *Coach K's Little Blue Book.*

ESPN Films/ACC Network, "The Class That Saved Coach K," 2019.

Joe Tiede, "Name of the Game Is Kre-Shef-Ski," *Raleigh News and Observer,* March 20, 1980.

CHAPTER 5. LOSER

Joe Tiede, "Duke Upsets Heels in OT," *Raleigh News and Observer,* March 1, 1981.

"Princeton Roars by Blue Devils 72–55," *Charlotte Observer,* December 13, 1981.

ESPN Films/ACC Network, "The Class That Saved Coach K," 2019.

Dick Weiss, with Jim Sumner, *True Blue: A Tribute to Mike Krzyzewski's Career at Duke* (New York: Sports Publishing, 2005).

John Feinstein, *The Legends Club: Dean Smith, Mike Krzyzewski, Jim Valvano, and an Epic College Basketball Rivalry* (New York: Doubleday, 2016).

CHAPTER 6. SAVING COACH K

Andrew Carter, "Coach K, Condoms, and the Evolution of Cameron Crazies," *Raleigh News and Observer,* February 14, 2020.

Stephanie Epstein, "Duke Fans Scorned Nationally," *The Chronicle* (Duke University), January 17, 1984.

Bill Brill and Mike Krzyzewski, *A Season Is a Lifetime: The Inside Story of the Duke Blue Devils and Their Championship Seasons* (New York: Simon & Schuster, 1993).

Weiss, with Sumner, *True Blue*.

Johnny Moore and Art Chansky, *The Blue Divide: Duke, North Carolina, and the Battle on Tobacco Road* (Chicago: Triumph Books, 2014).

Michael DeSisti, "Coach K. Sick of 'Double Standard'; UNC Is 14-0," *Daily Tar Heel* (University of North Carolina), January 23, 1984.

"Krzyzewski's New Duke Contract Ends Rumors" (AP and staff reports), *Charlotte Observer*, January 27, 1984.

Leonard Laye, Stan Olson, and Kevin Quirk, "Coach K the Cutup," *Charlotte Observer*, March 23, 1986.

Rich Radford, "Middies Weak at One Spot," *Newport News (VA) Daily Press*, March 23, 1986.

Joe Gergen, "This Game's Special for 'K,'" *Newsday* (Long Island, NY), March 23, 1986.

ESPN Films/ACC Network, "The Class That Saved Coach K," 2019.

J. D. Schulz, "Duke's Krzyzewski: Finally, a Time to Laugh," *Dallas Times Herald/Binghamton (NY) Press and Sun Bulletin*, March 31, 1986.

Bill Lyon, "Duke's Student-Athletes: The Way It Was Meant to Be," *Knight-Ridder Newspapers/Muncie (IN) Star*, March 31, 1986.

Tom Foreman Jr., "Pressure on Duke, but It Doesn't Show," Associated Press/*Allentown (PA) Morning Call*, March 31, 1986.

Brent Musburger and Billy Packer, CBS broadcast of the 1986 NCAA championship game, March 31, 1986.

Alwyn Featherston, *Tobacco Road: Duke, Carolina, NC State, Wake Forest, and the History of the Most Intense Backyard Rivalries in Sports* (Guilford, CT: Lyons Press, 2006).

CHAPTER 7. CAN'T WIN THE BIG ONE

Gene Wojciechowski, *The Last Great Game: Duke vs. Kentucky and the 2.1 Seconds That Changed Basketball* (New York: Blue Rider Press, 2012).

Alan Greenberg, "Laettner Makes Most of 2nd Chance," *Hartford Courant,* March 27, 1989.

"Smith Defensive to Reid Questions," *Raleigh News and Observer,* March 9, 1989.

"Final Four Notebook," *Indianapolis News,* April 3, 1989.

Chris Graham, "Men's Basketball Coach Blasts Chronicle Writers," *The Chronicle* (Duke University), January 17, 1990.

Jamie Rosenberg, "Krzyzewski: From Classy to Classless," *Daily Tar Heel* (University of North Carolina), January 18, 1990.

David Teel, "'Good Guys' vs. 'Bad Guys' Clash for Title," *Newport News (VA) Daily Press,* April 2, 1990.

Ian O'Connor, "Hurley Knows the Secret of K's Success," *ESPNNewYork.com,* November 15, 2011.

Ian O'Connor, "How a Loss Elevated Coach K," *ESPN.com,* January 24, 2015.

CHAPTER 8. CONQUEST

Ron Green Jr., "Duke Makes 4th Straight Final Four," *Charlotte Observer,* March 25, 1991.

Gary McCann, "Krzyzewski Expected to Meet with Celtics," *Greensboro (NC) News and Record,* June 1, 1990.

Feinstein, *The Legends Club.*

Thomas Golianopoulos, "25 Years Later, UNLV Players Still Feel the Heartbreak of Losing to Duke," *SBNation,* March 30, 2016.

Jim Nantz and Billy Packer, CBS broadcast of 1991 NCAA Final Four, March 30, 1991.

Milton Kent, "Coaches Cry Foul on Smith's Ejection," *Baltimore Evening Sun,* April 1, 1991.

Associated Press, "Krzyzewski Sheds 'Monkey' Off Back with Title," *Bedford (IN) Times-Mail,* April 2, 1991.

CHAPTER 9. DUKE-KENTUCKY

Ken Denlinger, "At Duke Success Is the Signature," *Washington Post,* April 26, 1992.

Ian O'Connor, "Hurley Knows Big Brother Is Watching," *ESPNNewYork.com,* February 15, 2012.

Wojciechowski, *The Last Great Game.*

Verne Lundquist and Len Elmore, CBS broadcast of the NCAA East Regional final, March 28, 1992.

Tim Layden, "A Game Worth Reliving; Duke's Victory One to Remember," *Newsday* (Long Island, NY), March 30, 1992.

Ian O'Connor, "Christian Laettner's Buzzer Beater Knocks Out Kentucky and Sends Duke to Another Final Four," *New York Daily News,* March 29, 1992.

Dana O'Neil, "From Hill to Laettner, 25 Years Later," *ESPN.com,* March 21, 2017.

Ian O'Connor, "Mr. Perfect," *New York Daily News,* March 31, 1992.

Don Markus, "These Two Are as Different as Knight and Krzyzewski," *Baltimore Sun,* April 2, 1992.

Alexander Wolff, "Blue Angel," *Sports Illustrated,* March 16, 1992.

Curry Kirkpatrick, "Boys to Men," *Sports Illustrated*, April 6, 1992.

Doyel, *Coach K: Building the Duke Dynasty*.

Jason Hehir, "The Fab Five," ESPN Films documentary, 2011.

CHAPTER 10. BREAKDOWN

Bob Valvano, *The Gifts of Jimmy V: A Coach's Legacy* (Chicago: Triumph Books, 2001).

Mike Krzyzewski, video letter, "Dear World," Jimmy V Foundation, 2016.

Larry Keech, "Coach K Thinks Twice, Ends Brief Flirtation with NBA: 'I Love Duke,'" *Greensboro (NC) News and Record*, June 1, 1994.

Jacobs, *Coach K's Little Blue Book*.

Skip Myslenski, "The 'K' in Duke Is Back," *Chicago Tribune*, October 18, 1995.

Charles Chandler, "For Tight-knit Krzyzewski Family, Basketball Is a Way of Life," *Charlotte Observer*, April 4, 1994.

Feinstein, *The Legends Club*.

Barry Jacobs, "How Health Trouble in '94–95 Made Coach K Today," *Rock Hill (SC) Herald*, January 5, 2015.

Mike Krzyzewski, telephone interview by Elizabeth Tennyson, Associated Press, March 30, 1995.

Mike Krzyzewski, "Mike Krzyzewski the Duke Coach Talks about the Price of Success and His Return to Courtside," *Sports Illustrated*, October 24, 1995.

Steve Politi, "Trials, Rewards for Duke," *Raleigh News and Observer*, March 13, 1996.

Krzyzewski, with Phillips, *Leading with the Heart*.

CHAPTER 11. AGONY

Ian O'Connor, "There's No Angel Guiding Blue Devils on March to Greatness," *Gannett Newspapers* (Westchester, NY), March 20, 1999.

Neil Amato, "After Helping Duke Get to the Final Four as a Player, Quin Snyder . . . ," *Durham Herald-Sun,* March 17, 2000.

A. J. Carr, "Perfect Fit: Carrawell, Duke," *Raleigh News and Observer,* March 4, 2000.

Andy Katz, "Duke's Secret? Recruiting Talent," *Fresno Bee,* March 29, 1999.

Chip Alexander, "Holding Court, the Battier Way," *Raleigh News and Observer,* March 22, 2001.

Mike Krzyzewski, "Mike Krzyzewski the Duke Coach Talks about the Price of Success and His Return to Courtside," *Sports Illustrated,* October 24, 1995.

Frank Vehorn, "Coach K Relax? Not Until Duke Wins a Title," *Virginian-Pilot* (Norfolk, VA), March 27, 1999.

Ron Green Jr., "Coach K's Journey Back," *Charlotte Observer,* March 4, 1999.

Larry Keech, "Double Trouble: Coach Mike Krzyzewski Gets Back into the Game," *Greensboro (NC) News and Record,* March 26, 1999.

Jim Nantz and Billy Packer, CBS broadcast of 1999 NCAA championship game, March 29, 1999.

CHAPTER 12. ECSTASY

Rick Bonnell, "Duke's Brand Takes 'Inevitable' Leap to Pros," *Charlotte Observer,* April 15, 1999.

Curry Kirkpatrick, "Blue Flew," *Chicago Sun-Times/ESPN The Magazine,* August 22, 1999.

Pat Forde, "Despite Family Image, Duke Has Its Squabbles, Too," *Louisville Courier-Journal,* July 18, 1999.

Wendell Barnhouse, "College Notes; Duke Absorbing Numerous Hits," *Fort Worth Star-Telegram,* May 1, 1999.

Feinstein, *The Legends Club.*

Mike Krzyzewski induction speech, Bob Knight presenting, Naismith Memorial Basketball Hall of Fame, October 5, 2001.

CHAPTER 13. GOLD

Aaron Beard, "Duke Cleared by NCAA in Player Case," Associated Press, April 2, 2004.

United States of America, Appellee, v. Myron C. Piggie, Appellant, Decided: September 16, 2002.

Jeff Donn, "UMass Stripped of '96 Final Four Finish," Associated Press, May 8, 1997.

Josh Peter, "Sweet Ride," *New Orleans Times-Picayune,* April 3, 2003.

Bob Ryan, "No Clean Getaways," *Boston Globe,* April 6, 2003.

Eddie Pells, "Connecticut 79, Duke 78," Associated Press, April 4, 2004.

Fred Mitchell, "Basketball Greats Tackle U.S.' Fate," *Chicago Tribune,* June 7, 2005.

Amy Shipley, "USA Takes a World View of Basketball; NBA Commitment Key to 2008 Games," *Washington Post,* July 27, 2005.

Ian O'Connor, "The Blame Game," *Gannett Newspapers* (Westchester, NY), August 28, 2004.

Jon Pessah, "Krunch Time," *ESPN.com,* December 3, 2007.

Harvey Araton, "At Duke, Coach K Avoids a Trap," *New York Times*, June 2, 2006.

Davis, *Getting to Us.*

Jay Williams, *Life Is Not an Accident: A Memoir of Reinvention* (New York: HarperCollins, 2016).

Dan Bickley, *Return of the Gold: The Journey of Jerry Colangelo and the Redeem Team* (New York: Morgan James Publishing, 2009).

Mike Krzyzewski, "In Depth with Graham Bensinger," interview by Graham Bensinger, November 22, 2014.

CHAPTER 14. LEAVING KNIGHT BEHIND

Jim Nantz and Clark Kellogg, CBS broadcast of 2010 NCAA championship game, April 5, 2010.

Greg Logan, "No 'Hoosiers' Ending, but Duke-Butler Still a Classic," *Newsday* (Long Island, NY), April 6, 2010.

Dan Shulman, Jay Bilas, and Bob Knight, ESPN broadcast of the 2011 Duke–Michigan State game, November 15, 2011.

Feinstein, *The Legends Club.*

LeBron James, Duke basketball video interview, August 13, 2008.

Adrian Wojnarowski, "NBA Needs to Pull Stars from USA Basketball, Which Is Showcasing Only Duke's Coach," *Yahoo!Sports,* September 15, 2014.

Ian O'Connor, "How Duke and Mike Krzyzewski Are Winning at Kentucky's One-and-Done Game," *ESPN.com,* November 17, 2015.

Mark Murphy, "Family, Faith Pave Semi Ojeleye's Path to Home with Celtics," *Boston Herald,* May 1, 2018.

Nick Martin and Emma Baccellieri, "Rasheed Sulaimon at Center of Sexual Assault Allegations Prior to Dismissal," *The Chronicle* (Duke University), March 2, 2015.

Jim Nantz, Grant Hill, and Bill Raftery, CBS broadcast of 2015 NCAA championship game, April 6, 2015.

Mike London, "Sports Legends: Local Resident Was Coached by Knight," *Salisbury (NC) Post,* May 28, 2020.

CHAPTER 15. LAST STAND

Greg Hadley, "Zion Williamson's Message to South Carolina, Clemson after Opting to Leave State," *The State,* January 20, 2018.

Jay Bilas and Dan Shulman, ESPN broadcast of the North Carolina–Duke game, February 20, 2019.

Jeff Manning and Brad Schmidt, "Marvin Bagley III and the Loyalty Game: How Sneaker Dollars Transformed Youth Basketball," *The Oregonian,* March 17, 2018.

Ian O'Connor, "A College Basketball Celebration at the Garden, and a Sport Grappling with Its Future," *ESPN.com,* November 6, 2019.

Dan Wetzel, "Would NCAA Even Dare to Investigate Zion Williamson Now That He's at Duke?," *Yahoo!Sports,* October 17, 2018.

Jim Nantz, Grant Hill, and Bill Raftery, CBS broadcast of 2019 NCAA East Regional final, March 31, 2019.

Mike Krzyzewski, interview, Blue Devil Sports Network/Learfield IMG College, March 2, 2020.

CBS broadcast audio, Duke-Oregon 2016 NCAA Sweet 16 game, March 24, 2016.

Mike Krzyzewski, video statement on Black lives matter, Duke basketball, June 26, 2020.

Steve Wiseman, "Duke's Coach K Says Trump Not Accountable to Anyone —
but He Should Be," *Herald-Sun,* October 18, 2017.

Seth Davis and Brendan Marks, "'Our Next Coach Is in This Room': Inside
Duke's Secret Search to Replace Coach K," *The Athletic,* June 21, 2021.

Jeff Goodman, "Coach K to Retire after 2021–22 Season," *Stadium,* June 2,
2021.

Andrew Bucholtz, "Jeff Goodman Talks Breaking the Coach K Retirement
News," *Awful Announcing,* June 16, 2021.

BIBLIOGRAPHY

BOOKS

Bickley, Dan. *Return of the Gold: The Journey of Jerry Colangelo and the Redeem Team*. New York: Morgan James Publishing, 2009.

Bilas, Jay. *Toughness: Developing True Strength on and off the Court*. New York: New American Library, 2013.

Brill, Bill, and Mike Krzyzewski. *A Season Is a Lifetime: The Inside Story of the Duke Blue Devils and Their Championship Seasons*. New York: Simon & Schuster, 1993.

Davis, Jeff. *Dean Smith: A Basketball Life*. Emmaus, PA: Rodale, 2017.

Davis, Seth. *Getting to Us: How Great Coaches Make Great Teams*. New York: Penguin Press, 2018.

Delsohn, Steve, and Mark Heisler. *Bob Knight: The Unauthorized Biography*. New York: Simon & Schuster, 2006.

Doyel, Gregg. *Coach K: Building the Duke Dynasty: The Story of Mike Krzyzewski and the Winning Tradition at Duke University*. Lenexa, KS: Addax Publishing, 1999

Featherston, Alwyn. *Tobacco Road: Duke, Carolina, NC State, Wake Forest, and the History of the Most Intense Backyard Rivalries in Sports*. Guilford, CT: Lyons Press, 2006.

Feinstein, John. *A March to Madness: The View from the Floor in the Atlantic Coast Conference.* Boston: Little, Brown, 1998.

———. *The Legends Club: Dean Smith, Mike Krzyzewski, Jim Valvano, and an Epic College Basketball Rivalry.* New York: Doubleday, 2016.

Isenhour, Jack. *Same Knight, Different Channel: Basketball Legend Bob Knight at West Point and Today.* Washington, DC: Potomac Books, 2003.

Jacobs, Barry. *Coach K's Little Blue Book: Lessons from College Basketball's Best Coach.* New York: Total/Sports Illustrated, 2000.

Knight, Bob, with Bob Hammel. *Knight: My Story.* New York: Thomas Dunne Books, 2002.

Krzyzewski, Mike, with Donald T. Phillips. *Leading with the Heart.* New York: Grand Central Publishing, 2001.

———, with Donald T. Phillips. *Five-Point Play: Duke's Journey to the 2001 National Championship.* New York: Warner Books, 2001.

———, with Jamie K. Spatola. *Beyond Basketball: Coach K's Keywords for Success.* New York: Warner Business Books, 2006.

———, with Jamie K. Spatola. *The Gold Standard: Building a World-Class Team.* New York: Business Plus, 2009.

McCallum, Jack. *Dream Team: How Michael, Magic, Larry, Charles, and the Greatest Team of All Time Conquered the World and Changed the Game of Basketball Forever.* New York: Ballantine Books, 2012.

Moore, Johnny, and Art Chansky. *The Blue Divide: Duke, North Carolina, and the Battle on Tobacco Road.* Chicago: Triumph Books, 2014.

Smith, Dean, with John Kilgo and Sally Jenkins. *A Coach's Life: My Forty Years in College Basketball.* New York: Random House, 1999.

Sumner, Jim. *Tales from the Duke Blue Devils Locker Room: A Collection of the Greatest Duke Basketball Stories Ever Told.* New York: Sports Publishing, 2020.

Valvano, Bob. *The Gifts of Jimmy V: A Coach's Legacy.* Chicago: Triumph Books, 2001.

Weiss, Dick, with Jim Sumner. *True Blue: A Tribute to Mike Krzyzewski's Career at Duke.* New York: Sports Publishing, 2005.

Williams, Jay. *Life Is Not an Accident: A Memoir of Reinvention.* New York: HarperCollins, 2016.

Wojciechowski, Gene. *The Last Great Game: Duke vs. Kentucky and the 2.1 Seconds That Changed Basketball.* New York: Blue Rider Press, 2012.

VIDEOS AND BROADCASTS

- CBS broadcasts of the 1986, 1991, 1992, 1999, 2001, 2010, and 2015 NCAA title games
- CBS broadcast of the 1992 Duke-Kentucky game
- CBS broadcast of the 2019 Duke–Michigan State game
- ESPN 1993 "ESPY Awards" broadcast, Jim Valvano's speech
- ESPN broadcast of the 2011 Duke–Michigan State game
- ESPN broadcast of the 2019 Duke–North Carolina game
- ESPN Films/ACC Network, "The Class That Saved Coach K," 2019
- Naismith Memorial Basketball Hall of Fame, Mike Krzyzewski induction, 2001

WEBSITES

- BallDurham.com
- CoachK.com
- DukeBasketballReport.com
- ESPN.com
- GoDuke.com
- Newspapers.com
- Nexis.com
- Sports-reference.com/cbb

INDEX